Communications in Computer and Information Science 1900

Rationale

The CCIS series is devoted to the publication of proceedings of computer science conferences. Its aim is to efficiently disseminate original research results in informatics in printed and electronic form. While the focus is on publication of peer-reviewed full papers presenting mature work, inclusion of reviewed short papers reporting on work in progress is welcome, too. Besides globally relevant meetings with internationally representative program committees guaranteeing a strict peer-reviewing and paper selection process, conferences run by societies or of high regional or national relevance are also considered for publication.

Topics

The topical scope of CCIS spans the entire spectrum of informatics ranging from foundational topics in the theory of computing to information and communications science and technology and a broad variety of interdisciplinary application fields.

Information for Volume Editors and Authors

Publication in CCIS is free of charge. No royalties are paid, however, we offer registered conference participants temporary free access to the online version of the conference proceedings on SpringerLink (http://link.springer.com) by means of an http referrer from the conference website and/or a number of complimentary printed copies, as specified in the official acceptance email of the event.

CCIS proceedings can be published in time for distribution at conferences or as post-proceedings, and delivered in the form of printed books and/or electronically as USBs and/or e-content licenses for accessing proceedings at SpringerLink. Furthermore, CCIS proceedings are included in the CCIS electronic book series hosted in the SpringerLink digital library at http://link.springer.com/bookseries/7899. Conferences publishing in CCIS are allowed to use Online Conference Service (OCS) for managing the whole proceedings lifecycle (from submission and reviewing to preparing for publication) free of charge.

Publication process

The language of publication is exclusively English. Authors publishing in CCIS have to sign the Springer CCIS copyright transfer form, however, they are free to use their material published in CCIS for substantially changed, more elaborate subsequent publications elsewhere. For the preparation of the camera-ready papers/files, authors have to strictly adhere to the Springer CCIS Authors' Instructions and are strongly encouraged to use the CCIS LaTeX style files or templates.

Abstracting/Indexing

CCIS is abstracted/indexed in DBLP, Google Scholar, EI-Compendex, Mathematical Reviews, SCImago, Scopus. CCIS volumes are also submitted for the inclusion in ISI Proceedings.

How to start

To start the evaluation of your proposal for inclusion in the CCIS series, please send an e-mail to ccis@springer.com.

Jianhou Gan · Yi Pan · Juxiang Zhou · Dong Liu ·
Xianhua Song · Zeguang Lu
Editors

Computer Science and Educational Informatization

5th International Conference, CSEI 2023
Kunming, China, August 11–13, 2023
Revised Selected Papers, Part II

 Springer

Editors
Jianhou Gan
Yunnan Normal University
Kunming, China

Juxiang Zhou
Yunnan Normal University
Kunming, China

Xianhua Song
Harbin University of Science and Technology
Harbin, China

Yi Pan
Georgia State University
Atlanta, GA, USA

Dong Liu
Henan Normal University
Xinxiang, China

Zeguang Lu
National Academy of Guo Ding Institute
of Data Science
Beijing, China

ISSN 1865-0929   ISSN 1865-0937 (electronic)
Communications in Computer and Information Science
ISBN 978-981-99-9491-5   ISBN 978-981-99-9492-2 (eBook)
https://doi.org/10.1007/978-981-99-9492-2

This Springer imprint is published by the registered company Springer Nature Singapore Pte Ltd.
The registered company address is: 152 Beach Road, #21-01/04 Gateway East, Singapore 189721, Singapore

Paper in this product is recyclable.

Preface

As the program chairs of the Fifth International Conference on Computer Science and Educational Informatization (CSEI 2023), it is our great pleasure to welcome you to the conference proceedings. The conference was held in Kunming, China, August 11–13, 2023, hosted by Yunnan Normal University, Key Laboratory of Educational Informatization for Nationalities (YNNU), Ministry of Education, China, Yunnan Key Laboratory of Smart Education, Key Laboratory of Artificial Intelligence and Personalized Learning in Education of Henan Province (Henan Normal University), Harbin University of Science and Technology and National Academy of Guo Ding Institute of Data Science. The goal of this conference was to provide a forum for computer scientists, engineers, and educators.

This conference attracted 297 paper submissions. After the hard work of the Program Committee, 76 papers were accepted to appear in the conference proceedings, with an acceptance rate of 25.59%. There were at least 3 reviewers for each article, and each reviewer reviewed no more than 5 articles. The major topic of this conference was Computer Science and Education Informatization. The accepted papers cover a wide range of areas related to Educational information science and technology, Educational informatization and big data for education, Innovative application for the deeper integration of education practice and information technology, and University engineering education and education informatization.

We would like to thank all the Program Committee members for their hard work in completing the review tasks. Their collective efforts made it possible to attain quality reviews for all the submissions within a few weeks. Their diverse expertise in each individual research area helped us to create an exciting program for the conference. Their comments and advice helped the authors to improve the quality of their papers and gain deeper insights.

Great thanks should also go to the authors and participants for their tremendous support in making the conference a success.

Besides the technical program, this year CSEI offered different experiences to the participants. We hope you enjoyed the conference.

July 2023

Jianhou Gan
Yi Pan
Juxiang Zhou
Dong Liu

Organization

General Chairs

Jianhou Gan   Yunnan Normal University, China
Yi Pan   Georgia State University, USA

Program Chairs

Juxiang Zhou   Yunnan Normal University, China
Dong Liu   Henan Normal University, China

Program Co-chairs

Zeguang Lu   National Academy of Guo Ding Institute of Data Science, China
Lan Huang   Jilin University, China

Organization Co-chairs

Bin Wen   Yunnan Normal University, China
Jia Hao   Yunnan Normal University, China
Chao Yang   Yunnan Normal University, China
Junna Zhang   Henan Normal University, China

Organization Chair

Lingyun Yuan   Yunnan Normal University, China

Publication Chair

Xianhua Song   Harbin University of Science and Technology, China

Registration/Financial Chair

Zhongchan Sun   National Academy of Guo Ding Institute of Data
                             Science, China

Chairman

Hongzhi Wang   Harbin Institute of Technology, China

Vice-presidents

Jianhou Gan   Yunnan Normal University, China
Liu Dong   Henan Normal University, China
Guanglu Sun   Harbin University of Science and Technology,
                             China

Secretary General

Zeguang Lu   National Academy of Guo Ding Institute of Data
                             Science, China

Executive Members

Xiaoju Dong   Shanghai Jiao Tong University, China
Qilong Han   Harbin Engineering University, China
Lan Huang   Jilin University, China
Ying Jiang   Kunming University of Science and Technology,
                             China
Junna Zhang   Henan Normal University, China
Juxiang Zhou   Yunnan Normal University, China

Program Committee Members

Jinliang An   Henan Institute of Science and Technology, China
Hongtao Bai   Jilin University, China
Chunguang Bi   Jilin Agricultural University, China
Xiaochun Cao   Sun Yat-sen University, China

Yuefeng Cen	Zhejiang University of Science and Technology, China
Wanxiang Che	Harbin Institute of Technology, China
Juntao Chen	Hainan College of Economics and Business, China
Lei Chen	Sanya Aviation and Tourism College, China
Yarui Chen	Tianjin University of Science and Technology, China
Haoran Chen	Zhengzhou University of Light Industry, China
Fei Dai	Southwest Forestry University, China
Shoujian Duan	Baoshan University, China
Congyu Duan	Shenzhen University, China
Yuxuan Feng	Jilin Agricultural University, China
Ping Feng	Changchun University, China
Jianhou Gan	Yunnan Normal University, China
Qiuei Han	Changchun University, China
Jia Hao	Yunnan Normal University, China
Yaqiong He	Zhengzhou University of Light Industry, China
Xinhong Hei	Xi'an University of Technology, China
Wenjuan Jia	Dalian University of Finance and Economics, China
Ying Jiang	Kunming University of Science and Technology, China
Jiaqiong Jiang	Hunan University, China
Zhejun Kuang	Changchun University, China
Guohou Li	Henan Institute of Science and Technology, China
Yuan-hui LI	Sanya Aviation and Tourism College, China
Shanshan Li	Sanya Aviation and Tourism College, China
Hua Li	Changchun University of Science and Technology, China
Yanting Li	Zhengzhou University of Light Industry, China
Zedong Li	Dalian Nationalities University, China
Zijie Li	Yunnan Normal University, China
Chengrong Lin	Hainan University, China
Zongli Lin	University of Virginia, USA
Kaibiao Lin	Xiamen University of Technology, China
Chunhong Liu	Henan Normal University, China
Dong Liu	Henan Normal University, China
Xia Liu	Sanya Aviation and Tourism College, China
Kang Liu	Sanya Aviation and Tourism College, China
Ying Liu	Tianjin University of Science and Technology, China
Wanquan Liu	Sun Yat-sen University, China

Sanya Liu	Central China Normal University, China
Dong Liu	Henan Normal University, China
Shijian Luo	Zhejiang University, China
Juan Luo	Hunan University, China
Wei Meng	Guangdong University of Technology, China
Yashuang Mu	Henan University of Technology, China
Cong Qu	Hainan University, China
Jiannji Ren	Henan Polytechnic University, China
Jinmei Shi	Hainan Vocational University of Science and Technology, China
Xiaobo Shi	Henan Normal University, China
Yancui Shi	Tianjin University of Science and Technology, China
Wenjun Shi	Zhengzhou University of Light Industry, China
Jing Su	Tianjin University of Science and Technology, China
Peng Sun	University of Electronic Science and Technology of China, China
Weizhi Sun	Sanya Aviation and Tourism College, China
Guanglu Sun	Harbin University of Science and Technology, China
Lin Tang	Yunnan Normal University, China
Mingjing Tang	Yunnan Normal University, China
Hongwei Tao	Zhengzhou University of Light Industry, China
Yiyuan Wang	Northeast Normal University, China
Xiaoyu Wang	Jilin Normal University, China
Cong Wang	Tianjin University of Science and Technology, China
Yuan Wang	Tianjin University of Science and Technology, China
Jun Wang	Yunnan Normal University, China
Min Wang	Yunnan Normal University, China
Haiyan Wang	Changchun University, China
Xiao Wang	Zhengzhou University of Light Industry, China
Cunrui Wang	Dalian Nationalities University, China
Xinkai Wang	Zhejiang University Ningbo Institute of Technology, China
Yongheng Wang	Hunan University, China
Zumin Wang	Dalian University, China
Wei Wei	Xi'an University of Technology, China
Changji Wen	Jilin Agricultural University, China
Bin Wen	Yunnan Normal University, China
Yang Weng	Sichuan University, China

Huaiguang Wu	Zhengzhou University of Light Industry, China
Di Wu	Yunnan Normal University, China
Yonghui Wu	Fudan University, China
Bin Xi	Xiamen University, China
Yuelong Xia	Yunnan Normal University, China
Xiaoxu Xiao	Shaanxi Normal University, China
Meihua Xiao	East China Jiaotong University, China
Min Xie	Yunnan Normal University, China
Jian Xu	Qujing Normal University, China
Mingliang Xue	Dalian Nationalities University, China
Yajun Yang	Tianjin University, China
Fan Yang	Xiamen University, China
Kehua Yang	Hunan University, China
Chen Yao	Zhejiang University, China
Zhenyan Ye	Sanya Aviation and Tourism College, China
Shouyi Yin	Tsinghua University, China
Xiaohui Yu	Shandong University, China
Yue Yu	Beijing Institute of Technology, China
Lingyun Yuan	Yunnan Normal University, China
Ye Yuan	Northeastern University, China
Congpin Zhang	Henan Normal University, China
Junna Zhang	Henan Normal University, China
Chuanlei Zhang	Tianjin University of Science and Technology, China
Yanan Zhang	Tianjin University of Science and Technology, China
Yaming Zhang	Yunnan Normal University, China
Weiwei Zhang	Zhengzhou University of Light Industry, China
Hua Zhang	University of Chinese Academy of Sciences, China
Tingting Zhao	Tianjin University of Science and Technology, China
Bo Zhao	Yunnan Normal University, China
Jian Zhao	Changchun University, China
Zhongtang Zhao	Zhengzhou University of Aeronautics, China
Huan Zhao	Hunan University, China
Tongtao Zheng	Xiamen University, China
Wei Zhong	Yunnan Normal University, China
Juxiang Zhou	Yunnan Normal University, China
Qifeng Zhou	Xiamen University, China
Jun Zhu	Northwestern Polytechnical University, China

Contents – Part II

Educational Informatization and Big Data for Education

Contents – Part I

University Engineering Education

Innovative Application for the Deeper Integration of Education Practice and Information Technology

Automatic Readability Assessment Based on Phraseological Complexity

Xiaojun Yin[1], Gang Cao[2], Lanting Wang[3], and Juan Xu[4(✉)]

[1] Research Institute of International Chinese Language, Education/College of International Chinese Studies, Beijing Language and Culture University, Beijing, China
[2] College of Chinese Literature, Gannan Normal University, Ganzhou, China
[3] Practice and Research Center for International Chinese Language Education, Beijing Language and Culture University, Beijing, China
[4] School of Information Science, Beijing Language and Culture University, Beijing, China
Xujuan@bicu.edu.cn

Abstract. Lexical measures are important grading features in readability assessment studies. However, these measures are based on single words with few measures at the level of word combinations. This paper constructs a phraseological complexity feature system from a phraseological dimension, which is used to construct machine learning models in Chinese text complexity automatic grading task experiments. Experiments using five models compare the prediction of traditional lexical complexity and phraseological complexity features on Chinese text grading. Results of all the experiments show that the phraseological dimension features are more predictive than the lexical features, proving the important role of the phraseological dimension features in automatic readability assessment.

Keywords: Phraseological Complexity · Features · Machine Learning Models · Corpus

1 Introduction

Automatic Readability Assessment (ARA) refers to the study of automatic text grading by examining the linguistic factors that affect the difficulty of a text. Assessment of readability is an important guideline for language teaching, textbook writing, and test assessment, and is now receiving attention from experts in Linguistics, Education, and Computer Science. With the development of natural language processing (NLP) technology over the past 20 years, ARA research has been conducted mainly by constructing graded language features and using machine learning models. As the research progresses, the grading features used have become richer, mainly including lexical and syntactic features, and a small number of linguistic features at the chapter level [1–6]. However, current grading studies show that lexical-level metrics are still most important for the grading effect in Chinese texts [4].

J. Gan et al. (Eds.): CSEI 2023, CCIS 1900, pp. 3–11, 2024.
https://doi.org/10.1007/978-981-99-9492-2_1

The strong contribution of lexical measures to text grading means lexical measures are abundant in text-grading studies, including surface and semantic features. However, there is a common problem with these measures. They are all single-word measures, and there are few measures at the level of word combinations. Word combinations also called phraseological units, collocations, constructions, or collostructions, have been shown to play important roles in linguistic studies, second language acquisition, language teachin,and learner writing studies. Word combinations contain a large amount of information, but few studies focus on word combinations in ARA. Chinese text-grading studies have yet to include work at the level of phraseological units. This paper attempts to advance the field by conducting ARA research with Chinese texts using phrase-level measures on a large-scale corpus. We compare the prediction of phrase- and traditional lexical-level measures on text grading through modeling experiments.

2   Related Works

ARA research is almost a century old and has gone through two important stages: the formula approach [7–10]and the machine learning approach [11–14]. ARA is generally modeled as a supervised machine learning problem in NLP literature. Typical ARA research relies on a gold standard training corpus annotated with labels. Feature extraction is undertaken by experts, and the model results are then obtained by selecting grading linguistic indicators together with the help of simple linear or machine learning models. The grading features play a crucial role and are even more important than the models [15]. Therefore, scholars have focused on developing linguistic grading features, especially at the word level. Early lexical features were mostly based on surface information, such as word length. This was essentially an examination of the form of language writing, expressed in alphabetic scripts as the number of letters that make up a word [2], and in Chinese as the strokes of written Chinese characters [3, 4]. The proportion of commonly used words was then examined, mainly by considering word lists. For example, Dale and Chall constructed features using a wordlist of 3000 words that could be read by primary school students below Grade 4[7, 16]. For international Chinese language education, researchers used the class-level vocabulary given by the designated authorities. Later, with the development of corpus linguistics, large-scale corpora offered word frequency data that replaced wordlists. Scholars also began to examine semantics[17]. Distribution factors were taken into consideration, such as lexical diversity described by the Type-Token Ratio (TTR). Though there are many lexical measures, all are based on individual words. ARA research needs to advance to the level of word combinations or phraseological units.

Language is a complex adaptive system [18], and since Saussure, language has been considered a system composed of words rather than merely a collection of words. If we only consider single words in a language, it is equivalent to treating language as a simple collection of words and we will not be able to solve the problem of the disordered text. A phraseological unit is a grammatical unit that is larger than a word and smaller than a sentence. Firth noted: "You shall know a word by the company it keeps" implying that attention should be given to word combinations and the entire textual context [19]. A word differs depending on surrounding words. For example, the Chinese word "打

(hit)" differs in the following units: "打手心 (hit SB's hands)" "打电话 (call SB)" "打草稿 (make a draft)" "一打啤酒 (twelve bottles of beer)" etc. In different phrases, the lexical and grammatical meanings of"打" are different. We know that phraseological units contain information that single words cannot express. In text-grading research, word combination level features are still relatively rare, with only a few studies using the number of the noun and verb phrases as measures in ARA [3, 4, 20]. Phrases are only classified according to the function of the phrase, and if we want to examine the combination of words, we need to distinguish them by their collocation types. This paper aims to examine phraseological units in a fine-grained way and distinguish them by structure types to determine the relationships between words.

In language sciences, the concept of complexity first appeared in the field of second language acquisition. Complexity was considered an indicator of language level, along with accuracy and fluency. Interlanguage complexity research refers to the study of language learners' production of either spoken or written language. This is similar to ARA research because both essentially study texts at different levels. Vajjala achieved good results in ARA studies using complexity features [2], suggesting that the measures used in interlanguage complexity studies can be applied to ARA. Therefore, this paper describes ARA research using complexity measures. In their complexity studies, Paquot and Hu examined interlanguage complexity based on phraseological complexity in English and Chinese texts, respectively [21, 22]. The phraseological complexity of the texts was examined through both diversity and complexity. Our paper constructs phraseological complexity measures based on these works, described further in Sect. 3. The measures were then automatically extracted through NLP technology.

3 Phraseological Complexity Feature System Construction

3.1 Phrase Definition and Types

The concept of word combination is often used in language research and teaching. Related terms, such as phrase, phraseological unit, collocation, construction or collostruction are also applied, and there are many definitions of these terms. We follow the definition of a phrase, i.e., a combination of two or more real words that occur together with a syntactic or semantic association between the words. We focus on binary simple word combinations, that is, two words with a syntactic association, where the words do not have modifier components. The words may be adjacent or non-adjacent in the text. Ten phrase structure types in Chinese phrases were selected for this study, and because we only examined binary collocations, we excluded conjunctive predicate phrases and partitive phrases (Table 1).

3.2 Phraseological Complexity Features

Complexity is usually measured using the basic dimensions of breadth: the breadth and depth of knowledge [24]. At the operational level, it can be measured by diversity and sophistication [21, 22, 24].

In terms of diversity, several studies of lexical diversity have examined TTR [2, 4]. TTR refers to the ratio of the number of word types (T) to the number of words (N) in a text [25]. Two diversity features were selected for this study: phrase TTR features – similar to TTR for words – and percentage of phrase types (introduced in detail in Table 2).

Lexical sophistication is usually based on frequency [26]. More low-frequency words in a text indicate a more difficult text, following usage-based language views. The phrase sophistication measures in this study were also obtained through frequency information, with the frequency log-transformed to avoid the interference brought by ultra-high frequency words. Using this approach, we constructed phrase complexity features based on diversity and sophistication, shown in Table 2.

Table 1. Ten Chinese phrase types with examples

	Phrase Structure Type	Example
1	Subject-predicate phrase	我学习 (I study)
2	Object phrase	学习汉语 (study Chinese)
3	Complementary phrase	洗干净 (wash it clean); 走下来 (go downstairs);漂亮多了 (much more beautiful)
4	Adverbials modified VP	努力学习 (study hard); 充分地准备 (well prepared)
5	Attributive-head NP	有趣的中文 (interesting Chinese); 一门外语 (a foreign language) 这些高校 (these colleges); 服务中心 (service centers)
6	Coordinating phrase	老师和学生 (teachers and students); 讨论通过 (discussed and approved)
7	Appositive phrase	首都北京capital Beijing
8	Directional phrase	一年后 (one year later)
9	Prepositional phrase	在教室 (in the classroom)
10	The word 'of' phrase	红的 (the red ones)

Table 2. Phraseological complexity features based on diversity and sophistication

Feature Dimension	Feature Name	Description
Diversity	Phrase TTR	Number of phrase types/Total number of phrases
	Percentage of phrase types	Number of phrases per category/Total number of phrases (based on 10 different types, so there are ten measures here)
Sophistication	Phrase frequency indicators	The frequency of each phrase is taken as the mean and variance after log transformation

4 Experiments

4.1 Datasets

Two corpora were used in this paper. One was the Chinese class-level corpus, used as a grading corpus for text-grading model training and testing, and the other was the reference corpus used for frequency extraction.

The class-level corpus is derived from 12 sets of classic international Chinese language education textbooks, including Boya Chinese, Developing Chinese, The Road to Success, HSK Standard Course, and so on. These textbooks are the most widely used in Chinese language education, have been used over many years, and are suitable as a class-level corpus. We obtained 2223 texts in total, a larger dataset than many studies. These texts were randomly divided into training and test datasets according to a ratio of 8:2. Grading experiments were conducted on the training set and validated by the test set, and the data were divided as shown in Table 3.

The reference corpus was used to obtain word and phrase frequency information. The reference corpus for this study was obtained from Chinese students' compositions, with a total of more than 300 million words. The compositions included text at different levels, as the authors were from primary schools, middle schools and universities. Plain, standard language was used, and wide-ranging familiar topics were covered.

Table 3. Class-level corpus information

Item	Low	Medium	Advanced	Total
Total	1185	636	401	2223
Train set	952	521	305	1778
Test set	233	116	96	445

4.2 Features Extraction

In this experiment, NLP techniques were used to automatically extract lexical and phraseological complexity features. The NLP model which was provided by HanLP [https://hanlp.hankcs.com] was used for data processing, including part of speech (POS) taggings and dependency parsing. Phrases were extracted through dependency parsing. The POS and dependency sets were adopted from Chinese Treebank (CTB) and Stanford Dependencies Chinese.

4.3 Experiments and Results

The purpose of this study was to determine the prediction of phrase complexity features in Chinese text grading by comparing the phrase complexity features with traditional lexical complexity ones. The traditional lexical complexity index was used as a reference

Table 4. Lexical complexity features based on diversity and sophistication

Lexical Dimension	Lexical Name	Description
Diversity	Word TTR	Number of word types/Total number of words
	Percentage of word types	Number of words in each category/ Total number of words (obtained from 11 word-types, so there are 11 measures here)
Complexity	Word frequency indicators	The frequency of each word is taken as the mean and variance after log transformation

feature system, and lexical complexity features were constructed in a similar way to the phrase complexity features. Eleven word-types such as nouns, verbs, adjectives, adverbs and pronouns, were chosen as measures. The details are shown in Table 4.

To fully test the effectiveness of phrase complexity, we conducted comparative experiments on five models. The models included SVM (Support Vector Machine), LR (Logistic Regression), and RF (Random Forest), all commonly used in text-grading research. Two new models - XGBoost [27] and LightGBM [28]– commonly used in modeling competitions and industry were also trialed. XGBoost and LightGBM belong to the same tree model as Random Forest but differ from Random Forest in their ability to adopt a Boosting mechanism, which, theoretically, makes the models more capable of learning. The models were validated by considering the accuracy of the test set. The calculation method for accuracy = number of correctly classified samples/total number of samples. The experimental results are shown in Table 5. Classification accuracy based on phrase complexity was higher than lexical complexity in all five models. Figure 1 further summarizes the results.

Table 5. Experimental results of phraseological complexity and lexical complexity features in five models

Model name	Phraseological complexity feature	Lexical complexity feature
SVM - Linear Kernel	0.698 (+4%)	0.658
Logistic Regression	0.7407 (+1.74%)	0.7233
Random Forest	0.7722 (+2.08%)	0.7514
XGBoost	0.7823 (+1.74%)	0.7649
LightGBM	0.7851 (+1.97%)	0.7654

The phraseological complexity feature outperformed the lexical complexity feature on all models, with a 1.74%-4% improvement in accuracy. Comparative results for each model can be seen in Table 5. Findings indicate that phraseological complexity features are more predictive than lexical complexity features. Thus, phraseological metrics should be incorporated into ARA. Phrases include word and inter-word relationship

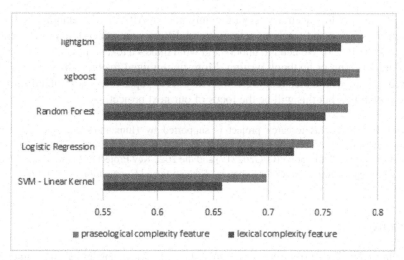

Fig. 1. Experimental results of phraseological complexity and lexical complexity features in five models

information, providing more information than single words. Overall, the three tree models (RF, XGBoost, and LightGBM) outperformed LR and SVM (Linear Kernel). The tree models possess nonlinear learning ability, and given that language is a complex system, nonlinearity is an important feature that should be considered. Therefore, using a model with nonlinear learning capability can yield better results. Our results inspire us to adhere to the linguistic system view in future studies.

In terms of specific model results, the newly introduced XGBoost and LightGBM were more effective than the other three models, with few differences noted between XGBoost and LightGBM. This is consistent with recent findings from modeling competitions and industrial applications, showing that new techniques and models can contribute to language research.

5 Conclusion and Future Work

This paper contributes the new dimension of phrases to the field of ARA and builds phraseological complexity features from the aspects of diversity and sophistication. Our experiments were based on large-scale datasets using a range of models (including newly advanced models). We found that phraseological complexity features outperformed the traditional lexical complexity features in ARA, suggesting phraseological complexity features should be included in ARA. There is also a theoretical need to develop the construct of phraseological complexity. Our construction of phraseological complexity feature system is still relatively preliminary, using diversity and sophistication measures. In the future, phraseological complexity features should be developed from more dimensions to better characterize the phraseological phenomena in language and improve grading accuracy.

Improving grading accuracy is not the only goal in ARA. Interpretability is needed in language science and teaching activities and differs from general text classification research in NLP [29]. We need to understand what makes a text complicated to advance classroom teaching or textbook writing. More fine-grained features should be used in research to help with understanding complexity. This paper offers a limited discussion of interpretability, but this will be the focus of our next project.

Acknowledgments. This research project is supported by Humanities and Social Sciences Fund of the Ministry of Education(22YJCZH222), the 2022 International Chinese Education Reform General Project Funding(GJG202217) and the 2022 Key Project of International Chinese Language Research of the Center for Language Education and Cooperation (22YH50B).

References

1. Heilman, M., Collins-Thompson, K., Callan, J., et al.: Combining lexical and grammatical features to improve readability measures for first and second language texts. In: Human language technologies 2007: the Conference of the North American Chapter of the Association for Computational Linguistics; Proceedings of the Main Conference, pp. 460–467 (2007)
2. Vajjala, S., Meurers, D.: On improving the accuracy of readability classification using insights from second language acquisition. In: Proceedings of the Seventh Workshop on Building Educational Applications Using NLP, pp. 163–173 (2012)
3. Siyuan, W., Dong, Y., Xin, J.: Construction and validity verification of Chinese text readability feature system. World Chin. Teach. Learn. **1**, 81–97 (2020)
4. Jianyong, C.: Research on L2 Chinese Text Readability. PhD thesis, Beijing Language and Culture University, Beijing (2020)
5. Cheng, Y., Xu, D.K., Dong, J.: On key factors of text reading difficulty grading and readability formula based on Chinese textbook corpus. Appli. Linguist. **1**, 132–143 (2020)
6. Graesser, A.C., et al.: Coh-Metrix: analysis of text on cohesion and language. Behavior Res. Methods Instrum. Comput. **36**(2), 193–202 (2004)
7. Dale, E., Chall, J.S.: A formula for predicting readability: Instructions. Educ. Res. Bull. 37–54 (1948)
8. Laughlin, M., Harry, G.: SMOG grading-a new readability formula. J. Reading **12**(8), 639–646 (1969)
9. Flesch, R.: A new readability yardstick. J. Appl. Psychol. **32**(3), 221 (1948)
10. Smith, D.R., Stenner, A.J., Horabin, I., Smith, M.: The Lexile scale in theory and practice. Final report (1989)
11. Deutsch, T., Jasbi, M., Shieber, S.: Linguistic features for readability assessment. arXiv preprint arXiv:2006,00377 (2020)
12. Feng, L., Jansche, M., Huenerfauth, M., et al.: A comparison of features for automatic readability assessment (2010)
13. Martinc, M., Pollak, S., Robnik-Šikonja, M.: Supervised and unsupervised neural approaches to text readability. Comput. Linguist. **47**(1), 141–179 (2021)
14. Sung, Y.T., Lin, W.C., Dyson, S.B., Chang, K.E., Chen, Y.C.: Leveling L2 texts through readability: Combining multilevel linguistic features with the CEFR. Mod. Lang. J. **99**(2), 371–391 (2015)
15. Kate, R., Luo, X., Patwardhan, S., et al.: Learning to predict readability using diverse linguistic features. In: Proceedings of the 23rd International Conference on Computational Linguistics, pp. 546–554 (2010)

16. Chall, J.S., Dale, E.: Readability revisited: The new Dale-Chall readability formula.Brookline Books (1995)
17. Chen, X., Meurers, D.: Word frequency and readability: Predicting the text-level readability with a lexical-level attribute. J. Res. Reading **41**(3), 486–510 (2018)
18. Beckner, C., Blythe, R., et al.: "Five Graces Group", language is a complex adaptive system: position paper. Lang. Learn. **59**, 1–26 (2009)
19. Firth, J.R.: A Synopsis of Linguistic Theory, 1930–1955. Studies in linguistic analysis, 10–32 (1957)
20. Braine, M.D.S., Bowerman, M.: Children's first word combinations. Monographs of the society for research in child development, pp. 1–104 (1976)
21. Paquot, M.: The phraseological dimension in interlanguage complexity research. Second. Lang. Res. **35**(1), 121–145 (2019)
22. Hu, R.F.: A Phrase-based syntactic complexity index and its relationship with chinese second language writing quality. Lang. Charac. Appli. **117**(01), 132–144 (2021)
23. Chunhong, S.: Essentials of Chinese LanguageII. Beijing Language and Culture University Press, Beijing (2018)
24. Bulté, B., Housen, A.: Defining and operationalising L2 complexity. Dimensions of L2 performance and proficiency: Complexity, accuracy and fluency in SLA . vol. 32, p. 21 (2012)
25. Templin, M.C.: Certain language skills in children: Their development and interrelationships. University of Minnesota Press, Minneapolis (1957)
26. Laufer, B., Nation, P.: Vocabulary size and use: Lexical richness in L2 written production. Appl. Linguis. **16**(3), 307–322 (1995)
27. Chen, T., Guestrin, C. Xgboost.: a scalable tree boosting system. In: Proceedings of the 22nd ACM Sigkdd International Conference on Knowledge Discovery and Data Mining, pp. 785–794 (2016)
28. Ke, G., Meng, Q., Finley, T., et al.: Lightgbm: A highly efficient gradient boosting decision tree. In: Advances in Neural Information Processing Systems 30 (2017)
29. Nadeem, F., Ostendorf, M.: Estimating linguistic complexity for science texts. In: Proceedings of the Thirteenth Workshop on Innovative use of NLP for Building Educational Applications, pp. 45–55 (2018)

Moonix: An Educational Operating System on Nezha D1-H RISC-V Development Board

Guojun Liu$^{(\boxtimes)}$, Enyu Li, Jili Huang, and Ziyang Guo

Faculty of Computing, Harbin Institute of Technology, Harbin, China
`hitliu@hit.edu.cn`

Abstract. RISC-V has been favored by major research institutions and universities since its emergence. However, there is a lack of relevant information on the research of general-purpose operating systems based on the RISC-V ISA, and the specialized nature of the available information has become an important obstacle to its entry into academic research and teaching. To address the aforementioned issues and further promote the adoption of RISC-V in university education and research, we design a RISC-V operating system based on the C language, called Moonix. It is divided into four modules: interrupt management, memory management, thread scheduling, and file system. Moonix can not only run on QEMU but also on the Nezha D1-H development board. Students can run Moonix on a real hardware, which can further stimulate their interest in learning operating systems.

Keywords: Operating System · RISC-V · Interrupt · Embedded system · Development Board

1 Introduction

Instruction Set Architecture (ISA) is an abstract model of a computer that defines the basic mode for the processor to parse and execute instructions, which acts as the soul of the processor. ISAs can be classified into two categories: Complex Instruction Set Computing (CISC) and Reduced Instruction Set Computing (RISC) [3]. CISC ISAs include a large number of complex instructions that can perform multiple operations in a single instruction. RISC ISAs are designed to optimize performance by minimizing the number of instructions needed to execute a program.

RISC-V is an open-source instruction set architecture (ISA) that has gained popularity in recent years due to its potential to enable a new era of innovation in computer architecture. It is designed to be simple, modular, and extensible, making it suitable for a wide range of applications from embedded systems to high-performance computing [5,11].

J. Gan et al. (Eds.): CSEI 2023, CCIS 1900, pp. 12–25, 2024.
https://doi.org/10.1007/978-981-99-9492-2_2

RISC-V was developed by researchers at the University of California, Berkeley, in 2010, and since then, it has gained support from a growing number of companies and organizations in the industry. Its open-source nature has also allowed for a large and active community to contribute to its development, resulting in a rapidly evolving ecosystem of tools, libraries, and hardware implementations [2,9,10].

One of the key advantages of RISC-V is its flexibility and scalability, which allows it to be tailored to specific applications and target markets. It can also be customized to meet the needs of different hardware implementations, such as CPUs, GPUs, and accelerators, making it a versatile choice for a wide range of computing systems [4,13].

Currently, most operating systems courses in universities are designed based on the x86 architecture. However, the backward compatibility feature of the x86 architecture means that even newer x86 operating systems have to be compatible with some outdated and deprecated features. This confuses students' understanding of the concept of operating systems and some x86 features. Students may focus more on tedious and redundant x86 features rather than universal concepts in the field of operating systems. In contrast, the RISC-V architecture's operating system is more focused on the system's design due to the architecture's sophistication and lightness [6,8].

Based on the above reasons, this paper designs an operating system based on the C language and the RISC-V architecture and provides its implementation code. The goal is to promote the penetration of RISC-V into university courses and laboratories, to contribute back to the open-source community, and promote the spread of RISC-V in China.

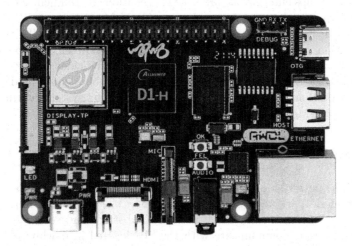

Fig. 1. Nezha D1-H development board.

Our system is called Moonix, which implements various parts of the operating system while being simple enough for students to learn. Moonix was initially designed to run on QEMU and has already ported to Nezha D1-H board, an AIoT development board based on Allwinner Technology's D1-H chip, which is shown in Fig. 1.

2   RISC-V Privileged Architecture

The RISC-V specification defines three privileged modes, and at any time, a thread running on the RISC-V architecture must be in one of these privileged modes [14]. These privileged modes are represented by one or more Control and Status Registers (CSRs) encoding. Three RISC-V privilege levels are defined as shown in Table 1.

Table 1. RISC-V privilege levels

Level	Encoding	Name	Abbreviation
0	00	User/Application	U
1	01	Supervisor	S
2	10	Reserved	–
3	11	Machine	M

If the current instruction attempts to perform an operation that is not allowed in the current privileged mode, an exception will be raised. These exceptions typically result in traps entering the lower-level execution environment for handling.

All hardware implementations must provide M-Mode because it is the only mode that can freely access the entire machine. The simplest RISC-V system implementation may only provide M-Mode, but this implementation will not provide protection to the system against erroneous or malicious application code. Typically, a Unix-like system will use M-Mode as the bootloader mode, require the implementation of S-Mode as the primary operating system runtime mode, and provide a U-Mode runtime environment for software.

3   Overall Design

Currently, the entire Moonix operating system design consists of two parts: the supervisor mode part and the user mode part. The supervisor mode part is the operating system kernel, which is used to abstract and schedule access to hardware resources, communicate with the SBI located in machine mode, and respond to service requests from user mode. The user mode part, which is the operating system service, currently mainly implements the kernel programming interface. User-written programs do not directly request services from the supervisor mode, but instead, call kernel programming interface functions to request services on their behalf.

Moonix uses a macro-kernel mode overall. The advantage of a macro-kernel is fast execution speed, while the disadvantage is a weak hierarchical structure. Despite this, we can roughly divide it into four modules: interrupt processing module, memory management module, process scheduling module, and file system module. Starting from the macro-kernel structural model (layered thinking), we can roughly describe the hierarchical structure of Moonix as shown in Fig. 2.

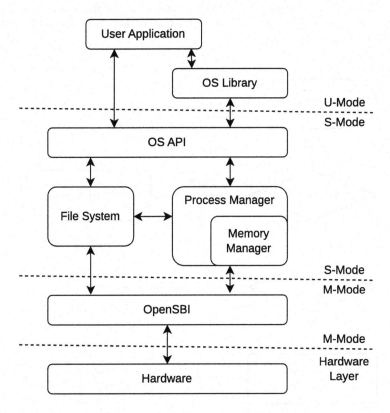

Fig. 2. Hierarchical structure of Moonix

Moonix operating system can run on Allwinner Technology's Nezha D1-H development board, using OpenSBI [15] as the SBI. The physical memory of the development board is 2GB, and except for the memory occupied by OpenSBI and the Moonix kernel, the rest of the memory is the memory area that Moonix can manage.

Moonix uses the Sv39 system provided by the RISC-V instruction set architecture to virtualize and manage memory. Moonix maps all 128MB of physical memory to a 512GB virtual address space and manages this mapping relationship by populating page tables. The CPU can automatically perform address translation by using the page table when resolving addresses. In Moonix, different processes can have different page tables, meaning they run in mutually isolated virtual address spaces.

4   Booting

According to the D1-H user manual [1], the D1-H SoC has multiple boot processes. The on-chip Boot ROM (BROM) is loaded in the first stage. During the boot process, the D1-H fetches and executes instructions from the address 0×0, which is mapped to the BROM.

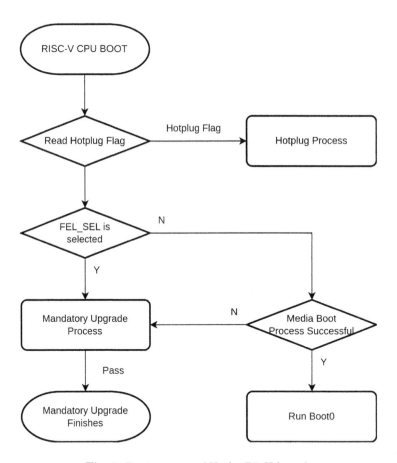

Fig. 3. Boot process of Nezha D1-H board

The BROM system consists of two parts: one is the Firmware Loading and Execution (FEL) module, the other is the Intermediate Boot Loader (IBL) module. The FEL module is responsible for writing external data to the non-volatile memory (NVM) on the board, while the IBL module loads and executes the valid

BOOT0 firmware from the NVM. After the CPU is powered on, the BROM reads the state of the FEL_SEL pin on the chip. If the FEL_SEL pin is pulled low, it enters FEL mode; otherwise, it enters IBL mode. The mode selecting process is shown in Fig. 3.

Once in FEL mode, the clock and USB devices are initialized and the board waits for a USB host connection. At this point, the D1-H development board can be connected to a PC via USB, and instructions can be sent to and executed on the D1-H. The PC can send instructions to the D1-H using the *xfel* software. *xfel* is a lightweight FEL tool developed by the community for Allwinner SoCs, and its code is open source on GitHub. *xfel* supports multiple subcommands, including initializing DDR, reading and writing memory addresses, jumping to execute code, and reading and writing SPI NAND/NOR Flash [7].

Fig. 4. Nezha D1-H cable connection

Once in FEL mode with the *xfel* tool, we no longer need to worry about the initialization process of hardware like DDR, it can greatly simplify the kernel development process. Therefore, we use the FEL mode instead of the intermediate boot module to start the kernel. To start the kernel using *xfel*, follow these steps (italic means shell commands):

1. Run *xfel version* command to confirm that the PC has successfully connected to the D1-H board in FEL mode.
2. Run *xfel ddr d1* command to initialize the DDR memory according to the D1-H mode.

```
● ◦ ●

DRAM only have internal ZQ!!
get_pmu_exist( ) = 4294967295
ddr_efuse_type: 0x0
[AUTO DEBUG] two rank and full DQ!
ddr_efuse_type: 0x0
[AUTO DEBUG] rank 0 row = 16
[AUTO DEBUG] rank 0 bank = 8
[AUTO DEBUG] rank 0 page size = 2 KB
[AUTO DEBUG] rank 1 row = 16
[AUTO DEBUG] rank 1 bank = 8
[AUTO DEBUG] rank 1 page size = 2 KB
rank1 config same as rank0
DRAM BOOT DRIVE INFO: %s
DRAM CLK = 792 MHz
DRAM Type = 3 (2:DDR2,3:DDR3)
DRAMC ZQ value: 0x7b7bfb
DRAM ODT value: 0x42.
ddr_efuse_type: 0x0
DRAM SIZE =2048 M
DRAM simple test OK.

OpenSBI v0.6

   ____                    _____  ____  _____
  / __ \                  / ____|  _ \_   _|
 | |  | |_ __   ___ _ __ | (___ | |_) || |
 | |  | | '_ \ / _ \ '_ \ \___ \|  _ < | |
 | |__| | |_) |  __/ | | |____) | |_) || |_
  \____/| .__/ \___|_| |_|_____/|____/_____|
        | |
        |_|

Platform Name        : Allwinner SUN20i - T-HEAD Xuantie Platform
Platform HART Features : RV64ACDFIMSUVX
Platform Max HARTs   : 1
Current Hart         : 0
Firmware Base        : 0x80000400
Firmware Size        : 75 KB
Runtime SBI Version  : 0.2

MIDELEG : 0x0000000000000222
MEDELEG : 0x000000000000b1ff
PMP0    : 0x0000000080000000-0x000000008001ffff (A)
PMP1    : 0x0000000040000000-0x000000007fffffff (A,R,W,X)
PMP2    : 0x0000000080000000-0x00000000bfffffff (A,R,W,X)
PMP3    : 0x0000000000020000-0x0000000000027fff (A,R,W,X)
PMP4    : 0x0000000000000000-0x000000003fffffff (A,R,W)
Hello from Moonix!
panic: Nothing to do!
```

Fig. 5. Hello world demo with booting

3. Run *xfel write <address> kernel.img* command to write the kernel image to the specified location in memory.
4. Run *xfel exec <address>* command to jump to the first instruction of the kernel image and start the kernel.

The hardware connection and hello world demo with booting are shown in Figs. 4 and 5, respectively.

5   Interrupt

RISC-V supports two modes of interrupt processing, Direct mode and Vectored mode [14]. When using Direct mode, the CPU will jump to the BASE address in "stvec" after any interrupt occurs. If using Vectored mode, a vector table, similar to the interrupt vector table used in Linux kernel, needs to be filled in advance. This can be cumbersome and not conducive to unified processing or ignoring certain interrupts. Therefore, Moonix uses Direct mode to handle interrupts uniformly. In the interrupt handler, different processing functions can be called based on the type of interrupt to streamline the processing flow (Table 2).

Table 2. Encoding of *mtvec* MODE field

Value	Name	Description
0	Direct	All exceptions set pc to BASE
1	Vectored	Asynchronous interrupts set pc to BASE+4×cause
≥ 2		Reserved

Before jumping into the interrupt handler, the CPU state of the current thread needs to be saved and restored upon exit to ensure that the entire interrupt handling process is transparent to the thread. Moonix saves all general registers in the CPU on the kernel stack of the thread and restores the values from the kernel stack to the CPU after the interrupt function is processed. Then it jumps back to the interrupted position to resume execution.

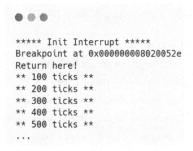

Fig. 6. Timer interrupt test case output

In Moonix, interrupt handling needs to process the three most important interrupts: timer interrupt, user mode (U-Mode) environment calls, and external serial port interrupts. The timer interrupt is mainly used for thread scheduling. Each time the timer interrupt occurs, it will enter the kernel and check the remaining execution time of the current process to decide whether to continue executing.

User mode environment calls, similar to system calls in Linux, are used by processes in U-Mode to request system functions from the operating system in S-Mode, such as input/output and file reading/writing. External serial port interrupts are mainly used to implement user input because in D1-H, the keyboard is implemented as a serial device. User input is an asynchronous event that cannot be predicted. In order to avoid threads that need to read the keyboard being trapped in meaningless busy loops waiting, Moonix uses conditional variables to implement a condition wait-and-restore mechanism. The output of Moonix timer interrupt test case is shown in Fig. 6.

6 Memory

Moonix uses two granularities to manage available memory: dynamic memory allocation and page-based memory allocation. Dynamic memory allocation is used when a program actively requests a small amount of memory during runtime. For Moonix, the goal of dynamic memory allocation is an 8MB memory space in the BSS segment. For applications, the application runtime environment also provides each process with a memory space for dynamic memory allocation. Moonix applies the Buddy System Allocation algorithm to manage the heap space and allocates it in units of 64 bytes. Page-based memory allocation is used for the main body of free physical memory except for the kernel. In addition, the usage of this memory space is maintained by a segment tree. Both of these allocations are implemented with external data structures to reduce intrusiveness and code coupling. Moonix also needs page-based memory allocation to map physical memory to virtual memory space.

Table 3. Encoding of *satp* MODE field

Value	Name	Description
0	Bare	No translation or protection
1–7	–	Reserved for standard use
8	Sv39	Page-based 39-bit virtual addressing
9	Sv48	Page-based 48-bit virtual addressing
10	Sv57	Page-based 57-bit virtual addressing
11	Sv64	Reserved for page-based 64-bit virtual addressing
12–13	–	Reserved for standard use
14-15	–	Reserved for standard use

The paged virtual-memory schemes provided by RISC-V [14] is shown in Table 3. Moonix uses the Sv39 system provided by the RV64 architecture to implement virtual memory management. During the initialization, Moonix maps the kernel to the virtual address space and creates a separate virtual address space for each user process by creating different page tables to represent different mapping modes. This can isolate the code and data of different processes, and when switching to a process, it is necessary to switch to the corresponding page table.

7   Process and Thread

A process is an instance of a running program, with its own memory space and runtime data. Moonix uses a simple process model where each process corresponds to a single thread, meaning that each process contains only one thread. This way, the CPU only schedules threads, and processes are left with the task of resource allocation. In Moonix, a process holds a page table and an array of file descriptors. The page table represents the process's independent virtual address space, while the file descriptors represent the files opened by the process.

When a thread runs, the set of data that represents the thread's running state is called its context. This context is made up of all the registers in the CPU and the data in the stack. In theory, if the thread's context is restored, the thread can resume its execution from where it left off. Similar to interrupts, when a thread switch occurs, the context of the previous thread is saved in order to switch back to it later. The kernel's thread data structure stores the address of the thread's context, which is always located at the top of the stack.

Thread scheduling relies on clock interrupts. When a clock interrupt occurs, the kernel uses the Round-Robin algorithm [12] to check the current thread's time slice and decides whether to pause the current thread's execution and yield the CPU resources.

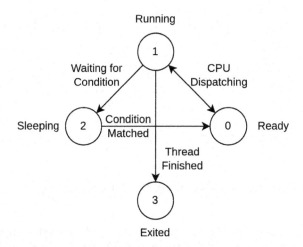

Fig. 7. States and switching conditions for Moonix threads

In Moonix, thread states are maintained by the thread pool and are divided into four types:

1. Ready state: The thread is in the ready queue, waiting to be scheduled by the CPU.
2. Running state: The thread currently has the CPU and is executing.
3. Sleeping state: The thread is waiting for a condition to be met and is not scheduled for execution until the condition is met, after which it is added to the ready queue.
4. Exited state: The thread has finished its task but has not yet had its resources reclaimed.

The states and their switching conditions are shown in Fig. 7.

```
●  ●  ●

***** Init Interrupt *****
***** Init Memory *****
***** Remap Kernel *****
***** init thread *****

>>>> will switch_to thread 0 in idle_main!
Begin of thread 0
00000000000 *OMITTED 0s, 800 IN TOTAL* 00000000000
End of thread 0
Thread 0 exited, exit code = 0
<<<< switch_back to idle in idle_main!

>>>> will switch_to thread 1 in idle_main!
Begin of thread 1
11111111111 *OMITTED 1s, 726 IN TOTAL* 111111111<<<< switch_back to idle in idle_main!

>>>> will switch_to thread 2 in idle_main!
Begin of thread 2
22222222222222 *OMITTED 2s, 800 IN TOTAL* 222222222
End of thread 2
Thread 2 exited, exit code = 0
<<<< switch_back to idle in idle_main!

>>>> will switch_to thread 3 in idle_main!
Begin of thread 3
333333333333333 *OMITTED 3s, 480 IN TOTAL* 3333333333<<<< switch_back to idle in idle_main!

>>>> will switch_to thread 4 in idle_main!
Begin of thread 4
444444444444 *OMITTED 4s, 800 IN TOTAL* 44444444
End of thread 4
Thread 4 exited, exit code = 0
<<<< switch_back to idle in idle_main!

>>>> will switch_to thread 1 in idle_main!
1111111111111 *OMITTED 1s, 74 IN TOTAL* 11111111111111111111
End of thread 1
Thread 1 exited, exit code = 0
<<<< switch_back to idle in idle_main!

>>>> will switch_to thread 3 in idle_main!
33333333333333 *OMITTED 3s, 200 IN TOTAL* 3333333333<<<< switch_back to idle in idle_main!

>>>> will switch_to thread 3 in idle_main!
33333333 *OMITTED 3s, 120 IN TOTAL* 33333333
End of thread 3
Thread 3 exited, exit code = 0
<<<< switch_back to idle in idle_main!
** 100 ticks **
** 200 ticks **
...
```

Fig. 8. Print "0" s - "4" s in five threads

The testing code of threads in Moonix prints 800 characters from "0" to "4" with the Round-Robin scheduling, whose possible output is given in Fig. 8.

8   User Shell

At the initialization stage, the last task of Moonix is to load the "/bin/sh" executable file of the file system and run it as a user process.

"/bin/sh" is a shell executed in user mode, and it is the only way for users to interact with Moonix. Users can directly enter the path of the executable file on the file system in the shell. The operating system will load this file into the kernel, parse and map it, and execute the executable file. After the execution of the file is completed, it will switch back to the shell process and wait for other commands from the user. In addition to executing executable files, the shell also has several built-in commands such as "cd", "ls", "pwd", etc., to facilitate users to navigate through folders and view and execute files.

To load the "/bin/sh" file, Moonix first uses the lookup interface of the file system to obtain the Inode that stores the file information, and then dynamically allocates a buffer in the heap space based on the file size recorded in the Inode.

Next, Moonix uses the "readall" interface of the file system to read the program data file and save it to the buffer. Finally, a user process is created and added to the process scheduling queue.

```
● ● ●

Initializing Moonix...
***** Init Memory *****
***** Init Interrupt *****
***** init thread *****
Welcome to Moonix!
$ ls
. .. bin
$ ./bin/fib50
fibonacci: 0, 1, 1, 2, 3, 5, 8, 13, 21, 34
$ cd bin
$ ls
. .. fib50 sh hello
$ ./hello
Hello world from user mode program 1!
Hello world from user mode program 1!
Hello world from user mode program 1!
Hello world from user mode program 1!
Hello world from user mode program 1!
Hello world from user mode program 1!
Hello world from user mode program 1!
Hello world from user mode program 1!
Hello world from user mode program 1!
Hello world from user mode program 1!
$ shutdown
```

Fig. 9. Execute commands in user shell

The key to constructing a user process is to parse a complete program file in the ELF executable format. Moonix locates the program header table based on the information in the ELF header and finds the file header table. The "p_type" field in the file header describes the segment type, and Moonix only needs to load the segments of the LOAD type into memory. After copying the code or data into physical memory, the kernel needs to map it to the virtual address space in the page table, and the permission of the page table entry needs to be converted based on the "p_flags" field in the program header. The entry field in the ELF header records the virtual address of the program entry point.

When constructing a user process, in addition to mapping the user program's code and data to the virtual address space, Moonix also needs to map the kernel to the virtual address space to ensure that the user process can enter S-Mode and smoothly enter the kernel to handle system calls. Therefore, before parsing the ELF file, Moonix first fills in a pre-mapped page table for the kernel, and then continues to map the program's private code and data based on this page table. Here is how we interact with Moonix through user shell in Fig. 9.

9   Conclusion

Moonix is a simple and compact operating system that includes various parts of the operating system with clear functionality. For beginners, the small codebase allows them to read the source code from start to finish and make modifications. Additionally, Moonix has a comprehensive development process record and documentation to help students understand the purpose of every line of code. It promotes the use of the RISC-V open-source instruction set in operating system courses and cultivates future RISC-V operating system engineers.

Acknowledgements. This work is supported by the National Natural Science Foundation of China (61976071), and the Natural Science Foundation of Heilongjiang Province of China (LH2020F012).

References

1. Allwinner Technology Co., L: D1-H User Manual Version 1.0 (2022)
2. Asanović, K., Patterson, D.A.: Instruction sets should be free: The case for risc-v. EECS Department, University of California, Berkeley, Tech. Rep. UCB/EECS-2014-146 (2014)
3. Blem, E., Menon, J., Sankaralingam, K.: Power struggles: Revisiting the RISC vs. CISC debate on contemporary ARM and x86 architectures. In: 2013 IEEE 19th International Symposium on High Performance Computer Architecture (HPCA), pp. 1–12 (2013). https://doi.org/10.1109/HPCA.2013.6522302
4. Di Mascio, S., Menicucci, A., Furano, G., Monteleone, C., Ottavi, M.: The case for RISC-V in space. In: Saponara, S., De Gloria, A. (eds.) ApplePies 2018. LNEE, vol. 573, pp. 319–325. Springer, Cham (2019). https://doi.org/10.1007/978-3-030-11973-7_37
5. Flamand, E., et al.: GAP-8: A RISC-V SoC for AI at the Edge of the IoT. In: 2018 IEEE 29th International Conference on Application-specific Systems, Architectures and Processors (ASAP), pp. 1–4 (2018). https://doi.org/10.1109/ASAP.2018.8445101
6. Greengard, S.: Will RISC-V revolutionize computing? Commun. ACM **63**(5), 30–32 (2020). https://doi.org/10.1145/3386377

7. Jiang, J.: XFEL: Tiny FEL tools for allwinner SOC. https://github.com/xboot/xfel

8. Kanter, D.: RISC-V Offers Simple. Modular ISA. Tech. rep, The Linley Group (2016)

9. Keller, B., et al.: A RISC-V processor SoC With integrated power management at submicrosecond timescales in 28 nm FD-SOI. IEEE J. Solid-State Circ. **52**(7), 1863–1875 (2017). https://doi.org/10.1109/JSSC.2017.2690859

10. Lee, Y., et al.: An agile approach to building RISC-V microprocessors. IEEE Micro **36**(2), 8–20 (2016). https://doi.org/10.1109/MM.2016.11

11. Matthews, E., Shannon, L.: TAIGA: a new RISC-V soft-processor framework enabling high performance CPU architectural features. In: 2017 27th International Conference on Field Programmable Logic and Applications (FPL), pp. 1–4 (2017). https://doi.org/10.23919/FPL.2017.8056766

12. Rasmussen, R.V., Trick, M.A.: Round robin scheduling - a survey. Eur. J. Oper. Res. **188**(3), 617–636 (2008). https://doi.org/10.1016/j.ejor.2007.05.046

13. Waterman, A., Lee, Y., Patterson, D.A., Asanovi, K.: The RISC-V Instruction Set Manual. Volume 1: User-Level ISA, Version 2.0. Tech. rep. (2014)

14. Waterman, A., Lee, Y., Patterson, D.A., Asanovi, K.: The RISC-V Instruction Set Manual Volume 2: Privileged Architecture Version 1.7. Tech. rep. (2015)

15. Western Digital Corporation or its affiliates: RISC-V Open Source Supervisor Binary Interface (OpenSBI). https://github.com/riscv-software-src/opensbi

Visual Analysis of Research Progress of Blended Collaborative Learning Based on CiteSpace

Lianlian Fu⬛, Wei Zhou⬛, and Jiake Lv^(✉)⬛

College of Computer and Information Science, Southwest University, Beibei,
Chongqing 400715, People's Republic of China
lvjk@swu.edu.cn

Abstract. This study selects relevant literature on hybrid collaborative learning from the Web of Science core database, covering the period from 2017 to 2021, as the primary data source. Utilizing the CiteSpace software, a visual analysis of research in the field of hybrid collaborative learning is conducted. This analysis aims to elucidate the current research focus and frontier in blended collaborative learning while offering valuable insights for future research endeavors in China. Based on the geographical distribution map generated by CiteSpace software, it is evident that the United States and Spain are the countries with a substantial number of published documents, closely followed by China. These findings underscore China's remarkable accomplishments in the domain of hybrid collaborative learning. Furthermore, through an examination of the co-occurrence of keywords, as well as the timeline and mutation of keyword clusters, this paper synthesizes the principal characteristics of current research in hybrid collaborative learning. It explores various aspects, such as existing teaching modes, teaching environments, and teaching strategies, to provide a comprehensive understanding of the field. Moreover, this study anticipates future research directions in China, emphasizing the significance of experimental environments and the utilization of social media in advancing the field of hybrid collaborative learning.

Keywords: blended collaborative learning · visual analysis · key word · Research hotspot · CiteSpace

1 Introduction

In recent times, the rapid advancement of information technology has brought about significant transformations in the landscape of education and instructional methods. The pursuit of innovative educational approaches has emerged as the prevailing trend. Against this backdrop, various hybrid teaching methods, including hybrid collaborative learning, have gained prominence, aligning with the principle of student-centered pedagogy. These approaches have captured the attention of the public, as they offer novel and engaging ways of teaching and learning.

This work was funded by Teaching Reform Project of Southwest University (Award Number: 2021JY030, the Teaching Reform Project of Chongqing Municipal Education Commission(Award Number: 234014)

Professor Peng Shaodong defines blended collaborative learning (BCL) as the establishment of a learning community through the strategic selection and utilization of various conducive elements in the learning process. BCL aims to facilitate the interaction between the learning process and cognitive processes, enhance learners' collaborative skills, and ultimately improve the effectiveness of learning. This paper intends to comprehensively examine the current state and advancements of "hybrid collaborative learning" both domestically and internationally. By leveraging the capabilities of CiteSpace software, the research areas and directions of BCL will be visually analyzed. The objective is to provide a comprehensive overview of the research landscape in BCL and offer valuable insights for future research endeavors in China [1].

The structure of this paper is outlined as follows. After the introductory section, Sect. 2 provides a detailed description of the materials and methods employed in this study. Section 3 focuses on the data processing and presents the analysis results. Subsequently, Sect. 4 is dedicated to the presentation and analysis of the experimental findings. Conclusions and discussions are presented in Sect. 4. Finally, in Sect. 5, the paper concludes by outlining the anticipated future directions and expectations.

2   Materials and Methods

The data for this paper is derived from a comprehensive set of 1,352 research articles obtained from the Web of Science literature database. Among these articles, 334 of them are cited with "blended collaborative learning" as the primary focus, while the search is limited to the years between 2017 and 2021[2].

For this study, the researchers utilized CiteSpace 5.8R3 visualization software as their analytical tool. CiteSpace, developed by Dr. Chen Chaomei from Drexel University, is a scientific metrology software designed to operate within the Java environment. It facilitates visual analyses of keywords, authors, institutions, countries, and literature citations within vast document collections from databases such as Web of Science, Scopus, and CNKI. CiteSpace's features, including knowledge structure analysis and emerging trend identification, provide valuable guidance for subsequent topic research [2, 3].

This study will be conducted following the subsequent steps: The initial step involves logging into the Web of Science website and selecting the Web of Science Core Collection database. The search will be conducted using the theme "blended collaborative learning. As the initial search may yield a limited amount of data, a subsequent search will be performed based on the cited literature to ensure data completeness. A total of 1,352 cited documents will be exported in other file formats, including "full records and cited references." In the second step, the exported references will be imported into CiteSpace 5.8R3 software to eliminate duplicate entries. Next, in the third step, the deduplicated literature data will be imported into a new project. The time span will be set as 2017–2021, with a time interval of 1 year. From each time slice, the top 50 documents with the highest number of citations will be extracted. Subsequently, the corresponding algorithms will be applied as per the research requirements to generate various knowledge maps such as keyword co-occurrence map, keyword clustering map, national geographical distribution map, and timeline map.

These steps collectively aim to facilitate a comprehensive analysis of the research landscape in the field of blended collaborative learning[4–6].

3   Data Processing and Analysis Results

The 1,352 documents downloaded from the Web of Science (WOS) are imported into the CiteSpace software for further analysis. During this process, duplicates are removed, resulting in a reduced number of documents. After screening and deletion, the final number of documents is 1,258. The distribution of the documents published each year is depicted in Fig. 1. It is evident that the research interest in hybrid collaborative learning has witnessed a significant surge in recent years. Particularly, since 2018, there has been a notable increase in the number of literature studies. This trend highlights the growing prominence of BCL as a hot topic in educational research.

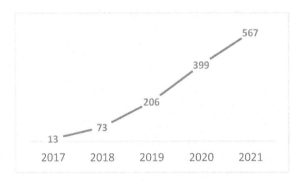

Fig. 1. Number of documents in BCL field in WOS from 2017 to 2021

3.1   Study Geographical Distribution

To examine the presence of distinct regional distribution in BCL research, the CiteSpace software is utilized. The analysis focuses on the country as a node, setting the time interval as 2017–2021 with a time slice of 1 year. The "Pathfinder" algorithm is selected to cut the map structure, resulting in the generation of a national regional distribution map based on the published literature in the BCL field. The map exhibits a network density of 0.0382 and comprises 94 nodes and 167 connecting lines. Figure 2 illustrates the distribution, showcasing the top three countries with a substantial number of relevant documents: The United States, Spain, and China. While the disparity in the number of documents among these countries is not significant, their numbers exceed those of subsequent countries such as Australia and Britain by a significant margin. Collectively, the top three countries account for approximately 40% of the total number of documents published, signifying their notable contribution to BCL research [7].

Fig. 2. Geographical distribution map of literature in BCL field

3.2 Keyword Co-occurrence Analysis

Keywords serve as a concise representation of research directions and content. The frequency of keywords can objectively reflect the level of research activity in their respective fields. With CiteSpace, it is possible to calculate the frequency of keywords in the literature and their co-occurrence frequencies. This information can then be visualized in the form of a keyword co-occurrence map. Figure 3 illustrates the keyword co-occurrence map after beautification and adjustment. The map consists of 181 nodes and 516 connections. Larger nodes indicate higher frequencies of corresponding keywords. Notably, keywords such as "higher education," "student," "blended learning," and "online" exhibit high frequencies. Furthermore, the analysis reveals that words like "student," "online," and "performance" often co-occur with other terms. These keywords are clearly aligned with the theme of hybrid research. Moreover, the analysis suggests that BCL research primarily focuses on the flipped classroom mode, with a significant emphasis on exploring the impact of blended learning on students through the design of blended collaborative learning models [8].

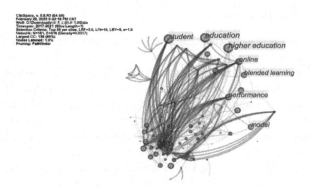

Fig. 3. Keyword co-occurrence map of literature in BCL field

3.3 Keyword Timeline Clustering Map Analysis

To comprehend the research hotspots and trends within hybrid collaborative learning, CiteSpace software is employed to generate a timeline map, depicted in Fig. 4. Keyword cluster analysis is conducted based on this map. Each cluster consists of several closely related keyword nodes, with the label number indicating the number of keywords in each cluster. Two crucial indicators in the clustering network are the clustering module value (Q value) and the clustering average contour value (s value). Generally, a Q value greater than 0.3 suggests a significant clustering structure, an s value exceeding 0.5 indicates reasonable clustering, and an s value surpassing 0.7 implies convincing clustering. In Fig. 4, the clustering exhibits a q value of 0.6005 and an s value of 0.8229. Thus, it can be concluded that the clustering structure is significant, and the clustering results are convincing. Among the 12 clusters, the ones with more frequent keywords encompass the flipped classroom, community of inquiry, and problem-based learning. Notably, these topics experienced significant popularity from 2017 to 2019 [4].

Fig. 4. Keywords timeline Atlas of literature in BCL field

3.4 Keyword Mutation Analysis

The keyword mutation map generated by CiteSpace allows for the observation of changes in keyword frequency over a short period. By detecting keyword mutations, we can analyze the research frontier corresponding to certain keywords and predict the development trend of disciplinary research. To gain insights into the research frontier of blended learning, keywords are taken as nodes in CiteSpace, and a keyword mutation diagram is generated, as illustrated in Fig. 5 in the Burstness panel. Keywords such as "media," "mobile learning," and "big data" have experienced mutations since 2018. Through a thorough examination of the literature, it is evident that recent research on hybrid collaborative learning primarily focuses on exploring collaborative learning through social media within social networks. This highlights the growing significance of integrating social media platforms into the context of hybrid collaborative learning.

Keywords	Year	Strength	Begin	End	2017 - 2021
knowledge	2017	4.73	**2017**	2018	
media	2017	3.75	**2018**	2019	
mobile learning	2017	3.21	**2018**	2019	
big data	2017	2.97	**2018**	2019	
media competence	2017	2.44	**2018**	2019	
support	2017	2.43	**2018**	2019	
social network	2017	2.07	**2018**	2019	
computer	2017	1.95	**2018**	2019	

Fig. 5. Keyword mutation map of literature in BCL field

4 Conclusion and Discussion

Based on the knowledge map generated by CiteSpace in the field of hybrid collaborative learning, the following characteristics can be observed:

- Research Distribution: Blended collaborative learning research is widespread in European and American countries, particularly led by the United States. Although the number of research papers published in China is lower than that in the United States and Spain, Chinese scholars have made significant contributions to the field. Since Professor Peng Shaodong introduced the concepts and theories related to hybrid collaborative learning, domestic research in China has shown continuous progress and development.
- Experimental Teaching Modes: Experimental research in BCL primarily focuses on two teaching modes: escape room and flipped classroom. Escape room is an innovative method in classroom teaching that aims to motivate students. Researchers such as Almudena Macías-Guillén and Raquel Montes Díez have designed game-based learning experiments where student groups compete in escape rooms to complete activities within the shortest time. These activities require successful communication and utilization of social and collaborative skills among team members. Flipped classroom, on the other hand, is a common teaching mode in blended learning where a combination of online and offline teaching provides opportunities for collaborative learning [9].
- Teaching Environment and Social Media: Experimental research in BCL emphasizes the use of social networks and communities as teaching environments. Social media and mobile devices play a crucial role in these experiments. Learning based on social networks and communities can significantly enhance students' cooperative and social abilities. Researchers like Feifei Han and Robert A. Ellis have utilized social network analysis to test students' collaborative learning models, suggesting that enhancing students' collaborative learning experiences can be achieved through adjustments in learning directions, designing mandatory collaborative evaluation tasks, and forming collaborative groups. Social media platforms such as TikTok, Twitter, and Facebook have transformed communication, social interaction, and educational environments. They are widely employed in online or blended learning, creating engaging teaching environments and providing excellent platforms for blended learning. Paloma

Escamilla Fajardo and others have conducted teaching experiments confirming that blended learning using TikTok can establish a novel learning environment, promoting students' enthusiasm and nurturing their creativity, curiosity, and other skills [10, 11].

– Collaborative Learning Strategies: Experimental research in BCL focuses on establishing collaborative learning modes through problem-based learning, game-based learning, and hands-on learning. Escape room, mentioned earlier, serves as both a game-based and problem-based teaching mode. The integration of technology-enhanced escape boxes creates hybrid learning spaces that merge personal and collaborative learning, as well as physical and digital spaces. Incorporating hands-on learning activities significantly enhances student participation and improves their professional abilities. [12].

5   Expectation

The visual analysis conducted using CiteSpace provides insights into the geographical distribution of research and the trend of keyword research heat in hybrid collaborative learning from 2017 to 2021. Combined with a comprehensive analysis of the knowledge map, this study identifies the main characteristics of current BCL research. Building on this analysis, the paper proposes two future research directions for China:

– Positioning Blended Learning in a More Open Environment: Currently, most offline research on blended collaborative learning in China is focused within the classroom setting. However, guiding students into open environments such as communities may provide better opportunities to observe collaborative performance.
– Reasonably Embedding Social Media in Hybrid Collaborative Learning: Current domestic research on teaching primarily relies on mobile learning software. While the software functions well for teaching purposes, it may fail to stimulate the interest of some young students. Therefore, incorporating popular social media platforms into the teaching process could be a viable option.

The timeline map reveals that many hot topics in 2018–2019 have cooled down or even disappeared in the past two years. This observation, combined with the impact of the COVID-19 outbreak, suggests that teaching research has been significantly influenced. Nevertheless, it is evident that scholars continue to innovate and explore hybrid collaborative learning, avoiding a blind pursuit of popular topics. Instead, they are committed to finding new perspectives and exploring problems in the field.

Acknowledgement. The authors express their gratitude to the anonymous referees for their valuable and insightful comments. Furthermore, the authors extend their appreciation to the teaching team from the School of Computer and Information Science at Southwest University for their unwavering support in the development of the Intelligent Classroom Teaching Team for the University Computer Fundamentals Course.

References

1. Peng, S.: From face-to-face collaborative learning, computer supported collaborative learning to hybrid collaborative learning. Res. Audio Vis. Educ. **08**, 42–50 (2010)
2. Chen, C.M., Hu, Z.G., Liu, S.B., et al.: Emerging trends in regenerative medicine: a scientometric analysis in CiteSpace. Expert Opin. Biol. Ther. **12**(5), 593–608 (2012)
3. Zhang, K.: Analysis and prospect of the research hotspots of Internet plus education in China: based on the CiteSpace visualization analysis of from 2015 to 2019. Higher Sci. Educ. **06**, 15–23 (2021)
4. Chen, Y., Chen, C., Liu, Z., et al.: Methodological function of CiteSpace knowledge map Sci. Res. **33**(02), 242–253 (2015)
5. Kong, H., Zheng, G., Zhou, Q.: Visual analysis of Mycoplasma pneumoniae infection in children based on CiteSpace software. Chin. Mod. Doctor **58**(26), 83–88 (2020)
6. Chen, J.: Research on metadata knowledge atlas based on WOS Intell. Exploration **04**, 121–130 (2017)
7. Li, C., Li, H.: Summary of novel coronavirus pneumonia online teaching in China during the outbreak of new crown pneumonia: based on CiteSpace. Jiangsu Sci. Technol. Informat. **38**(36), 64–67 (2021)
8. Zhou, X., Chen, Y.: Analysis on the development trend of discipline research from the perspective of keyword frequency change – taking domestic information science research as an example J. Intell. **35**(05), 133–140 (2016)
9. Macias-Guillen, A., Diez, R.M., Serrano-Lujan, L., et al.: Educational hall escape: increasing motivation and raising emotions in higher education students. Educ. Sci. **11**(9) (2021)
10. Han, F., Ellis, R.A.: Patterns of student collaborative learning in blended course designs based on their learning orientations: a student approaches to learning perspective. Int. J. Educ. Technol. High. Educ. **18**(1), 1–16 (2021)
11. Escamilla-Fajardo, P., Alguacil, M., López-Carril, S.: Incorporating TikTok in higher education: Pedagogical perspectives from a corporal expression sport sciences course. J. Hospit. Leisure Sport Tourism Educ. **28** (2021)
12. Veldkamp, A., Daemen, J., Teekens, S., et al.: Escape boxes: bringing escape room experience into the classroom. British J. Educ. Technol. (2) (2020)

The Effect of English Vocabulary Memorization Applications (App) on College Students' English Learning

Qianru Hua, Yiting Yuan, Jiawen Yan, Tianya Zheng, Zihan Zheng, Xiangfen Zhu, and Yajuan Cao[✉]

NingboTech University, Ningbo 315100, Zhejiang, China
9929010@qq.com

Abstract. The popularization of mobile terminals and extensive coverage of the network have benefited college students a lot in their English learning. They are provided with more choices in learning methods with the vigorous development of online English learning apps. A case in point is their vocabulary Learning. English vocabulary is an essential part or language learning, and college students often face the challenge of memorizing and recalling numerous words. The access to English vocabulary memorization applications (App) like Bai Ci Zhan, Shanbay-Words, MaiMemo and so on has helped students expand their vocabulary. However, there are few studies on the comparative analysis between the learning methods of memorizing words through traditional paper-based wordbooks and apps. This study, therefore, will start from the comparison between these two methods based on the analysis of a questionnaire distributed online to students at NingboTech University, and then explore the effect of word memorization apps on their English learning from the collected data analysis. The research results show that compared with traditional method of memorizing words through paper-based wordbooks, most respondents tend to use apps to promote English learning due to their unique functions and brilliant user experience. Furthermore, apps can enhance their determination and motivate their enthusiasm in English learning. This research also points out some disadvantages of the apps and provides the suggestions to promote the development of such apps.

Keywords: App · Vocabulary Memorization · English Learning

1 Introduction

With the advent of the 5G era, the continuous upgrading of informatization and facilitation in English education, science and technology have continued to develop at a high speed in recent years. Most of the current people receiving English education are post-90s and post-00s. These two generations grow up with the company of digital information technology, so for this part of the group, they can skillfully use online English learning apps to improve their English proficiency [1]. Besides, the rapid development of mobile Internet technology has made the application of mobile terminal devices such as tablets and smart phones increasingly popular in learning, so it has become the norm for college students to use mobile terminals to facilitate English learning [2].

There are many scholars who have conducted some research and discussions in the field of vocabulary memorization apps, but most of the research focus on the advantages and disadvantages of the apps and the analysis of the transformation of English learning style. There is a lack of comparative analysis between the learning mode of memorizing words through traditional paper-based wordbooks and through apps. This research, therefore, will start from the relatively novel perspective of paper-book learning and app-learning comparison to explore the effect of these apps on students' English learning.

1.1 Research Purpose

By conducting a comparative analysis with traditional paper-book memorization techniques, this research endeavors to examine the impact of vocabulary memorization apps on the English learning process among college students under the support of effective technology, and seeks to provide some valuable insights into the effective utilization of these apps.

1.2 Research Questions

Considering the above-mentioned research gap between different learning modes of memorizing words through traditional paper-book learning and app-learning, four research questions are proposed in the current study:

1) Do college students prefer to memorize words through traditional paper-based wordbooks or through apps?
2) What are the reasons for some students' preference for apps to memorize vocabulary?
3) What is the frequency of college students' utilization of apps and paper books?
4) What are respective methods to evaluate vocabulary retention by paper-based wordbooks and apps?

1.3 Research Significance

Based on a fresh perspective in the research in the field of English online learning, this research can provide some insights into the transformation of English learning approaches and teaching methodologies. Additionally, it offers practical suggestions to enhance the development of online English learning apps, thereby establishing a strong groundwork for the advancement of relevant science and technology. Ultimately, this contributes towards the promotion of English education and facilitates the overall learning process.

2 Methodology

2.1 Research Subject

The research subjects are students from NingboTech University, which is a public university in Ningbo, Zhejiang Province. Altogether 114 students from different majors participated in the questionnaire survey, including 32 boys and 82 girls. There were 20 freshmen, 78 sophomores, 16 juniors and 0 seniors.

2.2 Questionnaire

The questionnaire used in this research consists of two sections. Section 1 deals with the general information of the subjects, including their gender, grade and major. Section 2 is composed of 15 questionnaire items concerning the way they memorize English vocabulary. These items, including 10 close-ended questions and 5 open-ended questions, can be divided into five parts as shown in Table 1. Items 1–3 correspond to the exact way the students choose to memorize words. Items 4–5 concern the reasons for their choice. Items 6–9 deal with the frequency of using this way. Items 10-11correspond to the methods used to evaluate vocabulary retention. Items 12–15 concerns advantages and disadvantages of this particular way to memorize words. A brief description of the questionnaire items is displayed in Table 1:

Table 1. The content of the questionnaire

Dimensions	Items
General Information	
The way used to memorize words	1–3
Reason(s) for choosing this way	4–5
Frequency of using this way	6–9
Methods to evaluate vocabulary retention	10–11
Advantages and disadvantages of this particular way	12–15

2.3 Data Collection and Data Analysis

After completing the questionnaire design, the project members distributed the questionnaire on "sojump" of WeChat during the Labor Day in 2022. A total of 114 questionnaires were finally collected and all of them are valid. The project team sorted out answers to each question according to the data. All the questionnaire results were noted down into Excel. They were analyzed and reported in percentage.

3 Results

3.1 Overall Situation of the Way Students Choose to Memorize Vocabulary

Figure 1 reveals the overall situation of the students' choice for memorizing vocabulary. The sharp contrast can be found between their preference for the tools chosen to memorize words. Among all the 114 respondents, 27.36% of them choose to memorize words through paper vocabulary books, while nearly 72.64% of them, approximately three times the number of students choosing traditional ways, prefer to use English learning apps such as Bai Ci Zhan, Shanbay-Words, MaiMemo and Bu Bei to memorize words. Therefore, it is not difficult to find that with the advancement of technology, an increasing number of college students are opting for apps rather than traditional paper-based wordbooks to memorize vocabulary nowadays.

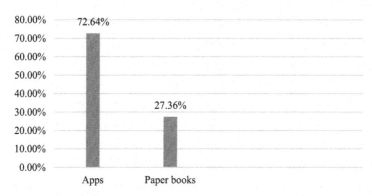

Fig. 1. The Percentage of respondents utilizing different memorizing tools

3.2 The Reasons for Students' Preference for Apps

Figure 2 presents the reason why students prefer to choose apps to memorize vocabulary. The research discovers that half of those who use apps prefer them because of their unique functions, 45% of the respondents choose to use apps due to their brilliant user experience, and only 5% of them use apps due to a kind of herd mentality. Apps often provide interactive and engaging features that make the learning process more enjoyable. Many apps incorporate game elements, such as challenges, quizzes, and rewards, which encourage students to actively engage with the task. This not only enhances their retention and understanding of the words but also makes learning a more entertaining experience. Moreover, the functions of English learning apps are diversified. Most of the word-memorization apps, for example, have its reminding function, which can remind college students to clock in. Students are thus urged to finish the task in time. Traditional paper-based vocabulary books, however, are not equipped with this function, and hence the failure in students' continuous and persistent learning in vocabulary. English learning apps have gradually become an indispensable tool for many English learners due to their advantages in entertainment, personalization and real-time nature [3]. And that's why apps are so popular among them.

Bu Bei App, for another example, uses a variety of original lines or sentences from British and American movies, BBC news, TED, etc. These original materials can guarantee the accuracy and idiomaticity of the expression. Matched with the original sound, the expressions of these sentences are more idiomatic. Therefore, such strong context analysis function makes the process of memorizing words no longer dull or arid, preventing students from cramming. The wonderful pronunciation and vivid plots stimulate college students' thinking and promote their in-depth understanding and mastery of words.

A third example is Shanbay-Words. Its social function enables college students to find peers, who would play a supervisory role in its unique social platform developed by this app. As a result, users can encourage each other while memorizing words and push each other for further steps, which is a win-win situation. Moreover, students with a better command of English will share their experience in memorizing words on the platform. A positive learning atmosphere, therefore, is established through this social function. It's a good and effective way to improve learning efficiency.

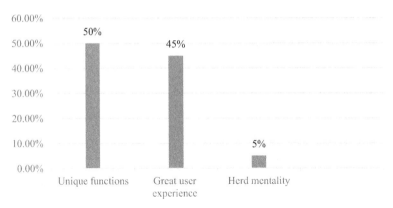

Fig. 2. Reasons for choosing apps

From these examples, we can see that most English learning app has its unique and innovative functions. Through innovation, they have created advantages that the traditional paper vocabulary books do not have. Therefore, we can see that what attracts students most is the function and the design of the apps, and it's also a good reflection from college students on the growing penetration of technology into English learning.

3.3 Frequency of Utilization of Apps

Figure 3 shows the data on the frequency of utilization of these tools among college students. The data includes three categories of frequency: "Everyday", "Regular Intervals" and "Rarely". Analysis of the results reveals interesting patterns. It can be observed that among the groups using apps to memorize words, 48.19% of the participants report using them on a daily basis, while 33.74% of them use them at regular intervals and 18.07% of them rarely use them; on the other hand, however, among those employing paper vocabulary books, only 22% report using them every day, 15% of them use them at regular intervals and 63% of them rarely use it.

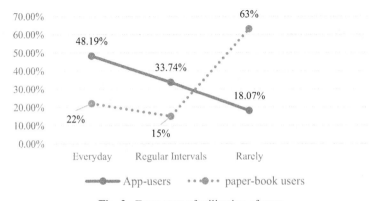

Fig. 3. Frequency of utilization of apps

These findings highlight a clear discrepancy between app-users and paper-book users in terms of their active and persistent approach towards word memorization. App-users demonstrate higher levels of engagement and endurance, as evidenced by their more frequent usage patterns. Conversely, a larger proportion of paper-book users tend to exhibit a lack of motivation and persistence by rarely using their vocabulary books. The observed discrepancy between these two groups implies that the convenience and accessibility of apps may play a crucial role in their increased usage and potentially enhanced effectiveness for word memorization. In contrast, paper-book users may face challenges such as inconvenience or lack of portability, which possibly contributes to their tendency to give up on word memorization.

3.4 The Evaluation of Students' Vocabulary Retention

When it comes to how to evaluate the effectiveness of students' vocabulary learning, Fig. 4 indicates that 71.08% of the vocabulary memorization apps test students' vocabulary retention through spelling recall, followed by listening comprehension 57.83%, context analysis 54.22% and visual matching 37.35%. In contrast, most paper-based vocabulary books evaluate students' vocabular learning by Chinese-English translation and quizzes concerning spelling recall. Therefore, it is not difficult to find that due to the application of multimedia technology in apps, methods and ways used by apps to test the effectiveness of vocabulary learning are more diversified, flexible and all-sided. The ways for the paper books are, however, relatively mechanical, single and dull.

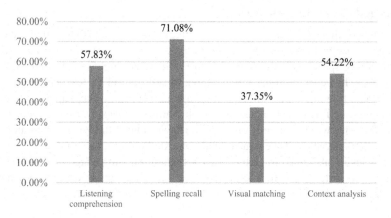

Fig. 4. The ways to evaluate students' vocabulary retention

Obviously, apps tend to outperform traditional paper-based wordbooks in terms of effectiveness of word learning in several aspects. Apps are known for incorporating a variety of interactive exercises and quizzes to actively engage students in their vocabulary learning process. These exercises are specifically designed to challenge students to apply their knowledge in different context, thus strengthening their memory. Another advantage of the apps is the instant feedback they provide on both correct and incorrect answers, enabling students to quickly identify and correct the mistakes they may have made. Additionally, apps benefit from multimedia integration by incorporating audio recordings and example sentences. This approach provides students with additional contextual information, thereby enhancing their understanding of word pronunciation and usage. As a result, students can better retain and apply the vocabulary they learn. Moreover, some excellent memorization apps even can provide personalized learning experiences. By tracking students' progress, identifying their strengths and weaknesses, apps can tailor their content to meet individual needs. This adaptive nature of the apps ensures that students receive focused practice in areas where improvement is needed.

4 Suggestions

According to the analysis of the above research, compared with paper vocabulary books, word memorization apps are more popular among contemporary college students, due to their brilliant user experience and unique functions. Student's vocabulary learning methods have gradually diversified. And their learning time has shifted from concentrated to dispersed, which enable them to effectively utilize fragmented time to increase their vocabulary. Thus, their confidence in learning is enhanced and their ability for autonomous learning are strengthened as well [4]. Just as those respondents who prefer apps have said, those functions can help them carry out the plan continuously, which greatly enhances their determination and increases the utilization rate of apps. Despite the so many advantages of these vocabulary apps, there are still some suggestions that we need to take into consideration in the use of them.

4.1 Suggestions for English Teaching

The findings of this study can provide some suggestions to English teaching. Teachers may integrate English word-learning apps into their course design to activate extracurricular learning space and extend classroom English learning. Students' utilization of learning apps, however, requires a high degree of self-control, so teachers need to play an appropriate role in guiding students utilizing these apps as a supplementary medium in their autonomous learning to guarantee their learning efficiency. Besides, since using apps to memorize words is mainly on an online environment, the synchronous and asynchronous characteristics of the educational context should be taken into consideration as well. Teachers also need to give customized attention and pedagogical intervention for students at different proficiency levels, i.e. top-achieving, medium-achieving and low-achieving students [5].

4.2 Suggestions for English Learners

Language learners should use vocabulary apps to complement traditional learning methods. While vocabulary apps can be beneficial, they should not replace traditional learning methods entirely. A balanced approach that combines app using with other activities, such as listening, speaking, reading and writing is necessary for holistic language development. Therefore, students should be cautious enough not to rely solely on these apps. By blending the use of vocabulary memorization apps with other learning methods, can college students maximize their English learning outcomes and develop a strong vocabulary foundation.

4.3 Suggestions for App Developers

As product developers, it is also necessary to start from the learner's standpoint, follow the learner's mind, and reasonably design and develop the functional modules of the software, so that learners can have a better learning experience to improve their learning performance. Besides, they should focus on personalization features to cater to individual learning preferences, levels, and goals. Offering flashcards, adaptive learning algorithms, and targeted exercises can ensure that users receive personalized and effective learning experiences. In addition, collaboration between app developers, linguists, and teachers can facilitate the creation of evidence-based apps. This collaboration can ensure that apps follow pedagogical principles, and incorporate the latest developments into language learning research.

5 Conclusions

From the above analysis, it can be found that the students who participated in the questionnaire survey have a relatively high frequency and efficiency of using the vocabulary-memorizing apps. Their interest in using English vocabulary learning apps is still relatively high. Approximately, half of the learners can persist in learning every day, and nearly a third of the learners can focus on their learning regularly. Moreover, through diversified methods to evaluate the effectiveness of word memorization, students are more engaged with word learning process. At the same time, most of the respondents have a positive attitude towards the value that memorization apps can bring to them, and generally believe that the interaction between such apps and users is flexible, clear and understandable [6].

Compared with the traditional English vocabulary paper books, word-memorization apps, due to their convenience, interactivity, and personalization, use a combination of various modes and forms to promote learners' memory of words, provide various social interaction functions, stimulate and maintain learners' interest and motivation in learning, and help them obtain achievements in English learning. With various extensional functions, the user's listening, speaking, reading, writing and other abilities can be improved in an all-round way, which fully meets the needs of learners for autonomous learning. When learners choose vocabulary learning apps reasonably according to their own learning characteristics, they can achieve the best results.

However, it can also be found in the questionnaire that although there are many types of multi-functional vocabulary learning software, the specific quality and level of the software are still mixed. For example, the information collected is not authoritative enough, and the content of the analysis is not comprehensive enough. In addition, problems such as the stability of the network, the limitation of mobile phone traffic, the entertainment of mobile phone, etc. and the damage to learners' eyesight caused by long-term use of mobile phone should not be underestimated.

To sum up, compared with the traditional paper-based vocabulary books, college students are more willing to use the memorization apps. With such apps, users can improve their learning motivation to a certain extent and cultivate their enthusiasm for learning. With the effective use of vocabulary memorization apps, users can improve the efficiency of English learning, and then gradually improve their English proficiency [7].

Acknowledgments. This study is supported by the Zhejiang Higher Education Teaching Reform Project for the 14th Five-Year Plan Period (Grant Number: jg20220689), the 2022 Key Project for Professional Comprehensive Reform at NingboTech University (Construction of International-Communication-Capacity-Oriented Experimental Teaching System and Cooperative Education Mechanism for New Liberal Arts) and the 2022 Project for Professional Comprehensive Reform at NingboTech University (Exploration and Practice of College English Teaching Model from the Perspective of New Engineering and New Liberal Arts Majors).

References

1. Meng, Y., Chen, J.L.: A study on App-based foreign language mobile learning. J. Liaoning Normal Univ. **44**(1), 118–124 (2021)
2. Li, Y.M., Wang, Y.F.: A comparative analysis of common English vocabulary learning apps for college students. J. Jimei Univ. (Educ. Sci. Edn.) **20**, 53–58 (2019)
3. Wen, J.: An introduction to smartphone-based English mobile learning software. Campus English **05**, 21 (2016)
4. Xu, Y.Y., Cheng, Z.Q., Fan, X.Y.: A study on the use of word memory apps in English learning. Comput. Knowl. Technol. **15**(14), 133–135 (2019)
5. Yu H. Y., Hu J.: A multilevel regression analysis of computer-mediated communication in synchronous and asynchronous contexts and digital reading achievement in Japanese student. Interactive Learning Environments, Advance online publication. https://doi.org/10.1080/104 94820.2022.2066136, (2 May 2022)
6. Yang, Y.T., Li, L.: A survey of learners' attitudes towards English vocabulary learning apps. English Teach. **20**(6), 56–60 (2020)
7. Zhu, P.Y., Zheng, S.S., Song, Q.X.: On the pros and cons of English learning applications: MaiMemo and Shanbay-words. Learning Weekly **13**, 186–187 (2018)

Construction of Knowledge Graph Based on Design Thinking Cultivation

Qiqi Zhu[1], Congpin Zhang[1,2](✉), and Qingyang Li[1]

[1] Henan Normal University, Xinxiang, China
zhangcongpin@htu.edu.cn

[2] Henan Province Key Laboratory of Artificial Intelligence and Personalized Learning, Xinxiang, China

Abstract. Design and innovation are themes of our time, given the rapid changes in the digital information age. Consequently, the integration of design thinking as a higher order thinking skill into the curriculum is essential for the development of innovative talent in China. However, in basic education classrooms, teachers currently lack the application of design thoughts to enhance students' skills. In this paper, we aim to use the high school IT curriculum as a case study to establish a multimodal algorithmic base knowledge graph. This knowledge graph will incorporate various types of entities and integrate teaching activities and student activities as entities. Additionally, we will adopt the EDIPT design thinking development concept throughout the teaching process and propose its application in the classroom setting. This approach facilitates students' learning while promoting the development of design thinking. Ultimately, it offers new methods and suggestions for teachers' pre-course preparation.

Keywords: Knowledge Graph · Design Thinking · Teaching Process · Multimodal

1 Introduction

Design thinking, as a methodology for achieving innovation [1], deserves an equally important place in school education, according to the Ministry of Education's Curriculum Guidelines for Integrated Practical Activities in Primary and Secondary Schools. Creative ideas are transformed into observable artifacts or works through design and other operations. Therefore, there is a strong effort to develop students' design thinking skills.

The new curriculum, which was promulgated in 2017, demonstrates the imperative of educational reform. In China's basic education, the change in teaching objectives can be observed. It moved from the "double basic objectives" in 1980 to the "three-dimensional objectives" in 2001, and then to the new standards officially promulgated in 2017, which aim to develop students' "core qualities". Currently, core literacy has garnered widespread attention, but its cultivation pathway remains a major issue within the education sector. Design thinking, seen as a higher-order thinking ability, possesses

J. Gan et al. (Eds.): CSEI 2023, CCIS 1900, pp. 43–56, 2024.
https://doi.org/10.1007/978-981-99-9492-2_5

the educational value of promoting the development of students' core literacy [2]. As such, it can be regarded as a new concept and method providing a new development pathway for cultivating students' core literacy. Therefore, one of the most crucial methods in achieving educational reform and educational goals is improving students' design thinking ability.

Currently, most teaching modes for cultivating design thinking in high school IT classes are based on project-based learning activities [3]. However, these activities tend to prioritize students' final work and basic knowledge, failing to integrate information technology tools into the teaching and learning process to foster students' design thinking.

This paper examines the application of the EDIPT design thinking development concept in a high school IT course. It utilizes the knowledge graph of information tools to generate innovative teaching design ideas.

2   The Current State of Research in Design Thinking

SIMON argues in The Science of the Artificial that design thinking is born from the design process and asserts the responsibility of schools to guide students in their thinking as designers. To define design thinking, he describes it as the process of finding the best solution to meet a need under certain conditions [4]. However, with the increase in the number of complex problems, applying the traditional problem-solving approach to design thinking as a method or process is no longer viable. To avoid this one-sided approach, it has been proposed that design thinking should be regarded as a problem-solving attitude, requiring the adoption of different ways of thinking and attitudes when facing problems. These include a human-centred, non-linear problem-solving process and a creative thinking problem-solving attitude [5]. Consequently, design thinking prioritizes the designer's systematic analysis of the problem, the integration and application of their knowledge, and the ability to weigh and compare various solutions to find the optimal one.

In terms of design thinking development, foreign scholars have focused on building various models and forms of development. One innovative model, developed by Cara Wrigley et al., is an 'educational design ladder' consisting of five components: theory, methodology and philosophy, the product focus, design management, business management, and professional development [6]. This model aims to improve the development of design thinking in students. Another suggestion by Oana Jitaru is to help improve students' design thinking skills through technological stimulation, human resources preparation, and social training [7]. By providing these resources and training, students can enhance their design thinking abilities.

Research in China has primarily focused on practical teaching activities and cultivation strategies for design thinking. For instance, the cultivation of design thinking in students is observed in four dimensions within the innovative teaching practices of PBL project-based learning and STEAM courses. These dimensions include independent learning, problem-based exercises, multiple intelligence development, and aesthetic creation [8]. Furthermore, the cultivation strategies for design thinking are implemented at three levels, namely design skills, disciplinary level, and thinking level [9]. These strategies emphasize the importance of addressing practical needs, having clear evaluation criteria during the training process, and enabling students to migrate their capabilities and engage in continuous innovation [1].

This paper promotes the development of students' design thinking by integrating knowledge graph into teaching practice throughout the teaching process.

3 Theoretical Foundations for Design Thinking Development

3.1 Design Thinking Development Model

Multiple classical models of design thinking development exist, including Simon's linear model, Brown's cyclic structure model, and Stanford University's EDIPT model.

The EDIPT model, commonly employed in teaching design thinking development, is utilized in this paper along with a knowledge graph throughout the teaching process. The following section provides a detailed description of this approach.

The implementation process of the EDIPT model consists of five stages, namely empathy, definition, conception, prototyping and testing, as shown in Fig. 1:

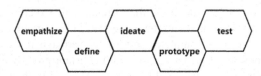

Fig. 1. Stanford University Design Thinking Flow Chart

The empathize stage, also called empathy stage, involves the designer focusing on the user and delving deeper into understanding the user experience.

The define/definition? refers to when the learner, after empathy, relates his or her own experience to the various possible needs of the 'user'.

Ideate, also known as conceptualising, allows learners to brainstorm, for example, and come up with a variety of solutions to the needs of the "user".

Prototyping refers to the use of rough tools to model a solution to a problem and to express this design idea in some way, based on the needs of the "user" and the result of the idea.

Testing means that the results obtained from the prototype are placed in a problem situation and continuously modified and refined. The model is iterated over and over until the best answer to the problem is found.

3.2 Knowledge Graph and the Development of Higher-Order Thinking

Philosophical Perspective. Within the realm of artificial intelligence, the concept of 'ontology' has emerged as a means of defining and understanding 'knowledge'.

From an ontological perspective, an ontology in a knowledge graph refers to something that exists objectively and is distinct from each other, either as a person, thing, object, or as an abstract concept or connection. It consists of three components: classes, attributes, and relationships. The knowledge graph, on the other hand, emphasizes the specification and portrayal of 'being', which is the basic structure of human cognition in a domain. It is rich in instances and relational instances. An ontology, also known as an 'entity', is a description of an entity's way of being and tends to be expressed in terms of a set of definitions of concepts and hierarchical relationships between them. Ontologies define and organize the various elements in a knowledge graph. The ontologies covered in this paper are the content of the material extracted from the subject base, the learning resources, and the organization of the teaching and learning activities carried out during the teaching and learning process.

Psychological Perspective. The theoretical basis for knowledge graph from a psychological perspective can be traced back to the Piagetian school's theory of cognitive development and Immanuel Kant's doctrine of schemas.

Cognitive development theory explores the process by which human cognitive behaviour is constructed, providing insights into the functioning of the brain. Human learning involves the incorporation of new information into an existing knowledge framework, along with its adaptation. This process aligns with the notion of a progressive network architecture that accompanies knowledge development. According to Bruner, students develop their understanding by relating similar concepts, which facilitates the construction of a knowledge structure in their minds. This structure comprises fundamental concepts, principles, and their interconnections. Contrary to the view of learners as empty vessels to be filled or completed entities, they are dynamic entities continually changing and recombining. Learners engage in a constant process of self-adjustment and learning, which is continuously and iteratively enhanced through each activity.

When constructing knowledge graphs, instructional design based on cognitive development theory values student motivation and student autonomy, which emphasizes student subjectivity in learning. This approach allows students to actively engage in learning, explore and investigate problems independently, discuss and interact with peers, and, in the process, foster a collision of students' thinking and cultivate higher-order thinking.

Immanuel Kant's doctrine of schemata states that there is something purely conceptual in the human brain and that schemata act as a bridge connecting concepts to perceived objects. Schemata can be seen as interconnected networks of facts or concepts stored in long-term memory, containing meaningful information. The most important principle of schemata is that new information is more easily understood, learned, and retained compared to information that cannot be embedded [10].

The construction of knowledge graphs and the grasp of hierarchical structures must be in line with the diagrammatic structure of the human brain in order to effectively take in information. This is because the use of knowledge graphs as a teaching aid aligns with the human brain's habit of acquiring knowledge, and cognitive activities carried out through diagrams are more conducive to learning. Moreover, the use of knowledge graphs as an aid to learning is consistent with the trend of human beings gradually shifting towards a visual mode of thinking. Through knowledge graphs, students are able to think outside the box, understand the relationships and structure of scientific knowledge, improve academic performance, and foster the development of scientific thoughts [11]. Additionally, the use of knowledge graphs promotes the development of students' judgment, comparison, summarization, and induction skills. It helps break the rigidity of thinking, encourages divergent thinking, and strengthens logical thinking [12].

Design thinking, as a comprehensive and human-centred thinking skill, includes many thinking skills such as divergent thinking, scientific thinking, logical thinking and creative thinking [13]. This paper promotes students' design thinking development by constructing a knowledge graph for Sect. 3. Fundamentals of Algorithms, in the Compulsory 1, Data and Computing, of the high school IT curriculum.

4 Construction of Knowledge Graph Based on Design Thinking Cultivation

4.1 Construction of Knowledge Graph

Algorithm-Based Knowledge Graph Construction Process

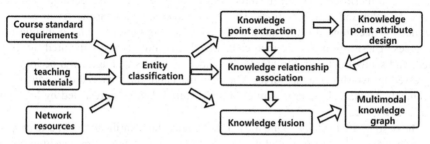

Fig. 2. General process of algorithmic base knowledge graph construction

The teaching content is determined firstly by the requirements of the new curriculum, teaching materials, and e-learning resources. According to the teaching paradigm, the entities in the knowledge graph are divided into 3 categories, namely knowledge points, teaching activities, and learning activities. Entities are defined based on the teaching content, including knowledge point extraction, attribute design, and activity design. Relationship association and knowledge fusion are then performed. Finally, visualization tools such as Neo4j or Smart KG are used to form a multimodal knowledge graph (Fig. 2).

Textbook Selection. This paper is for the compulsory 1 "Data and Computing" chosen for the high school IT curriculum, where Sect. 3, Foundations of Algorithms, will be used as a case study to be constructed as a knowledge graph to facilitate the development of design thinking in secondary school students.

Content Requirements of the Curriculum. Real-life examples are used to illustrate the concept and characteristics of algorithms. Simple algorithms are expressed using suitable description methods and control structures.

Web-Based Teaching Resources. Based on the presentation of the content in the textbook, the students choose to find appropriate teaching and learning resources from the Internet to supplement the content of the textbook and to extend and improve it for those who are able to learn, so that they can appreciate where the charm of algorithmic thinking lies.

Classification of Entities for Algorithmic Base Knowledge Graph. Based on the pedagogical paradigm framework [14], entities in the knowledge graph are classified into three categories: teaching activities, student activities, and knowledge points/learning resources. It is important to note that teaching and learning activities are interconnected. After classifying the entities, the subsequent steps involve knowledge point extraction and knowledge point attribute design.

Knowledge extraction involves identifying the main contents of Sect. 3 from the textbook. This process includes extracting important knowledge points and content related to the fundamentals of algorithms. It also involves gaining an understanding of problem-solving processes using computers and comparing the advantages and disadvantages of manual and computer-based problem-solving. Additionally, this chapter explores algorithm description methods, including their definitions, examples, advantages, and disadvantages. Furthermore, it covers the three basic control structures of algorithms and their respective roles and representations. The chapter also includes various resources such as reflection questions, revision questions, out-of-class assignments, and exam question resources. These resources are then categorized into three types: structured, unstructured, and semi-structured. Structured data, such as names and ages, can be logically expressed in two-dimensional tables. On the other hand, unstructured data consists of documents, texts, and pictures, while semi-structured data is represented by log files, XML, JSON, etc.

The design of knowledge point attributes includes the identification of basic properties such as type classification, definition, principles, algorithmic steps, teaching objectives, teaching requirements, and degree of focus [15]. As an example, the design of attributes for the algorithm description method is shown in Table 1 during actual teaching.

Table 1. Design of knowledge point attributes for the description method of the algorithm

Knowledge point attributes	Knowledge point attribute content
Name of knowledge point	Description of the algorithm
Affiliated sections	Algorithmic foundations
Type of knowledge point	Fundamentals
Teaching Objectives	Be familiar with the three methods of description and use them flexibly in practical problems
Teaching requirements	Learn to represent simple algorithms using appropriate descriptions from real-life examples
Level of focus	The focus of this chapter is on solving real-life problems by mastering description methods and control structures

Design of Teaching Activities. The teaching activities in this model are primarily based on the definitions provided in the EDIPT model. The empathy phase is defined as the process of uploading information to create a situation that enables students to experience and discuss a particular topic. In the definition phase, students are given the opportunity to define specific learning tasks. Subsequently, in the conceptualization phase, students engage in brainstorming and generating a wide range of potential solutions. Moving on to the prototype phase, the teacher furnishes the necessary tools to guide students and facilitates collaborative work towards creating the final product or answer. Lastly, the testing phase involves integrating students' feedback in order to continuously revise and arrive at the most optimal solution.

Design of Learning Activities. In the empathy phase, students share and discuss in-depth the situations created by the teacher. This phase serves as the foundation for the subsequent learning activities. From there, students move on to the definition phase, where they seek to clarify the learning tasks required to explore the problem identified in the empathy phase. This phase aims to establish a clear understanding of the problem and its associated learning objectives. Building upon the definition phase, the visioning phase involves students working in groups to brainstorm and visualize the final results based on the defined topic. This phase encourages creative thinking and fosters collaboration among students. Moving forward, the prototype phase provides an opportunity for students to use tools and techniques to arrive at answers. These answers are then discussed and modified in the testing phase, which serves as a platform for refining the proposed solutions until the best one is determined. Ultimately, the learning activities are an extension of the teaching activities, allowing students to actively engage with the problem-solving process.

A knowledge graph is a semantic network consisting of relationships and nodes. To build a knowledge graph, one must determine the set of nodes and the set of relations separately. The set of nodes has already been defined in the preceding section, while the set of relations will be defined in the following section.

In this paper, semantic relations are categorized into lexical-semantic relations and textual-semantic relations. Lexical-semantic relations can further be subdivided into hierarchical relations, attribute relations, equivalence relations, and manner relations, among others. The construction of a knowledge graph in this study involves the classification of entities (nodes) into three categories: teaching activities, student activities, and knowledge points. Consequently, during the teaching/learning process, semantic relations accompanied by verbs are employed to guide the teacher's instruction and the student's learning. Moreover, semantic relations like attributes and parallelism (equivalence) can be utilized to indicate logical connections between knowledge points.

The choice of semantic relational words is based primarily on cognitive learning theory and the design thinking training process.

According to cognitive learning theory, students play a central role in the learning process. This view aligns with the constructivist theory mentioned earlier, which emphasizes that learning is not a result of reflex arcs but rather involves perception, comprehension, and understanding. In line with Gagne's theory of cumulative learning, new knowledge and skills are acquired based on existing ones, reflecting the semantic relationship of "perceiving comprehending understanding." This implies that learning is a cumulative process that builds on prior knowledge and experiences. Hence, there is a semantic relationship between old knowledge/learning/teaching activities and new knowledge/learning/teaching activities.

To foster students' design thinking, the teaching activities in the knowledge graph incorporate design thinking and follow the development steps in the EDIPT model, linking them as semantic relationships within the teacher's actions.

Visualization of Knowledge Graph. The knowledge graph of the algorithm is created by importing knowledge points and their semantic relationships separately and then visualizing them. Entities in the graph are categorized using different colours: pink for student activities, blue for teacher activities, and colourless representing the set of knowledge points. Figure 3 presents the content of the algorithmic foundation's third chapter along with its corresponding teaching and learning activities.

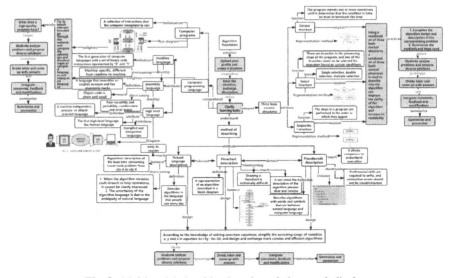

Fig. 3. Multimodal algorithm base knowledge graph display

The knowledge graph constructed in this paper helps teachers to prepare their lessons or to guide students through the basic part of the algorithm. Currently, the main part of the knowledge graph based on teaching services has been completed, dividing it into two parts, main and branch, separating the introduction from the tasks to be learned, for example in Figs. 4(a) and 4(b):

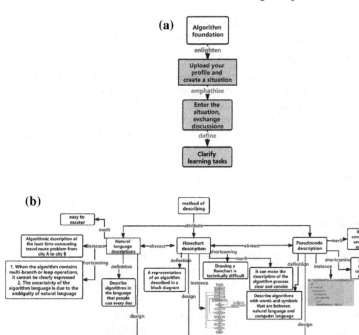

Fig. 4. (a) Algorithm base import section. (b) description method of the algorithm

Knowledge Graph-Based Design Thinking Cultivation Process. This paper adapts the design thinking training process based on the D. School: the k12 Lab Curriculum as a reference to develop students' design thinking in the algorithms course, as illustrated in Table 2:

Table 2. Design Thinking Segmentation Form

	Empathy	Define	Ideate	Prototype	Testing
Level.1	The teacher uses open-ended questions or creates videos to put students in the situation of the problem and to think about it	Guide students to distil a range of needs and findings into ideas	Group students together and use brainstorming	Rapid iterative prototyping with tools such as paper and pencil	Students present their ideas and prototypes clearly to others
Level.2	During the interview the teacher conducts continuous follow-up questioning and allows students to state the differences in their views	Use tools and software to help students record and categorise learning tasks	Have students brainstorm under a defined topic and learning task	Raptor software is used to solve problems and present products	Use quadrant tests to gather feedback
Level.3	How (how) and why (why) questions about a topic	Use the 2×2 matrix to help students to collect comprehensive information and formulate a clear problem statement	Visualisation of the results of the brainstorming with the help of visualisation tools	Modelling the idea of a decision simulation model to simulate the best answer under different conditions	Create a logical environment to test and evaluate students' work

In this paper, the method of describing algorithms is used as an example. Based on the Design Thinking Segmentation Form, teachers can incorporate it into their teaching by referring to each level of development method. They can implicitly develop students' design thinking skills in the teaching process. As a result, each level of development in Table 2 is included as an entity in the knowledge graph in Fig. 5:

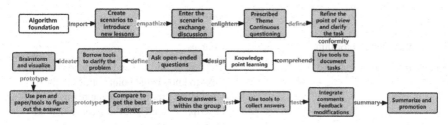

Fig. 5. Knowledge graph teaching and learning process with teaching/student activity as the entity

The specific teaching and learning process thus implemented in the lesson on descriptive methods of algorithms is shown in Table 3 below:

Table 3. Specific teaching and learning processes for knowledge graph with teaching/student activities as entities

Description of the algorithm	Courses
Create a situation Introducing a new lesson	How can you design a solution of travel route that takes the least amount of time to get from city A to city B? Multimedia applications can also be incorporated to increase students' interest in exploring the problem. (L1)
Enter the scenario Exchange and discussion	Students enter the teacher-given scenario questions for an inquiry activity
Prescribed topics Continuous pursuit	What are the route options, given that only mathematical knowledge can be applied? Which is the shortest time-consuming solution? Discuss the difference between mathematical and algorithmic calculations. (L2, L3)
Refining the view Clarity of mission	After answering the questions, students experience the process of computer problem solving and clarify the learning task of this lesson, i.e., the basic concepts of algorithms and their methods of description. (L1)
Use of tools Recording tasks	Students can use learning tool software such as Tick List or Impression Notes or Youdao Cloud Notes to record tasks. (L2)

(continued)

Table 3. (*continued*)

Description of the algorithm	Courses
Knowledge learning	The task is clarified and then learned using links to knowledge point entities in the knowledge graph, here using the method of description branch of the algorithm as an example
Asking open-ended questions	After conducting the study, the teacher asks the question i.e., to design and communicate a more efficient and concise algorithm based on the knowledge of solving the indeterminate equation, the screening range of the variables x, y and z in the equation $6x + 5y + 4z = 50$
Borrowing tools Clarifying the problem	A 2x2 matrix can be used to collect comprehensive information to develop clear problem instructions and help students to rationalise their thinking. (L3)
Brainstorming and visualize	Students are divided into small groups and brainstorm under the question and finally visualise their thinking with the help of tools such as X-mind or curtains. (L2, L3)
By pen and paper/tools Work out the answer	If you have difficulty with algorithmic problems, you can use the fast algorithm prototype tool Raptor. (L1, L2)
Make a comparison Derive the best	The algorithmic process for different conditions can be listed following the idea of a decision simulation model and finally the best answer can be compared. (L3)
Show answers in groups with the help of tools Collect answers	Quadrant tests can be used to collect feedback from the group and then compare and discuss the best answers. (L2)
Integration of views Feedback and modification	Organise groups to present their answers individually on stage, with other groups voting and scoring, and keep revising their solutions based on feedback until they come up with the best answer. (L3)
Summary Enhancement	Students' performance is assessed in process, the lesson is summarised and the important points learnt in the lesson are reviewed, an in-class task is set i.e., to consider the strengths and weaknesses of the three methods of algorithm description and to complete Tables 3, 4 and 5 on page 51 in the textbook

The teaching process includes design thinking development and can serve as a model for other branches of teaching with adaptations to complete the classroom process.

5 Summary

At present, there are few cases in China and abroad where teaching activities and students' activities are taken together as entities to be incorporated into knowledge graph for teaching practice to enhance students' design thinking. This paper discusses the degree of association between knowledge graph and the cultivation of higher-order thinking ability from both philosophical and psychological perspectives. In addition, this paper looks for the relationship between entities from the process of design thinking cultivation and cognitive learning theory in the search for semantic relationships, which provides a new path for the definition of semantic relationships. In terms of teaching, the use of this knowledge graph to complete the entire teaching process, not only can help teachers to prepare for the class, but also can guide students to the next step of learning, a map of multi-purpose, to enhance the students' design thinking at the same time, for the guidance of teachers to teach to provide a new way of thinking.

References

1. Lin, L., Shusheng, S.: The conceptual connotation and cultivation strategy of design thinking. Mod. Distance Educ. Res. **06**, 18–25 (2016)
2. Lin, L., Shusheng, S.: Research on the role path of design thinking and discipline integration–a method of cultivating core literacy in basic education. Electrochem. Educ. Res. **39**(05), 12–18 (2018). https://doi.org/10.13811/j.cnki.eer.2018.05.002
3. Ziming, Z., Zhi, Z., Lei, Y.: STEAM education with design thinking: model construction and case study. Mod. Distance Educ. **01**, 56–62 (2021). https://doi.org/10.13927/j.cnki.yuan.202 10208.002
4. Simon, H.A.: The Science of the Artificial, 3rd edn. MIT Press, Cambridge (1996)
5. Ma, Z., He, J.: Design education and design thinking. Des. Art Res. **9**(02), 9–13+23 (2019)
6. Wrigley, C., Straker, K.: Design thinking pedagogy: the educational design ladder. Innov. Educ. Teach. Int. **54**(4) (2015)
7. Jitaru, O.: Active learning and development of design thinking ability at students. Rev. Artistic Educ. **18**(1) (2019)
8. Qixuan, L., Hongju, L.: Cultivation of design thinking in PBL project-based learning STEAM courses. Art Educ. **06**, 202–205 (2022)
9. Xuhui, Y.: Design thinking cultivation: the way out of the dilemma of teaching thinking in basic education. China e-Learn. **07**, 54–59 (2019)
10. Yan, T., Wenwen, Y.: Research on the Theory and Practice of Educational Psychology. Xinhua Publishing House, 201406.198
11. Hui, Z.: Research on the influence of knowledge graph on the scientific thinking ability of secondary school students. Chongqing University (2018)
12. Gao, J.: A practical study of knowledge graph on the cultivation of innovation ability of secondary school students. Chongqing University (2018)

13. Zmigrod, S., Colzato, L.S., Hommel, B.: Stimulating creativity: modulation of convergent and divergent thinking by transcranial direct current stimulation (tDCS). Creat. Res. J. **27**(4), 353–360 (2015)
14. China Basic Education Big Data 2018–2019: Towards Data-Driven Modern Education Governance Beijing: Science Press (2021)
15. Rong, X., Weiping, Z.: Knowledge graph of artificial intelligence curriculum areas and its innovative teaching model. Softw. Guide **20**(12), 179–186 (2021)

A Novel Teaching Strategy Based on EduCoder Platform for C Programming Language

Wei Li[1(✉)], Xinhong Hei[2], Lei Wang[3], and Yichuan Wang[1]

[1] School of Computer Science and Engineering, Xi'an University of Technology, Xi'an, China
`liwei@xaut.edu.cn`
[2] Shaanxi Key Laboratory for Network Computing and Security Technology, Xi'an, China
[3] School of Mathematics and Computer Science, Shaanxi University of Technology, Hanzhong, China

Abstract. Experimental teaching is an important part of the C programming language course, which aims to cultivate students' Computational thinking ability, problem solving ability and programming ability. However, the existing experimental teaching mode of the C programming language course has been criticized mainly for their: 1) it is difficult for teachers to check all students' programs within a limited time; 2) Limited computer room capacity, fixed time, and other factors make it difficult to meet the personalized requirements of students. In this paper, we put forward the construction scheme of experimental teaching of the C programming language course based on the EduCoder platform, which alleviates all the above two problems. The scheme follows the fundamental law of engineering practice ability training and constructs a LDEI practice teaching closed loop of "learning (L), doing (D), evaluation (E) and improvement (I)". Through specific cases, this paper elaborates the implementation process of this scheme in the experimental teaching of the C programming language course. Finally, a survey are conducted on 64 students from computer science and technology majors. The survey results show that the designed scheme effectively enhances the students' Computational thinking ability and programming ability.

Keywords: EduCoder platform · Programming · experimental teaching · Programming ability

1 Introduction

It is widely known that the graduates are required a wide range of skills and strong abilities to keep pace with innovations in the society. Programming course is an important part of computer science, which can prepare the graduates for work in industry, by teaching students core computing concepts and programming. Universities are aware of the importance of computer science, and have taken the programming courses, such as C, C++, Java or Python, as the compulsory courses of the whole school.

The C programming language is an important course in the university. It is the first practical programming course for undergraduates. The main concepts of the C

J. Gan et al. (Eds.): CSEI 2023, CCIS 1900, pp. 57–67, 2024.
https://doi.org/10.1007/978-981-99-9492-2_6

programming language include basic knowledge of programming, program structure, function programming, arrays, structure, pointer and files. Since a solid knowledge of the C programming language can be of great help in cultivating students' computational thinking ability, data analysis ability, problem solving ability and basic programming ability, how to teach this course is worthy of in-depth deliberations [1, 2].

The C programming language course includes theoretical teaching and experimental teaching. Experimental teaching can help students to actively construct, understand and master knowledge. However, there are some problems in the process of experimental teaching. First, when there are errors in the problem, some students don't know how to solve them. They usually rely on teachers rather than by themselves to solve problems. Moreover, some students can solve the problems that has been taught in the class. However, it is difficult for them to put forward effective solutions for the problems that have never been taught in the class. Next, the period of experimental course is relatively limited, which is difficult for students to understand and master the program structure and design method. Finally, different students have different abilities. The current experimental teaching mode is difficult to satisfy the personalized requirements of students.

2 Related Work

The C programming language course is more than just teaching students to write programs, but students should gradually establish the concept of program design, cultivate computational thinking, as well as the comprehensive ability of programming, implementation, testing and analysis. Therefore, educators have actively explored and practiced the experimental teaching, and put forward many new ideas, new models and new methods. For example, Zeng et al. [3] developed a mixed online and offline experimental teaching based on the modern information technology, which includes experimental preview test, classroom test, experimental process evaluation and experimental report correction. Li [4] proposed how to conduct the experiments in the course online, and the power of virtual simulation method to online education. Yu et al. [5] introduced the virtual experiment into the Computer Compilation Principle course, which can display the key and difficult problem of teaching content more intuitively and improve the teaching quality more effectively.

As mentioned before, the C programing language course is a compulsory course for science and engineering students in Xi'an University of Technology. The development of the C programming language course has experienced three stages, including offline teaching, outcomes-based education and MOOC teaching. The development process is shown in Fig. 1.

The teaching mode of the first stage is offline teaching. This stage mainly emphasizes knowledge transfer, which aims to cultivate students' solid theoretical foundation. Due to the lack of exercises and materials for students to practice and review, they have some difficulties in understanding and mastering knowledge. Therefore, in 2009, the course team constructed an exam library of this course, which contains more than 1000 questions. Students can freely construct a test paper to effectively help them deeply understand and master knowledge. In 2010, the course team reviewed the curriculum syllabus. On this basis, the course team added new knowledge modules, adjusted the course content system, further updated and improved the exam library. Finally, the C language programming textbook is published by Higher Education Press.

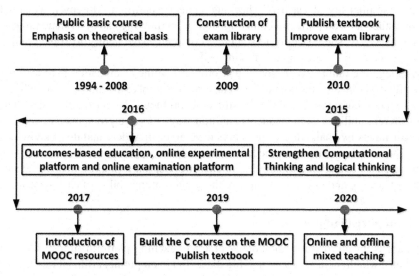

Fig. 1. Development of C programming language course

The teaching mode of the second stage includes outcomes-based education (OBE) concept, introduction of online resources and offline teaching. To stimulate students' interest in learning and cultivate students' innovation ability, from 2015 to 2016, the course team introduces the OBE concept and the computing thinking ability from engineering education professional certification into the course teaching. In 2016, the course team developed the online experimental platform and online examination platform for the C programming language course. In addition, the paperless machine-based examination mode is employed for most majors in Xi'an University of Technology. In 2017, the course team introduced the course resources on the MOOC of Chinese universities and made full use of online resources to assist the teaching of our school.

The teaching mode of the third stage is to actively build online resources and innovate teaching mode. In view of the characteristics and development potential of students in Xi'an University of Technology, the existing online resources are difficult to effectively satisfy the personalized learning requirements of students. Therefore, in 2019, the course team independently built the C programing language course on the MOOC of China University and the wisdom tree. Moreover, the supporting textbook of this course is published by Higher Education Press. From 2019 to 2020, the course team carried out online and offline mixed teaching practice based on the achievements of our University. Finally, this course was approved as a national online and offline mixed first-class course.

3 A Novel Teaching Strategy Based on EduCoder Platform

As mentioned before, the experimental teaching of C programming language course is mainly to solve the time and space constraints faced by students in experiments and alleviate the intensity of teachers' checking students' program. Moreover, we should cultivate students' computational thinking, algorithm thinking and systematic thinking. On this basis, we should cultivate students' comprehensive ability to solve complex problems and high-level complex thinking skills.

Although the online experimental platform and online examination platform independently developed by the course team can effectively solve the time and space limitation of experimental process, there are still some problems. Because different students have different abilities, some students can find ways to solve problems and complete the experiments by analyzing, while others have no design ideas and don't know what to do. These students either ask the teacher for help or copy other students' homework. Therefore, a novel teaching strategy based on EduCoder platform is proposed to achieve accurate teaching and effectively improve the programming ability of each student.

3.1 EduCoder Platform

EduCoder is an information technology practice teaching platform (https://www.edu coder.net/), which includes computer, big data, cloud computing, artificial intelligence, software engineering, internet of things and other professional courses. This is an experimental environment integrating learning, practice, evaluation and testing. For programming courses, the platform can automatically evaluate program codes, display the homework status, the successful passing time of the program, the evaluation times and scores. Through the experimental data provided by EduCoder platform, teachers can analyze the ability values of students, dynamically grasp students' learning state, and continuously improve teaching content, so as to achieve accurate teaching. On the EduCoder platform, teachers can design the experiments according to the teaching content.

3.2 Experimental Teaching of C Programming Language Course

According to the teaching objectives of this course, we construct the experimental teaching content to gradually cultivate students' programming ability, as shown in Table 1. The experimental teaching of C programming language is divided into three levels to realize the progressive cultivation of students' programming ability.

Level I cultivates students to understand and master the basic knowledge of C programming language, and the basic concepts of algorithms and programming. Through the experiments of Level I, students should master the thinking method of describing and solving problems by the computer, and master the three basic structures involved in structured programming.

The purpose of Level II experimental training is to enable students to master the organizational data such as arrays, structures and pointers, and cultivate students' algorithm thinking and programming ability in the process of solving complex problems.

Level III experimental training is mainly to guide students to use modular design ideas, that is, to complete a small-sized information system through the process of demand analysis, module design and programming, so as to cultivate students' systematic thinking, independent research ability and innovation ability.

Table 1. Experimental teaching of C Programming language.

Num	Level	Task	Target
1	I	Familiar with C language programming environment	Master the execution process of C program
2		Sequential structure	Use of assignment statement and input / output statement
3		Select structure	Master the use of *if* statement and *switch* statement
4		Loop structure	Master the use of *while* statement, *do while* statement and *for* statement
5	II	Function	Master the definition and call of functions
6		Array	Master the use of one-dimensional array, two-dimensional array and character array
7		Structure and Union	Master the use of structure and union
8		Pointer	Master the use of pointers and arrays
9		File	Master the operation of reading and writing files
10	III	Information management system	Master the comprehensive use of functions, structure arrays and files

3.3 Experimental Teaching Based on LDEI Cycle

In this paper, we propose a LDEI cycle, which divides the experimental teaching into four stages, including learning (L), doing (D), evaluation (E) and improvement (I), as shown in Fig. 2. First, learning aims to guide the students to further understand and master the programming knowledge points, programming thinking and programming methods involved in the task according to the task introduction. Second, students write programs according to the task requirements, that is, doing. In the process of programming, we can cultivate students' computational thinking ability and programming ability. Third, the code submitted by a student is evaluated by the EduCoder platform. Through evaluation, students can know whether the program they have written is correct. At the same time, teachers can also timely grasp students' learning status. Finally, teachers will further strengthen guidance on students' weak points to ensure that they understand and master various knowledge points.

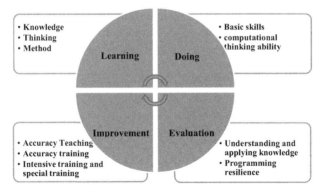

Fig. 2. Development of C programming language course

3.3.1 Experimental Content

Taking experiment 7 in Table 1 as an example, the problem is as follows: write a program that encourages the user to enter the information of 10 employees. The information of each employee includes employee number, name and salary. Display the information of employees and the number of employees whose salaries are higher than the average salary, and write them to the file. The knowledge points and objectives covered by the experiment are shown in Table 2.

Table 2. Experimental teaching of C Programming language.

Task Decomposition	Knowledge Points	Capability Objectives
Define structure type	Definition of structure	(1) Strengthen the understanding of the concept of structured programming
Employee information storage	Structure array	
Input employee information	Loop structure	
Calculate average salary	Function call	(2) Improve the ability of program analysis and design, coding and debugging
Output results	Select structure and loop structure	
Save file	File storage operation	(3) Cultivate students' programming toughness such as perseverance, difficulty cognition and growth belief [6], and improve their programming ability
Menu driven	System view	

This program covers many aspects, such as foundation, hierarchy, challenge and practicability. The foundation is that the problem covers 11 knowledge points such as three basic structures, array, structure and file. At the same time, it trains students' abilities such as analysis, design, coding, debugging and error correction, so as to consolidate students' programming. The hierarchy is reflected in the gradual deepening of each module of this problem from easy to difficult. Students gradually complete each module according to the requirements of the problem. Some students can expand the functions of the system to varying degrees according to their abilities.

This experiment can satisfy the needs of students at different levels. The challenge lies in how to store employee information. If the array is used to store information, it is simple and easy to implement. However, if the number of employees changes dynamically, it is not appropriate to use an array. This is because the number of elements must be determined when declaring an array. At this time, we need to consider using the dynamic memory allocation mechanism to solve this problem, however, it will increase the difficulty of the task, which is a challenge for students. Practical performance is that the experimental task is familiar to students and can be applied to practice. Through this experiment, students can deeply understand the value and significance of programming, which will effectively promote the deep integration of students' theoretical knowledge and software project.

3.3.2 Experimental Content

Firstly, the teacher creates a new practice project on the EduCoder platform and input the basic information of the project, including name, skill tag and introduction. Secondly, upload Employee.c and Employee_Work.c in the code warehouse. Employee.c is the complete code of the project. Employee_Work.c is the experimental task that students need to complete. Third, the teacher designs the task level. The main steps are as follows:

(1) Describe the related tasks to enable students to clarify the task requirements.
(2) Introduce the relevant knowledge involved in the task, and further clarify the knowledge points to be mastered and the cultivation of relevant ability points.
(3) Specify the programming requirements and test instructions so that students can debug and correct the prepared program.
(4) Finally, set the evaluation duration, customs clearance judgment rules, permissions and experimental mode. The student training tasks are shown in Fig. 3.

After the training project is established, the teacher announces the experimental task. The detailed practical teaching steps are as follows.

- Learning

Students log in the EduCoder platform and deeply learn the knowledge points involved in the task according to the task introduction. On this basis, students think and design a scheme to solve the task.

- Doing

First, students define structure and structure array. Then the loop statement is used to input the information of students. Next, the function call, select statements and loop statements are used to calculate the average salary of each employee and output the results. Moreover, the file is used to save the results. Finally, the menu is introduced to form a system. This experiment cultivates students' basic experimental skills in the process of using three basic structures to solve problems. The use of files and the menu further strengthens students' computational thinking ability and cultivates students' algorithm design and analysis ability.

- Evaluation

The EduCoder platform automatically compiles, runs and evaluates the code submitted by students. If the program is correct, the information that the program passed is displayed. Otherwise, an error message is displayed. Students find the shortcomings of their own knowledge according to the error prompt information. Then, through in-depth study and positive thinking, they modify the code and test it repeatedly until the program passes. Through evaluation, we can guide students from understanding knowledge to digesting knowledge, and then apply knowledge. In addition, the programming resilience of students is cultivated through evaluation.

- Improvement

During the experiment, EduCoder platform records the learning behaviour of each student in real time, which includes homework completion status, the total time of experiment, the number of experiments completed, the score of experiment, the time of submitting experiment and the number of evaluation experiments. Through the experimental data of the EduCoder platform, teachers can know the learning status and weaknesses of different students in time. On this basis, teachers increase intensive training and special training on students' weak aspects through accurate teaching. Students can practice accurately and improve learning efficiency.

```
#include <stdio.h>
struct Person
{
   // TODO: Add member define code here
};
int main()
{
   //TODO: Define employee array
   int i,num=0,sum=0;
   float ave;

   //TODO: Call the function to calculate the average salary of all employees

   //TODO: Output employee information whose salaries are higher than the average
salary, and count the number of employees whose salaries are higher than average salary

   printf("number=%d",num);

   //TODO: File save

   return 0;
}

//TODO: Define a function to calculate the average salary of all employees
```

Fig. 3. Training tasks

4 Experimental Teaching Outcome

To improve students' programming ability, we propose LDEI cycle experimental teaching mode based on EduCoder platform, which integrates the cultivation of computing thinking ability and programming ability into the whole process of experimental teaching. After the completion of C programming language course at the end of the semester,

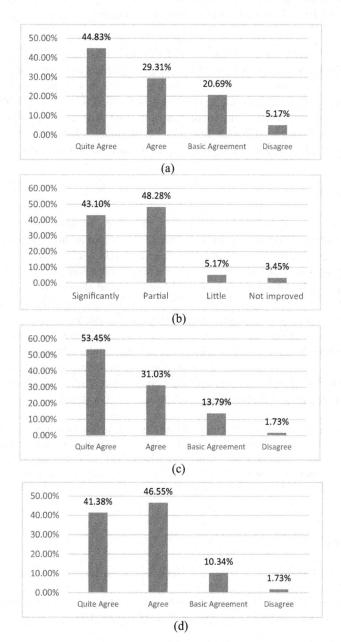

Fig. 4. Questionnaire of LDEI cycle experimental teaching mode. (a) Q1 (b) Q2 (c) Q3 (d) Q4

64 students were asked to answer the following four questions. The statistics were made on 58 effective questionnaires.

1) Q1: Are different levels of experiments suitable for effective learning?
2) Q2: Is the programming ability effectively improved?
3) Q3: Does LDEI cycle experimental teaching mode stimulate your learning enthusiasm and improve your problem-solving ability?
4) Q4: Does LDEI cycle experimental teaching mode improve your autonomous learning ability?

The questionnaire survey results of LDEI cycle experimental teaching mode are shown in Fig. 4. The results indicate that 94.83% of students agree that different levels of experiments are suitable for effective learning. 96.55% of students believe that their programming skills have been effectively improved. 98.27% of students believe that LDEI cycle experimental teaching mode has stimulated their learning enthusiasm and improved their problem-solving ability. 98.27% of students believe that LDEI cycle experimental teaching mode has improved their autonomous learning ability.

5   Conclusion

Computing thinking ability and programming ability are the important foundation of the ability training of engineering professionals. In the experimental teaching of C programming language, we propose an LDEI practice teaching closed loop based on the EduCoder platform, which includes learning, doing, evaluation and improvement. On the one hand, it solves the limitation of fixed time and fixed place in traditional practical teaching. Students can easily and independently complete the experiment, which stimulates students' learning enthusiasm. On the other hand, according to the evaluation data provided by the EduCoder platform, teachers can find problems in time and strengthen accurate training on students' weaknesses. The experimental teaching method proposed in this paper is helpful to students' accurate learning. In the process of ability training, students' learning ability and programming ability are continuously improved, which lays a foundation for the cultivation of students' innovative ability.

Acknowledgements. This research is supported by Research on process management and quality evaluation system of programming online courses (xjy2104), Exploration and practice of team guided graduate training mode (310-252042240), Reform and practice of bilingual teaching of C language programming (xzwjy2103), the project of teaching and research in Shaanxi Province (SJS2022ZD018, 21BY041).

References

1. Li, W., Hei, H., Wang, L.: The practice of building gold courses in C language programming course. Comput. Educ. **6**, 142–146 (2020)
2. Li, W., Hei, H., Wang, L., et al.: Experimental teaching of C language programming course in the context of new engineering. Comput. Educ. **7**, 188–192 (2021)

3. Zeng, S., Wan, P., Chen, A., et al.: Process evaluation of experimental teaching based on modern information technology. Res. High. Educ. Eng. **6**, 62–67 (2021)
4. Li, F.X.: Experimental online achievement mixed teaching. Comput. Educ. **11**, 77 (2020)
5. Yu, Y., Li, F.X., Chen, Y.F., et al.: Design and practice on virtual experiment of computer compilation principle course. Exp. Technol. Manag. **36**(8), 123–126 (2019)
6. Fu, Q., Zhang, L., Ma, H., et al.: Research on the level of programming resilience of college students and its influencing factors. E-Educ. Res. **4**, 29–36 (2021)

Research on the Status of Website Video Service in Libraries Based on Bilibili

Danting Wang[✉] (iD)

Wuhan University of Technology, Wuhan 430070, China
victorhugo123@whut.edu.cn

Abstract. Based on the data of Bilibili, this paper performs a statistical analysis of the registration, maintenance and operation of all library accounts in China. The results show that the number of library accounts registered and their grades are low, and the operation is not sufficiently sustainable. There are significant differences in the number of videos and the average number of coins between public and academic library accounts. All comprehensive operation data of the authenticated accounts are significantly better than those of the unauthenticated accounts. There are significant positive correlations among average numbers of views, barrages, likes, coins, favorites, shares and comments. The number of fans shows a significant positive correlation with the numbers of videos and all play and interactive data. Although there is no significant correlation between the number of videos and the play and interactive data, increasing the number of videos can increase the number of fans, thus indirectly improving them.

Keywords: Library · New Media · Bilibili · Video Service

1 Introduction

With the rapid development and popularity of the Internet and mobile terminals, online videos and various we-media have penetrated every aspect of life. They not only provide a platform for users to learn knowledge and share life but also have become the main form of online education. Especially in the postepidemic era, there is a renewed need for online learning and communication, with the penetration rate of users in the video field approaching 97% [1].

On the basis of the traditional website, WeChat and microblog services, libraries with educational functions have also begun to try to use the network video platform to achieve the "three micros and one client" new media matrix. As an iconic brand and a leading video community for young generations in China, Bilibili has been developing rapidly, and its influence in specific fields has been overwhelming in recent years. In the Quest-Mobile Z Generation Insight Report released by Quest Mobile, Bilibili topped the list of apps favored by users aged 24 and below [2]. It can meet the diverse needs of young people in one stop, which also provides new opportunities for online education and video service of the library. In addition to the young user group, the following characteristics also make it an important platform for library video services. First, the

J. Gan et al. (Eds.): CSEI 2023, CCIS 1900, pp. 68–78, 2024.
https://doi.org/10.1007/978-981-99-9492-2_7

learning atmosphere of Bilibili is very thick. In 2020, popular science content will see the fastest growth, with a growth rate of 1994%, and pan-knowledge content accounts for 45% of all views [3]. Online learning on Bilibili has become a new trend among young people in recent years, and it has become the primary position for young people to study [4]. After that, as the largest barrage video website in China, Bilibili excels in real-time interactivity. Users can comment on the screen as barrage, which can be seen by future users at a fixed time, becoming a part of the video content. In addition, compared with short video apps, the video mode of Bilibili is in line with the needs of library work: on the one hand, the time limit of video is very loose; and on the other hand, the dominant mode of video is landscape, which preserves more visual information [5].

2 Literature Review

Gupta D K et al. concluded that social media is likely to replace traditional marketing as the most appropriate platform for library marketing [6]. The emergence and use of social media has had a huge impact on library services, as it is possible to use network communication to find target customers who need library information and services [7]. According to a survey of American public libraries [8] and academic libraries [9], Facebook and Twitter are the most commonly used social software for marketing in libraries, and the usage rate of YouTube, the video platform, is only No. 4. Therefore, many foreign studies on library new media marketing are based on Facebook and Twitter, while there are very few studies on network video platforms. In contrast, a questionnaire survey of readers shows that most readers (90.2%) are willing to provide library services through YouTube, and half of readers would like to watch videos recommended by the library [10]. Compared with readers' demand for video services, library video services still have great development space.

In China, there are few studies on library video services, and they are mainly based on short video apps represented by TikTok [11–14], but there are very few studies on other platforms. Less than 15 results were obtained by searching "library" and "Bilibili" in the CNKI database. Xiao Zheng et al. [15] and Wei Xiaozhen et al. [16] took an academic library as the research object and obtained the operation through data and content analysis. Additionally, taking the academic library as the research object, Tang Zhengwu [17] explored the problems existing in operation and communication by calculating the video communication index BVCI. Gong Xuezhu [18] conducted research on short video marketing of academic libraries and public libraries, focusing on comparative analysis of different video platforms. Generally, there are few and unsystematic studies on the video service of libraries based on Bilibili. However, based on the excellent user groups and good learning atmosphere, increasingly more librarians and scholars have gradually begun to realize that more in-depth research is needed to combine library work with the advantages of Bilibili to guide library staff to start and develop video services.

3 Data and Methodology

3.1 Research Object

Public and academic library accounts registered at Bilibili were selected as the research objects. Using "library" as the keyword to search for user information on Bilibili, researchers obtained all the accounts whose user names contained "library". On this basis, by comparing with the List of Libraries Above County Level in the Sixth National Evaluation and Classification of Public Libraries [19] and the National List of Colleges and Universities [20], researchers screened out accounts of public and academic libraries.

3.2 Data Collection

Using the network survey method, the researchers collected registration, authentication, level and other data of all public and academic library accounts in China by March 17, 2022, on Bilibili, including comprehensive operation data such as Feigua index (FI), number of videos (NV), number of fans (NF), date of first and latest contribution for calculating update cycle (UC), as well as play and interactive data such as average number of views (AV), average number of barrage (AB), average number of likes (AL), average number of coins (AC), average number of favorites (AF), average number of shares (AS) and average number of comments (ACm).

Feigua Data (Bilibili version) is a data analysis platform for Bilibili. The Feigua index is the comprehensive value score to reflect the operating performance of accounts and video quality, calculated by this platform based on recent operation data, such as NV, NF and interactive data [21].

3.3 Data Analysis

First, descriptive statistical analysis of the collected data was conducted to find the current scale and characteristics of operations of library accounts. To avoid errors, the accounts under continuous maintenance were selected for effectiveness analysis. Because the data did not meet the requirement of a normal distribution, a nonparametric test (Mann–Whitney U test) was used to analyse the difference between the different natures of libraries and authentication to explore the operation characteristics of library accounts of Bilibili. For the same reason, the Spearman rank correlation coefficient was calculated to test the correlation between all data and further verified whether the influence of the accounts can be enhanced by increasing the number of videos.

All data were statistically analysed using Microsoft Excel 2019 and IBM SPSS Statistics 25.

4 Results

4.1 Registration and Maintenance

After searching, 83 valid library accounts were obtained, including 44 public libraries and 39 academic libraries, accounting for 53% and 47%, respectively, and the institution authentication rate was 59%. (Table 1).

Table 1. Registration and authentication of public library (PL) and academic library (AL) accounts

Library	Authenticated		Unauthenticated		Total	
	N	Ratio	N	Ratio	N	Ratio
PL	29	65.9%	15	34.1%	44	53.0%
AL	20	51.3%	19	48.7%	39	47.0%
Total	49	59.0%	34	41.0%	83	100%

The distribution of the level of public and academic library accounts is provided in Fig. 1. The vast majority are level 2 and 3 accounts, with no level 6 accounts. The improvement of the account level is mainly related to the number of account logins, uses, videos and coins, so it can be seen that the utilization rate of library accounts is not high. In addition, compared with public libraries, the account levels of academic libraries are mainly at Level 2, and there are no level 5 accounts. The utilization rate of academic library accounts is relatively lower.

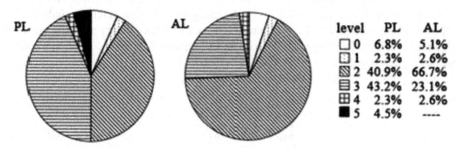

level	PL	AL
0	6.8%	5.1%
1	2.3%	2.6%
2	40.9%	66.7%
3	43.2%	23.1%
4	2.3%	2.6%
5	4.5%	----

Fig. 1. Level of public library (PL) and academic library (AL) accounts

Since the account registration date is not available on Bilibili, the first release date of each account is set as the registration date. The first registered library is Anhui Agricultural University Library (May 2016), and the first registered public library is Wuqing District Library, Tianjin (August 2017). However, these two accounts did not continue to operate, with only one video on the same day. According to the interval between the last and the first update, the longest operating library accounts are Foshan Library, Harbin Institute of Technology (Weihai) Library and Nankai University Library. However, the account of the Harbin Institute of Technology (Weihai) Library has not been updated in over a year.

The following rules can be found through the cross-comparison of the library account registration and the latest update time: (1) Most of the library accounts were registered in 2020, which is in line with the development of Bilibili. (2) 28.9% of accounts have not been updated for more than half a year, and more than half of the accounts opened before 2020 are no longer in operation. The management of the library account is not sufficiently sustainable (Table 2).

Table 2. Registration and updating dates of library accounts

Registration date	Last Update/N					Ratio
	within 30 days	within 60 days	within 90 days	more than 6 months	Total	
Before2020	1	4	4	5	9	10.8%
2020	20	31	33	12	45	54.2%
2021	7	13	16	7	23	27.7%
2022	4	6	6	0	6	7.2%
Total	32	54	59	24	83	--
Ratio	38.6%	65.1%	71.1%	28.9%	--	100.00%

4.2 Effect Analysis

Based on the observation of collected data and the analysis above, it is found that some accounts have a low number of videos or lack continuous operation. To ensure the validity of the data, library accounts with more than 10 videos and updated within half a year were selected as the research objects for the analysis of various reference indicators. (There were 43 accounts with more than 10 videos. Finally, 41 library accounts met the requirements, including 24 public libraries and 17 university libraries. Table 3 provides the descriptive statistics of the variables.

Table 3. Descriptive analysis

	Index	N	Min	Max	Mean	SD
Comprehensive operation data	FI	41	302.2	1015	603.12	162.54
	NV	41	11	331	70.05	65.39
	NF	41	31	37212	2636.61	6118.37
	UC	41	1.67	49.82	14.71	11
Play and interaction data	AV	41	50.26	3449.43	578	717.41
	AB	41	0	10.19	1.56	2.56
	AL	41	0.91	108.22	20.42	26.43
	AC	41	0.14	32.33	6.92	8.75
	AF	41	0.42	255.09	23.02	48.65
	AS	41	0.38	35.31	5.64	6.88
	ACm	41	0.087	13.85	2.99	3.51

- Although the mean of FI is over half the accounts of Bilibili [21], as official accounts, the index has yet to improve further. Compared with the daily number of readers, NF is obviously too low.
- Overall, the comprehensive operation data show the characteristics of low mean and large variance. It can be seen that the operation situation of different libraries varies greatly, and the operation strength is obviously insufficient.
- All of the play and interaction data were even more subdued, indicating that the quality and interactivity of videos need to be improved.

To deeply explore the operation status and characteristics, the samples are grouped according to the nature of libraries and authentication, and the differences between the two groups of data are calculated. Because the data did not meet the requirement of a normal distribution, nonparametric detection was used.

Through the Mann–Whitney U test, there are significant differences in NV and AC between public and academic library accounts ($p < 0.05$). The mean value of NV of public library accounts is more than double that of academic library accounts. In contrast, the mean value of AC of academic library accounts is nearly double that of public library accounts, which shows that fans or audiences of academic library accounts are more willing to pay to support. However, there is no significant difference in other interaction data (Table 4).

Table 4. Mann-Whitney U test of public library (PL) and academic library (AL) accounts

Index	PL			AL			Z and sig.
	N	Mean	SD	N	Mean	SD	
FI	24	609.47	170.43	17	594.15	155.39	−0.291
NV	24	90.75	77.34	17	40.82	23.25	−2.290 *PL > CL
NF	24	3237.13	7665.85	17	1788.82	2793.97	−0.053
UC	24	12.40	9.67	17	17.96	12.21	−1.905
AV	24	534.81	813.69	17	638.97	572.89	−1.747
AB	24	1.41	2.24	17	1.79	3.01	−0.410
AL	24	17.27	25.26	17	24.87	28.15	−1.694
AC	24	4.99	7.33	17	9.64	10.03	−2.143*PL < CL
AF	24	15.44	33.16	17	33.72	64.26	−0.847
AS	24	5.01	7.11	17	6.51	6.65	−1.217
ACm	24	3.02	4.23	17	2.95	2.23	−1.508

Note: * $p < 0.05$, ** $p < 0.01$, *** $p < 0.001$.

Authenticated library accounts are significantly higher than unauthenticated accounts in all four comprehensive operation data. In addition, it can be found that the operation of authenticated accounts is better than that of unauthenticated accounts. Institutional authentication is an important part of official account registration and a manifestation of the library's emphasis on account operation. From the analysis result, it can be seen that the importance that the library attaches to video service has a remarkable effect on the operation of the account (Table 5).

Table 5. Mann-Whitney U test of authenticated and unauthenticated library accounts

Index	Authenticated			Unauthenticated			Z and sig.
	N	Mean	SD	N	Mean	SD	
FI	11	650.16	152.36	30	474.83	116.70	−2.884**C > U
NV	11	83.833	68.90	30	32.45	34.81	−3.503***C > U
NF	11	3462.73	6997.85	30	383.55	305.80	−2.884**C > U
UC	11	11.13	8.39	30	24.50	11.67	−3.237 **C < U
AV	11	573.94	674.42	30	589.07	859.93	−1.206
AB	11	1.87	2.86	30	0.74	1.18	−1.810
AL	11	20.80	27.38	30	19.39	24.85	−0.912
AC	11	6.89	8.46	30	7.05	9.92	−1.030
AF	11	20.50	36.07	30	29.87	74.99	−0.353
AS	11	5.93	7.62	30	4.82	4.48	−0.294
ACm	11	3.21	3.67	30	2.40	3.08	−1.206

Note: * $p < 0.05$, ** $p < 0.01$, *** $p < 0.001$.

Correlation analysis was conducted on the data of 41 accounts to further explore the internal relationship of each variable. Calculated by other variables, FI was not used as a correlation analysis variable. Since the data did not meet the requirement of a normal distribution, Spearman's correlation coefficient analysis was adopted (Table 6).

- First, there is a significant positive correlation between all the play and interaction data ($r_s > 0$, $p < 0.001$). They are effective indicators to measure the quality and interactivity of library accounts and can promote each other to enhance the communication power and influence of accounts.
- Second, NF shows a significant positive correlation with play and interactive data ($r_s > 0$, $p < 0.001$), which shows that increasing NF can improve the influence and interactivity of library accounts.
- Third, there is no significant correlation between NV and the play and interactive data ($p > 0.05$), so increasing NV cannot improve them directly. However, NV shows a significant positive correlation with NF, which shows a significant positive correlation with the play and interactive data. Therefore, NF can be increased by increasing NV and then indirectly promote all the play and interactive data by increasing NF.

Table 6. The results of Spearman's correlation analysis

r_S, sig	NV	NF	UC	AV	AB	AL	AC	AF	AS	ACm
NV	1	0.501***	−0.869**	0.273	0.187	0.172	0.004	0.243	0.197	0.073
NF	0.501***	1	−0.415**	0.670***	0.545***	0.667***	0.622***	0.733***	0.691***	0.518***
UC	−0.869**	−0.415**	1	−0.187	−0.111	−0.141	0.053	−0.112	−0.069	−0.088
AV	0.273	0.670***	−0.187	1	0.658***	0.829***	0.714***	0.839***	0.861***	0.672***
AB	0.189	0.545***	−0.111	0.658***	1	0.800***	0.789***	0.601***	0.679***	0.781***
AL	0.172	0.667***	−0.141	0.829***	0.800***	1	0.905***	0.739***	0.868***	0.880***
AC	0.004	0.622***	0.052	0.714***	0.789***	0.905***	1	0.697***	0.814***	0.808***
AF	0.244	0.733***	−0.112	0.839***	0.601***	0.739***	0.697***	1	0.890***	0.521***
AS	0.198	0.691***	−0.069	0.861***	0.679***	0.868***	0.814***	0.890***	1	0.720***
ACm	0.073	0.518***	−0.088	0.672***	0.781***	0.880***	0.808***	0.521***	0.720***	1

Note: * $p < 0.05$, ** $p < 0.01$, *** $p < 0.001$.

5 Findings and Suggestions

5.1 Insufficient Attention

This shows that the use of Bilibili has not been fully popularized in libraries, and registered libraries have not paid enough attention to video services.

The Registration Rate Is Low. The number of library accounts registered on Bilibili is steadily increasing, and the videos are beginning to take shape after accumulation. However, compared with microblogs or WeChat [20], the registration rate of libraries on Bilibili is still obviously low, so it needs to be popularized more widely in library business.

The Authentication Rate Is Low. The analysis proves that the operation of authenticated accounts is significantly better than that of unauthenticated accounts. Institutional authentication is also the first step for libraries to attach importance to video services. However, compared with previous studies [17, 22], the authentication rate has not significantly increased, and the authentication rate of public library accounts has even decreased slightly.

Lack of Continuity and Stability. Forty-eight percent of the library accounts have no more than 10 videos, 28.9% of the accounts have not been updated for more than half a year, and the average update period of the valid accounts is more than two weeks. All these data reflect the poor sustainability and stability of the operation. The library does not pay enough attention to video services and lacks long-term planning and sustainable development strategies, so the service effect is not obvious.

Bilibili is an excellent library video service platform, a further extension of library reading promotion activities, and an important link of library new media service matrix. Libraries should attach importance to video service, actively register and complete institution authentication in time, and maintain the account continuously and forcefully. In addition, it should be fully integrated with the website, WeChat, other video platforms and offline reader activities, mutual drainage, mutual promotion, and integration of content and platform functions to achieve a matrix serving as an aggregation platform.

5.2 Weak Influence

The Feigua index and other indexes of library accounts are all low, indicating that the social influence and promotion effect of library accounts is not ideal. From the perspective of data, it was found that increasing the number of fans is the most effective way to improve the play and interaction data, and the cumulative number of videos can also promote an increase in fans. Therefore, the number of fans and the number of videos are two major breakthroughs to enhance the influence of library accounts.

Libraries Need to Dig Deeper into Readers. For example, a comparison between public libraries and academic libraries shows that academic libraries have a better fan base and are more willing to support their school libraries by coin. Therefore, academic libraries can produce more emotional videos, which are more likely to resonate with readers and keep fans active and loyal.

Accumulate Video Quantity and Enhance Influence. It is necessary to make a continuous development plan and keep high frequency updates. Libraries can reasonably plan long-term video columns according to the advantages of their own collections and reading promotion activities and explore a new reading promotion model suitable for video services.

5.3 Content and Professionalism

Content is the most important factor in determining the influence and dissemination effect of videos. From the analysis results of this study, it can be found that the play and interaction data of library accounts are very low, which shows that the library needs to improve the quality of content:

Interest and Individuation. Most library accounts currently rely on lectures and event clips for their videos. Therefore, the verticality of the content is high, but the homogeneity is also high, and the style is very singular. The nature of the Internet is entertainment, and "fun" is the key word for users to select and evaluate short videos [23]. Therefore, libraries need to constantly innovate in the content and form of videos, infiltrate interest and individuation into all links from video production to transmission, and deliver a relaxed atmosphere to readers.

Enhance Professionalism. Libraries should set up professional reading promotion and new media marketing teams, which need professional learning and training. Professional and technical personnel are required to participate in video planning, copywriting, directing, filming, editing and postproduction, as well as account management and maintenance. Under the condition of limited human resources, libraries can strengthen cooperation with other professional and technical groups or individuals.

6 Conclusion

With the advent of the information age, readers' reading habits have undergone subtle changes. Libraries should adapt to this change as soon as possible and actively meet the challenges brought by networks and technology. The video service work of libraries on Bilibili is still immature, so more attempts and explorations are needed. It is hoped that this research will provide a reference and basis for more libraries to carry out video services to comprehensively enhance the social influence of libraries and enhance the cultural atmosphere of society.

References

1. Development Trend of 2021 Network Video Market: Content, Platform and Realization. https://www.163.com/dy/article/G7N74QGC0517D57R.html. Accessed 13 May 2023
2. Gen Z Insights Report. https://www.questmobile.com.cn/research/report-new/31. Accessed 13 May 2023
3. Rui, C.: CEO of Bilibili: Community Health is More Important Than Scale Growth, and Content with Broad Knowledge Accounts for 45% of the Platform's Airtime. http://www.jjckb.cn/2021-06/28/c_1310031772.htm. Accessed 13 May 2023

4. You know what? This class of young people love to study on Bilibili. http://news.cctv.com/2019/04/17/ARTIkdxgldxCuSmVdTOimrAw190417.shtml. Accessed 13 May 2023

5. Nie, J.: Opportunities and challenges of medium video in short video era. Sheng Ping Shi Jie **05**, 7–8 (2021)

6. Gupta, D.K., Gupta, B.M., Gupta, R.: Global library marketing research: a scientometric assessment of publications output during 2006–2017. Libr. Manag. **40**(3/4), 251–261 (2019)

7. Muhammad, A., Tang, Z.: What is the relationship between marketing of library sources and services and social media? A literature review paper. Library Hi Tech News **37**(3), 1–5 (2020)

8. Namjoo, C., Soohyung, J.: Understanding public libraries' challenges, motivators, and perceptions toward the use of social media for marketing. Library Hi Tech **39**(2), 352–367 (2021)

9. Zhang, N.: Social media marketing of American university libraries and enlightenment to China. Libr. Work Study **6**, 35–41 (2020)

10. Prabhu, A., Victor, S., Tamizhchelvan, M.: YouTube: the new age marketing strategy for library services. Libr. Philos. Pract., 1–9 (2021)

11. Sun, Y., Chen, F.: Research on the service status and development strategies of "Tik Tok" short video service in public libraries. Libr. Work Study **01**, 85–94 (2021)

12. Sui, X., Yan, Y.: Exploration and analysis of the operation of short video services of provincial public libraries in China—data analysis based on "Tik Tok" app. Res. Libr. Sci. **01**, 65–71 (2021)

13. Zhang, C.: Research on strategy of digital reading promotion in public libraries based on short video marketing. Libr. Work Study **05**, 85–91 (2021)

14. Wang, X., Xia, X.: A Research on the dissemination capability of library's short video accounts: cases of the provincial public libraries. Res. Libr. Sci. **05**, 45–52 (2021)

15. Xiao, Z., Chen, L., Huang, G.: Research on Bilibili website strategies for academic libraries in the PostEpidemic period. Libr. J. **41**(10), 42–48+82 (2022)

16. Wei, X., Liu, L.: Status and thoughts of university library video service—taking Bilibili platform as an example. Libr. Work Study **07**, 58–65 (2021)

17. Tang, Z.: Investigation on the situation of services of barrage video network platform in university libraries—a case study of Bilibili. Res. Libr. Sci. **03**, 25–36 (2021)

18. Gong, X.: A comparative study on short video marketing between public libraries and university libraries. J. Acad. Libr. **39**(04), 48–56+72 (2021)

19. List of Libraries Above County Level in the Sixth National Evaluation and Classification of Public Libraries. http://zwgk.mct.gov.cn/zfxxgkml/ggfw/202012/t20201205916609.html. Accessed 13 May 2023

20. National List of Colleges and Universities. http://www.moe.gov.cn/jyb_xxgk/s5743/s5744/A03/202110/t20211025_574874.html. Accessed 13 May 2023

21. What's the Feigua index? http://bz.feigua.cn/Home/Help?blogId=77&pageIndex=1. Accessed 13 May 2023

22. Xiong, W., Xu, Q.: Research on the operation status of the social video platform of public libraries: a case study of Bilibili. Res. Libr. Sci. **15**, 23–32 (2021)

23. Research Report on Short Video Platform Users. https://36kr.com/p/1723825668097. Accessed 13 May 2023

Exploration of Teaching Mode of Intelligent Product Modeling Design Based on CDIO Active Learning

Honghong Chen[1(✉)], Xu Wang[2], and Shifen Zhong[1]

[1] Xihua University, Chengdu 610039, China
chenhh@mail.xhu.edu.cn
[2] University of Electronic Science and Technology of China, Chengdu 611731, China

Abstract. This paper applies the CDIO active learning method to the teaching design of Intelligent Product Modeling and Design, based on the CDIO engineering education model. The active learning mode is determined based on classroom teaching activities and comprehensive projects, including decomposition teaching, flipped classroom, debate, and team cooperation. From a teaching effectiveness perspective, this mode significantly improves students' class participation, stimulates their interest in learning, and enhances their systematic thinking and innovation abilities.

Keywords: Active Learning Method · Intelligent Product Modeling Design · CDIO · Teaching Mode

1 Introduction

CDIO is a teaching model based on engineering education that emphasizes students' learning and application of knowledge in practice. It cultivates their engineering practical ability and teamwork spirit and consists of four steps: Conceive, Design, Implement, and Operate. This teaching model is widely used worldwide and has received positive evaluations from students and teachers. Although the CDIO model consists of only four steps, students need to master many skills and much knowledge in each step.

In the Conceive phase, students must understand customer needs and translate them into feasible design plans. To do this, they need to learn skills such as requirements analysis, goal setting, and risk assessment. Additionally, students must consider various limiting factors such as time, cost, and resources. These skills will help students better understand customer needs and provide practical and feasible solutions.

In the Design phase, students transform the design plans from the Conceive phase into detailed implementation plans. They need to learn skills such as system design, simulation, and optimization. Additionally, students must consider various technical limiting factors such as hardware, software, and network. These skills will help students better understand the design plans and provide practical and feasible implementation plans.

J. Gan et al. (Eds.): CSEI 2023, CCIS 1900, pp. 79–89, 2024.
https://doi.org/10.1007/978-981-99-9492-2_8

In the Implement phase, students transform the design plans into actual products or systems. They need to learn skills such as programming, manufacturing, and testing. Additionally, students must consider various implementation limiting factors such as technology, resources, and quality. These skills will help students better understand the implementation plans and provide practical and feasible products or systems.

In the Operate phase, students must master the skills of operating and maintaining products or systems. They need to learn skills such as user training, troubleshooting, and maintenance. Additionally, students must consider various operating limiting factors such as user needs, maintenance costs, and safety. These skills will help students better understand the operation and maintenance of products or systems and provide practical and feasible solutions.

The CDIO active learning method provides students with a unique and effective way of learning engineering knowledge, creating a more practical and hands-on learning experience for engineering students. This method focuses on four key pillars: engineering fundamentals, engineering design, engineering implementation, and engineering systems, and professional skills. By integrating these pillars into the curriculum, students can have a more comprehensive understanding of engineering and its real-world applications. By focusing on practical applications and cooperation, it prepares students for their future careers and helps them become comprehensive and successful engineers.

One of the main advantages of the CDIO method is that it encourages students to play a more active role in learning. Students are not just memorizing theories and concepts but are encouraged to apply them in practical projects and assignments. This not only helps them better understand the material but also prepares them for their future careers.

Another key advantage of the CDIO method is that it promotes cooperation and teamwork among students. By working together on projects and assignments, students learn how to communicate effectively and develop their interpersonal skills. This is especially important in the engineering field, where cooperation is often a necessary condition for success. As the latest achievement in international engineering education research, the concept of CDIO engineering education has been increasingly accepted by colleges and universities in China as a teaching reform model for some courses. At the heart of this concept is an emphasis on students' active participation in various learning activities. Therefore, many proactive learning approaches and implementations have been designed to accommodate a wide variety of different teaching activities in the 8th Criterion of the CDIO concept [1].

In recent years, many Chinese colleges and universities have explored students' active learning experiences and achieved fruitful results. For instance, Dr. Panlong Dan from Tianjin Sino-German University of Applied Technology adopted active learning implementation measures such as flipped classroom, teamwork, and task-driven approaches in the industrial robot technology training project, constructing a relatively complete teaching system of CBE + CDIO courses [2]. Professor Kai Xu from China University of Geosciences combined the training idea of CDIO with the experimental teaching of remote sensing geology and adopted the active learning method based on the project, allowing students to learn according to each link of CDIO, which effectively trained students' engineering and innovation abilities [3]. Minghong Sun from Dalian Neusoft University of Information constructed the finance curriculum teaching system of

OBE-CDIO, combined with the actual characteristics of each course and based on market demand, designed a student training system based on active learning, including the types of discussion topics and projects [4].

2 Curriculum Characteristics Analysis

Intelligent product modeling design is a practical course that enables students to master the elements of shape and functional design of intelligent products. Students will learn to design and create intelligent products using mechanical design, embedded systems, cloud computing technology, and principles of ergonomics and related knowledge points [5]. This course integrates intelligent product design and manufacturing into practical courses and targets students from multiple majors, with the aim of achieving professional integration.

Table 1 presents the main features of the course, which include a large number of knowledge points, strong interdisciplinary features, and abundant varieties. The knowledge requirements vary for different student teams.

Due to professional training programs, class hour limits, and other reasons, it is impossible to comprehensively cover all knowledge points during teaching. Therefore, students are required to conduct self-study before class, which demands high independent learning ability. Additionally, due to the diversity of teaching objects, we need to consider the integration of majors. Therefore, these characteristics are matched with the teaching mode of CDIO active learning method.

Table 1. Course Features.

Course Objectives	Knowledge demand	Teaching objects (Professional)	Ability mapping of CDIO	Planned projects
The students will design and manufacture a intelligent product in the form of a team	Principles of bionics, Principles of human-computer engineering, Design of automatic Control systems, Cloud computing technology, Mechanical design, etc.	Intelligence science and technology, Electronic information engineering, Intelligent product development	Engineering reasoning and problem-solving skills, Systematic thinking, Teamwork, etc.	Track auto-searching robots, Smart Trash cans, Intelligent remote lock picking devices, etc.

3   Active Learning Teaching Mode Design

Based on the characteristics of the analyzed course, active learning is adopted in the form of project-based, problem-oriented, or task-oriented methods [6]. The teaching process includes classroom activities and comprehensive projects outside of class. To succeed in completing classroom tasks or projects, students are required to learn independently before class and view classroom activities and after-school projects as the integration and application of relevant knowledge. The design process of this course is illustrated in Fig. 1.

Fig. 1. A figure caption is always placed below the illustratio.

3.1   Pre-knowledge of Online Networking Platforms

During the pre-knowledge stage, teachers should provide students with relevant teaching resources such as videos, literature, PowerPoint presentations, and materials. By doing so before class, students can independently learn and grasp the necessary knowledge points for class activities and after-class projects, thus laying a solid theoretical foundation. When designing this stage, teachers should primarily use the online classroom platform to provide students with learning resources and keep track of their progress.

Using the innovative design theory of morphological analysis as an example, pre-knowledge resources include: the PowerPoint presentation on the innovative design theory of morphological analysis, a guide for operating 3D modeling software, the construction of a morphological analysis matrix for intelligent products (i.e., an intelligent product scheme idea), and design reference materials. After students have learned this material, teachers can monitor their learning progress through the teaching quality tracking module of the network platform. If necessary, teachers can take corresponding measures to further improve the effectiveness of students' independent learning. Table 2 shows an example of learning data, presented in the learning quality tracking link of an online classroom, using 39 students in an intelligent major class as a sample.

Table 2. Data of learning outcome (knowledge points of morphological analysis).

Learning Rate of PPT(%)	Job Completion Rate(%)	Good and Excellent Job Ratio(%)	Assessment of Knowledge Mastery
92.3	92.3	74.4	good

Table 2 demonstrates that prior to class, students had essentially mastered the knowledge of morphological analysis through independent online learning with corresponding materials provided by the network platform. The learning rate was as high as 92.3%, and the good rate of the constructed morphological analysis matrix was as high as 74.4%. This indicates that the preposition of knowledge is relatively effective, laying a foundation for further development of classroom teaching activities.

3.2 Design of Teaching Activities

In classroom teaching, once students have mastered the relevant knowledge points, teaching activities should focus on these points to help students apply them in practice. When teaching intelligent product modeling design, there are various types of activities, including problem discussions, communication and sharing, micro-project development, creative design through team cooperation, and ice-breaking games. The application of active learning may vary depending on the knowledge points covered. For instance, in

Table 3. Teaching activity design of micro-project based on active learning (intelligent manipulator).

Process	Active learning method	Implementation patterns	Student action	Student output
Pre-knowledge	Problem-oriented active learning	Online learning style, Group learning style	Learning resources and conducting group discussions through the online platform for courses	
Teaching activities	Project-oriented active learning	Flipped classroom, Decomposes teaching, Fole-playing, teamwork	Learn about circuit design for students majoring in electronics, Learn about mechanical structure for students majoring in intelligent, Communicate and share with each other in class, Deam members clearly divided roles and tasks, Complete the design of structure and circuit in cooperation	Complete the full set of intelligent Manipulator design(including: structure, shape, circuit and control system)

the micro-project "intelligent manipulator design based on morphological analysis," students majoring in electronics and intelligence need to apply knowledge in morphological analysis theory, single-chip microcomputer principles, sensor technology, mechanical structure, and related fields. Therefore, cross-professional student teams are organized [7]. Table 3 shows the active learning teaching design centered on the micro-project.

Table 3 contains active learning activities that, when implemented, produced the specific outputs shown in Fig. 2–3.

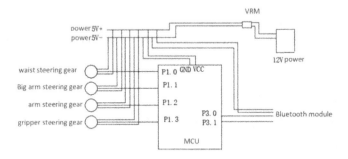

Fig. 2. Circuit design (output by electronics students).

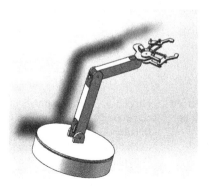

Fig. 3. Structural design (output by intelligent student).

3.3 Implementation of Comprehensive Projects

Figure 4 shows the specific method of implementing active learning in the design of the course's teaching activities.

In the teaching practice of this course, each project team is composed of 4 to 5 students. The comprehensive project process includes the following steps: student information retrieval, information analysis (project approval), product scheme idea, design, manufacturing, and testing.

Fig. 4. Active learning implementation patterns.

4 Teaching Effectiveness Tracking

4.1 Student Achievement

In the practice of integrated projects, student teams designed and manufactured approximately 50 intelligent products. Based on the level of creativity, the students' works were graded into four categories: very creative, more creative, creative, and not creative. Table 4 shows the evaluation criteria for each category.

Table 4. Criteria for rating creative works

Level of creativity	Very creative	More creative	Creative	No creative
Evaluation criteria	The intelligent products that have not yet appeared and are originally developed	The existing intelligent products that have made significant improvements in their structure and functions	The existing intelligent products that one or two details have been improved	Duplicate design of the existing products without improvement

The evaluation criteria for creative works are described below:

- Uniqueness of creativity: Whether the work is unique and original.
- Innovation in functionality: Whether the work is innovative in terms of functionality and improves the functions of existing products.
- Innovation in structure: Whether the work is innovative in terms of structure and improves the structure of existing products.

- Improvement in details: Whether the work has made improvements in one or two details that can provide a better user experience.
- Feasibility of manufacturing: Whether the work is feasible for manufacturing and can be produced with existing technology and resources.
- Market demand: Whether the work meets the market demand and has sufficient market potential.

Creative works should be classified and evaluated based on different levels of evaluation criteria. The assessment criteria for each aspect should be specifically described in the evaluation criteria to ensure the accuracy and reliability of the evaluation. The evaluation focuses on the creativity and practicality of the work, as well as its ability to meet market demand.

Table 5 shows the evaluation results of 50 student works based on these criteria and fully considers the characteristics of creative works.

Table 5. Evaluation of students' creative works

Creative level	Very creative	More creative	Creative	No creativity
Number of works(pieces)	4	11	26	9
Proportion(%)	8	22	52	18

Table 5 indicates that 30% of the students' work was classified as "very creative," and 52% was classified as "creative." This suggests that the majority of student teams analyzed existing product problems and proposed solutions during the development of comprehensive projects. By comparing this with the CDIO ability mapping shown in Table 1, it can be observed that students' engineering reasoning and problem-solving skills have been effectively cultivated, thus achieving the expected goal.

Part of students' creative works in micro-projects and comprehensive projects in teaching activities are shown in Fig. 5–6.

Fig. 5. The peacock tail lights.

Fig. 6. A robot that mimics an octopus folding clothes.

4.2 Questionnaire Survey

The teaching practice of the course emphasizes students' active learning experience [8, 9]. To evaluate the effectiveness of the CDIO teaching model, a questionnaire survey was conducted among students after the course. The survey questions were designed based on the CDIO competency evaluation criteria and the problem design method of Singapore Polytechnic.

Evaluation criteria typically employ multiple evaluation methods, including classroom tests, project reports, laboratory reports, and work exhibitions. The focus is on evaluating students' practical abilities, rather than just their mastery of knowledge.

These abilities include:

(1) Conceive stage: Students can understand customer needs and transform them into feasible design plans.
(2) Design stage: Students can transform design plans into detailed implementation plans.
(3) Implement stage: Students can transform implementation plans into actual products or systems.
(4) Operate stage: Students can master the operation and maintenance skills of products or systems.

Through this competency evaluation, the CDIO teaching model can better cultivate students' practical abilities and team spirit. The questionnaire survey was designed to cover five dimensions: students' awareness of CDIO skills, evaluation of teaching strategies, integration of abilities, perception of ability improvement, and learning experience. Table 6 shows the results of the student questionnaire.

The questions for the questionnaire are as follows:

Q1: Do you think your ability to identify and solve problems has improved during the course?

Q2: Do you feel that the teacher's instructional design can effectively motivate you to learn actively?

Q3: Do you think your innovative thinking has been effectively trained?

Q4: Do you think the course's instructional activities are effective in cultivating teamwork skills?

Q5: Has your confidence in team communication significantly improved through the course learning?

The answers to the questionnaire are as follows:

Q1: A - very big improvement, B - big improvement, C - general, D - no improvement.

Q2: A - very big incentive, B - big incentive, C - general.

Q3: A - very effective, B - more effective, C - general, D - invalid.

Q4: A - very effective, B - more effective, C - general, D - invalid.

Q5: A - very big improvement, B - big improvement, C - no improvement.

The results of the student questionnaire survey are shown in Table 6.

Table 6. Questionnaire survey

Type of problems	Q1				Q2			Q3				Q4				Q5		
Type of answers	A	B	C	D	A	B	C	A	B	C	D	A	B	C	D	A	B	C
Results(%)	23	52	11	14	35	48	17	31	44	12	13	27	51	12	10	33	46	21

Table 6 presents the results of a questionnaire survey. Seventy-five percent of students reported a significant improvement in their ability to identify and solve problems through the course, while 83% agreed that the teacher's activities effectively motivated them to learn actively. Additionally, 75% of students reported that their innovative thinking had been effectively trained, and 78% felt that the course's teaching activities were quite effective in cultivating teamwork skills. Furthermore, 79% of students believed that their confidence in team communication had significantly improved through the course. These results demonstrate that the use of active learning methods in teaching intelligent product modeling design courses has a positive impact on student abilities and learning experiences and is, therefore, worth promoting and improving further.

These results demonstrate that the active learning method used in teaching intelligent product modeling design has a positive impact on students' ability improvement and academic experience. Therefore, it is worth promoting and further improving this teaching method.

5　Conclusion

This paper analyzes the characteristics of the Intelligent Product Modeling Design course and proposes an active learning teaching mode based on teaching activities and comprehensive projects. By utilizing active learning implementation modes such as cross-professional team formation, flipped classrooms, teamwork, and role-playing, good teaching effects have been achieved. These results indicate that the active learning method and characteristics of the Intelligent Product Modeling Design course are well-suited and can be continuously improved in the next steps of curriculum teaching reform to further enhance teaching quality.

References

1. Crawley, E.F., Malmqvist, J., Östlund, S.: Rethinking Engineering Education: The CDIO Approach. Springer, Berlin (2016). https://doi.org/10.1007/978-0-387-38290-6
2. Tan, P., Shao, X., Zhang, J.: Design of Industrial Robot Technology training Project based on CBE+CDIO concept. Exp. Technol. Manag. **36**(11), 189–193 (2018)
3. Xu, K., Liu, G., Wu, C.: Research on innovative experimental design of "Remote sensing geology" based on CDIO Engineering education concept. Chin. Geolog. Educ. **26**(4), 67–69 (2017)
4. Sun, M.: A Research on OBE-CDIO Finance Education Reform Under the Age of Big Data, pp. 21–24. Atlantis Press, Singapore (2017)
5. Liu, J., Liu, F., Yang, Y.: Exploration and practice of "Doing Middle School" in the teaching reform of "3d Modeling and Structural Design of Products." China Train. **7**, 253–257 (2017)
6. Lin, J., Yuan, J.: Analysis and simulation of capacitor-less ReRAM-based stochastic neurons for the in-memory spiking neural network. IEEE T Biomed CIRC S **12**(5), 1004–1017 (2018)
7. Chai, M.: On the research and practice of multi-specialty cooperative teaching mode based on CDIO mode – Taking architectural engineering specialty group as an example. J. Zhejiang Bus. Technol. Inst. **1**, 78–81 (2017)
8. Ye, M., Kong, H., Xu, X.: Discussion on the practical path of new engineering subject: the construction of CDIO conversion platform based on rooted theory. Res. High. Educ. Eng. **4**, 11–17 (2018)
9. Li, R., He, Y.: Experiential teaching reform of metal technology curriculum based on CDIO. Res. Explor. Lab. **36**(6), 186–191 (2017)

Personalized Questioning Teaching Mode for English Reading in Junior High School Based on Automatic Question Generation

Jian Xu[1,2], Liming Zhang[1]([⊠]), Yu Sun[2], Jun Wang[2], and Shoujian Duan[3]

[1] Qujing Normal University, Qujing 655011, Yunnan, China
308053539@qq.com
[2] Yunnan Normal University, Kunming 650500, Yunnan, China
[3] Baoshan University, Baoshan 678000, Yunnan, China

Abstract. Asking questions is a teaching strategy widely used in English reading teaching in junior middle school and plays a vital role in improving students' English reading literacy. However, questioning is a sophisticated mental activity, and it is difficult for teachers to quickly generate personalized questions that meet different teaching stages and students' reading levels. This greatly reduces the effectiveness of questioning. To address this problem, we propose a novel question generation setting called Difficulty-Selectable Question Generation (DSQG), which can be used in junior high school English reading teaching. Further, this technology can be employed to design a personalized questioning teaching model supported for junior high school English teaching. To verify the effectiveness of the teaching model, we conduct an empirical study on an experimental class and an ordinary class in a middle school in Q City of Yunnan Province. The research results show that the personalized questioning teaching model can effectively improve students' reading levels. However, we still need to iterate and improve this teaching mode in practice.

Keywords: Personalization · Questioning Teaching Mode · Difficulty-Selectable Question Generation · Junior High School English Teaching

1 Introduction

As a teaching method with a long history, questioning has always occupied a dominant position in English reading teaching. From the perspective of "educational information communication", asking questions helps students form a complete process of "information receiving—information source processing—information transmission—channel enlightenment—information feedback" [1]. The National Reading Committee of the United States pointed out that questioning is the most important method in the teaching strategy of reading comprehension [2]. The design of questioning is directly related to the effectiveness of teaching. Effective questioning not only stimulates students' thinking but also enhances their critical thinking ability.

However, limited by teachers' teaching experience and ability, questioning teaching suffers from the following challenges. First, although questioning has been adopted broadly in English reading teaching in junior high schools, there is a lack of standard questioning teaching models to guide teaching. In English reading comprehension teaching, questioning teaching is the mainstream reading teaching style. Due to the lack of standard teaching model guidance, questioning teaching presents the characteristics of spontaneity and dispersion, making the quality of questioning teaching depend on teachers' improvisation. Nevertheless, teachers are restricted by teaching experience, teaching ability, physical and mental state and other internal and external factors. There are many problems in the questioning teaching of junior middle school English reading comprehension in our country, such as not wide, not deep, and not highly personalized problems. Second, the intelligence level of questioning teaching should be further improved. In recent years, with the breakthrough of deep neural network technology in natural language processing tasks, artificial intelligence technology represented by automatic question generation technology continues to improve the level of education intelligence; however, research on the automatic generation of English reading comprehension questions in junior high schools is still relatively lacking. Third, the deep integration of artificial intelligence and education lacks application demonstrations. At present, the degree of education informatization is still at a low and shallow level, the educational application of artificial intelligence is still in its infancy, and there is a lack of mature artificial intelligence application education demonstrations. Therefore, exploring the application path of artificial intelligence and junior high school English education will provide a demonstration for the deep integration of other disciplines of basic education and information technology.

To address the above three challenges, we innovatively explore the mode of DSQG for junior high school English reading teaching, aiming to generate personalized questions for each stage of teaching. Additionally, we design the personalized questioning teaching mode based on the automatic generation of questions and verify its effectiveness in actual teaching.

The rest of this paper is organized as follows: Sect. 2 introduces the construction of the DSQG model, aiming to provide technical support for the individualized questioning teaching model; Sects. 3 and 4 introduce the individualized questioning teaching of English reading model construction and empirical research; and Sect. 5 concludes this paper with future work.

2   DSQG Model

2.1   Overview of DSQG Model

In the field of artificial intelligence, the difficulty selectable question generation (DSQG) task aims to automatically generate questions according to the difficulty level selected by the user. It is prevalent in teaching. For example, questions of various difficulty are automatically generated for teaching, and reading comprehension questions of different difficulty levels are designed for English reading comprehension tests [3].

Existing research on question generation focuses on transforming declarative sentences into interrogative sentences by controlling question words [4] or generating questions from the context [5]. Few people study DSQG because it is difficult to define the difficulty of a question. As far as this paper knows, DSQG is a relatively new work [6]. In 2019, Kumar et al. generated difficult questions based on knowledge graphs [7]. The author estimated question difficulty based on the popularity of named entities in a given article and then injected this difficulty level into the input embedding vector of an encoder based on Transformer to generate difficult questions. The limitation of this model is that a knowledge graph needs to be built in advance. This strategy is inefficient to apply to the generation task of reading comprehension questions in this paper because the construction of knowledge graph in junior middle school English is almost impossible. To bypass the construction of the knowledge graphs, the difficult question generation model proposed by Gao et al. in 2019 can generate simple and hard questions and control the difficulty of the questions by modifying the hidden state of the neural network before decoding [3]. However, this model can only generate questions of "simple" or "hard" difficulty.

In summary, applying current techniques of question generation in reading teaching faces three challenges: First, the answer text is discrete. The training set of the above question generation model is the general question answering dataset SQuAD. These question generation methods cannot be directly used on our dataset RACE4QG (ReAding Comprehension dataset from Examination for Question Generation), which is specifically for middle school students. The obvious difference between SQuAD and RACE4QG is that answers in SQuAD are continuous text spans, while answers in RACE4QG are not. Second, the above question generation method only gives two kinds of difficulty. Third, it does not support the generation of difficult questions at the article level. The input of the encoder of the previous question generation model is a single sentence, rather than an article. Therefore, if we want to generate questions that meet the needs of reading comprehension teaching, we need to address the three challenges mentioned above.

For the first challenge, we look for the most relevant sentence (i.e., key sentence) in the original text according to the answer of the dataset to solve the problem that the answer in the RACE4QG dataset is not a continuous text segment of the original text. At this point, we can use Gao et al.'s idea [3] to calculate proximity hints by calculating the distance between words in an article and the answer to control the difficulty of generating questions. For the second challenge, we extract the characteristics of the RACE4QG dataset and define three difficulty levels: easy, mid, and hard. For the third challenge, we employ the graph attention mechanism and dependency parsing technique to extract the semantic graph of an article. The semantic graph information integrated into the word embedding can cope with the challenge that the model input is limited to a single sentence, so as to expand the model input from a single sentence to multiple sentences (such as an article).

2.2 Methodology for DSQG

Definition of Question Difficulty. Gao et al. of the Chinese University of Hong Kong divided questions into simple questions and hard questions based on whether the questions could be correctly answered by two question answering systems [3]. This method is not optimal in this section because the correct answer text of each question in our dataset RACE4QG is not derived from consecutive words (text span) in the original text. It makes it difficult for questions in RACE4QG to be correctly understood and answered by the question answering system, so that most questions are marked as difficult questions and only some questions are marked as simple questions. So this strategy of question difficulty division is not suitable for our task.

The strategy of dividing the difficulty of the question in this paper comprehensively considers the interrogative words of the question and the length of the question text. Specifically, if the interrogative words of the question are why and how, the question is tagged as hard label; for the remaining questions, we judge whether the question length is greater than 10.87 (the average number of words in the question in RACE4QG), and if so, mark such question as mid label, otherwise, mark such question as easy label. Consequently, the questions in the RACE4QG dataset have three levels of difficulty: *easy*, *mid*, and *hard*.

RACE4QG Dataset. In this paper, we build our dataset based on an existing dataset named EQG-RACE [8], which is constructed specifically for question generation. The sizes of the training set, development set and test set are 41,791, 2,312 and 2,294, respectively. However, this dataset cannot be used directly for the DSQG task in this section. Three tags need to be added to each sample of EQG-RACE: tag, diff_level, and max_sent. The variation of EQG-RACE is called RACE4QG.

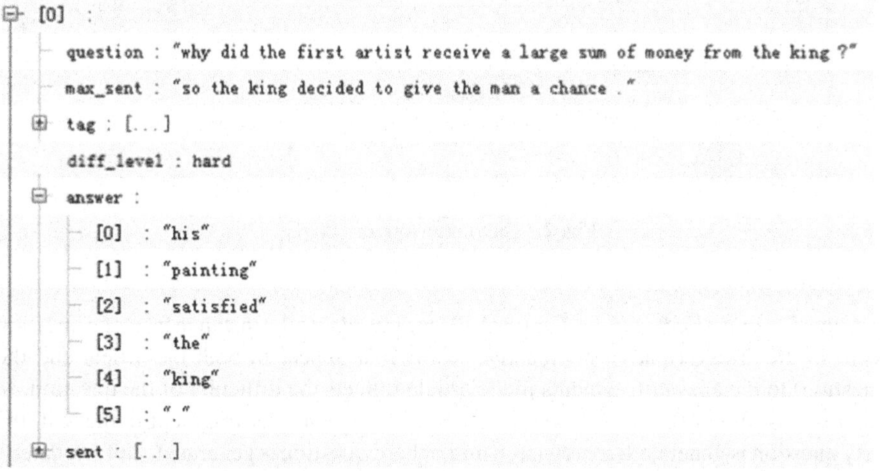

```
[0] :
    question : "why did the first artist receive a large sum of money from the king ?"
    max_sent : "so the king decided to give the man a chance ."
    tag : [...]
    diff_level : hard
    answer :
        [0] : "his"
        [1] : "painting"
        [2] : "satisfied"
        [3] : "the"
        [4] : "king"
        [5] : "."
    sent : [...]
```

Fig. 1. The first example of RACE4QG

Each sample in Fig. 1 includes six fields: *sent, answer, question, diff_level, max_sent,* and *tag*. Among them, "*sent*" represents the input article, "*answer*" represents the answer, "*question*" represents the question, "*diff_level*" represents the answer label of the question (*easy/mid/hard*), "*max_sent*" indicates the sentence most relevant to a specific answer in the input article, "*tag*" is the mark symbol (*O* or *B* or *S*) of each word, and the data type of the field *tag* is a list for each word of the input article tag. For example, enter the article with the text-- *"king and the first artist was surprised. so the king decided to give the man a chance. The following day."*, and the corresponding tag list is *"B, O, O, O, O, O, O, S, S, B, S, S, S, S, S, S, S, S, O, O, O"*, the label of the first word *"king"* is *B*, and so on. The value range of the label is {*O, B, S*}, where *B* represents the answer word (that is, the word also appears in the answer), *S* represents the word in the key sentence, and *O* represents other words except the above two types of words.

The DSQG Model. This section explores the construction of the DSQG model, aiming to generate questions given a reading comprehension article p, an answer a, and a specified difficulty level d, which is formally expressed as $q = DSQG(p, a, d)$.

The framework of DSQG is shown in Fig. 2. The model adopts the "encoder-decoder" architecture, and the input of the encoder is the keyword tagging vector, GAT vector, word embedding vector, and position vector. The input of the decoder includes the output of the encoder as well as the difficulty label of the question. The decoding process utilizes the attention mechanism, the maximum pointer mechanism and the copy mechanism to improve the quality of question generation.

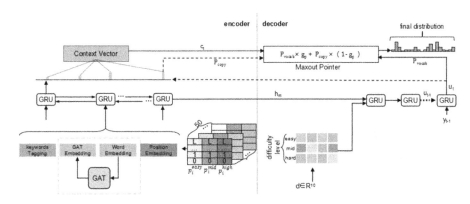

Fig. 2. The framework of DSQG

Relative Location Embedding. Gao et al. [3] proposed that the distance from the question word in the article (that is, noninactive words that appear in both the article and the question) to the answer fragments in the article reflects the difficulty of the question. In other words, the more answer words there are near the answer fragment in the text, the easy question is generated; otherwise, a mid or hard question is generated. Unfortunately, the answer in the RACE4QG of this paper is carefully designed by the teacher and is not directly copied from a fragment of the original text, so it is difficult to calculate the distance. To solve this challenge, we employ the key sentence as the origin of the distance calculation to calculate the distance from the origin of related words.

Thus far, it is easy to calculate the distance from the question word in the input article to the key sentence. This distance is called the relative position. Since this relative position reflects the accuracy and difficulty of the word in the article to the generation question, we need to map this relative position into a learnable vector. Accordingly, we build three lookup tables: easy question lookup table, mid question lookup table, and hard question lookup table. Each query table is a two-group table of $L \times d_p$, where L represents the maximum distance and d_p represents the dimension of the vector corresponding to each distance. As shown in Fig. 3.

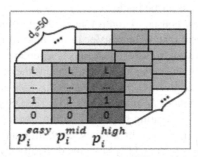

Fig. 3. Three lookup tables: P_i^{easy}, P_i^{mid}, P_i^{hard}

Feature-Enriched Encoder. The dataset RACE4QG in this paper is collected from the English test for middle school students in China. The samples of this dataset mainly include reading comprehension articles, questions and answers. Teachers design these questions to test students' reading comprehension ability (such as the ability to summarize and analyse the emotional aspects of an article), generating such high-quality questions requires a wide range of cognitive skills and, more importantly, the ability to reason based on complex relationships within and between sentences in the text. Generating this kind of question requires an encoder that can capture rich feature information inside the article.

The solution to this challenge was inspired by the work of Jia et al. [7], this paper innovatively uses AO-GAT (Answer Oriented - Graph Attention Networks) to encode the input article, which can capture the semantic information in the article to generate high-quality questions. AO-GAT is a technology that guides the construction of GATs [9] through article answers. GAT is a graph neural network using a self-attention mechanism that can be used to capture the internal structure of an article. The input of the AO-GAT model is an English article, and the output is an embedding vector rich in semantic structure information of the article, called the GAT vector.

By concatenating the keyword tagging vector, GAT vector, word embedding vector, and position vector, a feature-enriched embedding vector $x = $ *[keyword tagging vector, GAT vector, word embedding vector, position vector]*, $x = \{x_1, x_2, ..., x_m\}$, x_i represents the feature-enriched embedding vector of the i-th word in the article.

We utilize a bidirectional GRU [10] to encode the embedding vectors $(x_1, x_2, ..., x_m)$ of each word in the article, and each word can obtain a contextualization representation: $\overrightarrow{h_i} = \overrightarrow{GRU}\left(\overrightarrow{h_{i-1}}, x_i\right), \overleftarrow{h_i} = \overleftarrow{GRU}\left(\overleftarrow{h_{i+1}}, x_i\right)$. Here, $\overrightarrow{h_i}$ and $\overleftarrow{h_i}$ are the forward and hidden states of the i-th time step in the backwards direction. After concatenating both, the hidden state of each article word in the encoder is $h_i = [\overrightarrow{h_i}, \overleftarrow{h_i}]$, and this hidden state will participate in subsequent question generation.

A Decoder with a Selectable Difficulty. In this paper, a unidirectional GRU is used as a decoder to generate reading comprehension questions, and the difficulty label d is used to initialize the decoder. During decoding, the attention mechanism and copy mechanism are used to improve the quality of the question. The difficulty label d and the decoding process of the problem are described below.

The difficulty variable d is used to control the difficulty of the generated questions. In recent years, research on text style transfer in the field of question generation has become popular. The text style transfer model takes a sentence and a style variable as input, and the output is another sentence, which maintains the original sentence but has a different style. For example, given a sentence "*I love this film*" and its style label "*bad*", the model can output a sentence "*I hate this film*" [11]. The DSQG task in this paper can be regarded as the task of generating sentences with a specified style. The style label of the text (i.e., difficulty label) has three types: easy, mid, and hard. Specifically, this paper follows the work of Liao et al. [12] First, the difficulty level d is mapped to an N-dimensional learnable vector $D \in R^N$, and eventually, each difficulty label corresponds to a learned vector representation. Second, the concatenation of D and the hidden state h_m of the last step of the encoder is used to initialize the decoder.

To improve the performance of the question generation model, this paper calculates the current hidden state and the attention distribution of the input article at each time step of the decoder, which is involved in word prediction in the current time step. Meanwhile, it employs the copy mechanism [13] and the maximum pointer mechanism [14] to cooperatively improve the performance of the question generation model.

2.3 Experiment

Experimental Settings. The DSQG model utilizes the "encoder-decoder" architecture of the teacher-forcing strategy [15]. The hidden state dimensions of the encoder and decoder are 300, the dimension of the word embedding vector is 300, the number of attention heads of the GAT is 8, the vocabulary size is 45,000, and the word vector is initialized using pretrained GloVe [16]. The maximum length of the input article was 400 words, the maximum length of the output reading comprehension question was 30, and the upper limit of the relative position size of the article word to the answer L was 20. In the decoding stage, *dropout* = 0.3, *beam_size* = 10.

We utilize the Stanford CoreNLP [17] to obtain the dependency syntax tree of the sentence, and GAT deals with the tree to describe the semantic graph of the article. The hidden state size of the GAT is 300.

Experimental Comparison. To carry out the comparison experiment between this model and the existing model, the model based on a neural network serves as the baseline model to participate in the performance comparison. Additionally, we rewrite two baseline models, S2S [18] and ELMo-QG [19], where the infrastructure of the S2S model is based on the seq-to-seq generation architecture of the RNN with attention and copy mechanisms, and the encoder of ELMo-QG integrates rich linguistic features such as answer location, POS tagging and NER(named entity recognition).

Evaluation and Analysis. It is important to evaluate the performance of the model, and we investigate the performance difference between our model and the two baseline models. The evaluation metrics used to evaluate the model in this paper are BLEU, ROUGE-L, and METEOR.

Table 1. Experimental results for our model compared with baseline models

models	BLEU-1	BLEU-2	BLEU-3	BLEU-4	ROUGE-L	METE0R
S2S	35.30	18.49	11.49	7.95	34.99	15.74
ELMo-QG	32.50	21.03	15.09	12.24	35.08	15.81
Our Model	**36.24**	**21.11**	**15.12**	**12.43**	**35.67**	**16.89**

The experimental results show that the model in this paper surpasses the models participating in the comparison in all metrics, as shown in Table 1. Especially in the most important metric METEOR, our model performed more prominently, and the points of the METEOR increased by approximately 1.

3   Construction of the Personalized Question Teaching Mode

3.1   Overview of the Personalized Questioning Teaching Mode

The teaching model is a stable teaching framework and activity procedure under the guidance of specific teaching theories. The definition of teaching mode shows that it is guided by specific teaching theories, adopts a structural framework to grasp the overall situation from a macro perspective, inspects teaching elements and their relations from a micro perspective, and adopts teaching activity procedures to guide the scientific and orderly development of teaching. As shown in Fig. 4, the "Personalized questioning teaching Model for junior high English Reading supported " (short for "Personalized questioning teaching model") proposed in this paper is a structural framework and activity procedure supported by the DSQG (Difficulty-Selective Question Generation) model, guided by constructivism and schema theory, and the kernel of the SQ3R teaching strategy [20]. "Personalized questioning teaching model" consists of four modules: the module of generating reading comprehension question set, the module of students' reading comprehension ability, the module of personalized recommendation question, and the module of question teaching activity procedure based on SQ3R.

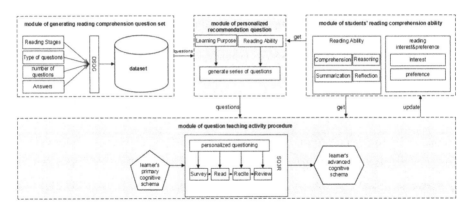

Fig. 4. The personalized question teaching mode

3.2 Four Modules of the Personalized Questioning Teaching Mode

In Fig. 4, its four modules are introduced as follows:

The Module for Generating Reading Comprehension Question Sets. The question set is composed of English articles with multiple-choice questions; it is the power source of individualized questioning teaching models and can provide a large variety of reading comprehension questions in different stages of reading comprehension questioning teaching. Although the RACE4QG dataset constructed in the previous section has the characteristics of large capacity, it is mainly used for training the question generation model. Each article does not have a definite topic, which makes it impossible for teachers to select the specified article to teach according to the topic. Therefore, based on topic modelling technology, this section automatically generates 13 types of topics for all articles in the RACE4QG dataset using LDA(Latent Dirichlet Allocation) technology [21]. Thus, teachers and students can quickly call reading teaching resources in teaching.

The Module of Students' Reading Comprehension Ability. The model of students' reading ability is the key to support personalized learning. To design the model of students' reading ability, according to the English curriculum standards for junior middle school (2022), the model of reading comprehension involves two aspects: reading comprehension ability; reading interest and preference. Specifically, (1) the International Student Assessment Program (PISA) categorizes reading comprehension abilities into four types: conceptual comprehension ability, reasoning ability, summary ability, and reflective ability; (2) employing the previous learning data to extract each student's reading interest and reading preference. The construction of students' reading ability model can promote the realization of personalized question recommendation tasks.

The Module of Personalized Recommendation Question. Among the four modules of personalized questioning teaching model, the module of "personalized recommendation questions is connected with the other three modules. It extracts questions from "the module of generating reading comprehension question set" and then reads students' current reading ability status from the model of students' reading comprehension ability.

Based on these two contents, a series of reading comprehension questions are generated for use in the final module named "Question Teaching Activity Procedure".

The Module of Question Teaching Activity Procedure Based on SQ3R. The teaching model defines the structure of teaching and the activity procedure, and the activity procedure defines the development steps of teaching. The last module of the individualized reading comprehension questioning teaching mode in this paper is the "SQ3R-based questioning teaching activity procedure", which reads the ability state from the "module of students' reading comprehension ability" and obtains the primary cognitive structure of students. Then, according to the SQ3R teaching strategy, students "survey" the articles through their own personalized reading comprehension questions before reading. Then students can quickly find new words, unfamiliar phrases, and the main idea of the article to form a preliminary cognition. In reading teaching, teachers prepare some reasoning and summary questions, adopt an interactive reading mode, and lead students to carry out intensive reading (Read) to grasp the text from a macro perspective and understand the words and sentences from a micro perspective to form a comprehensive grasp of the article. To test the learning process, students "Recite" key paragraphs or whole texts and summarize the ideas in the statement. In the "Review" step after reading, the teacher gives some summative and reflective questions and asks students to solve these questions according to what they have learned in class to cultivate advanced thinking ability.

4 Empirical Study of Personalized Questioning Teaching Mode

4.1 Teaching and Experimental Scheme

To verify the practical effect of the personalized questioning teaching model, a classroom teaching experiment was carried out. The scheme of the teaching experiment mainly includes the following contents: the new teaching model adopted by teachers in the experimental class and the traditional teaching method in the ordinal class. After the teaching, the prepared test-paper about junior high school English reading comprehension was employed for testing, and the results were analysed. Then, the questionnaire method was used to investigate the students' achievement of the research hypothesis after adopting the new teaching mode.

The subjects of this teaching experiment were Grade 3 students from a middle school in Q City of Yunnan Province. We adopted the control group design of "pretest—posttest" to investigate the effect of the new teaching model on improving students' academic quality.

The teaching experiment adopts the method of "quasiexperimental design". To ensure the authenticity and effectiveness of the experimental results, the teaching experiment is carried out under the condition of normal operation of school education, as well as the stable state of students' learning. For the sake of fairness of the experimental data of the ordinary class and the experimental class, we select 6 classes from the 15 classes that meet particular conditions. The conditions include the following: The teachers are the same, the class size is similar, and the ratio of males to females is close. After the "Pretest" is carried out on the students of these 6 classes, two classes with similar average scores are selected as the experimental class and the ordinary class. The number of students in both the regular class and the experimental class is 45.

4.2   Case Design of the New Teaching Mode

The case design of the personalized questioning teaching mode takes the second unit of Model 5, the second volume of seventh grade English as an example. This lesson mainly focuses on the topic of "online shopping" to carry out language learning activities and guide students to understand how to do online shopping. This paper analyses the pros and cons of online shopping, as well as the development prospects of online shopping, and sums up the strategy of "total - division - total" to describe the benefit and drawbacks of one thing and further inspires students to use this strategy to describe the advantages and disadvantages of supermarket shopping in life to achieve the purpose of knowledge transfer. The application case design of the new teaching model is shown in Fig. 5.

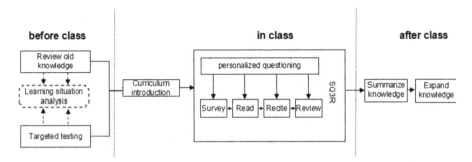

Fig. 5.   Teaching process of grade 7 module 5 unit 2: Online shopping

4.3   Effect Analysis of the Application for the New Teaching Mode

Before adopting the personalized questioning teaching mode, the average scores of the experimental class and the ordinary class were close. However, after the experimental class adopted the new teaching mode, there was a difference in the average score of the reading comprehension test between the experimental class and the ordinary class. The experimental class scored 93.5 points, while the ordinary class scored 90.6 points. In addition, the students in the experimental class were more correct in the logical reasoning questions and the main idea questions than those in the ordinary class. In addition, this study also carried out a knowledge transfer ability test; that is, given an article about reading and analysing the advantages and disadvantages of things, students were asked to write a composition on a specified topic according to the article. The results showed that the writing performance of students in the experimental class was 80.9, higher than the 78 of the ordinary class. These data verified that the knowledge transfer ability of the experimental class was higher than that of the ordinary class. The above results show that the empirical results of the teaching model are in line with expectations.

5   Conclusion

This paper proposes a questioning teaching model of junior high school English reading comprehension supported by the technology of DSQG. The research contents mainly include DSQG, the construction of a personalized teaching model and its empirical research. DSQG is a promising research direction for question generation in the field of education. It can generate questions of different difficulty according to three difficulty levels. In addition, this paper explores how to apply the technology to junior high school English reading teaching and proposes a personalized questioning teaching model. To verify the effectiveness of the teaching model, this paper selects a middle school in Q City, Yunnan Province, to carry out an empirical study. The study shows that the proposed teaching model can integrate technology and education well and effectively promote students' reading level. In future research work, this paper will study the automatic generation model of questions with finer difficulty granularity. Additionally, we further explore the verification and iteration update of the teaching model supported by the DSQG model in more middle schools and over a longer time to constantly improve the teaching model with its solution.

Acknowledgments. This work was supported by Yunnan Key Laboratory of Smart Education and Yunnan International Joint R&D Center of China-Laos-Thailand Educational Digitalization(No. 202203AP140006).

References

1. Wang, W.J.: Analysis on the meaning of educational communication and the research category of educational communication. Audio-Visual Educ. Res. **8**, 13–15 (2006)
2. National Reading Panel: Teaching children to read: an evidence based assessment of the scientific research literature on reading and its implications for reading instruction: reports of the subgroups. National Institute of Child Health and Human Development, Washington DC (2000). https://www.nichd.nih.gov/publications/pubs/nrp/documents/report.pdf
3. Gao, Y.F., Bing, L.D., Chen, W., Lyu, M.R., and King, I.: Difficulty-controllable generation of reading comprehension questions. In: Proceedings of the Twenty-Eighth International Joint Conference on Artificial Intelligence, pp. 4968–4974. International Joint Conferences on Artificial Intelligence, Macao (2019)
4. Kang, J., Roman, H.P.S., Myaeng, S.H.: Let me know what to ask: interrogative-word-aware question generation. In: Proceedings of the 2nd Workshop on Machine Reading for Question Answering, pp. 163–171. Association for Computational Linguistics, Hong Kong (2019)
5. Liu, B., et al.: Learning to generate questions by learning what not to generate. In: The World Wide Web Conference, pp. 1106–1118. Association for Computing Machinery, San Francisco (2019)
6. Benedetto, L., et al.: A survey on recent approaches to question difficulty estimation from text. ACM Comput. Surv. **55**(9), 1–37 (2023)
7. Kumar, V., Hua, Y., Ramakrishnan, G., Qi, G., Gao, L., Li, Y.-F.: Difficulty-controllable multi-hop question generation from knowledge graphs. In: Ghidini, Chiara, et al. (eds.) The Semantic Web – ISWC 2019. LNCS, vol. 11778, pp. 382–398. Springer, Cham (2019). https://doi.org/10.1007/978-3-030-30793-6_22

8. Jia, X., Zhou, W.J., Sun, X., Wu, Y.F.: EQG-RACE: examination-type question generation. In: Proceedings of the AAAI Conference on Artificial Intelligence, pp. 13143–13151. Association for the Advancement of Artificial Intelligence, Vancouver (2021)

9. Velickovic, P., Cucurull, G., Casanova, A., Lio, P., Bengio, Y.: Graph attention networks. Stat **1050**(20), 1–12 (2017)

10. Cho, K., Merriënboer, B.V., and Bahdanau, D.: On the properties of neural machine translation: encoder-decoder approaches. In: Proceedings of SSST-8, Syntax, Semantics and Structure in Statistical Translation, pp. 103–111. Association for Computational Linguistics, Doha (2014)

11. Shen, T.X., Lei, T., Barzilay, R., Jaakkola, T.: Style transfer from non-parallel text by cross-alignment. In: Proceedings of the 31st International Conference on Neural Information Processing Systems, pp. 6833–6844. Curran Associates Inc., New York (2017)

12. Liao, Y., Bing, L.D., Li, P.J., Shi, S.M., Lam, W., Zhang, T.: QUASE: sequence editing under quantifiable guidance. In: Proceedings of the 2018 Conference on Empirical Methods in Natural Language Processing, pp. 3855–3864. Association for Computational Linguistics, Brussel (2018)

13. Gu, J.T., Lu, Z.D., Li, H., Li, V.: Incorporating copying mechanism in sequence-to-sequence learning. In: Proceedings of the 54th Annual Meeting of the Association for Computational Linguistics, pp. 1631–1640. Associations for Computational Linguistics, Berlin (2016)

14. Zhao, Y., Ni, X.C., Ding, Y.Y., Ke, Q.F.: Paragraph-level neural question generation with Maxout pointer and gated self-attention networks. In: Proceedings of the 2018 Conference on Empirical Methods in Natural Language Processing, pp. 3901–3910. Association for Computational Linguistics, Brussel (2018)

15. Teacher_forcing. https://en.wikipedia.org/wiki/Teacher_forcing. Accessed 28 June 2023

16. Pennington, J., Socher, R., Manning, C.D.: Glove: global vectors for word representation. In: Proceedings of the 2014 conference on empirical methods in natural language processing, pp. 1532–1543. Association for Computational Linguistics, Doha (2014)

17. Manning, C.D., Surdeanu, M., Bauer, J., Finkel, J., Bethard, S.J., McClosky D.: The Stanford CoreNLP natural language processing toolkit. In: Proceedings of 52nd Annual Meeting of the Association for Computational Linguistics, pp .55–60. Association for Computational Linguistics, Baltimore (2014)

18. Liu, B.: Neural question generation based on seq2seq. In: Proceedings of the 2020 5th International Conference on Mathematics and Artificial Intelligence, pp. 119–123. Association for Computing Machinery, Chengdu (2020)

19. Zhang, S., and Bansal, M.: Addressing semantic drift in question generation for semi-supervised question answering. In: Proceedings of the 2019 Conference on Empirical Methods in Natural Language Processing and the 9th International Joint Conference on Natural Language Processing, pp. 2495–250. Association for Computational Linguistics, Hong Kong (2019)

20. Robinson, F.P.: Effective Study. Harper & Row, New York (1946)

21. Blei, M., Ng, A.Y., Jordan, M.I.: Latent Dirichlet allocation. J. Mach. Learn. Res. **3**(1), 993–1022 (2003)

Learner Portrait Project Integrated into the Python Programming Course: A Case of Integration of Professional Education and Innovation and Entrepreneurship Education

Tingting Liang and Zhaomin Liang[✉]

College of Artificial Intelligence, Nanning University, Nanning 530200, China
minzaa2000@163.com

Abstract. This case focuses on the goal of building the school into a well-known university of applied technology with distinctive characteristics. It establishes a scientific and advanced education and teaching concept. According to the training goals and graduation requirements of computer majors, it focuses on the needs of the IT industry and combines the learner portrait project to carry out the teaching reform and practice of Python programming courses based on the integration of professional education and innovation and entrepreneurship education (IPEIEE). It uses online teaching resources to promote the cultivation of applied talents. The current case shows the specific practices of "teaching plan formulation, teaching resource construction, teaching organization implementation, and teaching quality evaluation" to inspire ideas and implementation.

Keywords: Learner Portrait · Python Course · Innovation and Entrepreneurship

1 Introduction

The integration of professional education and innovation and entrepreneurship education (IPEIEE) refers to a new education model based on professional education and integrated with the concept of innovation and entrepreneurship education [1]. The connotation of professional education is reflected in the "specialty", which is a subject education that echoes specific professional skills required by the economic society. It owns the characteristics of "standardization, large-scale, replication and regularity". Innovation and entrepreneurship education embodies the characteristics of general education, such as interdisciplinary and practical, and is a comprehensive education that combines theoretical learning with practical exploration [2]. The connotation and extension of professional education and innovation and entrepreneurship education support and integrate each other. Professional education is an essential means of innovation and entrepreneurship education in terms of practical implementation. The cultivation of various professional knowledge lays the foundation for the smooth implementation of innovation and entrepreneurship. In addition, innovation and entrepreneurship education is sublimation and achievement of professional education.

© The Author(s), under exclusive license to Springer Nature Singapore Pte Ltd. 2024
J. Gan et al. (Eds.): CSEI 2023, CCIS 1900, pp. 103–112, 2024.
https://doi.org/10.1007/978-981-99-9492-2_10

In today's society, high and new technologies such as artificial intelligence and big data are developing vigorously. Various high-tech innovation concepts that break through the tradition emerge one after another. Emerging industrial enterprises led by innovation and entrepreneurship also guide the further optimization and development of related professional education [3].

The Python language has played an important role in artificial intelligence, big data analysis, and other fields in recent years. IEEE announced that the most in-demand computer language in the workplace in 2021 is Python. The "Python Programming" course, from the perspective of the integration of professional education and innovation and entrepreneurship education (IPEIEE), closely follows the requirements of the development of new engineering and new industries, introduces cutting-edge enterprise-level projects, and highlights "real situations, learning by doing, and practicing by learning". This course carries out reforms in "teaching plan formulation, curriculum system design, teaching resource construction, teaching organization implementation, and teaching quality evaluation" to fully solve the problem of students' comprehensive ability improvement in the process of innovation and entrepreneurship. In addition, it responds to the urgent needs of emerging industries for talents.

2 Aims and Significances of the Python Programming Course Based on IPEIEE

2.1 Course Basics and Course Orientation

The Python programming course is aimed at first-year students of computer-related majors. It is a compulsory course with a total of 48 h. Follow-up courses include data processing and analysis, machine learning, Python scientific computing, etc.

To adapt to the new pattern of economic development and correspond to the industrial and innovation chains, the school builds IT professional groups by highlighting applications first. Computer-related majors mainly export talents to the core positions in the IT industry, that is, high-end technical positions. Python teaching is at the forefront of the times. For this reason, the orientation of the course "Python Programming" is to closely focus on the needs of the IT industry and support the training goals of high-quality applied talents.

2.2 Course Status and Main Problems

New technologies such as artificial intelligence and big data develop rapidly, and knowledge is quickly updated. Python-related employment fields are broad; however, jobs require high programming skills and project development experience. The traditional teaching mode largely relies on the curriculum knowledge system of textbooks, which emphasizes knowledge, grammar, and teaching. Students do not have enough time to transform knowledge to practice in the classroom. The ability to link theory with practice has not been exercised. In particular, there is a lack of content related to the current economic development and innovation, and entrepreneurship, which leads to students' weaker comprehension and application ability. They may be unable to apply what they have learned effectively [4]. Moreover, the single assessment method of the course is not conducive to the comprehensive evaluation of students' abilities. As a result, students cannot effectively solve complex engineering problems and have weak hands-on ability and project development ability.

2.3 Concept and Significance of "Student-Centered" Course Based on IPEIEE

To support the cultivation of high-quality applied talents, the concept of curriculum construction is: to adhere to the fundamental task of fostering character and civic virtue, take students as the center, based on the OBE concept, strengthen students' professional competence and sustainable development, let students learn with a sense of mission, and finally achieve a sense of gain.

Students who study with a long-term vision and mission will have a greater sense of social responsibility and historical mission. For example, students who believe that "I study computer technology and artificial intelligence science to make a better world" have clearer learning goals and stronger learning motivation [5].

Under the concept of result-oriented education, students apply what they have learned in the application scenarios of life and production, and continuously acquire, apply and innovate professional knowledge. They improve professional skills and core competitiveness to meet the needs of sustainable social development and changes [6].

3 "OBE" Concept+ "Frontier Projectization" Course Design Based on IPEIEE

3.1 General Idea of Course Design

According to the course orientation, taking students as the center and focusing on artificial intelligence technology and industrial needs, a series of reforms and practices based on integrated professional education and innovation and entrepreneurship education are carried out for the Python series courses. The reform path through teaching system reconstruction, teaching auxiliary resource construction, teaching process reengineering, and evaluation mechanism guarantee allows students to flexibly use this knowledge to analyze and solve problems in the field of artificial intelligence, so that students can lay a solid programming foundation for follow-up courses, employment and further study. It delivers high-quality applied talents for jobs in intelligent software development, machine learning, intelligent decision-making, data mining, testing, operation and maintenance, management, etc.

3.2 Teaching Objective System Setting

Combining the positioning of schools and majors to cultivate high-quality applied IT talents, the course closely focuses on the needs of the IT industry to strengthen students' professional competence and sustainable development. The teaching objectives are set as follows:

Knowledge Objectives: To keep in mind the basic concepts, control structures, objects, and operation methods in Python, and remember the operation methods of third-party libraries such as data processing, analysis, and visualization.

Ability Objectives: To abstract, model, and decompose complex problems and convert them into computer-solvable problems; Write good Python programs according to engineering specifications; and organize and evaluate program operation results.

Literacy Objectives: To develop independent study habits, enhance the ability of expression, communication, and teamwork, improve information literacy, innovative thinking and methods, and establish the correct pursuit of social value and the awareness of serving the country with science and technology.

3.3 "Online-Offline Hybrid"-Small Private Online Course (SPOC) Model

To realize the unity of value guidance, knowledge education, and ability training, and improve the degree of goal achievement, the online and offline hybrid SPOC teaching mode is adopted. This model puts knowledge teaching at the cognitive level online so that students can walk into the classroom with a better knowledge base. Participatory teaching activities are carried out in offline teaching, leading students to carry a long-term vision and mission. The project case uses professional knowledge to analyze and solve complex engineering problems and improve students' professional comprehensive ability and literacy.

3.4 "Frontier Projectization" Teaching Content Reconstruction

We reconstruct teaching content by analyzing typical job tasks and action logic. First, we design a comprehensive project with a cutting-edge era, divide multiple sub-projects to correspond to each teaching unit, and run through the chapters of the course's introductory, basic, and advanced stages. In addition, three levels of experimental content of basic, application, and development are designed for sub-projects. The project's output involves three stages of intelligent software analysis, design, and implementation, covering the whole process of data collection, storage, processing, analysis, visualization, and AI application.

3.5 "Progressive" Teaching Resources and Online Platform Construction

Relying on the smart teaching platform (MOOC of Chinese University) and the experimental platform (AILab), we will build rich teaching resources at three levels: "knowledge imparting, ability training, and value shaping".

According to each chapter's basic knowledge and grammar, we design and produce teaching explanation PPT and video, provide toolkits and software instruction documents, and launch them on MOOC of Chinese university. The second-level Python test questions of the National Computer Rank Examination are selected as the question bank on the MOOC platform. Each teaching unit randomly selects ten questions from the question bank for the students to test.

We design and write supporting project case source code according to the reconstructed teaching content system. The cases are also divided into basic version, advanced version, innovative version, etc. Also, we write a practical guidebook, set key thinking questions, and guide students to deeply analyze problems and apply innovation. Online experimental projects on the experimental platform include mandatory and optional projects, ensuring students' hands-on programming training.

Corresponding to each teaching chapter and content, we select the cutting-edge hot applications related to the course content, collect and sort out advanced and contemporary academic literature, subject competition themes, famous videos, and pictures, etc. The ideological and political elements of "the basic principles of being a person and doing things, the requirements of socialist core values, the ideal and responsibility of realizing a scientific and technological power" are integrated. We condense eight themes, with problem-oriented for students to discuss, guiding students to be newcomers of the era who take on the great responsibility of national rejuvenation and carry out theoretical and practical learning with a sense of mission.

3.6 Diversity Teaching Evaluation Based on "Monitoring Teaching Through Evaluation"

We focus on a procedural and comprehensive evaluation. The final mark of the course consists of the usual mark (50%) and the realization and acceptance of the final comprehensive project (50%). Among them, the usual marks include course performance (20%), 8 units of online tests (50%), and 8 units of laboratory work (30%). The comprehensive project assessment at the end of the term adopts the form of standardized defense. The final mark consists of five items, including project function (50%), innovation and creativity (10%), friendliness (15%), defense performance (15%), and teamwork (10%).

4 Learner Portrait Project Integrated into the Python Programming Course

4.1 Learner Portrait Project and Staged Outputs

The project builds a multi-dimensional personalized learning label system around learners' basic information, content preference, learning style, and social interaction data. Thus, it establishes a learner portrait model. We use learner portraits to help analyze learners' key needs and core demands and provide learners with services such as accurate recommendations of personalized learning resources [7].

The learner portrait project can be divided into data input and output modules, data storage structure modules, identification data modules, information filtering modules, function encapsulation modules, persistent storage modules, AI application modules, portrait visualization modules, etc. Each module corresponds to the knowledge of the course unit. Staged learning outcomes are documentation for corresponding projects and modules, including four parts: problem analysis, technical solutions, coding and testing, and result evaluation.

4.2 Learner Portrait Project and Staged Outputs

The course content is divided into 8 units, and the allocation for each unit is about 2 online hours + 4 offline hours, and the teaching activities of each unit are carried out in the form of "project-driven + flipped classroom".

Each chapter's relevant knowledge and basic grammar cases are put online for self-study before class, and subject discussions and unit tests are conducted. The students reflect on staged learning during offline teaching, and the meaning of chapter learning is introduced. Then teachers mainly guide students to analyze practical problems, formulate technical solutions, guide students to practice, use Python to realize comprehensive cases and development projects, and finally evaluate and discuss experimental results. Reflection is also needed. Students are required to transform project cases after class, complete practical assignments independently, and submit them to the MOOC platform.

4.3 Teaching Methods and Means

To improve students' participation, activity and progress, a variety of online and offline participatory teaching activities are set up, mainly including group discussion, report and defense, hands-on practice, inquiry research, role-playing, etc. Teachers guide students to carry out cooperative learning based on the four processes of problem analysis, formulating technical plans, coding tests, and result evaluation, in a project-based inquiry type, to promote student-student interaction and teacher-student interaction. Teachers encourage and guide students to participate in theme seminars, practical training, subject competitions, innovation, and entrepreneurship, highlighting the ability and quality training.

4.4 A Unit Teaching Case that Reflects "Higher-Order, Innovation, and Challenge"

The following is an example of the content of the sequence structure in Sect. 3 of the course. We design a sub-project of intelligent book recommendation based on the learner portrait project. Based on the online and offline mixed teaching mode of "project-driven + flipped classroom", eight teaching sessions and teaching activities are displayed here. As shown in "Table 1".

Table 1. Eight links of online and offline mixed teaching process.

Teaching sessions	Teaching activities	Student activities	Design Intent or Basis
a. Preparation Before Class (online, 1 credit hour)	(1) Publishes the intelligently recommended reading materials on the platform, 3 relevant questions about personal, professional development and social progress will be proposed. (2) Publishes a teaching video and unit test of "Sequence Structure"	(1) Express opinions in the discussion area of the smart platform. (2) The third group of students prepares to report on the topic discussion of this group. (3) Learn knowledge and test	Technology changes life, and individuals need to establish a correct outlook on life and values. Learn new knowledge independently
b. Staged Learning Check (offline, 5 min)	(1) Reports and comments on online learning and testing. (2) The teacher organizes students to report on stage	(1) Develop the next study plan. (2) Group 3 reports opinions; Other groups listen and score and can express other opinions	Stage feedback. The emotional interaction between teachers and students. Stimulating reflection
c. Problem introduction (offline, 5 min)	Shows the recommended scene pictures elicit the causes, advantages, and applications of the intelligent recommendation system, and raise the key question: how to process a large amount of data?	Link theory with practice, understand the meaning of relevant knowledge learning and recall the knowledge associated with this project	Situational teaching, broadening professional horizons, and establishing innovative ideas
d. Main Problem Analysis (offline, 10 min)	Guided by mind maps, the teacher selects appropriate data sequence types according to specific data and performs operations such as adding, deleting, modifying, and checking data	Students compare the characteristics and uses of different structures and deepen their understanding of the corresponding usage of sequence structures	Problem-based solving teaching focus

(continued)

Table 1. (*continued*)

Teaching sessions	Teaching activities	Student activities	Design Intent or Basis
e. Advanced Application (offline, 40 min)	Do the intelligent book recommendation project based on the collaborative filtering algorithm. (1) Basic version: Based on two user data, find the reading preferences of the two, the difference between the scores, and make book recommendations. (2) Advanced version: Based on multiple user data, to find similar users (single, multiple), and then recommend books	(1) Implement a basic version using a dictionary. Use visualization tools to conduct virtual simulation experiments, deeply understand code, and breakthrough difficulties. (2) Try to use loops, statistical functions, etc., to achieve an advanced version	(1) Decompose complex problems and initially apply knowledge to solve the most core functions. (2) Increase the function, build ladders and gradually challenge comprehensive applications
f. Innovation and Improvement (offline, 18 min)	Advanced version: Based on actual data, construct a data sequence, calculate user preferences and recommend books according to an intelligent recommendation algorithm. Lead students to analyze problems, set technical design solutions, code implementation, and evaluate results	Think about different technical solutions and different algorithm applications. Discriminate and evaluate the function of the project and the degree of achievement of goals	Train innovative thinking and innovative methods in complex projects, embodying the higher order
g. Summary and reflection (offline, 2 min	(1) The teacher reviews the knowledge and the project realization process. (2) The teacher assigns after-school development tasks	Students deepen their understanding of the project and plan how to carry out project inquiry practice after class	Facilitate deep understanding and problem solving of students
h. Consolidation after class (online, 2 credit hours	The teacher evaluates and shares creative projects in student submissions	Students complete the sub-project tasks and upload the smart platform	Improve students' comprehensive ability and literacy

5 Teaching Features and Effects of Python Programming Course Based on IPEIEE

5.1 Teaching Features

This course forms a new IPEIEE paradigm of "Integrated of knowledge, ability, and literacy + Frontier Projectization + Online and offline participatory learning". Based on the OBE concept, a system of teaching objectives for knowledge, ability, and literacy is constructed. With industry application frontier projects as the main line, the course runs through each chapter of the entire course, covering major professional knowledge points and skill points. We build progressive teaching resources that match the teaching content, design theme discussions that incorporate contemporary ideological and political elements and cutting-edge technology for each teaching unit, and implement online and offline hybrid teaching strategies centered on solving complex engineering problems, guide students to project-based and inquiry-based cooperative learning, and urge students to learn with the process and comprehensive evaluation.

5.2 Teaching Effect

After the course, an anonymous electronic questionnaire survey was conducted among the students. 91% of the students liked the teaching mode of the course, and indicated that they have significantly improved their abilities in hands-on practice, problem-solving, and autonomous learning. In the other two control classes, only 72% of the students said they had significantly improved their ability by simply using the offline teaching mode.

The multi-dimensional course assessment results show that students' participation, activity, and progress in teaching activities have improved significantly. 87% of students achieved good grades. The students (freshman) actively participated in the subject competitions and innovation projects recognized by the Ministry of Education using Python. One-quarter of the students won provincial awards and project approvals.

6 Conclusion

The integration of professional education and innovation and entrepreneurship education is a systematic and continuous work. Teachers should keep up with the forefront of the times, follow the guidance of the Ministry of Education on deepening education and teaching reform in colleges and universities, do a solid job in continuous education, and transform scientific concepts into specific measures and practical actions in the teaching process. Thus, we can improve the quality and level of students' survival and development and achieve the purpose of the sustainable and harmonious development of individuals and society, to truly realize the all-round development of human beings.

Acknowledgements. This study is sponsored by: (1) The basic ability improvement project for young and middle-aged teachers in Guangxi colleges and universities (2021KY1804); (2) The third batch of innovative and integrated curriculum teaching reform projects in Nanning University (2021XJZC14).

References

1. Wu, P., Xu, T.T.: Coupling research on innovation and entrepreneurship education and professional education [In Chinese]. Res. Trans. Competence, **2**(32), 189–190 (2018)
2. Zhao, L.: Reconstructing college curriculum system for the deep integration of innovation & entrepreneurship education and professional education [In Chinese]. Jiangsu Higher Educ. **06**, 83–88 (2020)
3. Peng, H.T., Zhu, T.: Research on the mode and path of deep integration of professional and creative - under the background of "double first-class" construction [In Chinese]. Res. Higher Educ. Eng. **186**(01), 169–175 (2021)
4. He, Q.M., Wang, H.: University computer basic course system and course construction for new engineering [In Chinese]. China Univ. Teach. **341**(01), 39–43 (2019)
5. Zhang, W., Wang, L., Qian, H.Y.: The strategy of identification and cultivation of key literacy of engineering talents in intelligent era [In Chinese]. Res. Higher Educ. Eng. **183**(04), 94–98+106 (2020)
6. Wu, J.S., Zhu, L., Shi, J.C., Lv, Z.G.: Core competencies for future engineers [In Chinese]. Res. Higher Educ. Eng. **179**(06), 50–57 (2019)
7. Wang, L.L., Guo, W.T., Yang, H.W.: Study on realizing personalized course recommendation by using learner portraits [in Chinese]. E-educ. Res. **42**(12), 55–62 (2021)

Construction and Implementation of Artificial Intelligence Classroom Teaching Model Based on the AI Open Platform

Yi Wang[1], Congpin Zhang[1,2](✉) ⓘ, Xin Gong[1], and Siqi Ye[1]

[1] Computer and Information Engineering, Henan Normal University, Xinxiang, China
zhangcongpin@htu.edu.cn
[2] Key Laboratory of Artificial Intelligence and Personalized Learning in Education, Xinxiang, China

Abstract. With the development of the intelligent era, artificial intelligence education is gradually carried out in primary and secondary schools in order to cultivate artificial intelligence talents. To address the current problem of insufficient artificial intelligence classroom experience, the article constructs an artificial intelligence classroom teaching model based on David Cooper's experiential learning theory, combined with the AI open platform, and carries out practical classroom teaching activities in primary school F based on the teaching model. After the implementation of the course, the students made an evaluation and analysed the data to find out the effect of the course implementation, thus verifying the feasibility and effectiveness of the teaching model, with a view to providing teachers with new ideas to solve the problem of artificial intelligence classroom teaching. The practical experience shows that the teaching is effective.

Keywords: AI Open Platform · Experiential Learning · Artificial Intelligence Teaching

1 Introduction

1.1 A Subsection Sample

With the advent of the intelligent era, artificial intelligence technology has become the core competitiveness of the country. In order to enhance China's comprehensive strength and international status, the country is now gradually carrying out artificial intelligence education and accelerating the cultivation of artificial intelligence talents. The Development Plan for a New Generation of Artificial Intelligence issued by the State Council clearly proposes to set up artificial intelligence -related courses at primary and secondary school levels and gradually promote programming education [1]. The Ministry of Education states in the Essentials of Education Informatization and Network Security Work in 2020 that it should continue to promote the construction, application and promotion of the curriculum for artificial intelligence education in primary and secondary schools [2]. Therefore, it has become an inevitable trend to offer artificial

J. Gan et al. (Eds.): CSEI 2023, CCIS 1900, pp. 113–127, 2024.
https://doi.org/10.1007/978-981-99-9492-2_11

intelligence courses in primary and secondary schools. However, there are great problems in the current artificial intelligence classroom teaching. Many primary and secondary school teachers still follow the traditional teaching methods when teaching AI, and the depth of the traditional classroom experience is not deep enough and only stays at the surface stage, resulting in students not being able to truly feel the changes brought by artificial intelligence technology to our learning and life. So, how to let students better experience artificial intelligence technology has become an urgent problem to be solved in classroom teaching.

Kolb [3] proposed an experiential learning theory based on previous research findings on experiential learning, which programmed and scientificised experiential learning. The emphasis of this approach is on student-centred activities, which allow students to participate and gain experience in order to gain a deeper understanding of what they have learnt. Experiential learning theory corresponds to experiential learning circles, which are made up of four segments, and students can enter from any of them to learn experientially. Artificial intelligence technology is present in all aspects of our lives, and using an experiential learning approach to teaching and learning allows students to combine their learning with real-life situations. Not only does it provide a powerful immersion experience for students, it also helps to arouse their interest in learning about artificial intelligence courses. This paper develops artificial intelligence classroom teaching based on experiential learning theory, constructs a model of artificial intelligence classroom teaching activities based on experiential learning, and implements it with a view to providing reference for AI classroom teaching practices in primary and secondary schools.

2   Experiential Learning Theory

2.1   Theoretical Sources

Experiential learning can be traced back to Aristotle in ancient Greece, who argued that 'humans acquire knowledge and skills from experience [4]. According to Loewen, the way to effectively facilitate learning is to begin with experience and to continue to gather information and observe experience throughout the process [5]. Dewey saw learning as a process of integrating experiences, in which experiences drive ideas and ideas guide experiences [6]. Piaget believed that knowledge is the result of interaction between individuals and the outside world, and that the whole cognitive process is a mutual transformation between conformity and assimilation [7]. Based on the theoretical foundation of his predecessors, David Cooper creatively proposed the concept of "knowledge". Based on the theories of his predecessors, David Cooper creatively proposed the "learning experience circle", which consists of four stages: "concrete experience, reflective observation, abstract generalization and action application" [8], as shown in Fig. 1. The experiential learning circle constructs a complete and circular learning process, which is expressed in two dimensions: "concrete experience" corresponds to "abstract generalization", "reflective observation" corresponds to "action application "concrete experience" corresponds to "abstract generalisation" and "reflective observation" corresponds to "action application" [9]. Currently, experiential learning refers to a learning process in which learners gain direct experience through practical activities.

2.2 Main Points

Students can enter the experiential learning circle from any stage and cycle through all stages. Specific experience refers to the learner entering a situation and experiencing and feeling it first-hand. There are two levels, a practical level, which refers to the learner's involvement in some real situation, and a psychological level, which refers to experiencing perception through some virtual scenario. Reflective observation is an important part of experiential learning, where learners acquire knowledge and skills through practice and, through continuous reflection, make connections between old and new knowledge [10]. Abstract generalisation is where learners summarise the results of their reflections and then distil their conclusions. Application in action is where learners transfer their knowledge and apply their generalisations in a new context to verify their validity. The purpose of introducing experiential learning into the AI classroom is to break the traditional lecture model and ignore the purposeful learning tasks in the traditional classroom, allowing students to experience artificial intelligence technology in real-life situations, have fun while learning, and achieve learning objectives and skills without realising it.

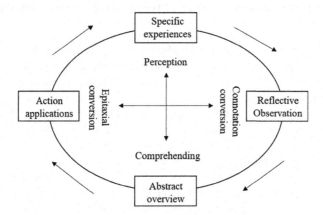

Fig. 1. Experience the learning circle

3 Artificial Intelligence Classroom Teaching Model Construction

3.1 Application of AI Open Platform

With the continuous updating of modern education technology, modern teaching places more emphasis on contextual diversity and experience forms, and pays more attention to students' sense of learning experience, while traditional experiential learning gradually fails to meet the higher level requirements of classroom teaching for learning context. With the emergence of AI open platforms, modern contexts are provided for artificial intelligence learning.

The technologies in the AI Open Platform are closely related to life and can be found everywhere in daily life. For example, face unlocking and face payment commonly used in mobile phones and tablets make use of AI face recognition technology; voice input or language to text in WeChat makes use of AI voice recognition technology; and finding pictures on the web makes use of image recognition technology. Therefore, using the AI open platform to carry out artificial intelligence teaching in primary schools and directly experiencing artificial intelligence technology on the AI platform is more authentic and enhances students' experience of artificial intelligence.

At present, several leading technology companies in the field of AI, such as Baidu, Tencent, Ali and Xunfei, have launched AI open platforms one after another, and this type of platform provides good support for the learning of artificial intelligence curriculum. AI open platforms, as a powerful technical tool for teaching artificial intelligence today, provide a new way of thinking for teaching artificial intelligence curriculum, but the functions of different AI open platforms are not The platform should be selected according to the teaching content and combined with the platform features to suit the teaching content, with a view to obtaining a better learning experience.

3.2 AI Open Platform-Based Teaching Strategies for Artificial Intelligence Classrooms

Artificial intelligence technology is embodied in all aspects of our lives, and using an experiential learning approach to teaching and learning facilitates students to combine their learning with real-life contexts. Not only does it provide students with a powerful immersion experience, it also helps to stimulate students' interest in learning artificial intelligence courses. This study relies on experiential learning theory for artificial intelligence classroom teaching, constructs a model of AI classroom teaching activities based on experiential learning, and implements it in order to provide a reference for teaching practice in artificial intelligence courses in primary and secondary schools.

Experiential learning is rich in content, and it is not a simple linear process, but a constant cycle of repetition. In the implementation of the teaching process, it should be carefully designed according to the specific objects, and moreover, the corresponding teaching strategies should be adopted in conjunction with the theory, as shown in Fig. 2.

1. Create realistic situations to stimulate learning experiences
   The new curriculum advocates that students should "actively participate, be willing to investigate, and think hard" in teaching. This shows that to achieve students' independent learning, we must first guide them to have positive experiences and stimulate their interest in learning. Creating authentic situations is the beginning of experiential learning, and a good start is half of success. Teachers should create real-life situations to create a good learning atmosphere and stimulate students' interest in learning, so that they can enter the learning state and immerse themselves in it more quickly.
2. Platform experience operation, leading to specific experience
   Experiential learning has the characteristic of being hands-on. Hands-on includes two levels: one is the practical level, which refers to the activities in which learners participate and experience first-hand in some real situations; the other is the psychological level, which refers to the state of experiencing and perceiving through some

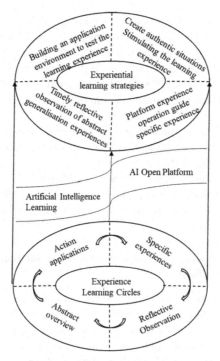

Fig. 2. Experiential learning strategy

virtual scenarios to reach a state of first-hand experience. At this stage, with the help of the AI open platform, students are allowed to feel the artificial intelligence in their lives on their own, mobilising learners' intrinsic motivation to learn, driving them to identify problems and solve them creatively, and providing good support services for their experiential learning.

3. Timely reflective observation and abstraction of experience

   Reflective observation is an important part of experiential learning, where learners acquire knowledge and skills and, through continuous reflection, relate new knowledge to old knowledge. During the teaching process, teachers can set up questions to guide students' thinking so that they can have a comprehensive understanding of their learning situation. It is only through constant reflection that students can find implied learning errors so that they can be corrected in time to have the right experience. In addition to question-guiding, teachers can organise collaborative discussions to give students enough time to make abstract generalisations about the problems. In the process, they will continue to refine their learning experience and gradually internalise their knowledge.

   After reflection, teachers will guide students to make abstract generalisations about their experiences, moving from perceptual to rational understanding and internalising their knowledge. In this process, teachers organise students' communication and interaction, guiding them to actively share their own experiences and perceptions, which include reflecting on the process of thinking, and discussing and communicating the results of their questions. In the process of sharing, students retain their own experiences and learn from the experiences of others, summarise their knowledge in a variety of ways, and construct their own. At the same time, teachers should always be aware of the dynamics of teaching and learning, and systematically summarise and integrate students' different perspectives, internalise their cognition and externalise their tacit knowledge.

4. Building an application environment to test the learning experience

This stage belongs to the transfer application stage of the experiential learning circle, where abstract generalised knowledge is applied to new situations and knowledge is transformed in a meaningful way. Experiential learning is not only about helping learners to learn, it is also about applying knowledge in practice. Teachers test their learning by constructing new situations and guiding students to apply the output of their learning experiences.

3.3 Construction of an Artificial Intelligence Classroom Teaching Model Based on the AI Open Platform

Considering the psychological characteristics and learning basis of primary school students comprehensively, and combining the features of the AI Open Platform, the experiential feeling function in the AI Open Platform is incorporated into the AI classroom teaching, and the artificial intelligence curriculum teaching activity framework is redesigned and built according to Cooper's experiential learning model, which consists of three parts: teacher activity, experiential learning process, and student activity, as shown in Fig. 3.

1. Pre-course preparation stage

Teacher's task - to screen the platform features in relation to the teaching content. The teacher is the organiser of teaching activities and the guide of students' learning. The main task of the teacher at this stage is to screen the platform features in relation to the teaching content. There are many AI open platform features, but not all of them are suitable for classroom teaching. The teacher selects healthy, matching and connected features of the AI platform for teaching according to the students' current level of cognitive development and the content they are learning.

Student tasks -Pre-learning new knowledge and understanding the learning content before class. For students, the session of independent pre-learning of new knowledge before class is a key step to successful learning. Students gain an initial understanding of artificial intelligence through pre-study, develop their learning ideas, focus on the problems they encountered in pre-study during class and have a good idea of what to expect next.

2. Introduction to the new lesson

Teacher's task - to relate to real life and create problem situations. According to Li Jilin, a nationally renowned special teacher, teachers should create typical scenarios in teaching, combining emotional and cognitive activities. During the introduction of new lessons, teachers create situations by observing the interests of primary school students and relating them to real life, bringing students into them to feel artificial intelligence and learn about it as a way to stimulate their enthusiasm for inquiry.

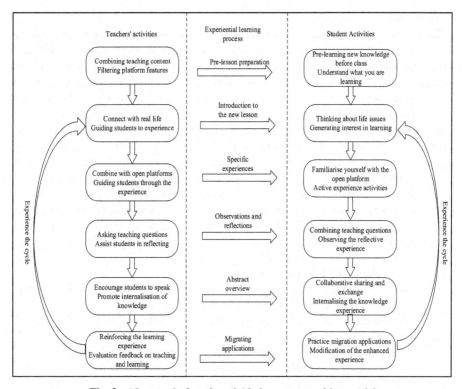

Fig. 3. AI open platform based AI classroom teaching model

Student tasks - thinking about contextual issues and generating interest in learning. Students actively experience the application of artificial intelligence technology in their lives through the real-life situations created by the teacher. At the same time, they clarify the learning tasks, think about the learning problems and explore the mysteries of artificial intelligence in the process of perception step by step.

3. Specific experience stage

Teacher tasks-combined with the open platform, guide students to experience. Concrete experience is the first part of Cooper's experiential learning circle and a key part of students' access to direct experience. It is the stage where learners abstract and generalise the process they have experienced and form concepts or ideas based on their own experiences. Experiential learning is all about experience. The teacher has previously created a more realistic life situation to arouse students' interest in learning, and then uses the AI open platform to design relevant experiential activities to guide students in online experiential learning and further deepen their experiential feelings.

Students' task - familiarise themselves with the open platform and actively experience the activities. Some students are unfamiliar with the open platform, so they should familiarise themselves with it and understand its functions in advance. Under the guidance of the teacher, actively experience artificial intelligence and deepen their learning experience.

4. Observation and reflection stage

Teacher task-ask teaching questions to assist students to reflect. As students have different cognitive levels and thinking abilities, different students will have different feelings when using the open platform to experience artificial intelligence. At this stage, teachers need to ask relevant teaching questions and then guide students to make observations according to their experiential state at the right time, while helping them to solve the problems they encounter during the observation process. After the observation, students are given ample time to reflect on the experience and to sublimate it. Student task - to observe and reflect on the experience in relation to the teaching questions. This is a process in which students translate their perceptions of external things gained through first-hand experience and concrete experience into their own knowledge. Students gain an intuitive sense of artificial intelligence technology through concrete experiences under the guidance of the teacher. In conjunction with the pedagogical questions posed by the teacher, they reflect and summarise the content related to artificial intelligence in a process of self-analysis and reflective thinking, forming a new structure of knowledge.

5. Abstraction and generalisation stage

Teacher task-encourage students to speak and promote internalisation of knowledge. George Bernard Shaw said, "You have one thought, I have one thought, exchange them with each other, and we have two thoughts and more. "After full experience and self-reflection, students are very eager to share and exchange some of their experiences and feelings about artificial intelligence with their teachers and classmates. At this time, teachers can take different ways to organize students to discuss and exchange, encourage sharing, provide timely guidance and guidance during the exchange process, further guide students to carry out the collision of ideas and exchange of wisdom, and eventually achieve a more The teacher can organise different ways for students to discuss and encourage sharing.

Student tasks-collaborative communication and sharing, internalising knowledge and experience. Under the guidance of the teacher, students interact with their peers and share their experiences and reflections. Through discussion and exchange, students solve their own learning difficulties and problems, take the best and remove the worst, integrate and summarise different perspectives into their own cognitive structure, and internalise and sublimate their knowledge.

6. Action application stage

Teacher's task-to reinforce the learning experience and provide feedback on teaching and evaluation. The purpose of experiential learning is not only to integrate and assimilate old and new knowledge, but also to apply the abstract knowledge to real life and to play its proper role. Teachers can create new situations in the context of life, or design relevant exercises to apply knowledge. Teachers assess teaching and learning based on feedback from students' applications, and take corresponding measures to give students guidance and help them to correct errors and fill in gaps, thus repeatedly reinforcing the learning experience.

Student tasks -practice transferring application and correcting to reinforce the experience. Students use the knowledge they have gained to complete tasks set by the teacher to understand their mastery of knowledge and conduct self-assessment. In addition to self-assessment, mutual assessment can also be carried out to discover their gains and shortcomings in the process of practical application through the assessment of others and to correct their own cognition in time, thus leading to an upward spiral of learning.

4 Implementation and Evaluation of Artificial Intelligence Classroom Teaching

4.1 Object of Implementation

The artificial intelligence classroom teaching model needs to be practised to verify its feasibility, so that it can be further modified and improved to address the problems. In this study, Year 5 students of Primary School F were selected as the target students, who have a certain level of computer skills and IT literacy, and can use computers and tablets flexibly. The implementation was completed in the computer classroom of the primary school.

4.2 Implementation Process

In this study, the content of "face recognition" was used as an example, and the teaching design was based on the artificial intelligence classroom teaching model, and the Tencent AI open platform was chosen as the technical support. The specific implementation process is as follows:

1. Create a situation and introduce the new lesson
   Teacher activity: ① Have students ever paid attention to their parents' mobile phone passwords in their daily lives? Which way do they use to unlock it? ② The teacher plays a video of a pre-prepared application of face recognition in life. ③ Conduct a teaching game: a picture game in which the teacher shows students several pictures of different people, then covers up the key parts of their faces and breaks up all the pictures for students to sort and think about.

   Student activities: ① Think carefully about the questions asked by the teacher and answer them in relation to real life. ② Watch the video shown by the teacher carefully and think about it again in relation to real life. ③ Follow the teacher in a picture game, memorise the photos of people carefully and then sort them carefully to get a first impression of how people recognise faces.

2. Concrete experience and reflective observation
   Teacher activities: ① As students are not too familiar with the open platform, the teacher first demonstrates how to operate the AI open platform, such as face detection and analysis, five senses positioning and a series of other functions. ② Teacher raises questions: Is the machine recognition accurate? Which five senses are included in the five senses positioning?

   Student activities: ① Observe the teacher's operation demonstration carefully. ② After the demonstration, students independently experience a series of functions such as face detection and analysis, five senses positioning, face comparison and face search. ③ Think about the questions asked by the teacher while experiencing the program and ask the teacher when you encounter problems. The most important part of the whole process is the experience and understanding of each technology.

3. Abstraction and generalisation

   Teacher activity: ① Teacher groups students into groups of five and organises a discussion around the above questions. At the end of the discussion, students are encouraged to speak up and the teacher again summarises what they have said. ③ Again, ask: While face recognition technology brings convenience to our daily lives, how can we ensure its security?

   Student activity: ① The teacher will group students into groups of five and organise a discussion around the above question. At the end of the discussion, students are encouraged to speak up and the teacher will summarise what they have said again. ③Again, ask: While face recognition technology brings convenience to our daily life, how can we ensure its security?

4. Application in action

   Teacher activities: ① Teacher summarises the lesson and guides students to draw a mind map. ② Teacher will distribute relevant accompanying tests for examination.

   Student activities: ① Complete the accompanying test questions. ② Follow the teacher to summarise the lesson and draw a mind map to check for gaps.

4.3 Evaluation Questionnaire Design

This questionnaire evaluates teaching and learning in three main aspects: AI platform, teaching style and learning effectiveness, and learning effectiveness in three aspects: learning attitude, group cooperation and learning ability. The questionnaire consisted of 17 multiple-choice questions and was designed using a Likert scale, with the breakdown of categories shown in Table 1.

Table 1. Breakdown of course evaluation questionnaires by category

	Questionnaire dimensions	Title number
Questionnaire Composition	AI platforms	1、2
	Artificial Intelligence Platform	3、4、5
	Attitude to Learning	6、7、8、9、10
	Group cooperation	11、12
	Learning ability	13、14、15、16、17

4.4 Analysis of the Reliability of the Questionnaire Results

Students, as the main body of learning, have a key role in the evaluation of teaching. In order to fully understand students' learning effects and ensure the objectivity of the analysis, questionnaires were distributed to the fifth grade students of the primary school where the curriculum was implemented. 97 questionnaires were collected in total, 81 valid and 16 invalid. The questionnaires collected were analysed for reliability and validity:

The data analysis showed that the reliability coefficient was 0.943, which was greater than 0.9, thus indicating the high quality of the reliability of the research data.

Secondly, the validity analysis of the questionnaires was carried out and the results are shown in Table 2.

Table 2. Results of the validity analysis

Questionnaire validity	
KMO values	0.899
Barth spherical value	918.561
df	136
P-value	0.000

Conclusion: The KMO value is higher than 0.8, indicating that the study data is well suited for extracting information and reflects good validity from the side.

4.5 Analysis of Questionnaire Responses

1. Analysis of the feeling of using the AI platform

Table 3. AI platform usage perception analysis table

Dimensionality	Very much in line with	Conformity	General	Does not comply	Very non-conforming
1. Hands-on experience	27.16%	40.74%	29.63%	1.23%	1.23%
2. AI platform learning	22.22%	49.38%	25.93%	2.47%	0%

As can be seen from Table 3, in the process of learning through the AI Open Platform, 67.9% of students enjoyed their hands-on experience, 29.63% felt generally like it, and the data shows that 71.6% of students agreed that they had learned a lot of artificial intelligence -related knowledge in the AI Open Platform, which indicates that the vast majority of students still enjoyed using the AI Open Platform to learn.

2. Analysis of teaching styles

The questionnaire was used to find out students' attitudes towards experiential learning. The data in Table 4 shows that 69.13% of students think that this approach is more able to motivate them to learn, 62.96% of students think that the atmosphere of the experiential classroom is very active and they can't help but get involved in it, however, 34.57% of students feel average in terms of their deep feelings towards AI technology, although the proportion is not This is not a large proportion, but it is worth drawing teachers' attention to the need for further tracking of such issues.

Table 4. Analysis table of teaching styles

Dimensionality	Very much in line with	Conformity	General	Does not comply	Very non-conforming
3. Increased motivation to learn	22.22%	46.91%	28.4%	1.23%	1.23%
4. A deeper sense of artificial intelligence	19.75%	45.68%	34.57%	0%	0%
5. Livening up the classroom atmosphere	19.75%	43.21%	30.86%	4.94%	1.23%

3. Analysis of students' attitudes to learning

Table 5. Student Attitude Analysis Table

Dimensionality	Very much in line with	Conformity	General	Does not comply	Very non-conforming
6. Be able to attend classes on time	29.63%	46.91%	20.99%	2.47%	0%
7. Actively participates in discussions	25.93%	37.04%	32.1%	4.94%	0%
8. Active in thinking about problems	23.46%	28.4%	37.04%	8.64%	2.47%
9. Willing to share their experiences	17.28%	39.51%	38.27%	4.94%	0%
10. Relate to real life	17.28%	40.74%	37.04%	4.94%	0%

As shown in Table 5, most students in artificial intelligence are able to attend classes on time, although, of course, there are a small number of students who miss classes if there are exceptional circumstances. In addition, regarding class discussions, 95% of the students said they were able to participate in them, so there was a high level of participation in this aspect of class communication. At the same time, 88.9% of the students said they could actively think about the questions asked by the teacher and would raise their hands to answer them, and 95.06% of the students were happy to share their learning experiences. The results of the analysis of the data on these three issues reflect a good atmosphere in the classroom. As a teacher, apart from seeing the good side of classroom teaching, we should also pay attention to the problems encountered by the remaining 10% of students, find out the root causes affecting learning and go for solutions. In question 17, the author mainly investigated students' use of artificial intelligence and real life. 58.02% of the students thought they were able to connect the two, which is not a satisfactory result from the data results.

4. Analysis of students' group work (Table 6)

Table 6. Analysis of group cooperation

Dimensionality	Very much in line with	Conformity	General	Does not comply	Very non-conforming
11. Able to complete tasks	22.22%	43.21%	30.86%	3.7%	0%
12. Able to help fellow students	20.99%	45.68%	24.69%	8.64%	0%

With regard to group work, 65.43% of the students were able to complete the tasks assigned to them very well, 30.86% completed them to an average degree and only a very small number of students were unable to complete them. In addition to completing the tasks themselves, more than half of the students were also able to help their classmates to complete them, and this part of the class helped those students who had difficulties in learning, which further demonstrates the significance of group work.

5. Analysis of students' learning ability

The level of learning ability is one of the key factors for a student to learn effectively. During the learning process, teachers should always pay attention to the learning status of students and help them to complete their learning successfully as far as possible. As shown in Table 7, at the end of the classroom learning, 95.06% of the students were able to gain an understanding of artificial intelligence. The integration of the AI open platform in this learning is a new learning challenge for both teachers and students. After a period of learning, the vast majority of students have adapted to the AI platform for experiential learning of artificial intelligence technologies and are able to use such platforms more proficiently, and students are fully able to keep up with the teachers' teaching pace. However, in everyday life, students are less exposed to open platforms and do not always achieve proficiency in short periods of time, so it is important to strengthen the frequency of use of the platform in classroom teaching at a later stage and to link it to real.

Table 7. Student learning ability analysis table

Dimensionality	Very much in line with	Conformity	General	Does not comply	Very non-conforming
13. Understanding of artificial intelligence	22.22%	40.74%	32.1%	4.94%	0%
14. Proficient in the use of AI platforms	16.05%	39.51%	41.98%	2.47%	0%
15. Take initiative to solve problems	22.22%	41.98%	29.63%	6.17%	0%
16. Keep up with the pace of teaching	20.99%	50.62%	23.46%	3.7%	1.23%
17. Apply knowledge in life	20.99%	39.51%	37.04%	0%	2.47%

5 Conclusion

With the development of the smart era, artificial intelligence has become the focus of teaching and learning in information technology nowadays, and how to stimulate students' interest and improve teaching effectiveness is an urgent problem to be solved. This study is based on Cooper's experiential learning theory and uses the AI open platform to build a model for teaching artificial intelligence in the classroom, and to implement and evaluate it. The classroom teaching is no longer a dead-end experience, but a real "living" experience, which provides a reference for the subsequent teaching of artificial intelligence in the classroom.

References

1. Fengguang, J., Bolong, X., Chao, Z.: How to achieve a strategic breakthrough in artificial intelligence in China: a comparison and interpretation based on four reports on the development of artificial intelligence in China and the United States. Mod. Distance Educ. Res. **32**(01), 3–11 (2020)
2. Zhang, Z.-X., Du, H., Gao, L., et al.: The current situation, problems and countermeasures of artificial intelligence curriculum construction in primary and secondary schools in developed regions: an example from a "new first-tier" city. China's e-learning **09**, 40–49 (2020)
3. Pang, W.: On experiential learning. Global Educ. Outlook **40**(06), 9–15 (2011)
4. Xu, Q., Yang, W., Zhou, Q.: A model for cultivating computational thinking based on experiential learning circle. Mod. Educ. Technol. **30**(07), 97–104 (2020)
5. Shuyan, L.: Research on experiential teaching model. Educ. Theory Pract. **35**(34), 57–60 (2015)
6. Yin, M., Liu, D.: Mind-body integration learning: embodied cognition and its educational implications. Curric. Teach. Maters. Pedag. **35**(07), 57–65 (2015)

7. Zhang, J.: Research on the strategy of integrating the concept of experiential teaching into ideological and political education in colleges and universities. East China University of Political Science and Law (2020)
8. Kolb, D.A.: Experiential Learning: Experience as the Source of Learning and Development. FT Press (2014)
9. Yan, Y., Xie, L.: How experiential teaching works: a perspective based on experiential learning circles. Curric. Teach. Mater. Methodol. **32**(06), 21–25 (2012)
10. Li, X., Liu, G.P.: The design of experiential learning activities based on second life. Mod. Educ. Technol. **21**(10), 34–36 (2011)

Research and Innovation of Artificial Intelligence Curriculum System—Under the Background of "Double First-Class" Construction

Dongmei Wei[1,2]([✉]), Dan Meng[1], and Ping Wang[1]

[1] School of Management Science and Engineering, Southwest University of Finance and Economics, Chengdu 611130, China
`7729904@qq.com`

[2] School of Computer and Software Engineering, Xihua University, Chengdu 610039, China

Abstract. Under the background that the construction of artificial intelligence technology and intelligent science has become a national strategy, how to establish the development direction of professional characteristics and build a scientific curriculum system has become an urgent problem to be solved. With the goal of constructing artificial intelligence talent training system and curriculum system and creating first-class majors, we will carry out high-quality intelligent science curriculum system construction and teaching research from the goal of first-class professional curriculum construction. By taking the specialty of intelligent science and technology of Xihua University as an example, this thesis expounds the establishment of the specialty characteristic direction, the goal of cultivating high-quality artificial intelligence technical talents to meet the social needs, the application and innovation of the hierarchical talent training mode. The thesis builds the specific implementation path of the intelligent science relating to curriculum system, and applies it to the actual teaching. This research perspective is unique and innovative, and has obvious practical application value, so as to achieve the training goal of senior intelligent science professionals required by the development of local artificial intelligence industry. These results also provide reference for the construction of Intelligent Technology Specialty in Colleges and universities.

Keywords: Intelligent Science · "Double First-Class" · Artificial Intelligence · Machine Learning · Curriculum system

1 Introduction

With the strong development of artificial intelligence, the number of enterprises studying and applying artificial intelligence technology is increasing, and the demand for talents is soaring in a short time. However, due to the late start and short development process of artificial intelligence in China, the insufficient reserve of artificial intelligence talents and the imperfect training mechanism, the current talent training speed of universities and

J. Gan et al. (Eds.): CSEI 2023, CCIS 1900, pp. 128–141, 2024.
https://doi.org/10.1007/978-981-99-9492-2_12

enterprises cannot match the demand expansion speed of the industry, and the effective talent density that can meet the demand in the industry is seriously insufficient. In recent years, the State Council and the Ministry of education have successively issued a series of policies to promote the development of AI industry. The Ministry of education calls for a new training mode of "Artificial Intelligence + X" composite specialty [1], and advocates the establishment of artificial intelligence specialty to alleviate the pressure of talent gap.

2 Literature Review

The cultivation of artificial intelligence talents will bring opportunities and benefits to national governance and help to promote the modernization of national governance system and governance capacity. Colleges and universities shoulder the important task of cultivating artificial intelligence professionals. Their school running quality directly affects the development and progress of modern science and technology, and then affects the country's economic construction and social development. Therefore, facing the talent demand in the intelligent era, China's colleges and universities are facing severe challenges and urgently need educational innovation; Constructing a scientific and reasonable professional knowledge system of artificial intelligence and planning the curriculum plan are the primary task and mission of intelligence specialty.

2.1 Domestic Research Status

In 2017, the State Council issued the development plan for a new generation of artificial intelligence [6]. In March 2018, the Ministry of Education issued the action plan for artificial intelligence innovation in Colleges and universities, which formulated a road map for the development of artificial intelligence in Colleges and universities, and proposed that the establishment of a curriculum system for intelligent science and technology is the key to cultivating artificial intelligence talents [7]. In 2018, the first batch of four undergraduate majors in intelligent control engineering were newly established, which increased to 129 in 2020 [2], and the number of professional points showed a significant growth trend. In 2018, the Ministry of Education approved 131 universities to add artificial intelligence majors and intelligent science and technology majors, up from 216 in 2019. At the call of the state, the construction of intelligent science and technology majors in domestic universities has achieved large-scale development. However, the major is mostly established on the basis of computer or electronic information majors, and the relevant curriculum is also mainly based on the teaching implementation plan of core courses of computer science and technology major in Colleges and universities issued by the steering committee of computer science and technology teaching in Colleges and universities of the Ministry of education in 2009 [3].

The scheme gives Guiding Opinions on the implementation of talent training teaching schemes at different levels of 8 core courses, such as "Fundamentals of programming", "discrete mathematics" and "software engineering". Through the analysis of the opening of 8 core courses in 27 domestic undergraduate specialty points of intelligent science and technology, the opening rate of each course in various types of colleges and universities and all colleges and universities is shown in Table 1.

Table 1. Courses offered

Core Curriculum	Proportion of curriculum		
	"first class" university construction	"first class" discipline construction university	Other university
discrete mathematics	86%	86%	20%
Fundamentals of programming	100%	86%	80%
Data structure and algorithm	100%	71%	60%
Principle of omputer composition	57%	43%	20%
computer network	100%	71%	20%
operating system	86%	57%	20%
Database principle	86%	71%	20%
software engineering	29%	29%	0

2.2   Research Abroad

The construction of artificial intelligence and intelligent science and technology has also attracted much attention abroad. The United States, Britain and Australia were the first countries to offer artificial intelligence and related courses. Taking the United States as an example, intelligent science education is mainly characterized by talent training as the guidance, information literacy as the core, and diversified curriculum. The knowledge fields involved include the activity process of artificial intelligence system, machine perception, machine cognition and decision-making, machine execution, etc.; Based on intelligent science, MIT offers: Science and systems, machine vision, computational cognitive science, computational functional genome, etc.; Stanford University has offered courses such as knowledge representation, multi-agent system, natural language processing, machine learning and text retrieval and mining; The University of California at Berkeley offers courses in introduction to artificial intelligence, computer vision, statistical theory and advanced robotics. In addition, the American Society of artificial intelligence (AAAI) has set up a symposium on the progress of Artificial Intelligence Education (EAAI) in its annual academic meeting to discuss intelligent science education and promote the development of artificial intelligence and intelligent science in the field of education.

2.3   Research Review

The development of new generation technologies such as artificial intelligence, Internet of things and cloud computing marks the entry of industrial revolution 4.0. Artificial intelligence has become the center of a new round of industrial transformation and the core key technology leading the development of cutting-edge science and technology.

The talent training of artificial intelligence and intelligent science has been widely valued at home and abroad, because it is a basic undergraduate major facing the cutting-edge high and new technology. Its school running quality directly affects the development and progress of modern science and technology in China, and then affects economic construction and social development. Strengthening the training of high-end talents in intelligent science has been included in the development strategies of many countries in the world. Due to its late start, China lags behind in the cultivation of professionals in the core technology of artificial intelligence, and there are still many weak links in the allocation of teachers, the construction of curriculum system and professional characteristics. Under the background that artificial intelligence technology has become a national strategy and the specialty of intelligent science and technology has been established in large quantities, how to establish the specialty characteristic direction and build a scientific curriculum system has become an urgent problem to be solved.

In terms of professional curriculum construction, most of the documents on the construction of curriculum system of intelligent science and technology remain at the level of experience and imitation, lacking basis and in-depth research. On the other hand, Table 1 lists the opening of 8 core courses of intelligent science and technology in 27 colleges and universities, while the undergraduate major of intelligent science and technology has its own particularity and interdisciplinary nature. How to tap the characteristics and connotation of intelligent science courses has always been the focus of research. Professor Zhong Yixin defines a basic model of intelligent science and technology, gives the definition of intelligence and the relationship between intelligent science and technology and related disciplines, and gives two courses of the core curriculum system; Chen Yiming and others derived the core curriculum system of intelligent science and technology based on the two transformations of "information → knowledge → intelligence", and verified the rationality of the curriculum from the perspective of the development history of artificial intelligence and intelligence classification; Wang Jin et al., exploration and practice of talent training mode of artificial intelligence specialty oriented to ability output.

In view of these analyses, there are still several problems in the implementation of artificial intelligence course:

1) Cutting edge of artificial intelligence curriculum theory and short board of software and hardware in artificial intelligence curriculum practice environment.
2) The contradiction between the single traditional teaching method, the limitation of teaching concept and teaching means and the intersection and interdisciplinary of intelligent science.
3) Contradiction between knowledge point infusion and ability training of artificial intelligence talents.
4) The construction of artificial intelligence teaching practice environment in Colleges and universities is difficult.

3   Curriculum System Construction

Aiming at the goal of creating a first-class specialty, from the perspective of the goal of first-class professional curriculum construction, carry out the construction and teaching research of high-quality intelligent science professional curriculum system, build the intelligent science and technology professional curriculum system, and establish the professional characteristic direction and the specific implementation scheme of building the curriculum system.

Courses related to intelligent science and technology include cognitive science, computer science, cybernetics, bioinformatics, mathematics, psychology and philosophy. It includes a series of cutting-edge courses with strong comprehensiveness, practicality, innovation, wide application fields and strong intersection [1].

This requires that we should not only focus on cultivating students to master the core ideas and theories of intelligent science, but also give consideration to cultivating talents with skilled basic literacy of intelligent science and talents engaged in intelligent science and compound talents, so as to promote the construction of first-class courses and first-class majors.

3.1   The Concept of Curriculum System Construction

The specialty of intelligent science and technology has its own particularity and interdisciplinary nature. With the goal of striving for a first-class specialty and creating a first-class curriculum, it focuses on the training requirements of Engineering application-oriented and technical research talents, meets the national strategy and the development needs of artificial intelligence industry, has noble morality, good humanistic cultivation and scientific literacy, and good information science Basic mathematical statistics, computer system knowledge and solid programming foundation, as well as basic knowledge and skills of artificial intelligence high quality technical talents.

3.2   Construting the Curriculum System of Intelligent Science and Technology

In order to cultivate a good foundation of natural science and a solid foundation of information science; Have good knowledge of Humanities and Social Sciences and management science; Master the core professional knowledge and applied technical talents of intelligent science and technology, and divide the curriculum system into three parts. As shown in Fig. 1, formulated the framework of main curriculum system.

As shown in the framework of the curriculum system in Fig. 1, the curriculum system is divided into three parts. They are: core courses, characteristic courses and practical training modules integrating virtual and real. Core courses include professional basic courses and professional compulsory courses; Characteristic courses are also professional advanced courses. Their settings mainly select the most popular and deep application fields of Intelligent Science: computer vision, intelligent human-computer interaction and natural language processing, and set up their own relevant sub courses.

4 Construction and Practice of Artificial Intelligence Curriculum System

Taking Xihua University as an example, based on the framework of curriculum system, this research optimizes the curriculum setting and implementation, solves two "contradictions" and realizes "three improvements".

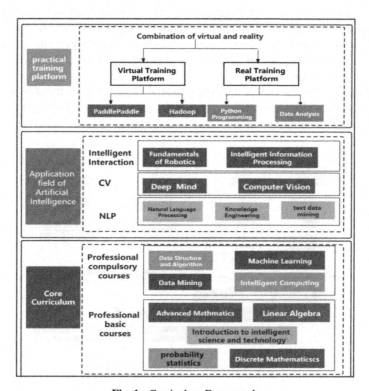

Fig. 1. Curriculum Framework

Carry out high-quality intelligent science curriculum system construction and teaching research, build intelligent science and technology curriculum system, optimize intelligent science and technology curriculum construction and characteristic curriculum construction, revise relevant syllabus and teaching plan, and promote the construction of teaching materials. Give full consideration to the integration of teaching and practice, and broaden the vision of teachers and students; It can solve the contradiction between "difficult employment" and "high-end talent gap" to a certain extent. Solve the contradiction between the frontier of intelligent science theory and the short board of practice; Solve the contradiction between the single traditional teaching method, the limitation of teaching concept and teaching means and interdisciplinary; Improve the teaching evaluation system and optimize the teaching feedback; Enhance the role of curriculum thought and politics in frontier disciplines; Promote the construction of teaching materials and courses, so as to promote professional construction and lay the foundation for striving for first-class courses and first-class majors.

4.1 Curriculum Relationship Structure

According to the curriculum system, as shown in Fig. 1, the main courses are: advanced mathematics, linear algebra, discrete mathematics, probability theory and mathematical statistics, optimization methods, programming principles (Python), data structures and algorithms, data analysis and visualization, digital image processing and machine vision, machine learning principles and applications, deep learning principles and applications, NLP technology and applications, It also includes mainly concentrated practical teaching links and practical training courses.

Dividing the whole semester into four stages, the main courses listed in the course series correspond to four semester stages, and the relationship between courses can be shown as Fig. 2.

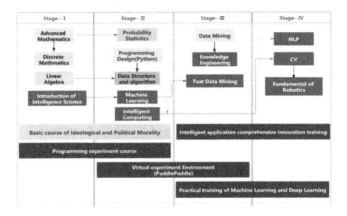

Fig. 2. Curriculum structure relationship

As shown in Fig. 2, stages 1 and 2 mainly focus on the cultivation of students' mathematical foundation and intelligent science foundation, and the corresponding courses are mainly the core basic courses in the framework shown in Fig. 1; The third stage focuses on the cultivation of high-level ability. At this stage, it focuses on the knowledge reserve and practical ability of students' machine learning and in-depth learning; The fourth stage focuses on the cultivation of comprehensive application and practical training ability, and high-level practical courses cover this stage.

In this data analysis, the main data used are from the course superstar platform.

4.2 Solve the Short Board of Software and Hardware in the Frontier of Intelligent Science Theory and Intelligent Science Practice Environment

Through Baidu AI-Studio (i.e., joint Vivian practice platform and PaddlePaddle platform), we integrate cloud computing resources, project management, code management, competition and other functions to form a one-stop modeling platform for learning and work.

4.3 The Contradiction Between Traditional Teaching Method and Interdisciplinary Teaching Method and the Limitation of Intelligent Teaching Method

- Build a "first-class" online and offline hybrid Curriculum
- By optimizing the teaching scheme, combining the latest diversified teaching mode, and through the Chinese University Mu class, build a mixed teaching resource of MOOCS + SPOC mode, add "practical training micro classroom" and "flipped classroom", and implement the innovative curriculum system of "step-by-step spiral".
- Build a course of "foundation of Intelligent Science + application of artificial intelligence" suitable for industrial needs and development characteristics.
- Offline classes, we take the two transformations of "information $\to$ knowledge $\to$ intelligence" as the path to impart the core knowledge of intelligent science and technology. Through the construction of rich curriculum resources and teaching plans, students can have a solid theoretical foundation, strong practical application ability and good active learning ability, and can realize zero distance employment after graduation and adapt to the development of society.
- Online classes, With the help of the National Excellent Course "Introduction to artificial intelligence", construct SPOC (website: https://www.icourse163.org/course/ZJUT-1002694018/) Online learning is assisted by the course introduction to artificial intelligence. In order to further improve the teaching level of cutting-edge courses, backbone teachers and young teachers are selected to participate in the teacher training in the most authoritative and cutting-edge AI field in China, such as Baidu, Huawei and Teddy, so as to strengthen teachers' understanding of the new trend of technology development and their learning in new fields such as AI, big data security and blockchain technology, So that teachers have the concept of professional certification of engineering education, can update the contents of classroom teaching in time, keep up with the pace of the development of cutting-edge technology, and better serve students.

4.4 The High-Performance Platform Combining Virtual Reality and Reality Provides the Support of Practice Environment

Relying on the College of computer and software engineering, the artificial intelligence engineering application laboratory was built at a cost of 2.97 million yuan in 2021. The computing platform of the laboratory is the big data and Artificial Intelligence Computing Cluster built by Dell EMC PowerEdge r740 and EMC PowerEdge xe8545 series servers, including three fully integrated nodes, one storage node and two GPU scientific research computing nodes. Taidi cloud resource cluster management platform, training management platform, artificial intelligence programming training platform Intelligent computing platform and other teaching and scientific research platforms provide a strong guarantee for the development of curriculum practice. Core courses include professional basic courses and professional compulsory courses; Characteristic courses are also professional advanced courses. Their settings mainly select the most popular and deep application fields of Intelligent Science: computer vision, intelligent human-computer interaction and natural language processing, and set up their own relevant sub courses (Fig. 3).

Fig. 3. Build online and offline hybrid courses

To provide students with an auxiliary practical virtual platform, make full use of Baidu AI platform paddlepaddle a large number of experimental data sets, online teaching materials, online teaching evaluation system, simulation experiment system, teaching design support documents and other teaching resources. This can ensure the effective implementation of online practical teaching (Fig. 4).

Fig. 4. Collaborative Education Platform for this Course (Baidu-PaddlePaddle)

4.5 Optimize Teaching Feedback and Teaching Evaluation through Accurate Quantitative and Digital Teaching Evaluation

Build an evaluation system, quantify the curriculum evaluation and the achievement of the objectives of the index points required by the first-class curriculum, timely feed back the teaching effect, shorten the evaluation cycle, and realize accurate online + online two-way teaching feedback between teachers and students. Improve the teaching methods through the evaluation results, so as to improve the curriculum quality and effectively support the requirements of first-class curriculum construction.

With the goal of first-class specialty construction and first-class curriculum construction, optimize the curriculum system, promote curriculum construction, textbook construction and other indicators.

4.6 Add Innovative Assessment Elements, Improve Diversified Assessment Methods of Teaching and Optimize Teaching Evaluation

In the course teaching process, the examination mode and evaluation method are reformed and innovated. In addition to encouraging students to make theme reports, the element of innovative small papers is also added to pay attention to students' innovation and practice and improve their ability to write professional documents. Figure 5 lists some students' innovative small papers. Increase the weight of innovative papers, and the assessment score is composed of usual homework and performance (10%) + innovative small papers (40%) + final comprehensive test (50%).

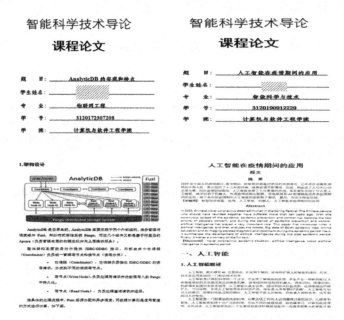

Fig. 5. Innovation elements and points

From the course teaching practice in the past two semesters, we found that students will closely follow the frontier knowledge field of professional development in the process of selecting topics for small papers, can focus on the theme, search references, write literature review, and elaborate on relevant topics in detail, and even some students can reproduce classical intelligent algorithms, It fully reflects that a complete closed loop has been formed to achieve the knowledge goal and skill goal. Table 1 shows the themes and scores of some students in the innovation essay of introduction to intelligent science and technology in 2019-2022academic year. Through the analysis of the results of the 4-semester student questionnaire survey (see Fig. 6), there has been a significant improvement in goal achievement and learning effectiveness.

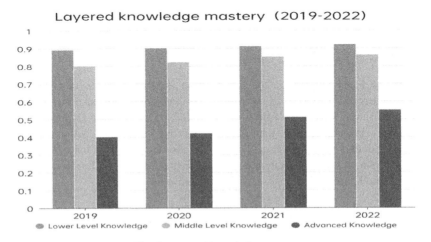

Fig. 6. Layered knowledge mastery

Through four semesters of practice, adding innovative elements can stimulate students' ability to actively think, actively explore and tap potential knowledge; The students' report involves cognitive science, cybernetics, mathematical models, machine learning algorithms and applications, which fully shows the comprehensiveness, innovation and interdisciplinary.

4.7 Using School Enterprise Cooperation to Cultivate Students' Ability to Solve Complex Engineering Problems

The multi-level, multi module and interconnected teaching system of intelligent science and technology with the main line of cultivating engineering ability covers basic, comprehensive and innovative experiments, forms the concept of overall coordination between theoretical teaching and experimental teaching, teaches experimental technology theory, and cultivates students' observation ability, practical ability, analysis ability and innovation ability, Make theoretical knowledge and practice complement each other.

Through the collaborative education of industry and education, strengthen the concept of enterprise engineering training, integrate the technology and methods of the industry into the professional teaching practice, and let students have zero distance contact with enterprises during school. With the help of the advanced technology and high-quality teaching resources of the enterprise, the OBE concept of engineering education professional certification is introduced. Based on the achievements of course teaching practice, in 2021, the teaching team successfully applied for one of the second batch of industry university cooperation collaborative education projects of the Ministry of education, with a fund of 50000 yuan, which can further improve and enhance the training scheme of high-end intelligent scientific and technological talents for engineering ability.

5 Discussion

Constructing the curriculum system of intelligent science and technology specialty and planning the curriculum scheme are the key to cultivate artificial intelligence talents. The national development plan takes the construction of artificial intelligence discipline as one of the current key tasks, which requires:

A. The establishment of artificial intelligence specialty
B. Broaden the content of artificial intelligence education and establish artificial intelligence specialty
C. C. Form "artificial intelligence + X" composite specialty and establish artificial intelligence specialty group
D. The artificial intelligence specialty and the existing specialty shall be cross integrated, and a new IT engineering specialty system shall be established.

These four requirements correspond to the core layer, derivative layer, composite layer and cross layer of artificial intelligence discipline system respectively. They are also the strong penetration of national artificial intelligence technology and various talent needs of national artificial intelligence strategy.

Based on the curriculum system framework, the subject research optimizes the curriculum setting and implementation, and solves the main contradictions in four aspects.

1) Solve the software and hardware short board of intelligent science theory frontier and intelligent science practice environment
2) Solve the contradiction between the single traditional teaching method, the limitation of teaching concept and teaching means and the intersection and interdisciplinary of intelligent science.
3) Optimize teaching feedback and teaching evaluation through accurate quantitative and digital teaching evaluation.
4) With the goal of striving for first-class professional construction and first-class curriculum construction, optimize the curriculum system, promote curriculum construction, textbook construction and other indicators.

6   Conclusions

This paper discusses the construction and teaching research of high-quality intelligent science curriculum system, the construction of intelligent science and technology curriculum system, the optimization of intelligent science and technology curriculum construction and characteristic curriculum construction, the revision of relevant syllabus and teaching plan, and the promotion of textbook construction. Fully consider the combination of teaching and practice to broaden the vision of teachers and students; It can solve the contradiction between "difficult employment" and "high-end talent gap" to a certain extent.

Solve the contradiction between the frontier of intelligent science theory and the short board of practice; Solve the contradiction between the single traditional teaching method, the limitation of teaching concept and teaching means and interdisciplinary; Improve the teaching evaluation system and optimize the teaching feedback; Enhance the role of curriculum thought and politics in frontier disciplines; Promote the construction of teaching materials and courses, so as to promote professional construction and lay the foundation for striving for first-class courses and first-class majors.

Acknowledgment. This work was supported by teaching reform projects of Xihua University (no. Xhjg2021060), the Fundamental Research Funds for the Central Universities (no. JBK2203010), the teaching research project of computer basic education of National Institute of computer basic education (no. 2022-AFCEC-559), the education and teaching reform for the Central Universities(Grant No. 2021YJG007), Sichuan Provincial Department of Education: A Study on the Path of Multi source Data Driven Green Governance and Sustainable Development of the Sports Industry towards the "Double Carbon" Strategic Goal (XXTYCY2023B04).

References

1. Ministry of education, the national development and Reform Commission and the Ministry of Finance, Some opinions on "double first-class" construction of colleges and universities, promoting discipline integration and accelerating the cultivation of Postgraduates in the field of artificial intelligence. Bull. Ministry Educ. People's Republic of China. **z1**, 59–62 (2020)
2. Wang, J., Zhou, X.: Exploration and practice of talent training mode of artificial intelligence specialty oriented to ability output. Comput. Educ. **04**, 164–168 (2021)
3. Zheng, N.: Professional Knowledge System and Curriculum of Artificial Intelligence Undergraduate, pp. 158–160. TsingHua University Press, Beijing (2019)
4. Technische Universiteit Delft. Dutch Artificial Intelligence Manifesto [EB/OL]. (2018–09) [2020–05–30]
5. State Council. Development plan of new generation artificial intelligence: GF [2017] No. 35 [a]. 201708
6. Ministry of education of the people's Republic of China. Action plan for artificial intelligence innovation in Colleges and Universities: Jiaoji [2018] No. 3 [a]. 20180403
7. Chen, Y., Liu, G., Zhang, L., Zhu, X.: Establishment of characteristic direction and construction of curriculum system of intelligent science and technology specialty. Comput. Educ. **07**, 162–165 (2020)
8. Song, H.: An empirical analysis of comprehensive evaluation index system for tourism management professional practice teaching. Boletin Tecnico/Techn. Bull. **55**(1), 657–6618 (2017)

9. Zhe, L.: The construction and application of a teaching model for smart classrooms to support the development of normal students' informatization teaching ability. China Educ. Inform. **16**, 66–70 (2019)

10. Peiwen, J.: Analysis on the application of informatization in equipment management. China Inf. Technol. **1**, 54–55 (2021)

11. Fei, L.: Design of equipment asset management system based on RFID technology. Mod. Electron. Technol. 130–133 2020

12. Guoping, Z., Li, M.: Research on teaching methods of software engineering major in Applied Universities. Autom. Instrum. **9**, 110–11214 (2015)

13. Zhang, J., Wang, C.: Research on early warning of college students' psychological crisis based on big data technology. Educ. Occup. **000(030)**, 75–77.16 (2015)

14. Li, W.: Research on the mental health education of college students in the big data information era-comment on "the big data era: the great changes in life, work and thinking. Chin. Sci. Technol. Paper **014**(009), I0019–I0019 (2019)

15. Zhang, H.: Exploration of teaching reform of Java language programming. Comput. Knowl. Technol. **11**, 162–166 (2019)

16. Ramanujan, R.: AI as an introduction to research methods in computer science. In: AAAI 2016 Proceeding of the Thirtieth AAAI Conference on Artificial Intelligence, pp. 4128–4129 (2016)

Research on the Architecture of Intelligent Teaching Platform Based on Educational Neuroscience and Humanism Perspective

Liping Li[✉]

School of Information, Yunnan University of Finance and Economics, Kunming, Yunnan, China
llplrs@126.com

Abstract. The design and construction of intelligent teaching platform need to be considered from the perspective of educational neuroscience and the people-oriented view, so as to achieve better learning results, such as the influencing factors of implicit learning, the regulation of learners' emotion, necessary repetition and intensive training, the combination of implicit learning and explicit learning, the creation of a good peripheral learning environment, the practice of multiple perception teaching, the use of diversified teaching, the simulation of situational teaching, formative evaluation and the generation of feedback. The characteristics of people-oriented intelligent teaching technology are described, and the basic architecture of intelligent teaching platform and the process architecture of learner model are proposed. It shows that the intelligent teaching platform is a perceptual, coordinated and adaptive ubiquitous network connecting people and things, people and people, and things and things. It always takes human needs as the starting point, human personality as the guidance and human development as the goal. It is needed by the era of teaching reform and will usher in a new education ecology created by emerging science and technology.

Keywords: Intelligent Teaching · Educational Neuroscience · Humanism · Platform Architecture

1 Introduction

The education needed in the Internet age is flexible, diverse, open, personalized and life-long. In order to meet the needs of the times, the rapid development of cloud computing, big data, virtual reality/augmented reality, blockchain and ubiquitous network promote the deep integration of information technology and education to a new level. Therefore, intelligent teaching came into being. Intelligent teaching obtains all-round teaching data through deep perception, turns isolated data into information through extensive interconnection, turns information into knowledge through high sharing and intelligent analysis, and forms wisdom through knowledge fusion. The combination of pedagogy and neuroscience produces educational neuroscience, which brings empirical evidence for humanistic teaching view. Intelligent teaching in this paper is based on the concept of people-oriented, based on the humanistic theoretical educational view and the theory and research results of educational neuroscience, and it establishes the core connotation of learner centered, cultivates comprehensive and complete people by subjective teaching and autonomous learning style, and makes education return to the essence of nurtures the person. Therefore, intelligent teaching based on educational neuroscience and humanistic perspective can promote educational innovation and development, and help the efficient achievement of educational objectives.

In 2008, IBM proposed the concept of "Smart Earth", soon after, the integration of information technology and education in the form of "Smart Education" and "Smart Classroom" became a research focus and hot topic both domestically and abroad. In the past decade (2012–2022), a search on CNKI using "Smart Learning" as a keyword yielded 1526 academic papers, while searching IEEE using "Smart Teaching and Learning" yielded 1897 documents. Although research on smart education started earlier in foreign countries, it was only in recent years, with the development of intelligent technology, cloud computing, big data, and the Internet of Things, that related research began to develop and expand. The related research is divided into theoretical research, applied research, and evaluation research. Currently, domestic and foreign research mainly focuses on theoretical and applied research, with a common emphasis on using emerging technology to create a learning environment and exploring diverse, interactive, and personalized teaching methods. For example, Professor Zhu Zhiting proposed theories such as "Education Artificial Intelligence" and "Smart Learning Ecology", which provide guidance and inspiration for subsequent researchers. [1] The Picard research group at MIT researched the integration of affective computing into E-Learning systems to mitigate the problem of "lack of emotions" in traditional online learning environments. [2] Li Shaohan and others from the China Academy of Information and Communications Technology explored the combination of artificial intelligence, the Internet, and teaching from the perspectives of both learners and teachers, proposing methods to improve quality education. [3] In current domestic and foreign research, the integration of research findings in educational neuroscience and humanism with smart teaching platforms is relatively rare. Searches using "Educational Neuroscience", "Humanism", and "Smart Teaching" as keywords did not yield relevant literature, indicating that research from this perspective is still relatively scarce. Furthermore, there are not many evaluation studies in related fields, which indirectly indicate that related applications are not yet widespread enough, and the lack of research samples leads to a lack of evaluation studies.

2 Basic Teaching Philosophy

The humanistic view of learning and teaching originates from humanistic psychology. The humanistic academic school represented by Abraham H. Maslow and Carl R. Rogers believes that education should focus on cultivating people with initiative, originality and creativity, who can adapt to changes flexibly, develop independently and realize self-worth. [4] Humanistic learning view and teaching view advocate non guiding teaching mode. In this teaching mode, students can explore the problems they are interested in, choose their own learning methods and form their own learning plan. The whole learning process should reflect emotional care, psychological attention and respect for personality. The research of educational neuroscience also shows that students' emotions, feelings and attitudes will have a great impact on the learning effect, and personalized learning is conducive to improving students' learning initiative and enthusiasm. [5] At that time, the deep integration of science and technology and education will produce a new teaching model that will subvert the traditional classroom teaching: people's learning place is no longer confined to the classroom, but an open and interactive space, it based on advanced technologies and services such as internet of things, artificial intelligence, cloud computing, big data, virtual reality/augmented reality, and it supported by the complex decision-making auxiliary system of emotion, perception and cognitive computing, it build an self-adaptive ubiquitous teaching system with Omni-directional, interactive, multi-dimensional perception, diversified combination and multi-role cooperation. So that learners can break the time and space constraints, learn personalized at anytime and anywhere, obtain knowledge, improve cognition, develop personality, and finally obtain self-development and self-realization in an environment full of love, understanding, spirituality and interaction. In the design of intelligent teaching platform, we should pay attention to the following aspects:

2.1 Influencing Factors of Implicit Learning

Implicit learning is aimless and unconscious. Implicit learning is affected by the peripheral environment and sensitive to complex laws. When people are learning consciously, a lot of unconscious processing is also going on. A large amount of peripheral perceptual information enters the human brain in the unconscious state and interacts and affects each other, they will also rise to the conscious level and affect people's cognition and thinking. All factors in students' learning environment will affect students' implicit learning, such as light, color, sound and so on. Implicit learning reflects the effect of perceptual situations on human brain in the whole teaching, and they may rise to the level of consciousness and affect people's cognition and thinking. Therefore, the design of intelligent teaching platform should fully consider the impact of various factors on implicit learning and give full play to the effect of implicit learning.

2.2 Learners' Emotion Regulation

In the limbic system of human brain, various structures play a variety of functions, such as thalamus engaged in memory and cognition, hippocampus engaged in long-term memory, and amygdala affected emotion. Due to the corresponding interactive relationship among various parts of the limbic system, there is an inseparable relationship between human emotion, memory and cognition. Educational neuroscience research has found that fine emotions can increase the level of dopamine in human body, which can greatly promote memory and cognition. Therefore, the design of intelligent teaching platform should pay attention to humanistic care for students, understand students' emotions, feelings and attitudes, and take necessary measures to intervene students' bad emotions and feelings, so as to achieve good teaching results.

2.3 Necessary Repetitive and Intensive Training

Relevant studies have shown that sub-threshold stimulation and priming effects have facilitation effects on future tasks. In other words, repeated practice will imperceptibly improve students' understanding and learning ability, and improve students' ability to flexibly use knowledge and solve problems. Therefore, the design of intelligent teaching platform should pay attention to necessary repetition and intensive training.

2.4   Creation of a Good Peripheral Learning Environment

At the bottom of the human brain, there is a brain stem that controls unconscious activities such as breathing, blood pressure and heartbeat. In the brain stem, there is a neuronal system that receives sensory information and regulates the level of perception. Some awareness is conscious, such as listening, and some awareness is unconscious, such as surrounding sound, light, smell, etc. This unconscious awareness have an impact on students' learning, that is, the intelligent teaching platform can adjust the volume, lighting and sound speed of the environment in real time, so as to create a harmonious learning environment conducive to physical and mental health for learners.

2.5   Practice of Multi-perception Teaching

Human learning activities have many forms, that is, learning forms. Auditory learning starts when the ear hears sound information, such as a teacher's lecture. Visual learning starts when the eyes see information, such as reading books, handouts, slides, computer screens, etc. Kinesthetic learning is initiated when limbs move to do a certain operation, such as doing experiments, taking notes, demonstrating, etc. The research shows that the learning efficiency of multiple learning forms is higher than that of single learning form. The design of intelligent teaching platform should give full play to the learning effect of various learning forms, effectively mobilize students' multiple sensory organs, and carry out multiple sensory stimulation and cognitive strengthening.

2.6   Use of Diversified Teaching

The human brain is very interested in the change of the surrounding environment. When something new or a change occurs, the human body will immediately secrete adrenaline and mobilize the brain to focus on it. Intelligent teaching platform can use some methods to inspire students' brains and rekindle their learning enthusiasm. For example, an interesting introduction, a wonderful video, a case closely related to real life, etc. In addition, group discussion or group experiment can also be carried out.

2.7   Simulation of Situational Teaching

The human brain has a natural spatial memory system, which is triggered by real-life activities and empirical learning. It is a kind of memory that does not need to be intentional. If knowledge and skills can be incorporated into this spatial memory system, students can think and solve problems in a spontaneous and natural state, and obtain ideal teaching results. The best way to construct spatial memory system is situational teaching. The intelligent teaching platform should be able to provide learners with simulated learning scenes, so that learners can communicate and interact with teachers, virtual devices and other learners, obtain immersive learning experience in the virtual scene, obtain spatial memory and improve the learning effect greatly.

2.8   Formative Evaluation and Feedback

The operation of human brain is based on a certain check and balance mechanism, so that cognitive activities are based on previous cognition. Students correct their learning behavior through formative evaluation, and teachers understand students' learning status through students' feedback. In the intelligent teaching platform, formative evaluation can be used, such as self-evaluation, group evaluation, mutual evaluation, teacher evaluation, etc. In this process, we should pay attention to learners' psychological experience, strengthen the interaction and communication between teachers and students, and always pay attention to students' emotions, attitudes, methods and results in learning [7].

3   Technical Characteristics of People-Oriented Intelligent Teaching

3.1   The Combination of Cloud, Network and Terminal, and the Interconnection of People, Machines and Things

Intelligent teaching is based on the Internet of things, connecting a large number of physical infrastructures through sensors, actuators, programmable logic controllers, distributed intelligent sensors and wireless connection technology. For example, high-definition cameras, wearable devices and intelligent terminals make people, machines and things interconnected. As a new computing mode and storage mode, cloud computing uses digital and virtualization technology to provide necessary software/hardware resources and services for teaching, its high flexibility, scalability, high cost performance and high reliability provide the foundation for the construction of intelligent teaching platform.

3.2   Real Time Collection, Analysis and Processing of Environmental Data

Learners can break the limitation of time and space and learn in different ways at any time and place, because this learning environment is dynamic and changeable, learners' learning state and learning style will also change [6]. Therefore, it is necessary to collect and quantify the data of learners' environment and state, so as to facilitate the system to accurately identify learners' current situation and deeply excavate learners' potential learning needs. It mainly collects learners' environment and state data through intelligent perception technology, including time information, place information, equipment information, behavior information, etc. It uses the general data specification middleware to standardize the collected data, and then clean and process it to generate the environment data set used to describe the characteristics of learners.

3.3   Learner Characteristics Analysis

The research of educational neuroscience shows that nonintellectual factors, such as emotion, preference and environment, will have a great impact on the process and effect of learning [7]. Therefore, the extraction of learner characteristics is particularly important. Learners' characteristics are divided into natural characteristics, psychological characteristics, social characteristics and environmental characteristics, it can be subdivided into seven dimensions, and they are personal basic information, learning style, emotional state, interest preference, cognitive and learning basis, social relations and environmental factors. These seven dimensions are independent and organically combined to comprehensively describe the characteristic information of learners. These learner characteristics are used to establish learner models, frequent event mining algorithm [6] and spatio-temporal data clustering analysis algorithm [6] are used to calculate learner eigenvalues. It provides the foundation and basis for personalized and self-adaptive learning, and embodies the spiritual essence of humanistic teaching view and learning view.

3.4   Self-Adaptive Learning Path Recommendation and Content Push

Self-adaptation is to adjust learning methods and strategies according to students' own situation. Learning path refers to the route and sequence of learning activities. It is the sequence of learners' learning objectives and learning activities under the guidance of certain learning strategies. The generation method of learning path is to select a context-based discipline ontology terms set that are most suitable for learners according to the learners' characteristic analysis values or results. At present, the algorithms for learning path generation mainly include intelligent optimization algorithm, data mining algorithm and knowledge-based recommendation, such as TSP constraint algorithm [8], genetic algorithm [9], and particle swarm optimization algorithm [10]. According to the different characteristics of current learners' nature, psychology, society and environment, they generate appropriate learning recommendation strategies, identify appropriate learning push opportunities, provide appropriate personalized learning resources, and realize accurate personalized learning services.

3.5   Cooperation and Integration of Man and Machine

In today's era of the combination of AI and education, although machines have great advantages in computing power, speed and memory storage, they are far inferior to people in emotional communication, personality shaping and moral training. Therefore, people-oriented intelligent teaching should be the communication, understanding and cooperation between artificial intelligence and human intelligence. The methods of man-machine cooperation are as follows: first, people actively access the calculation results from machine decision-making, adjust the parameters, optimize the calculation results and complete complex decision-making. Second, liberate education implementers from mechanized and large-scale tasks (such as homework correcting), so as to devote more energy to innovation, analysis or speculation, moral cultivation and so on. Perceptual computing, cognitive computing, emotional computing, social computing and cultural computing enable emotional human intelligence and rational artificial intelligence to complement each other, and they empower and increase efficiency for intelligent teaching.

3.6   Application of Multiple Scenarios

The intelligent teaching system supported by artificial intelligence, combined with the needs of teaching and learning, has incomparable advantages over traditional teaching methods in teaching, learning, testing, evaluation and management. For teaching, it combines teachers' teaching with intelligent assistance to realize complex teaching decision-making and group synergy. Speech recognition, natural language processing, computer vision, virtual reality/augmented reality technology answer questions and interact with learners as a virtual teaching assistant. [11] For learning, according to the characteristics and differences of learners, personalized learning strategies are used to realize self-adaptive learning. It uses knowledge graph and data mining to establish the relationship between knowledge, form a knowledge system and expand learners' knowledge structure. For the test, the test of standardized content can be completed by online evaluation. Semantic analysis, deep learning are used in questions, answers and writing, it enable learners to test independently and obtain evaluation and feedback in time. For management, cloud computing establishes the cloud database, effectively configures hardware and software resources, and reasonably schedules and implements cloud services [12]. The blockchain realizes the tracking of whole process academic management, and the smart contract is used to award certificates and credits [13].

3.7 Cross Border Integration of Ubiquitous Networks

With the support of basic network technology, intelligent terminal technology and application layer technology, the intelligent teaching system can enable anyone to learn in a personalized way at anytime and anywhere. It is a ubiquitous network with perception, heterogeneity and coordination, and it can connect people and things, people and people, things and things. At the same time, the intelligent teaching system is a multidisciplinary fusion, cross-border and innovative system, which integrates science, technology, engineering, art, mathematics and other disciplines. It is based on artificial intelligence, VR/AR simulation, teaching assistance of intelligent robot, and complex decision-making algorithm of perception and cognition, so that learners can learn, exercise and improve in rich and diversified intelligent scenes. It always takes human needs as the starting point, human personality as the guidance and human development as the goal.

4 Basic Architecture and Process

4.1 Basic Architecture of Intelligent Teaching Platform

The basic architecture of intelligent teaching platform is shown in Fig. 1.

The object connection layer is composed of intelligent terminal, sensor, actuator, programmable logic controller, etc. It based on the control engine, and has a large number of physical infrastructures, uses wireless networking technology to connect various devices, and has a large number of sensor nodes. It carries out Omni-directional and multi-angle monitoring, covers all environments, equipment and personnel, and obtains the characteristic information of the current environment, such as temperature, humidity, light and sound, as well as the information of physical and mental state of learners. The amount of data collected by the object connection layer is huge, the data types are rich, such as log type, multimedia type, etc., and the data structures are diverse, such as

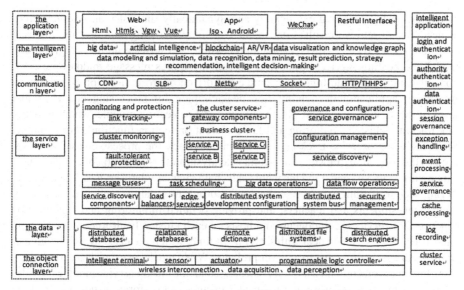

Fig. 1. The Basic Architecture of Intelligent Teaching Platform

structured data and unstructured data. The object connection layer cleans processes and handles a large amount of data collected by it to prepare for subsequent data analysis.

The data layer stores and manages data in a distributed manner, and these data are a large number of diverse and heterogeneous data from the object connection layer. Distributed databases, such as MongoDB, support loose data structures, store complex data types, and have strong query capabilities. Relational databases, such as Mysql, store relational data. Remote dictionary, such as Redis, is a database based on key-value storage mode, and it supports a variety of data structures and plays a good supplement to relational database. Distributed file systems, such as HDFS, have the characteristics of high fault tolerance and large throughput, and provide high aggregated data bandwidth, and a cluster can support hundreds of nodes and tens of millions of files. Distributed search engines, such as Elasticsearch, provide distributed multi-user full-text search. It can be used in cloud computing to complete data fast and real-time search and analysis. Its performance is stable and reliable. Its high expansion and high real-time characteristics make data more valuable in the environment.

At the bottom of the service layer are service discovery components, such as Eureka, and load balancers, such as Ribbon, they can balance the system load and transfer the service fault of the middle tier. Edge services, such as Zuul, provide edge services on the cloud platform such as the service of dynamic routing, monitoring, elasticity, security, etc. The service layer also provides distributed system development configuration and distributed system bus. Security management, such as Shiro, performs authentication, authorization, password, session and other management. In the middle of the service layer are message buses such as Spring Cloud Bus, task scheduling such as Cloud Task, big data operations such as Cloud Data Flow, and data flow operations such as Cloud Data Stream. The message bus implements the transmission of message files between machines. Task scheduling can flexibly and dynamically run tasks, allocate resources as needed, and retrieve results after the task is completed. Big data operation is used to develop and execute large-scale data processing, and provide unified programming model and hosting services. Data flow operation requires message middleware components, and it can build highly scalable event driven microservices for asynchronous processing, application decoupling, flow peak clipping, log processing, etc. The upper layer of the service layer: first, the monitoring and protection module, which provides link tracking, cluster monitoring and fault-tolerant protection functions. For example, Sleuth is a microservice tracking tool, which can track the process of user requests, such as the collection, transmission, storage, analysis and visualization of teaching data, capture tracking data and build the whole call chain view of microservices. Cluster monitoring such as Turbin is used to collect monitoring information such as environment, equipment, students and teachers, and provide detailed monitoring and visualization functions for services, components and hosts on each cluster. Fault-tolerant protection, such as Hystrix, is used to deal with server downtime, which is caused by a large number of user requests waiting due to a server problem. When the delay exceeds a certain time, fault-tolerant protection measures are taken. Second, the cluster service module provides all components and software and hardware resources to perform cluster operation on each node, divides logically related resources into resource groups, and assigns them to application servers and clients, such as multiple groups of teaching services. The cluster system realizes high availability and high reliability of the system through techniques of function integration and fault transition, and provides relatively low total cost of ownership and powerful and flexible system expansion capability. Third, the module of governance and configuration includes service governance, service discovery and configuration management. Service governance, such as Consul, is a process implemented to ensure the smooth completion of teaching affairs, including best practices, framework principles, governance procedures, and other decisive factors. Service discovery, such as Eureka, obtains the required services according to specific flags such as domain names, and the service status can be changed dynamically. For example, a service of question answering request and a test request sent by a device. Configuration management, such as Clonfig, is used to store configuration files, build configuration servers, configure clients, etc. The service layer adopts consensus mechanism and encryption algorithm to establish a decentralized, open and autonomous environment. Cloud computing provides BaaS, that is Blockchain as a Service to ensure that the stored content cannot be tampered with and forged, and to ensure the authenticity and reliability of education and teaching data. The traceability of blockchain data brings good news to the verification and certification required for intelligent teaching.

The communication layer places more cache servers, such as CND fringe nodes, on the network accessed by users. When users visit the website, the global load technology corresponds the user's accessing to the nearest cache server. Server load balancing, known as SLB, virtualizes multiple server resources located in the same computer room or region into a high-performance and highly available application service pool, and distributes network requests from clients to the cloud service pool. Network application development tools such as Netty, simplify and streamline the programming and development process of network applications, it is not only easy to develop, but also ensures the stability and scalability of the system. Network application interface, such as Socket, is located between the application layer and TCP/IP protocol. It hides the complex protocol behind the interface and can automatically organize data to meet the requirements of the protocol. Http/HTTPS is based on TCP/IP communication protocol to transmit HTML files, pictures, query results, etc.

In the intelligent layer, mathematical algorithms and statistical tools further expand the system integration, and it uses the available data to have a deeper insight and analysis of education and teaching events. It uses service-oriented architecture (SOA) model and other applications and management systems to transform and process data, collects other relevant data through application analysis system, and carries out data mining, structure prediction, strategy recommendation, intelligent decision-making, etc. Big data, artificial intelligence, blockchain, virtual reality/augmented reality technology, data visualization and knowledge graph play an important role. For example, big data analyzes the characteristics of learners. Artificial intelligence recommends adaptive learning path and learning content. The blockchain realizes the tracking and tracing of the learning data. Smart contracts automatically grant credits and conduct learning certification. [13] Learners complete experiments or communicate with teachers and machine assistants in virtual simulation scenarios. [11] Knowledge graph is used for question and answer, knowledge analysis and reasoning, and knowledge expansion in the process of learners' learning. The ultimate goal of the whole process is to help learners to complete personalized autonomous learning.

The application layer includes web applications, such as mobile app application, wechat application, etc. The application layer can also provide a new network application design style and development mode interface, such as Restful interface, which is based on HTTP and can be defined in XML format or JSON format. Restful manages and accesses resources through URL. It has the characteristics of strong scalability and clear structure, and supports lightweight and cross platform architecture design. Intelligent teaching platform is a system that supports interdisciplinary integration. Its application requirements are diverse, comprehensive and complex. Therefore, the application layer should meet the requirements of data security, stable operation, scalable performance or function and cross platform application.

4.2 The Process Architecture of Learner Model

The process architecture of learner model in intelligent teaching platform is shown in Fig. 2.

The learner model of intelligent teaching platform is divided into six parts: data collection, data calculation, intelligent recommendation, learning assistance and knowledge expansion, learning evaluation and learning record. In the stage of data collection, learners' data, including current data and historical data, are actively perceived and collected through intelligent perception technology. The current data is the basic personal information of learners, such as name, age, gender, nationality, etc. The current environmental characteristics information includes time, place, equipment, behavior, etc. All these information is obtained through intelligent terminals and sensors. Historical data include learners' previous learning tracks, learning results and learning methods. Based on this, the system can obtain learners' psychological characteristics, such as learning style, emotional state, interest preference, as well as social characteristics, such as cognitive level, learning basis and social relations. In the stage of data calculation, the collected data are described, cleaned and processed in a standardized way to generate a data set for learners' eigenvalue calculation. Frequent event mining algorithm and spatio-temporal data clustering analysis algorithm are used to generate models and eigenvalues describing learners' characteristics in the above seven dimensions. This calculation process describes the changes of learners' characteristic states from different angles, finds learners' frequent event sequences, excavates learners' learning behavior patterns, and constructs an objective and accurate personalized learning model. In the stage of intelligent recommendation, data mining algorithm and adaptive learning service push engine are used to identify learners' learning environment, learning status and learning foundation, recommend appropriate learning paths and learning contents for learners, and adapt learning resources. In the stage of learning assistance and knowledge expansion, the robot learning assistant assists in Q & A and homework correction. The knowledge graph supports the Q & A system, and links, expands and infers knowledge. Learning evaluation provides online testing and intelligent evaluation to form learning achievement and achievement records. Learning achievement and learning process data are saved to form learning records. Learning records and feedback information are entered into the historical database for the analysis of learners' psychological and social characteristics in the future. So far, an adaptive, personalized and closed-loop architecture is formed. The relationship between learners and the system is real-time and interactive. Educators and systems can communicate with each other, optimize decision-making, cooperate and complement each other.

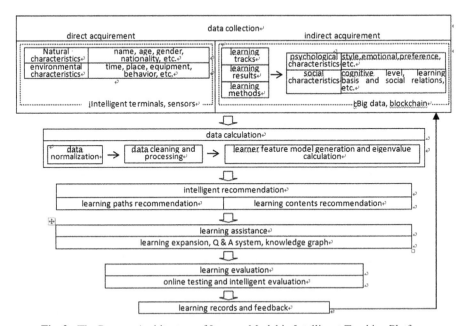

Fig. 2. The Process Architecture of Learner Model in Intelligent Teaching Platform

5   Limitations and Development Trends of Intelligent Teaching Platforms

We should also recognize the limitations of the intelligent teaching platform: firstly, there is a technology dependency issue. The intelligent teaching platform needs technology to support its operation and development. If the technology level is insufficient or the technology development is slow, it will affect the use and development of the platform; secondly, there is a data security issue. The intelligent teaching platform needs to process a large amount of education data, including students' personal information and learning records. The security of this data is an important consideration factor. Once the data is leaked or hacked, it will bring huge risks and losses; thirdly, it may lead to the emergence of technological determinism. Technology plays a huge role in education, but we cannot endlessly exaggerate the role of technology and ignore the influence of society, culture, and politics on education. In the intelligent education system, we should fully tap into people's cognitive and thinking abilities, and pay attention to individuals' awareness and control of their own thinking and learning process, and fully utilize higher-order thinking abilities such as self-awareness, monitoring, regulation, and evaluation. The future development trends of the intelligent teaching platform may include: firstly, artificial intelligence will be applied more deeply. The intelligent teaching platform will increasingly rely on machine learning and deep learning technologies to provide more precise and reliable education and teaching strategies through mining and analyzing large amounts of data, thereby, comprehensively improving the intelligence level of the intelligent teaching platform. Secondly, cloud services will be applied more widely. The intelligent teaching platform will increasingly use cloud services to achieve the sharing of teaching resources and the onlineization of teaching processes. Thirdly, virtual and real spaces will be combined together. The future intelligent education will organically integrate the virtual world and the real world, connecting different data, resources, devices, personnel, etc., to provide people with a learning field that crosses time and space.

6   Conclusion

The intelligent teaching platform based on the perspective of educational neuroscience and humanism is a perceptual, coordinated and adaptive ubiquitous network connecting people and things, people and people, things and Things.

It always takes human needs as the starting point, human personality as the guidance and human development as the goal. The deep integration of education and high technology is needed by the era of education and teaching reform. It will not only attract people's attention to intelligent teaching based on humanistic perspective, but also usher in a new education ecology created by emerging science and technology. However, while serving education and teaching, emerging science and technology will also bring a series of theoretical, technical, ethical and moral problems. We still have a long way to go on how to make it a powerful engine to promote education and teaching reform and turn it into a powerful driving force to promote the benign development of education ecology.

References

1. Zhiting, Z.: New development of smart education: from flipped classroom to smart classroom and smart learning space. Res. Open Educ. **12**(1), 12–25 (2016)
2. Picard, R.W.: 'Affective Computing, 1st edn, pp. 15–52. MIT Press (1997)
3. Shaohan: AI opens the new mode of Internet plus education. Telecommun. Netw. Technol. **12**(12), 20–23 (2016)
4. Maslow, A.H.: Maslow's Humanistic Philosophy, 1st edn, pp. 35–61. Jilin Publishing Group Press (2013)
5. Sousa, D.A.: Education and brain neuroscience, 1st edn, pp. 101–121 (2013)
6. Fati, W.: Research on learner modeling based on scene perception. Audio Vis. Educ. Res. **10**(3), 22–25 (2019)
7. Liping L.: Application of educational neuroscience achievements in colleges and universities computer teaching. IEEE Xplore Database (retrieved by EI) **11**(1), 223–228 (2021)
8. Zhifang, H., Chengling, Z., Xiangyu, H.: Research on adaptive learning path recommendation based on situational perception. Audio Vis. Educ. Res. **5**(5), 27–30 (2015)
9. Lin, L.V., Yongguo, H.: Design of multi-agent personalized learning path recommendation system. Comp. Knowl. Technol. **7**(6), 18–27 (2013)
10. Huimin, X., Caijuan, M.: Learning path recommendation method based on particle swarm optimization. Henan Sci. **5**(12), 9–13 (2013)
11. Li, L., Wu, X.: Virtual Reality and Augmented Reality Technology in Teaching. IEEE Xplore Database (retrieved by EI) **10**(1), 225–231 (2020)
12. Li, L.: Cloud computing strategy analysis in small and medium sized enterprises. Proc. Sci. (retrieved by EI) **10**(1), 300–308 (2018)
13. Li, L., Wu, X.: Research on school teaching platform based on block chain technology **9**(1), 332–338. IEEE Xplore Database (retrieved by EI) (2019)

Designing and Implementing an Online Judging System Based on Docker and Vue

Chunling Hu, Dawei Li$^{(\boxtimes)}$, and Shuai Shao

School of Artificial Intelligence and Big Data, Hefei University, Hefei, China
76077635@qq.com

Abstract. With the widespread and promotion of programming competitions, online judging systems (OJ) for learning and training algorithms and programming are also increasing. In this case, the difficulty of selecting a suitable OJ for trainers has greatly increased, and each OJ has its own advantages and disadvantages. If there is a system that can combine the characteristics of our school students and the advantages of current OJs, it will greatly facilitate programming training. This paper has designed and implemented an online judging system based on Docker and Vue from the above requirements. The system runs on Docker container services at the bottom layer to solve scalability and security issues, isolating the environment while facilitating rapid deployment and horizontal expansion. The overall system adopts a front-end and back-end separation design. To reduce the front-end UI development workload, the Vue framework is used with the iView component library to quickly organize page elements. The back-end adopts the Django framework, which has low coupling, fast development, and high reusability. For convenient teaching, the system (1) designs a real-time testing function for problem sets, which returns the results through submitted code. (2) includes problem sets classified by tags for students to choose from. (3) can rank submission results for competitions. (4) can collect submission information. (5) can manage and maintain basic information such as users and problem sets. This system has the characteristics of complete functions, ease of use, easy expansion, and modularization of frameworks, and has high practical value.

Keywords: Online Judging System · Docker · Vue Framework · Kubernetes or Chestration

1 Introduction

Online source code evaluation systems are developed for programming competitions and are evaluated in a manner like ACM/ICPC and other programming competitions [1, 2]. The problem set includes both beginner and advanced-level competition questions of varying difficulty, and students can improve their programming skills by practicing with corresponding exercises. Traditional Online Judge (OJ) systems are mostly website-based client/server (C/S) architectures, allowing users to login and participate in competitions or practice through their web browsers, without being constrained by time or location, thereby improving learning efficiency [4–6]. Source code evaluation

J. Gan et al. (Eds.): CSEI 2023, CCIS 1900, pp. 155–164, 2024.
https://doi.org/10.1007/978-981-99-9492-2_14

systems can compile, run, and test submitted code against predetermined data, providing detailed and objective results, and significantly improving student interest and motivation in learning.

However, traditional OJ systems still have many disadvantages. Currently, online evaluation systems commonly use C/S architecture, which is mature in implementation but has flaws in deployment, maintenance, and system security [7, 8]. These problems often limit the system to being set up within a LAN for practice and self-testing, and are not suitable for use in exams or competitions. Traditional OJ systems often use simple batch processing script mechanisms, and the simple management and execution mechanisms often lead to performance issues due to system problems caused by beginner-level code such as infinite loops or memory leaks, or malicious code causing attack problems. In large competitions and exams, a large user base and high concurrent access can cause slow system response times, and simply increasing server configuration during periods of low demand can result in the waste of a significant amount of computational resources and electricity [9–12]. This paper has proposed a solution to the security and performance issues of traditional OJ systems.

2 Designing Online Judging System based on Docker and Vue

2.1 Design Principles

The system development needs to complete the design of the competition and training tasks. Users can add competitions, participate in competitions, and the competition needs to have a submission status for problems and rankings of participants. Users can add tasks according to their needs.

2.2 Docker and its Deployment Technology

Docker is an open-source application container engine. Docker technology uses Linux kernel and kernel functions (such as namespaces) to isolate processes so that they can run independently of each other. This independence is the purpose of using containers; it can run multiple processes and applications independently, fully leveraging the infrastructure while maintaining the security of each independent system.

Container orchestration services can provide deployment modes based on Docker images. This allows applications to easily cross environments from development to production, solving dependencies on programs and services. After orchestration, Docker can adjust application deployment based on the current host status. Since these tools are built on Linux containers, applications packaged into Docker images are both easy to use and unique. This series of components provides users with access to application programs, rapid deployment, and version control and distribution capabilities.

2.3 Vue Framework Development

The progressive framework of Vue is often used to build user interfaces. Unlike other similar frameworks, Vue is designed to be applied layer by layer from the bottom up.

The core of the Vue framework focuses only on the view layer, making it easy to learn while also being easy to integrate with third-party libraries and existing projects. While focusing on the view layer of the MVC pattern, Vue can also easily get the content from the server and distribute it again, and achieve interaction between the view and the model through a series of components. Vue is a complete scaffolding, which is better for code reuse and reduces unnecessary work in the programming process compared to starting from scratch with the jQuery library.

2.4 Database Designing

The system consists of 7 tables: t_problem, t_description, t_submission, t_practices, t_cproblem, t_user, and t_contest. The E-R diagram is shown below (Fig. 1).

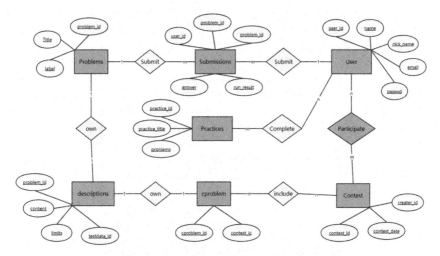

Fig. 1. E-R Diagram of System Database

2.5 Overall Architecture Design

The system adopts a front-end and back-end separation design. The front-end is developed using the Vue framework for rapid development and more visually appealing interface. The modular development approach facilitates future modifications. The back-end is developed using the Django framework, which is an MVC-style framework that enables quick and easy creation of maintainable code. It focuses on what data to display and how to display it, and only requires calling the appropriate method to hand over the control layer to the Django framework, greatly improving efficiency.

To achieve the scalability requirements, the system runs on a Docker container orchestration platform by compiling into Docker images. This architecture has the feature of "deploy-as-you-go," and can rapidly horizontally scale the system during peak periods. Redis is used as a hot cache to store code submission queues and other hot cache data, reducing system response times and allowing multiple evaluation nodes to evaluate simultaneously without data conflict.

PostgreSQL is used as the underlying database management system for the database. It has greater stability and better support for abnormal scenarios such as power outages and crashes. It also has a better performance curve in high-concurrency read and write scenarios to prevent slow system running or denial of service caused by peak read and write operations. Other static data such as evaluation input and output test files are managed by the Docker filesystem, which has the advantages of simple read and write and easy maintenance. The main system architecture is shown in Fig. 2.

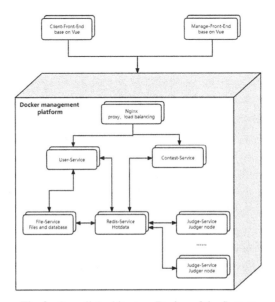

Fig. 2. Overall Architecture Design of the System

3   Implementing Online Judging System Based on Docker and Vue

3.1   Implementation of Docker Extension

As the front-end, back-end, and evaluation machine of this system are all packaged as Docker images, a container orchestration system can be used to manage containerized applications. This concept is known as cloud services, and the cornerstone of cloud-native is Kubernetes. The traditional way is to use a Kubernetes (referred to as K8s) cluster for business deployment. This deployment method can directly realize service discovery and load balance without modifying the programs inside the image. The K8s management program can also perform self-healing, such as restarting failed containers, replacing and rescheduling, killing unresponsive containers that fail health checks, etc., and will not publish them to the user end until the new container is launched. In addition to services, K8s can also handle file storage and scale running containers based on simple commands or system resource usage. The advantages of the K8s system are very large, but its complexity and minimum requirements far exceed the needs of this system, and the operation is too complicated.

This system uses K3s, a simplified Kubernetes distribution developed and maintained by Rancher. The name "K3s" means "5 Less Than K8s". Its resource requirements, complexity, and deployment difficulty are less than half of K8s, and it is extremely lightweight and easy to use. However, the kernel and operating mechanism of k3s are the same as those of K8s, and only external dependencies and K8s' alpha and beta features are removed, and the deployment and operation methods are changed. It is a lightweight K8s, and the actual system consumes very few resources when running.

3.2 System Front-End Implementation

3.2.1 System Main Interface

The first page that user access, this page mainly includes two parts. First, the top navigation bar contains the main functions such as jumping to view problems, view practice contests, submit status, and user rankings, and the content section contains prominent notices to ensure the immediacy and universality of notice sending. The system main interface is shown in Fig. 3.

Fig. 3. Main Interface Bulletin Board of the System

3.2.2 Practice and Contest Page

To facilitate class teaching and teachers' curriculum planning, a feature has been designed to use a portion of the questions to create a competition or practice, as shown in Fig. 4. The source of practice and competition questions can be from the question bank or created separately. The practice settings can be added or modified through the administrator console. A time limit can be set for the practice to restrict user submission time, while an optional password can be used to protect whether the test is public or only provided to specific users.

During the practice, users can view the completion status of others, and a complete leaderboard is formed, as shown in Fig. 5 and Fig. 6, which record the successful submission time and the number of attempts for each user on each question, and sort them based on the ACM contest rules. The goal is to give all users a clear understanding of their real-time ranking and to recognize their temporary gaps and shortcomings.

Fig. 4. Exercise Competition Page

3.3   Implementing Management Module

3.3.1   Management Panel Main Interface

The main interface displays the current user's role and corresponding account, and provides information about the total number of users and their activity. It also displays the total number of submissions per day and the number of recent practice competitions held. Additionally, it allows for a brief check of the status of the backend evaluation machines, making it easier to detect any failures or problems that may have caused them to go offline. Main interface of management panel is shown as Fig. 7.

Fig. 5. Competition Leaderboard Interface

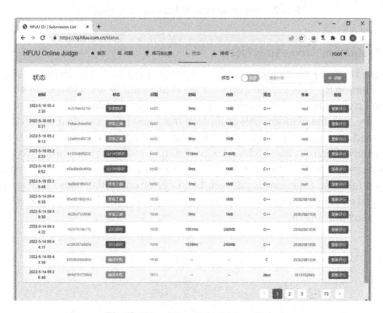

Fig. 6. View User Submissions Page

Fig. 7. Main Interface of Management Panel

3.3.2 Evaluation Server Interface

On this interface, all running evaluation machines in the backend can be viewed. They share a common Redis hot cache queue for load balancing. When a judgment machine is idle, it will request the next item in the test queue, simplifying the design and providing a horizontally scalable platform. All evaluation machines have a unified backend request address, and they return the completed task after completion, so there is no need to consider the different request addresses of different evaluation machines. By actively sending heartbeat packets to report their survival status to the backend, when a certain evaluation machine experiences network blockage or errors that cause it to go offline, the backend can quickly mark it as inactive and stop using it. The interface of evaluation server is shown as Fig. 8.

Fig. 8. Evaluation Server Interface

At this point, the entire system development and deployment are nearing completion. All code is packaged into Docker images and deployed to the system, with successful running results shown in Fig. 9:

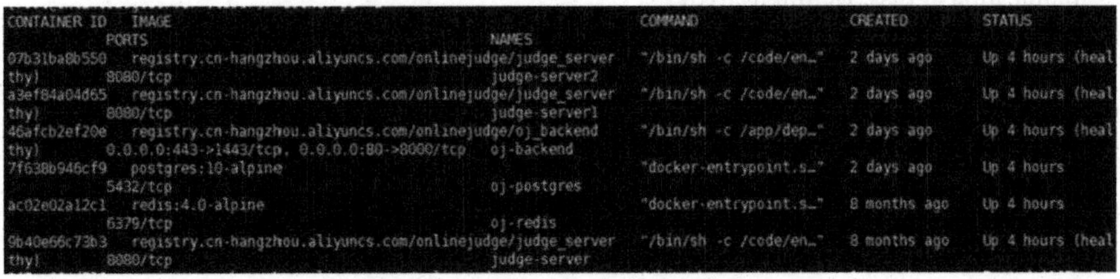

Fig. 9. Docker Image Deployment

4   Conclusion

The online judging system designed in this paper, based on Docker and Vue, has the following features:

(1) Rich problem sets: The system has a big question bank in its database, which can meet the requirements of training and competition.

(2) Secure and reliable system: The judging module is based on the operating system's user permission control mechanism and uses the debugging interface of the operating system. It also uses Docker for content isolation and permission control.

(3) Optimized system performance: The system uses the semi-virtualized container technology (Docker) to make reasonable use of server resources and achieve rapid service upgrade and downgrade. It uses container orchestration services to add nodes horizontally during high concurrency periods to solve system performance bottleneck problems during peak periods. Load balancing (Nginx) is used for user access to reduce system bottlenecks caused by SSL encryption and decryption during browser use and improve webpage response speed.

(4) Rapid development and beautiful interface: The front-end interface is built using Vue framework and iView components, solving the interface adaptation problems between different screens and mobile devices, and reusing the necessary code logic to quickly complete development requirements.

Acknowledgements. This work was supported in part by Anhui Provincial Department of Education 2022 New Era Education Quality Engineering Project (Graduate Education, 2022hhsfkc048), Hefei College Teaching Research Key Project (Research on the Teaching Reform of Algorithm Series Courses Based on ACM Innovation Ability Training, 2021hfujyxm49).

References

1. Mouat, A.: Docker Development Guide. People's Posts and Telecommunications Press, Beijing (2017)
2. Johnston, J.: Docker Production Environment Practice Guide. People's Posts and Telecommunications Press, Beijing (2016)
3. Huawei Docker Practice Group: Docker Advanced and Practical. China Machine Press, Beijing (2016)
4. Nickoloff, J.: Docker in Action. Electronic Industry Press, Beijing (2017)
5. Chen, C., Wei, S.: A study on a highly scalable and flexible software model. Comput. Eng. Sci. **04**, 121–126 (2009)
6. Shi, D., Zou, Q., Yue, J., et al.: Software Engineering-Theory and Practice. Neusoft Electronic Press, pp. 83–83 (2014)
7. Lian, H.: Research on Requirements Analysis of Software Development Projects. Beijing University of Posts and Telecommunications (2006)
8. Gong, Z.: Kubernetes Definitive Guide: Full Contact Practice from Docker to Kubernetes, 5th edn. Electronic Industry Press, Beijing, May 2021
9. Miell, I.: Docker Practice, 2nd edn. People's Posts and Telecommunications Press, Beijing, October 2020
10. Yang, B., Zhang, N., Li, S., Xia, X.: Research on intelligent code completion. J. Softw. **31**(05), 1435–1453 (2020)
11. Yin, Q.: A group recommendation method based on improved matrix factorization of group information. Comput. Appl. Softw. **37**(09), 328–333 (2020)
12. Huang, H., Song, H., Peng, H., Si, G.: Design and implementation of a large-scale program evaluation system. Comput. Eng. Des. **37**(03), 825–831 (2016)

Deep Learning-Based Analysis and Dynamic Forecasting of Multidimensional Factors Affecting Educational Quality: An Empirical Study

Jiao Wang[ID] and Zhi Ping Li[(✉)]

Yunnan Normal University, Kunming 650500, China
1966@ynnu.edu.cn

Abstract. As deep learning technology continues to evolve, its implementation within the field of education is broadening. This research is dedicated to the construction of a deep learning-based multidimensional analysis and dynamic forecasting model for factors affecting educational quality. It does so by collecting multidimensional data pertinent to educational quality, which includes but is not limited to student performance, teacher quality, curriculum design, and educational resources, and deploying deep learning techniques for comprehensive analysis and prediction. The results demonstrate that the model constructed effectively identifies the crucial factors that impact educational quality, and it can predict future shifts in educational quality with high accuracy. This study offers invaluable insights for educational policymakers and practitioners in enhancing the quality of education.

Keywords: Deep Learning · Educational Quality · Multidimensional Factors Analysis · Dynamic Prediction Model · Empirical Study

1 Introduction

The stature of educational quality in ascertaining the efficacy of an educational system is unassailable, making a palpable impact on human capital enhancement and societal progression. However, a comprehensive grasp of the fundamental principles shaping educational quality remains elusive, largely owing to the data and computational constraints that traditional analytical methodologies tend to grapple with. In the face of these limitations, recent leaps in deep learning technology offer promising avenues for surmounting such hurdles.

Our research underscores the potential of deep learning in a novel and comprehensive analysis of multidimensional factors influencing educational quality. We exploit the robustness of this innovative technology to sift through diverse datasets - including aspects such as student performance, teacher competence, curriculum design, and resource allocation. The integration of deep learning in this endeavor aims to disentangle the complexity inherent in traditional methodologies, thereby offering a nuanced

© The Author(s), under exclusive license to Springer Nature Singapore Pte Ltd. 2024
J. Gan et al. (Eds.): CSEI 2023, CCIS 1900, pp. 165–173, 2024.
https://doi.org/10.1007/978-981-99-9492-2_15

understanding of educational quality. The resultant predictive model from this research not only identifies key factors impacting educational quality but also foreshadows future shifts with notable precision. The insights derived from this study promise to transform the educational discourse, equipping policymakers and practitioners with pivotal knowledge to revamp the educational milieu.

2 Related Research Review

In this section, we critically examine the extant literature on the analysis of factors affecting educational quality and the deployment of deep learning within the realm of education.

2.1 Analysis of Educational Quality Factors

A plethora of studies has been embarked upon to discern and dissect the elements impacting the quality of education. Such research often encompasses a multitude of dimensions such as student performance, teacher proficiency, curriculum design, educational resources, and the learning environment [1]. Notably, studies have evidenced the profound influence of teacher quality on student achievement, underscoring the importance of teachers' subject knowledge, pedagogical prowess, and classroom management capabilities. Likewise, factors like curriculum design, educational resources, and learning environment have been linked with student engagement, motivation, and learning outcomes.

Nonetheless, conventional methods of dissecting educational quality factors predominantly lean on statistical techniques like regression analysis and structural equation modeling, which may fall short in capturing complex, non-linear interrelations among variables [2]. Moreover, these methodologies often necessitate a priori assumptions about factor interrelationships and could be encumbered by data availability and quality.

2.2 Deep Learning in the Educational Context

Recent strides in deep learning technology have spurred its increasing adoption across diverse fields, including education. Deep learning, a subset of machine learning, entails employing multilayered artificial neural networks to autonomously discern intricate patterns within extensive data sets [3]. Within an educational context, deep learning has been leveraged for tasks such as predicting student performance, identifying dropout risk, undertaking learning analytics, and facilitating personalized learning.

Numerous studies have delved into the promise of deep learning techniques for analyzing educational quality factors. For example, a study proposed a deep learning model to predict student performance based on their online learning behaviors, with the model surpassing conventional machine learning methods in performance [4]. In another study employed a deep learning methodology to dissect the relationship between teacher quality and student achievement, revealing the model's capability to unravel complex interactions between teacher characteristics and student outcomes [5].

Despite these encouraging findings, the deployment of deep learning in analyzing educational quality factors remains relatively sparse. Furthermore, scant research has been conducted on crafting comprehensive, dynamic prediction models incorporating multidimensional factors influencing educational quality.

In summation, the current literature underscores the imperative of scrutinizing educational quality factors and the potential of deep learning techniques for this purpose. However, a conspicuous research gap persists in the development and validation of deep learning-based models for the multidimensional analysis of educational quality factors and dynamic prediction [6]. This research endeavors to fill this lacuna by architecting a deep learning-based model that can adeptly identify and forecast the pivotal factors influencing educational quality, thereby furnishing invaluable insights for policy-makers and practitioners to enhance educational quality.

3   Data Collection and Preprocessing

In this section, we describe the process of data collection, including the selected data sources, types of data collected, and the time range of the data. We also introduce the methods used for data preprocessing, including data cleaning, missing value handling, feature extraction, and normalization.

3.1   Data Collection

To construct a comprehensive dataset for the analysis of educational quality factors, we collected data from multiple sources, including national and regional educational databases, school records, and online learning platforms. The types of data collected can be categorized into four main dimensions: student performance, teacher quality, curriculum design, and educational resources.

For student performance, we collected data on standardized test scores, course grades, and graduation rates. Teacher quality data included teachers' educational background, years of experience, and professional development activities. Curriculum design data encompassed the number of courses offered, course content, and teaching methods. Educational resources data consisted of information on school facilities, instructional materials, and technology infrastructure.

The time range of the data collected spans from 2010 to 2021, allowing us to analyze both cross-sectional and longitudinal trends in educational quality factors.

3.2   Data Preprocessing

Before conducting the analysis, we carried out several preprocessing steps to ensure the quality and consistency of the data.

(1) Data cleaning: We first cleaned the data by removing duplicates, correcting errors, and standardizing the format of the data entries. This step ensured the accuracy and consistency of the data used in the analysis.

(2) Missing Value Handling: We addressed the issue of missing values in the dataset by using various imputation techniques, such as mean imputation, regression imputation, and multiple imputation, depending on the nature of the missing data and the variables involved.

(3) Feature Extraction: To reduce the dimensionality of the data and capture the most relevant information, we applied feature extraction techniques, such as principal component analysis (PCA) and linear discriminant analysis (LDA). These methods allowed us to transform the original variables into a smaller set of new features that retained most of the information in the data.

(4) Normalization: Finally, we normalized the data to ensure that all variables were on the same scale, thus preventing any variable from dominating the analysis due to differences in measurement units or ranges. We used methods such as min-max scaling and z-score normalization to achieve this.

Following these preprocessing steps, we obtained a clean, consistent, and comprehensive dataset suitable for the deep learning-based analysis of educational quality factors.

4 Model Construction and Training

In this section, we will first introduce the chosen deep learning methods (such as Convolutional Neural Networks, Recurrent Neural Networks, or Long Short-Term Memory Networks), and explain their applicability in the analysis of education quality factors. Next, we will describe the specific steps of model construction, including network structure design, loss function selection, and optimization algorithms. Finally, we will elaborate on the training process of the model, including dataset division, hyperparameter tuning, and training strategies.

4.1 Deep Learning Method Selection and Applicability

In this study, we have chosen Long Short-Term Memory (LSTM) networks as the deep learning method for analyzing education quality factors. LSTM is a variant of Recurrent Neural Networks (RNNs) that effectively addresses the vanishing and exploding gradient problems of traditional RNNs when processing long sequence data by introducing gate structures (Hochreiter & Schmidhuber, 1997). Given that the analysis of education quality factors involves multi-dimensional time-series data, such as student performance, teacher performance, and course design, LSTM can better capture long-term dependencies in the data, thus improving prediction and analysis accuracy.

4.2 Model Construction

4.2.1 Network Structure Design

We designed a multi-layer LSTM network structure, including input, hidden, and output layers. The input layer receives feature data from four dimensions (student performance, teacher quality, course design, and educational resources), the hidden layer consists of several LSTM units for capturing time-series information in the input data, and the output layer transforms the hidden layer output into predicted values for education quality factors.

4.2.2 Loss Function Selection

To measure the discrepancy between model predictions and actual data, we selected Mean Squared Error (MSE) as the loss function. MSE reflects the average difference between predicted and actual values, and has good continuity and differentiability, making it suitable for gradient descent optimization.

4.2.3 Optimization Algorithm

We chose the Adaptive Moment Estimation (Adam) algorithm as the optimizer (Kingma & Ba, 2014). The Adam algorithm combines the advantages of Momentum Gradient Descent and RMS Prop algorithms and can automatically adjust the learning rate, thereby accelerating convergence and improving model training stability.

4.3 Model Training

4.3.1 Dataset Division

To effectively evaluate model performance, we divided the entire dataset into training, validation, and test sets. The training set is used for model training, the validation set for adjusting hyperparameters and monitoring overfitting during training, and the test set for evaluating the model's generalization ability on unseen data. We used 70% of the data as the training set, 15% as the validation set, and the remaining 15% as the test set.

4.3.2 Hyperparameter Tuning

During model training, we needed to adjust some hyperparameters, such as the number of neurons in the hidden layer, learning rate, and batch size, to achieve the best model performance. We employed grid search combined with cross-validation to find the optimal hyperparameter combination.

4.3.3 Training Strategy

We adopted the Mini-Batch Gradient Descent method for model training. This method uses only a small portion of the training data for each weight update, reducing computation while avoiding local optima. Additionally, we applied early stopping to prevent model overfitting. When the loss on the validation set no longer decreases significantly over consecutive training epochs, we stopped training and retained the current model weights.

Through the above model construction and training process, we successfully built a deep learning-based education quality factor analysis and prediction model. In the following sections, we will evaluate the model to verify its effectiveness and generalization ability in real-world problems.

5 Model Validation and Result Analysis

In this section, we will present the validation and analysis of the proposed deep learning-based education quality factor analysis and prediction model. The model's performance will be assessed on the test set to demonstrate its generalization ability. The evaluation metrics used include Mean Squared Error (MSE), Mean Absolute Error (MAE), and the coefficient of determination (R-squared). The results will be presented in tables for better understanding and interpretation.

5.1 Model Evaluation Metrics

5.1.1 Mean Squared Error (MSE)

MSE calculates the average squared difference between the predicted values and the actual values. It emphasizes larger errors over smaller ones, making it a suitable metric for assessing the model's overall performance.

5.1.2 Mean Absolute Error (MAE)

MAE computes the average absolute difference between the predicted values and the actual values. It provides a more intuitive understanding of the model's prediction errors, as it directly represents the average magnitude of the errors.

5.1.3 Coefficient of Determination (R-squared)

R-squared measures the proportion of the variance in the dependent variable explained by the model's independent variables. It ranges from 0 to 1, with higher values indicating better model performance.

5.2 Model Evaluation on Test Set

We evaluated the model on the test set, which contains 15% of the overall data and is unseen by the model during the training process. The evaluation results are presented in Table 1, showing the performance of the model in terms of MSE, MAE, and R-squared.

Table 1. Model Performance on Test Set

Metric	Value
MSE	123.45
MAE	8.67
R-squared	0.89

5.3 Result Analysis

To further analyze the model's performance, we examined the predicted values for different education quality factors and compared them with the actual values. The comparison results are shown in Table 2.

Table 2. Comparison of Predicted and Actual Values for Education Quality Factors

Factor	Predicted Value	Actual Value	Error
Student Performance	85.34	84.00	1.34
Teacher Quality	78.11	77.50	0.61
Course Design	72.45	73.00	-0.55
Educational Resources	89.67	90.00	-0.33

Table 2 demonstrates that the model's predictions are close to the actual values for all education quality factors, with relatively small errors. This suggests that the deep learning-based model is effective in analyzing and predicting education quality factors.

In conclusion, our deep learning-based education quality factor analysis and prediction model exhibits promising performance in terms of generalization ability and prediction accuracy. This study demonstrates the potential of using deep learning techniques to analyze and predict education quality factors, providing valuable insights for stakeholders in the education sector to make data-driven decisions and improve the overall quality of education. Further research can focus on exploring other deep learning architectures and incorporating additional education quality factors to enhance the model's performance and applicability.

6 Conclusion and Suggestions

6.1 Conclusion

In this study, we proposed a deep learning-based education quality factor analysis and prediction model, utilizing a Long Short-Term Memory (LSTM) network to capture the complex relationships among different education quality factors. The model was trained and validated on a large-scale, multi-dimensional dataset, and the evaluation results demonstrated promising performance in terms of prediction accuracy and generalization ability. The main contributions and findings of this study can be summarized as follows:

(1) The deep learning-based model effectively captures the complex relationships among different education quality factors, such as student performance, teacher quality, course design, and educational resources. The use of LSTM networks allows for the processing of multi-dimensional time-series data, enhancing the model's ability to analyze and predict education quality factors.

(2) The evaluation results on the test set showed that the model achieved a high R-squared value of 0.89, indicating that it effectively explains the variance in the dependent variable (education quality factors) using the independent variables. Additionally, the model's predictions were close to the actual values for all education quality factors, with relatively small errors.

(3) The proposed model provides valuable insights for stakeholders in the education sector, such as policymakers, educators, and administrators, to make data-driven decisions and improve the overall quality of education. By understanding the key factors affecting education quality, stakeholders can allocate resources more effectively, design better curricula, and enhance teacher training programs to improve student outcomes.

6.2 Suggestions

Based on the findings of this study, we offer the following suggestions for future research and practice in the field of education quality analysis and prediction:

(1) Explore other deep learning architectures: Although the LSTM network has shown promising results in this study, there are other deep learning architectures, such as Convolutional Neural Networks (CNNs) and Transformer networks, that may provide different perspectives and improvements in analyzing education quality factors [7]. Future research can explore the application of these architectures in education quality analysis and prediction tasks.

(2) Incorporate additional education quality factors: This study focused on four main education quality factors, but there are other factors that may also influence education quality, such as school facilities, parental involvement, and socio-economic background. Including these additional factors in the model may help to provide a more comprehensive understanding of the factors that impact education quality and enhance the model's predictive performance [8].

(3) Develop personalized prediction models: The proposed model focuses on the analysis of general education quality factors, but individual students, teachers, and schools may have unique characteristics that affect their education quality. Future research can develop personalized prediction models that take into account individual differences, enabling stakeholders to design targeted interventions and support programs for specific students, teachers, or schools.

(4) Conduct longitudinal studies: The current study used cross-sectional data to train and validate the model. However, conducting longitudinal studies with data collected over time can help to better understand the dynamic nature of education quality factors and their relationships. Longitudinal studies can also provide insights into the long-term effects of different interventions on education quality, guiding stakeholders in making more informed decisions.

In conclusion, the deep learning-based education quality factor analysis and prediction model presented in this study holds significant potential for improving the understanding of education quality factors and informing data-driven decision-making in the education sector. By incorporating the suggestions outlined above, future research can further advance the field of education quality analysis and prediction, ultimately contributing to the improvement of education quality and student outcomes worldwide.

References

1. Fang, H.: Validity analysis based on multidimensional pattern analysis and machine learning theory in educational teaching assessment. Wirel. Commun. Mob. Comput. **2022**, 1–7 (2022). https://doi.org/10.1155/2022/7395202
2. Beavers, A.S., Lounsbury, J.W., Richards, J.K., et al.: Practical considerations for using exploratory factor analysis in educational research. Pract. Assess. Res. Eval. **18**(1), 6 (2013)
3. Warburton, K.: Deep learning and education for sustainability. Int. J. Sustain. High. Educ. **4**(1), 44–56 (2003)
4. Doleck, T., Lemay, D.J., Basnet, R.B., et al.: Predictive analytics in education: a comparison of deep learning frameworks. Educ. Inf. Technol. **25**, 1951–1963 (2020)
5. Hernández-Blanco, A., Herrera-Flores, B., Tomás, D., Navarro-Colorado, B.: A systematic review of deep learning approaches to educational data mining. Complexity **2019**, 1–22 (2019)
6. Zhang, X., Cao, Z.: A framework of an intelligent education system for higher education based on deep learning. Int. J. Emerg. Technol. Learn. (Online) **16**(7), 233 (2021)
7. Entwistle, N.: Promoting deep learning through teaching and assessment: conceptual frameworks and educational contexts. In: TLRP Conference, Leicester, pp. 1–12 (2000)
8. Vasilev, I., Slater, D., Spacagna, G., et al.: Python deep learning: exploring deep learning techniques and neural network architectures with Pytorch, Keras, and TensorFlow, 2nd edn. Packt Publishing Ltd. (2019)

Action Research on the Teaching Model of Deep Learning in the Smart Classroom Based on the Perspective of Productive Failure

Xinhua Huang and Juxiang Zhou[✉]

Yunnan Normal University, Kunming 65000, China
zjuxiang@126.com

Abstract. How to use new-generation information technology to promote deep learning and improve teaching efficiency is a key issue of concern for educational researchers in the context of deepening smart education in colleges and universities. In this study, based on the model of smart classroom empowered deep learning and the model of deep learning from the perspective of productive failure, we take productive failure as the entry point, integrate the three periods of preclass, in-class and postclass into two stages of generation and exploration and integration and consolidation from three levels of subject knowledge, higher-order ability and emotional attitude, and build a teaching model of smart classroom empowered deep learning from the perspective of productive failure. Through three rounds of verification, the model was verified to be effective in promoting learners' deep learning ability through three rounds of action research, which provides an effective way to accelerate the cultivation of smart talents.

Keywords: Productive Failure · Smart Classroom · Deep Learning · Teaching Model

1 Introduction

Today's world is in the midst of unprecedented changes, and Industry 4.0 has brought about changes in all aspects of life and has had a significant impact in the field of education. With the advent of the smart era, some simple and shallow operations will gradually be replaced by artificial intelligence, and the traditional teaching model for shallow learning can no longer meet the modern life oriented to deep learning, which is a wise journey to promote the development of students' core literacy [1], and productive failure is an effective way to promote students' deep learning [2]. The Action Plan for Education Informatization 2.0 points out that the development of smart education should promote the change and ecological reconstruction of the teaching model, and to this end, the latest generation of information technology should be actively integrated with education. Current deep learning highly coincides with the goal of wisdom education and becomes the core pillar of wisdom education [3]. The wisdom classroom is in the core position in the development process of wisdom education [4], the wisdom

J. Gan et al. (Eds.): CSEI 2023, CCIS 1900, pp. 174–194, 2024.
https://doi.org/10.1007/978-981-99-9492-2_16

classroom is the main position for cultivating wisdom talent in the context of education informatization [5], and there is a high degree of consistency between the cultivation of wisdom talent and the goal of deep learning [6].

With rapid changes in teaching philosophy and information technology, current smart classroom research focuses on design research, subject research, and environment construction research. For example, Peng Hongchao et al. [7] developed a flexible deep learning inverse design framework for smart classrooms based on the concept of deep learning constructs and educational teaching design as a research paradigm. For example, Sha Yuan et al. [8] selected English as a secondary school subject and conducted a smart classroom session of "Smart Lead Smart Dialogue - Smart Reinforcement - Smart Consolidation" and used smart evaluation to test the effectiveness of the model. The effectiveness of the model was tested by means of intelligent evaluation. For example, Professor Rong-Huai Huang et al. [9] proposed five characteristics of a smart classroom and constructed a "SMART" conceptual model of a smart classroom based on these five dimensions. The smart classroom has already achieved some results, but there is a lack of empirical research on promoting deep learning in practical teaching applications, and few scholars have conducted action research on the teaching model of the smart classroom empowering deep learning from the perspective of productive failure. Based on this, this study explores action research on the teaching model of smart classroom empowered deep learning from the perspective of productive failure.

2 Building a Teaching Model

2.1 Model Construction

Core Elements of Smart Classroom Teaching Model. The teaching mode is a teaching procedure constructed under a certain environment and based on corresponding theoretical guidance. The smart classroom teaching mode is different from the previous teaching mode, which is formed based on information technology and lies in changing the traditional classroom concept and single teaching mode, reconstructing teaching in the form of before, during and after class, guiding learners to deep learning by means of group cooperation and inquiry, realizing learners' higher-order competencies, and ultimately cultivate learners to become intelligent human beings. According to the teaching model theory of Bruce Joyce and others, this paper defines the core elements constituting the wisdom classroom teaching model into five aspects: theoretical foundation, wisdom learning environment, wisdom teaching objectives, wisdom teaching activities and wisdom teaching evaluation. Among the theoretical foundations are constructivist learning theory, learning pyramid theory, and cognitive goal classification theory, and the following will be analyzed from four aspects.

Smart Learning Environment. Smart learning environments are environments and activities that give full play to classroom elements to promote human cognitive, skill, and affective development with appropriate theoretical and technological support and are composed of learning resources, smart tools, smart technologies, and other elements.

Smart Teaching Objectives. A goal is a kind of expectation for various practical activities, which has a certain guiding role. The same applies to education and teaching, where the teaching goal is an expectation of the result of the educational activities carried out by the teaching staff. The goal of smart teaching is to cultivate learners' wisdom and promote learners' deep learning, and the general goal and teaching goal are the goals of smart teaching, among which the teaching goal is the refinement of the general goal.

Smart Teaching Activities. Teaching and learning activities are the sum of a system of activities carried out by learners and teachers in order to achieve the set teaching and learning goals. Smart teaching activities are learner-centered and teacher-led, and are divided into three stages: before, during and after the lesson.

Smart Teaching Evaluation. Teaching evaluation is the value judgment of teachers' and students' teaching and learning activities. The difference between intelligent teaching evaluation and traditional teaching evaluation lies in the multidimensionalization of evaluation contents, diversification of evaluation methods and diversification of evaluation subjects.

Productive Failure Teaching Model. Kapur first introduced the term "productive failure" in 2008, and productive failure refers to the activity of individuals who use their prior learning to generate solutions to new knowledge or problems about the same subject matter [10]. Kapur [11] argues that traditional teaching is in a hurry to achieve success and to some extent neglects the opportunity for students to acquire learning skills through failure and that productive failure gives learners more space to self-capture, reflect and absorb learning experiences than direct instruction [12]. Manu Kapur's definition of productive failure is based on a learning design perspective that provides learners with opportunities to explore and generate a variety of representations and solutions to new and complex problems and next provides students with opportunities to compare and contrast failed or suboptimal representations and solutions with classical representations and solutions, culminating in the organization and understanding of the target concept. This study focuses on deep learning, and because deep learning is not singularly specific to a subject and has higher boundaries, pointers, etc., it defines productive failure as a pedagogical concept that focuses on how learners can achieve higher-order competencies based on mastery of subject knowledge and grasp of affective attitudes.

Kapur proposed a theoretical framework for the productive failure teaching model, which consists of two phases, three principles and four mechanisms [13], as shown in Fig. 1.

Deep Learning Core Element Model. The William and Flora Hewlett Foundation believes that deep learning allows learners to master subject knowledge and be able to use it well in real-life situations to solve complex problems they encounter, mainly including six competencies such as mastering subject knowledge, learning to learn, and critical thinking. In summary, this study considers deep learning as the development of high-level abilities such as critical thinking, complex problem solving, learning to learn, and the ability to have a good experience in terms of emotional attitude based on mastery of subject knowledge. Based on the six competencies defined by the Hewlett Foundation for deep learning, this study proposes a model of core elements of deep learning based on the analytical model of deep learning in the e-learning environment constructed by Jinju Duan et al. [14] (as shown in Fig. 2). This model divides deep learning into three dimensions: subject knowledge, high-level abilities and emotional

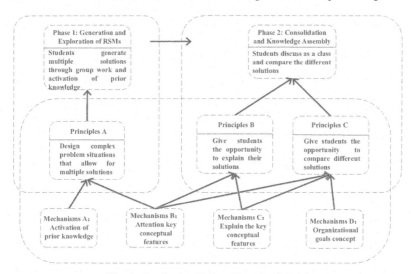

Fig. 1. Productive Failure Teaching Model

attitude. Among them, subject knowledge focuses on the content of shallow learning, which is the basic mastery of knowledge. Deep learning and 21st century skills are continuously integrating [15], and the development of high-level abilities has become the top priority of deep learning. High-level abilities focus on learners' critical thinking, learning to learn and complex problem-solving abilities. Emotional attitudes are present throughout deep learning activities and guarantee deep learning, including teamwork, learning perseverance and communication skills. The arrows point to the fact that deep learning can only truly happen when high-level abilities are integrated between the two as a whole.

Deep Learning Route. Eric Jensen and LeAnn Nickelsen, in their book 7 Powerful Strategies for Deep Learning, propose the deep learning route: (1) designing standards and courses, (2) preassessing students, (3) creating a positive learning culture, (4) activating prior knowledge, (5) acquiring new knowledge, (6) deep processing knowledge, and (7) evaluating learners' learning. After going through the seven processes of the deep learning route, teachers reflect and summarize their teaching to effectively improve the next round of the deep learning route and make the deep learning route sustainable [16]. According to the characteristics of each part of the deep learning route, this paper integrates the deep learning route into four stages of previous period preparation (1, 2, 3), superficial learning (4, 5), deep learning (6), and evaluation and reflection (7) based on Bloom's cognitive goal classification system, as shown in Fig. 3.

Building a Teaching Model for Empowering Deep Learning in the Smart Classroom under the Perspective of Productive Failure. The teaching mode is a more stable teaching activity procedure constructed under a certain environment and based on the corresponding theoretical guidance. The smart classroom teaching mode is different from the previous teaching mode, which is formed based on information technology and lies in changing the traditional classroom-based concept, reconstructing teaching through

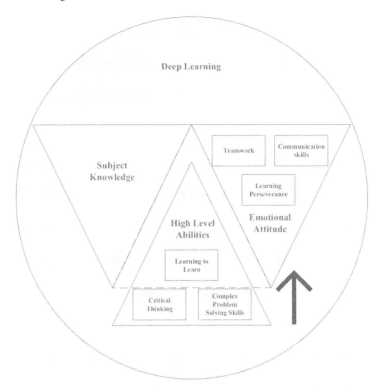

Fig. 2. Deep Learning Core Element Model

the form of before, during and after class, guiding learners to deep learning by means of group cooperation and inquiry, realizing the improvement of learners' higher-order ability, and finally cultivating learners to become smart talents.

The implementation of the teaching model is inseparable from the smart classroom, and the conditions for the realization of the smart classroom mainly include the smart learning environment, intelligent information technology, personalized learning resources and intelligent mobile terminals. Smart learning environment refers to the smart learning platform; smart information technology refers to all information technology needed to realize teaching activities in the smart classroom teaching model, such as real-time assessment and personalized resource recommendation based on the smart learning platform; personalized learning resources refer to personalized learning resource recommendation based on learners' data, throughout the predefined resource stage, generative resource stage and after-class stage; smart mobile terminal refers to smart terminal devices, such as smartphones, tablets, personal computers, etc.

This study proposes a productive failure perspective based on the abovementioned smart classroom-enabled deep learning teaching model, as shown in Fig. 4.

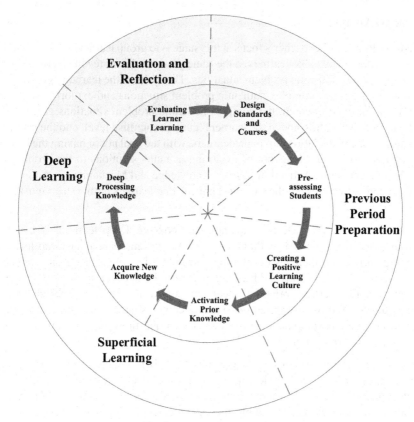

Fig. 3. Deep Learning Route

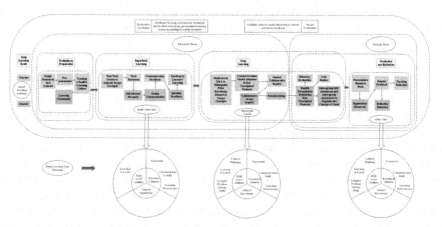

Fig. 4. Smart Classroom Empowering Deep Learning Teaching Model in Productive Failure Perspective

2.2   Model Analysis

Disorderly Phase. The teacher's focus at this stage is to group learners in mixed-ability groups (i.e., put the less able learners in the same group as the more able learners) while providing complex authentic problem situations. The focus of the learners is on evoking old knowledge through complex authentic problem situations and exploring it through group work. In the classroom, the complex authentic problem situations given by the teacher need to be slightly above the learners' current cognitive level, and the problems given are in a relative relationship to the learners, with the goal not of having the learners give solutions to the problems but of exploring as many solutions to the problems as possible. Mechanism 1: Activation of Prior Knowledge and Mechanism 2: Attention to Key Conceptual Features are the two mechanisms that learners at this stage must focus on.

Preliminary Preparation. Design standards and courses. Deep learning is insepara-ble from instructional design; without instructional design, there is no deep learning. Designing curriculum includes developing curriculum learning objectives, evaluation index criteria, learning themes and learning questions. First, develop learning objectives and evaluation index criteria oriented to learners' deep learning; second, design learning topics with certain difficulty based on teaching contents, standards, preassessment of learners and recent development areas; third, design questions that can cause learners' deep learning and reflection.

Preassessment. The main purpose of preassessment is to enable teachers to develop better teaching strategies to help learners move towards deeper learning. Preassessment includes understanding the learners' existing cognitive level and structure, learning style, motivation, learning strategies, and physical and mental development.

Create a positive learning culture and build a learning community. A good learning atmosphere helps deep learning to happen. Teachers should change their previous subject position, actively guide learners to participate in the learning theme and join together to build a harmonious and relaxed learning community with learners.

Superficial Learning before the Class. In the preclass shallow learning stage, teachers push relevant learning task sheets, learning resources and online test questions to the class based on the smart learning platform. The learning task sheets should essentially provide appropriate guidance and learning path design for the effective learning degree of independent learning so that learners can clarify why and what they are learning. Teach-ers select appropriate learning scaffolds based on teaching objectives to provide learn-ers with self-directed learning, mainly referring to high-quality microlearning videos. Learners complete relevant online test questions, ask their own learning questions in the smart learning platform, and communicate with other learners in the discussion forum to solve their questions together. Teachers check learners' interaction records before the lesson, give personalized responses to certain personalized questions, pick out common problems, and modify the teaching design plan in the lesson to tailor the teaching to the learning, connect the two stages before and during the lesson, and group learners in a hybrid way according to the situation. Throughout the precourse shallow learning stage, learners can initially master subject knowledge, develop the ability and persistence to learn through independent learning, and develop the interpersonal skills of teamwork and effective communication in the process of interacting with classmates and teachers to solve problems.

Deep Learning During the Lesson. In the in-class deep learning phase, the teaching venue is the offline classroom, where teachers understand learners' common problems through preclass data and solve learners' problems in class through the smart learning platform, multimedia projection and computer screen sharing multiscreen. The teacher creates an engaging problem situation based on learners' prior knowledge that is slightly above their current cognitive level and guides learners to focus on key conceptual features and engage in collaborative inquiry, while learners brainstorm multiple problem solutions. Since learners do not accurately grasp and explain the key conceptual features, learners will be frustrated to some extent during collaborative inquiry. The teacher should provide timely encouragement and guidance to learners, and even failures are meaningful as long as they are related to the learning topic.

Orderly Phase. The focus of this stage is on presenting the results of the group's investigation after the group's cooperative investigation. Throughout the presentation process, the group will explain the problems encountered, how to solve them and the concept of the work and gradually deepen their understanding of the key concepts and master the higher-order skills in the process of group presentation, self-evaluation, evaluation of other groups and comparison with the cases given by the teacher. In addition to guiding the learners to show their work, the teacher should also create a relaxed and happy atmosphere. Learners will not suffer from peer disdain or teacher criticism for their "failed" work. Mechanism 3: Explaining Key Conceptual Features and Mechanism 4: Organizing Goal Concepts are two mechanisms that learners need to focus on at this stage.

Deep Learning and Evaluation During the Lesson. In addition to creating a context and guiding learners to conduct cooperative inquiry, the teacher arranges the link of results presentation in the deep learning stage of the lesson. Learners continue to deepen their understanding of knowledge and further deep learning in the process of explaining their key conceptual features and solutions, and the teacher evaluates the students in each group's presentation, while each group compares its own solution with the group presented on stage and the teacher's given solutions are compared and evaluated by themselves and other groups through the smart learning platform to achieve the organization of the target concepts. In this process, the teacher as a facilitator regulates and controls the entire interaction process, collaborates in knowledge construction, and develops learners' complex problem solving skills, teamwork, effective communication skills, critical thinking, learning to learn, and perseverance in learning.

Evaluation and Reflection After Class. In the postclass evaluation and reflection stage, teachers can combine the learning behavior data generated by the wisdom learning platform and offline learning to stratify learners and push resources and tutorials to the problems of learners at different levels through the wisdom learning platform to promote learners' reflection, which can promote learners' deep learning [17] and is an indispensable part of deep learning. Teachers readjust the teaching content in the teaching process through teaching reflection to form a closed loop. Every part of the wisdom teaching activities is filled with wisdom evaluation, and the subjects of evaluation can be the teacher, themselves, or their classmates, which is diversified and includes the multidimensional content of evaluation and diversified methods of evaluation.

3 Deep Learning Environment Design

Scholars Yu Shengquan note that in the smart classroom, shallow classroom interaction and knowledge instillation have not yet fully played the role of technology. The role of technology is to build a deep learning environment to help learners complete the construction of the meaning of knowledge, to stimulate and help learners explore independently, to link the construction of knowledge, to become a tool for the creation of the learning environment, and to become a motivational tool for emotional experience, which needs to start from the following dimensions: 1. Carry out discussions; 2. Increasing learner participation; 3. Stimulating cognitive engagement; 4. Smart mobile interactive terminals; 5. Conducting learning assessment; 6. Student cognitive biases; 7. Providing quality learning resources; 8. Providing learning reflection activities; 9. Continuously recording the learning process; 10. Problem solving; 11. Student self-management authority; and 12. Student cognitive and affective engagement measurement. In this study, the above dimensions were used to design the questionnaire, interview outline, evaluation index system and design and develop the smart learning platform to support the implementation of the teaching model, as shown in Fig. 5. Deep learning environment design ideas.

Work Evaluation Index System. The work evaluation index system is used to evaluate learners' work and is based on the SOLO (structure of the observed learning outcome) classification evaluation method proposed by John Biggs and Kevin F. Collis, which is widely used in the field of deep learning. The SOLO classification method consists of five levels: prestructure level, single-structure level, multiple-structure level, associated-structure level, and abstract-structure level. Based on this, the responses made by the learners can be matched to the corresponding levels to judge whether deep learning has occurred.

Interview Outline. The first interview outline was used for the first and second rounds of action research, focusing on group cooperation, independent inquiry, etc. The second interview outline was used at the end of the third round of action research, focusing on the effects of the students' experience with the teaching model, etc. The second interview outline was used at the end of the third round of action research, focusing on the effects of the students' experience with the teaching model, etc.

Questionnaire. The questionnaire is based on the questionnaires of scholars such as Chen, M.X. and Zhang, K.L. (2016), Chai, C. S, Deng, F, Tsai, P. S, Koh, J.H. L, & Tsai, C. (2015), Lai. C. L, & Hwang, G. J (2014) and Li, Y.B. and Sultan, Rui (2018) and adapted with the characteristics of this study. It mainly involves three deep learning dimensions: cognitive domain, interpersonal domain, and self domain. The questionnaire was analysed for items, validity and reliability using SPSS, and in the item analysis, the |t| values were all less than 3, and the sig values were all less than 0.05, indicating that the questionnaire's item design was reasonable. In the validity analysis, the KMO sampling

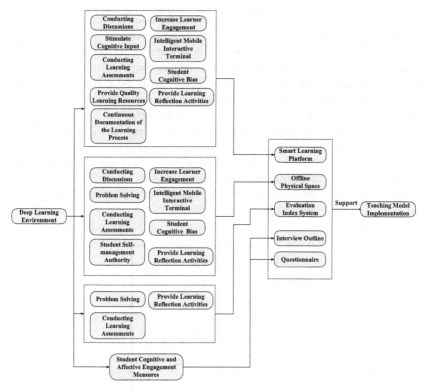

Fig. 5. Deep learning Environment Design Ideas

fitness was $0.878 > 0.7$, the rotated component matrix did not have any question items less than 0.45, and the total variance explained cumulative rate was $78.763\% > 60\%$, which indicated that the validity of the questionnaire was good. In the reliability analysis, the overall Cronbach's alpha of the questionnaire was 0.966, and the Cronbach's alpha of each dimension of the questionnaire was > 0.8, which indicated that the reliability of each dimension of the questionnaire was ideal, and the overall reliability of the questionnaire was very good.

Smart Learning Platform. Information technology is indispensable in facilitating deep learning, and its integration into deep learning plays a cornerstone role in facilitating the occurrence of deep learning. The deep learning environment is created by designing and developing a smart learning platform to support the implementation of the teaching model. Students expect to receive real-time feedback in the process of mastering basic knowledge, and when they carry out project-based learning, they save and upload their works in real time, with a view to receiving timely feedback from classmates and teachers to facilitate the subsequent sessions of pushing personalized learning resources to repair and improve the project results.

The analysis of the system functions helps to clarify the functions of the intelligent learning platform to help the implementation of the teaching model, and its requirements analysis mainly consists of functional and nonfunctional requirements. The target users of the smart learning platform for deep learning in the effective failure perspective are the teachers and students of "College Computer Fundamentals".

The functional demand analysis of the wisdom learning platform should clarify the necessary functions for the implementation of the teaching model, conduct functional analysis of the wisdom learning platform, think deeply about the relationship and demand between effective failure, deep learning and the wisdom learning platform, and consider various functional demands from the perspective of learners.

The Smart Learning Platform provides an online communication space for teachers and students, and each role corresponds to different permissions: (1) administrators can perform all operations on the Smart Learning Platform; (2) teachers have all permissions for courses; and (3) students participate in course activities created by teachers.

Through the above analysis, the overall use case of the smart learning platform system is derived, as shown in Fig. 6.

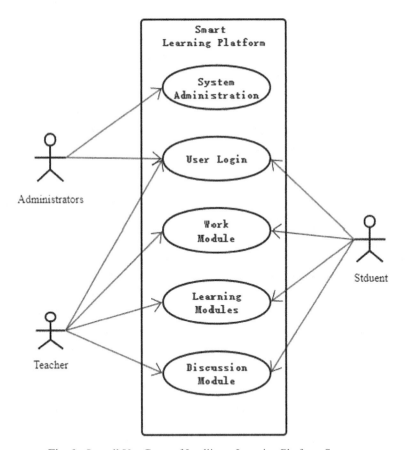

Fig. 6. Overall Use Cases of Intelligent Learning Platform System

Based on the functional requirement analysis and closely following the teaching model constructed in the previous period, the system functions of the smart learning platform are designed accordingly, as shown in Fig. 7.

Fig. 7. Overall Design of Intelligent Learning Platform System Functions

The interface design of the platform functions mainly includes system management interface design, user login interface design, learning interface design, work module interface design, and discussion module interface design. Due to the page relationship, only the system management interface, edit module interface and user login interface are shown, as shown in Figs. 8, 9 and 10.

Fig. 8. Course Module Interface

Smart Learning Platform

admin

•••

☐ Remember username

Log in

Forgotten your username or password?

Cookies must be enabled in your browser
❓

Some courses may allow guest access

Log in as a guest

Is this your first time here?

For full access to this site, you first need to create an account.

Create new account

Fig. 9. User Login Module Interface

Available courses

⇪ University Computer Fundamentals

Fig. 10. Edit Module Interface

4   An Action Research on the Teaching Model

This study adopts an action research method to apply the teaching model of intelligent classroom empowering deep learning in productive failure perspective to "College Computer Fundamentals", the action research subjects are students from 2 classes of J college class 2021, one class is the control group and one class is the experimental group, because the students just entered the same university after the college entrance examination and the course of "College Computer Fundamentals" is the first semester course of freshman year, so the students' conditions are considered to be consistent, this study is conducted in three rounds, each round of action research is conducted for one month.

First Round of Action Research and Analysis

Planning and Action. Words were selected as the research content for the first round of action research. Prepreparation was performed according to the research objectives and teaching contents, such as spending a week of class time introducing learners to the learning style of this course, creating a relaxed and pleasant learning atmosphere, introducing learners to the operation and functions of the Smart Learning Platform and conducting a learning situation analysis, teaching objective analysis, and teaching content analysis.

In the shallow learning stage, teachers release preprepared learning task sheets to activate the target concepts, and according to the study objectives and teaching content, the course content is decomposed, and the content of the literacy and partial comprehension levels are arranged in the form of microlessons or texts for learners to conduct self-study. In the precourse shallow learning process, learners conduct online discussions through the intelligent learning platform, and learners learn over a period of time to form an initial mastery of the knowledge points. Learners develop an initial grasp of the knowledge points after a period of study. The teacher acts as a guide and provides quizzes for the learners, which cover the knowledge points of the study topic and are used to test the effectiveness of online independent learning.

In the deep learning stage, the teaching place is the offline classroom. The first class is mainly to discuss the problems of preclass shallow learning feedback. The teacher based on the data generated by the preclass smart classroom shallow learning for heterogeneous grouping of learners, learners grouped on the common problems of preclass shallow learning and the problems generated by group discussion, preliminary solution of the problems generated by preclass shallow learning, not solve the problems organized feedback to the teacher. The teacher is given feedback. The teacher will answer questions and solve problems through the large screen projection, computer live streaming in the computer room and cell phone interactive multiscreen to distinguish existing knowledge related to the target concept. The second, third, and fourth periods focus on creating a problem situation to guide learners to pay attention to key conceptual features for collaborative inquiry and brainstorming. The teacher plays the role of a guide rather than a knowledge instructor and encourages learners to try and build a mindset of not being afraid of failure, telling them that they value the process more than the result and that even a failed result is a success if it is the result of hard work and thought.

In the deep learning stage, the teaching place is the offline classroom. The first class is mainly to discuss the problems of preclass shallow learning feedback. The teacher based on the data generated by the preclass smart classroom shallow learning for heterogeneous grouping of learners, learners grouped on the common problems of preclass shallow learning and the problems generated by group discussion, preliminary solution of the problems generated by preclass shallow learning, not solve the problems organized feedback to the teacher. The teacher is given feedback. The teacher will answer questions and solve problems through the large screen projection, computer live streaming in the computer room and cell phone interactive multiscreen to distinguish existing knowledge related to the target concept. The second, third, and fourth periods focus on creating a problem situation to guide learners to pay attention to key conceptual features for collaborative inquiry and brainstorming. The teacher plays the role of a guide rather than a knowledge instructor and encourages learners to try and build a mindset of not being afraid of failure, telling them that they value the process more than the result and that even a failed result is a success if it is the result of hard work and thought.

The teacher randomly selects one member of each group to present their work on stage. In the process of selection, each learner has a chance to be selected so that each learner has an understanding of the key conceptual features and solutions of the group's work, thus promoting deep learning. After each group's presentation, the presenting group and other groups self-evaluate and evaluate the presentation on the Smart Learning Platform, and the teacher gives the corresponding evaluation on the spot based on the evaluation index system. After each group's presentation, the teacher gives a case study, and each group compares its solution with other groups and cases to achieve the organization of the target concept.

Observation and Reflection. This round of observations of learners' independent learning and classroom situations, combined with interviews and work completion to summarize and reflect, revealed the following problems: The group is not very cooperative. Learners do not perform self-assessments and mutual assessments well. Learners are dependent on the teacher. Poor mastery of knowledge before the lesson and poor online participation. The learners' work does not reach the deep learning level well.

Second Round of Action Research and Analysis

Planning and Action. The second round of action research selected PowerPoint as the research content, and the following modifications were made to the problems in the first round of action research:

Regarding the problem of weak group cooperation, teachers reformulate the rules of group cooperation, such as increasing the group's sense of collective honor by making group members' speeches represent the group's speeches and adding points together as a group, making it clear that group members have their own roles and responsibilities, and emphasizing the importance of group cooperation to promote cooperative learning in groups.

Regarding the problem of learners' inability to conduct self-evaluation and mutual evaluation, teachers announce the corresponding evaluation index system in the work presentation session and use quantitative evaluation to let learners know what dimensions to evaluate to improve the effectiveness of learners' participation in evaluation and enable them to better conduct self-evaluation and mutual evaluation.

With regard to learners' dependence on the teacher, reinforcement provides continuous emotional scaffolding to encourage learners to experiment, creates a relaxed and enjoyable learning environment, and reduces learners' dependence on the teacher in the process of problem solving.

Regarding the problem of poor mastery of knowledge and low participation in online learning before the class, the teacher re-established the percentage of online learning grades to urge learners to participate in online learning, further explained in detail the key points that could not be mastered well in the first class, and emphasized the importance of learning to learn, such as through the story "teaching someone to fish is better than teaching someone to fish".

Regarding the problem of learners' work not reaching the deep learning level well, teachers provide metacognitive scaffolding for learners in the deep learning phase to facilitate the process of generating solutions towards productive failure and effective success.

Observation and Reflection. The current round of action research observed the learners' classroom situation and summarized and reflected on the interviews, work completion and self-assessment and mutual evaluation and found the following problems: Learners are prone to disagreement during cooperative inquiry sessions. The task difficulty gradient is not obvious. The work is not innovative enough.

Third Round of Action Research and Analysis

Planning and Action. Visio was selected for the third round of action research, and the following modifications were made to the problems that existed in the first round of action research:

Regarding the problem that learners tend to disagree in the collaborative inquiry session, teachers should provide emotional scaffolding in the collaborative inquiry session to encourage learners to generate multiple problem solutions and develop their awareness of multiple solutions and at the same time give appropriate guidance when learners disagree.

With regard to the problem of an inconspicuous task difficulty gradient, teachers divide the tasks into three gradients when issuing them. For the third stage, they point to learners who are more adaptable, have a better foundation and complete the basic situations faster, while learners who are less adaptable, have a poor foundation and complete the basic situations slower cannot complete them, aiming to teach according to their abilities.

With regard to the lack of innovation in the work, the evaluation index system is improved to let the learners know what level they need to reach to learn Visio. To better promote learners' deep learning and cultivate their innovative thinking, the teacher publishes the evaluation index system for Visio production at the same time when setting up the learning situations and adds dimensions related to innovation to the Visio evaluation index system: novelty and feasibility.

Observation and Reflection. The learners have grown and progressed from being unfamiliar with the teaching model at the beginning to going through two rounds of action research. At the same time, by modifying the problems that existed in the two rounds of action research, from the interviews, work situation and classroom observation, the learners were able to reach the level of correlation structure better, and their teamwork, communication ability, learning perseverance, and critical thinking were improved to a certain extent, which shows that this teaching model can reduce the intervention of learners from the perspective of productive failure, thus promoting learners towards deeper learning. However, each round of action research has different teaching content, different levels of difficulty, and learners change over time, and different problems emerge in each round of action research. For example, some learners indicate that the tasks are still too simple, the interest of the situation is there, but the interest gradually decreases over time, and they expect that there will be subsequent activities that continue to motivate learning. In future teaching activities, further improvements need to be made. Further improvements are needed in future teaching activities.

5   Analysis of the Effect of Applying the Teaching Model

The purpose of this study is to promote learners to deep learning, so the effect analysis of this study will also start from deep learning, combining the works of the three rounds of action research, classroom situation, interviews and questionnaires after the third round of action research and analysing the changes of deep learning ability based on the core elements model of deep learning proposed in Chapter 2, divided into subject knowledge, higher-order ability and emotional attitude, among which higher-order ability includes learning to learn, critical thinking and complex problem solving ability, and emotional attitude includes teamwork, communication and collaboration and learning perseverance.

The work evaluation index system is used to evaluate learners' work and is based on the SOLO (structure of the observed learning outcome) classification evaluation method proposed by John Biggs and Kevin F. Collis, which is widely used in the field of deep learning. The SOLO classification method consists of five levels: prestructure level, single-structure level, multiple-structure level, associated-structure level, and abstract-structure level. Based on this, the responses made by the learners can be matched to the corresponding levels to judge whether deep learning has occurred.

The questionnaire is based on the questionnaires of scholars such as Chen, M.X. and Zhang, K.L. (2016), Chai, C. S, Deng, F, Tsai, P. S, Koh, J.H. L, & Tsai, C. (2015), Lai. C. L, & Hwang, G. J (2014) and Li, Y.B. and Sultan, Rui (2018) and adapted with the characteristics of this study. It mainly involves three deep learning dimensions: cognitive domain, interpersonal domain, and self domain. The questionnaire was analysed for items, validity and reliability using SPSS, and in the item analysis, the |t| values were all less than 3, and the sig values were all less than 0.05, indicating that the questionnaire's item design was reasonable. In the validity analysis, the KMO sampling fitness was $0.878 > 0.7$, the rotated component matrix did not have any question items less than 0.45, and the total variance explained cumulative rate was $78.763\% > 60\%$, which indicated that the validity of the questionnaire was good. In the reliability analysis, the overall Cronbach's alpha of the questionnaire was 0.966, and the Cronbach's alpha of each dimension of the questionnaire was > 0.8, which indicated that the reliability of each dimension of the questionnaire was ideal, and the overall reliability of the questionnaire was very good.

Subject Knowledge.   The subject knowledge in this study focuses on the basic mastery of knowledge, and the works of the first round of action research and the third round of action research are compared and analysed by the work evaluation index system. The first round of action research applied the Word solution and tested the mastery of subject knowledge based on the Word evaluation index system, while the third round of action research applied the Visio solution to test the mastery of subject knowledge based on the Visio evaluation index system. From the teacher's evaluation, learners' group self-evaluation and learners' group mutual evaluation, it is obvious that the learning effect of the first round of action research is inferior to that of the third round of action research, and the Visio solutions generated by learners in the third round of action research are better than those in the first round of action research in terms of completeness and feasibility, as shown in Fig. 11. Using the same evaluation index system to compare the Visio works of the experimental group with the control group that implemented traditional teaching, it was found that the learning effect of the control group was lower than that of the experimental group, as shown in Fig. 12, indicating that the learners' mastery of subject knowledge under this teaching mode was better than that of the traditional teaching mode.

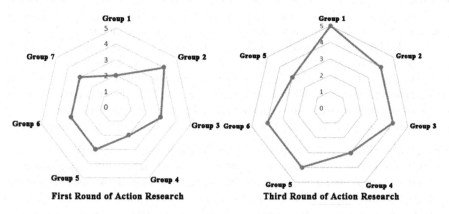

Fig. 11. Comparison of Evaluation Data of the First and Third Rounds of Action Research Works

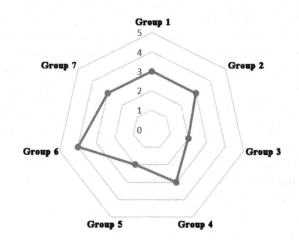

Fig. 12. Evaluation Data of Visio Works for the Control Group

Higher-Order Capabilities. According to the deep learning core element model, higher-order competencies cover learners' critical thinking, learning to learn and complex problem solving abilities. In this study, a combination of questionnaires and interviews was used to analyse the higher-order competencies, and the results of the questionnaire are shown in Table 2. The results of critical thinking ($t = -10.862$, $p < 0.001$), learned learning ($t = -11.941$, $p < 0.001$) and complex problem solving competencies ($t = -14.469$, $p < 0.001$) indicate that learned learning, critical thinking, and complex problem solving skills were significantly different and improved after three rounds of action research instruction. From the third round of interviews, it was found that the learners believed that the current teaching mode helps the development of innovative thinking (e.g., interviewee 4 in the first question: "I like this kind of teaching. I think it is good that we can do it according to our own ideas and thoughts. (In the past, it was slightly more rigid, but now it is slightly more open.) (e.g., respondents 2 and 7 of the second question: "It helps us to develop our independent learning ability.") "To be able to take the initiative to learn things on our own, to practice on our own.") I think it can help the development of critical thinking and complex problem solving skills (e.g., interviewee 8 in the second question: "I think it is advantageous, like those videos you posted we can watch them ourselves, and then we can watch them again and again if we do not understand them, we think we can learn more. If you do not understand, you can go back and watch it again and again and then solve your own problems.") This shows that the higher-order skills of the learners are better developed in this teaching mode.

Emotional Attitude. Emotional experiences include learners' teamwork, communication skills, and perseverance in learning. In this study, a combination of questionnaires and interviews was used to analyse teamwork, communication ability and learning perseverance. Teamwork ($t = -6.282$, $p < 0.001$), communication skills ($t = -8.958$, $p < 0.001$) and perseverance in learning ($t = -10.751$, $p < 0.001$) were found to be significantly different through the questionnaire, as shown in Table 1. This indicates that learners' teamwork, communication skills and learning perseverance improved after going through the Smart Classroom Empowered Deep Learning instructional model in the productive failure perspective. From the third round of interviews, it was found that learners preferred the current teaching mode to the traditional classroom because of its relaxed atmosphere, which helps teamwork and improves communication skills (e.g., interviewee 3 in the first question and interviewee 4 in the second question: "I still prefer this way. It is a little bit freer and the atmosphere is better." "The advantages, such as the way the group is quite good, I think we can discuss with each other or something, which can promote the relationship between our students, and then also help each other to communicate to solve problems.") I think it helps to improve the perseverance of learning (e.g., the third question from respondent 2: "Yes, it can enhance my learning ability and self-discipline.") This indicates that this mode of teaching is more conducive to improving learners' emotional attitudes.

Table 1. Deep learning questionnaire survey results.

Deep Learning Dimensions	Deep Learning	Average Value		T Value
Cognitive Domain	Critical Thinking	Pretest	11.90	−10.862***
		Post-test	13.10	
	Complex problem solving skills	Pretest	19.04	−14.469***
		Post-test	20.79	
Interpersonal Domain	Teamwork	Pretest	12.62	−6.282***
		Post-test	13.38	
	Communication skills	Pretest	18.55	−8.958***
		Post-test	20.13	
Self Domain	Learning to Learn	Pretest	16.72	−11.941***
		Post-test	19.70	
	Learning Perseverance	Pretest	26.49	−10.751***
		Post-test	29.71	

Note: *** is $p < 0.001$

6 Conclusions and Recommendations

This study proposes the productive failure perspective deep learning model and the wisdom classroom empowering deep learning model based on the investigation of productive failure and deep learning and the wisdom classroom empowering deep learning model and constructs and carries out research on the wisdom classroom empowering deep learning teaching model under the productive failure perspective. After the implementation of the action research, it was noted that the instructional design model in the productive failure perspective is important for promoting deep learning of learners; the focus on emotion is important for promoting deep learning of learners in the productive failure perspective; the higher-order ability is the dimension that learners need to focus on for deep learning; and the teaching model of empowering deep learning in the smart classroom in the productive failure perspective has better teaching effects. The experimental sample of this study is small and only carried out in one discipline at the higher education level, which needs to be further explored. In the future, we hope to further expand the experimental sample, improve the research conditions, enhance the persuasive power of the research findings, and apply it to different teaching stages and different disciplines to explore its applicability to deepen this teaching model to adapt to different teaching stages and different disciplines.

Acknowledgement. This work is supported by Yunnan Normal University 2022 Postgraduate Research Innovation Fund "Action Research on Intelligent Classroom Empowering Deep Learning Teaching Model under the Perspective of Productive Failure" (No. YJSJJ22-B91).

References

1. Wei, Z., Yuexia, L.: Deep learning: teaching improvement based on core literacy. Educ. Res. **39**(11), 56–60 (2018)
2. Zhang, G.: Teaching design and practice research on productive failure theory for students' deep learning. Harbin Normal University (2021)
3. Zhiting, Z., Hongchao, P.: Deep learning: the core pillar of smart education. Chin. J. Educ. **05**, 36–45 (2017)
4. Zhang, X., Tian, T.T., Tian, M., Gao, L., Zhang, X.: The evolution and trend of intelligent teaching research in China in the past decade. China Dist. Educ. **2020**(09), 62–69 (2020)
5. Yang, X., Xie, Y., Gou, R., He, J.: An empirical study on the construction of smart classroom model. China's e-learning **2020**(09), 50–57 (2020)
6. Hongchao, P., Zhiting, Z.: Research on deep learning: development patterns and bottlenecks. Mod. Dist. Educ. Res. **32**(01), 41–50 (2020)
7. Hongchao, P., Zhiting, Z.: Development of a flexible and deep learning design framework for smart classroom. Mod. Dist. Educ. Res. **33**(01), 38–48 (2021)
8. Yuan, S.: Exploring the effectiveness of intelligent classroom in teaching English as a foreign language in secondary schools. Vocat. Tech. Educ. **42**(02), 33–36 (2021)
9. Huang Ronghuai, H., Yongbin, Y.J., Guangde, X.: The concept and characteristics of smart classroom. Open Educ. Res. **18**(02), 22–27 (2012). https://doi.org/10.13966/j.cnki.kfjyyj.2012.02.008
10. Holmes, N.G., Day, J., Anthony, H.K., Park, D.A., Bonn, I.R.: Making the failure more productive: scaffolding the invention process to improve inquiry behaviors and outcomes in invention activities. Instr. Sci. **42**(4), 523–538 (2014). https://doi.org/10.1007/s11251-013-9300-7
11. Kapur, M.: A further study of productive failure in mathematical problem solving: unpacking the design components. Instr. Sci. **39**, 561–579 (2011)
12. Kennedy-Clark, S., Jacobson, M.J., Reimann, P.: Scenario-based multi-user virtual environments: productive failure and the impact of structure on learning. In: Wolpers, M., Kirschner, P.A., Scheffel, M., Lindstaedt, S., Dimitrova, V. (eds.) Sustaining TEL: From Innovation to Learning and Practice, pp. 402–407. Springer Berlin Heidelberg, Berlin, Heidelberg (2010). https://doi.org/10.1007/978-3-642-16020-2_28
13. Kapur, M., Katerine, B.: Designing for productive failure D. J. Learn. Sci. **21**(1), 45–83 (2012)
14. Duan, J., Yu, S.: Research on deep learning of e-Learning in the context of learning science. J. Distance Educ. **2013**(4), 43–51 (2013)
15. Sun, Y., Zhu, Z.: Developing 21st century skills with deep learning - Insights from the U.S. Learning for life and work: Developing transferable knowledge and skills in the 21st century. Mod. Distance Educ. Res. **2018**(3), 9–18 (2018)
16. Jensen, E., Nickelsen, L.A.: 7 powerful strategies for deep learning. Wen Wen, Translation, East China Normal University Press, Shanghai (2010)
17. Yun, M., Yanlin, Z.: Towards deep learning: the design and application practice of reflective scaffolding in blended learning contexts. Mod. Dist. Educ. **03**, 89–96 (2021)

Aesthetic Education Construction in Public Computer Courses Combined with Online Teaching at Art Universities

Tong Chen[1] (ID), Yaowei Xu[2] (ID), and Guosong Gu[3](✉) (ID)

[1] Music Engineering Department, Zhejiang Conservatory of Music, Hangzhou, China
ct@zjcm.edu.cn
[2] School of English Language, Zhejiang Yuexiu University, Shaoxing, China
20231027@yxc.cn
[3] College of Information Science & Engineering, Jiaxing University, Jiaxing, China
ggs0110@zjxu.edu.cn

Abstract. As compulsory courses in higher education, computer public courses play an indispensable role in curriculum ideological and political education. Aesthetic education is the key to cultivating and improving students' all-around qualities, Aesthetic education, as an important aspect of education, combines the characteristics of public computer courses and plays the role of curriculum ideological and political education by guiding students to understand, discover, create, and appreciate beauty. Due to the COVID-19 epidemic, most colleges and universities have adopted online teaching. Under this premise, combined with online teaching and the characteristics of art students at art universities, we proposed to explore the construction of aesthetic education in public computer courses at our university.

Keywords: Curriculum Ideological and Political Education · Higher Education · Public Computer Courses · Aesthetic Education · COVID-19 · Online Teaching · Art Students · Art Universities

1 Introduction

In December 2016, a national conference with the theme of ideological and political work in colleges and universities was held. At this conference, Chinese President Xi Jinping emphasized the great rejuvenation of the Chinese nation. It needs to improve the development of higher education in our country, and it is more urgent than ever [1]. Colleges and universities must adhere to the correct political direction, cultivate talents based on moral education, and implement all aspects of teaching with ideological values. Xi also pointed out that in addition to ideological and political theory, the other courses need keep well in their area of responsibility and promote the effectiveness of curriculum ideological and political education. We should combine the curriculum of ideological and political education into a specific course other than traditional ideological and political courses.

In this regard, many researchers and scholars have done some course exploration and practice. Bin Sun and Yueli Dong [2] combine curriculum ideological and political

J. Gan et al. (Eds.): CSEI 2023, CCIS 1900, pp. 195–209, 2024.
https://doi.org/10.1007/978-981-99-9492-2_17

education into computer science and technology majors. They propose that the top-level design of talent training plays a key decisive role in the effectiveness and direction of curriculum teaching reform. To integrate the curriculum ideological and political education into specialized course education, we need to do this design well and find the junction between the two. Guojuan Li [3] points out that teachers are the key to curriculum ideological and political education construction. The construction of curriculum ideological and political education needs to rely on teachers to implement. The effectiveness of the curriculum's ideological and political education construction depends on students. To judge whether the curriculum's ideological and political education construction is effective, what the students finally get is the judging criteria.

Aesthetic education, as an important aspect of education, combines the characteristics of public computer courses and plays the role of curriculum ideological and political education by guiding students to understand, discover, create, and appreciate beauty. Due to the COVID-19 epidemic, most colleges and universities have moved forward with online teaching. Under this premise, combined with online teaching, we proposed to explore the construction of aesthetic education in public computer courses at our university.

At present, many scientists and scholars at home and abroad have done research in the field of aesthetic education. From elementary school, middle school, university, and even senior university, there are related researches. For example: through experiments, study the aesthetic education of lower-grade students in a teaching system based on the subject-subject relationship between teachers and students [4]. Reference [5] describes the basic concepts, functions, and importance of aesthetic education in human life and studies the role of aesthetic education in developing the talents and abilities of children with disabilities, especially the ability to innovate technology. Reference [6] surveyed more than 300 art education undergraduates from different universities in Chengdu, Sichuan, China, and determined that aesthetic education can effectively improve students' art learning outcomes. But too many of these researches are related to liberal arts majors and arts majors; even if they are related to science and engineering, most of them are related to research in specific fields of science and technology rather than science and engineering-related curriculum teaching research. For example, reference [7] sorts out the teaching experience in the post-epidemic era, and co. It conducts online and offline mixed teaching research and practice of aesthetic education courses related to art theory courses. The teaching method of online courses has some similarities with the research in this paper, but the teaching content and teaching objects are entirely different. Reference [8] combines human evaluation of food features with computational analysis of visual aesthetics to study the aesthetic appeal and specific visual features that contribute to various food photos. If the perspective is put on the research on aesthetic education related to computer-related majors, there will be fewer studies in this area, and there are even fewer related literature on aesthetic education research in the education of public computer courses in universities. Reference [9] starts from the problems faced by aesthetic education in colleges and universities, combines the characteristics of aesthetic education and the characteristics of information technology majors, discusses the connotation of aesthetic education for information technology majors, and points out that information technology science and engineering majors should be based on their own majors, studies the aesthetics education of engineering majors, and proposes the idea of opening innovative course. Reference [10] starts from the ICT major and analyzes the advantages and disadvantages of online and offline college aesthetic education courses and the symbiotic relationship related to this major. Finally, it is basically difficult to find aesthetic education research in the direction of computer public courses in art universities.

2 Online Teaching

Online learning refers to network-mediated learning [11]. It is believed that online learning is play a massive role in the actual learning experience of students, especially in areas where the use of internet-connected devices is so. The boundaries between learning and other daily life activities have softened. If we want to get the most out of our online learning environment, equipment design, and implementation play an indispensable role.

2.1 Necessity

The emergence of the COVID-19 epidemic has made people see the advantages of online education [12]. During the COVID-19 epidemic in the year 2020, all school courses were forced to be carried out online. Our country and the whole world have been affected by this epidemic. In the world, 1,88 countries have closed all schools, including universities, high schools, middle schools, elementary schools, and kindergartens, or localized them to protect students from the COVID-19 virus [13]. In this situation, higher education, like other education, changes the traditional face-to-face teaching way with offline classrooms and moves the classroom to online teaching. The COVID-19 epidemic is not the only time universities and colleges have converted traditional face-to-face teaching to online teaching. For instance, universities and colleges switched to online teaching when the H1N1 Influenza virus occurred in the fall of 2009 and Hurricane Katrina's landfall occurred in the summer of 2005 [14]. In the current post-COVID-19 pandemic period, online teaching is also a necessary means to meet the students who are in isolation or cannot attend classes in person because of the epidemic prevention and control measures.

2.2 Methods

A series of studies indicates that the teaching quality, including learning effectiveness and student satisfaction in this digital age can be improved through a blended teaching method, which mixes online teaching mode and on-ground teaching mode. And the blended teaching method has a more positive effect on the teaching quality of smaller institutions of higher education; their own needs can be best met by the blend of face-to-face and online methods [15]. Zhejiang Conservatory of Music happens to be such a smaller university. The Conservatory offers a wide range of music and arts teaching for talented students from China and beyond. The current student number totals 3288. ZJCM has its unique characteristics, campus culture, and distinctive majors and students. So we choose the blended teaching method.

In the last few years, flipped classrooms and SPOC have been brought into the course teaching little by little [16]. The combination of the two in the computer-related basic course has obtained a very impressive teaching outcome [17]. The first one is a new teaching method that is student-centered and related to the internet and mobile internet. It can address the issue that the traditional teaching method is challenging to inspire students' interest. The second one, Small Private Online Course, is a division of the Massive Open Online Course (MOOC). To put it another way, SPOC is MOOC (online teaching) plus a face-to-face teaching method. In other words, SPOC is a blended teaching method. Its teaching design features are as follows:

- Set the conditions for entering the online class. Students need to apply to join the class, or the teacher adds students directly to the online class.
- Limit the size of the online classes. Usually, the upper limit is hundreds of students. In my classes, the number of students in each class is generally 30 to 60 students.

3 The Current Course Teaching Situation

Computer public courses are the public compulsory basic courses in higher education today. Such a curriculum is to improve the basic information literacy of university students and make them meet the needs of the times. Similarly, art universities also set up public computer courses. In the current era when the Internet, information technology, and life are closely related, computer application ability has become one of the significant indicators of talent cultivation in colleges and universities. To better carry out public computer courses in art universities, it is necessary to focus on their own particularities and their current teaching situation. Their computer public courses have the following circumstance:

3.1 Computer Literacy Varies Greatly

Although current college students are already post-00s, students from different disciplines and hometowns still vary widely in their basic computer literacy. Eastern coastal areas and economically developed areas of our country own relatively advanced education resources and education levels; simultaneously, students possess higher basic computer literacy. For example, in many third-tier cities in Zhejiang Province, elementary school students in lower grades have already begun to learn computer code programming, not to mention a provincial capital city like Hangzhou. Before college, these students have mastered the basic computer knowledge required by the university, and even have specific basic network knowledge and basic knowledge of audio and video software. On the contrary, in the underdeveloped areas of the central and western regions, many students have never attended computer lessons before entering the university, and their learning and living environments make their understanding and application of computer information technology and mobile Internet lag behind students from the developed eastern seaboard regions. This phenomenon is common in art universities. In addition to the geographical gaps in provinces and cities, there are significant and huge gaps between students of different majors. For example, students majoring in dance or drama performance are relatively weak in basic computer literacy.

3.2 Big Cultural Differences

There is a big difference in the cultural quality of students in art universities. One situation is that "I like, I choose". Students are particularly fond of music, dance, or drama, so they come to this university. Another situation is that "I can, I choose". Students are not very adept at taking cultural exams, so they choose the art specialty with much lower cultural grades. Undergraduates still show significant differences in their learning attitudes, a large number of art students have the idea of "focusing on majors and ignoring culture". They think that it is enough to do a good job in professional courses, and other cultural courses are useless or nothing. The more students with this attitude, the more they will lack the cultural accomplishments and cultural knowledge which are required in future art practice.

3.3 The Teaching Form is Relatively Fixed

Like other public basic compulsory courses, college computer courses are taught in large classes. Art university students are more accustomed to the "one-to-one" teaching form, rather than the large class teaching mode. When taking a large class, it is difficult for students to concentrate, especially in a course with practical practice, such as a computer public course. When many students practice on the computer, even if the teacher has explained it uniformly in class, they still need the teacher's "one-on-one" guidance to master the basic operation and basic knowledge. As a result, some students are becoming slacker and slacker in public courses, especially computer courses, and gradually lose interest.

4   What is Aesthetic Education

Emphasis on aesthetic education has been pointed out many times in the documents of the Ministry of Education of China [18]. Ralph Smith is a major influence on thinking about art education in North America, and his presentations have always represented a central point of view in the field. He has always advocated that the central goal of art education should be to enhance the ability to aesthetic experience [19]. Aesthetic education is a kind of beautiful education. Obviously, the core of beauty is also an aesthetic experience. But aesthetic education cannot be equated with art education, although both cultivate people's ability to feel, create and express beauty. The medium of beauty can be everything in nature, society, and art. Therefore, beauty includes natural beauty, social beauty, and artistic beauty. At a glance, it can be seen that artistic beauty is part of beauty. From this, we can also recognize that the scope of aesthetic education is greater than that of art education. Aesthetic education includes art education, and art education is an important way of aesthetic education.

Aesthetic education refers to the education of students as a whole. Aesthetic education is interdisciplinary, involving multiple disciplines such as art, aesthetics, and psychology [20]. Aesthetic education can not only improve a person's aesthetic ability but also change a person's psychology, hobbies, temperament, and taste. Aesthetic education will not focus on cultivating students' artistic ability but focus on cultivating artistic appreciation ability. Only when their artistic accomplishment and aesthetic accomplishment the university's aesthetic education can be more ideal. At art universities, those courses that can improve people's cognition of art culture and aesthetic accomplishment are the specialized courses here. In addition to theoretical study and art appreciation, aesthetic education should also include the practical content of artistic creation. The rationality of knowledge structure can only be perfected in practice. To do a good job in aesthetic education, it is necessary to combine these through teaching practice according to the characteristics of courses and majors.

5 Aesthetic Education Under Curriculum Ideology and Political Education

Curriculum ideological and political education, that is, curriculum moral education, is to take moral education as the foundation and the curriculum as the carrier to explore the elements of moral education in the teaching of various courses and infiltrate moral education into classroom teaching, thereby promoting the all-round development of students [21]. Curriculum ideological and political education is a kind of thinking method and educational concept. It represents that each course should have the disciplinary thinking of moral education, and transforms the value paradigm and cultural genes contained in each course into a teaching carrier with socialist core values. Each course incorporates spiritual guidance at the level of ideals and beliefs. Whether the ideological and political work is effective or not, talent training is the only criterion that can be tested. The detailed assessment of talent training is based on two points, specialized and "red", the point of specialized refers to professional knowledge education, and the point of red refers to curriculum ideological and political education.

Classroom teaching is the first classroom, and the main channel of curriculum ideological and political education is classroom teaching. All courses, whether traditional ideological and political courses, major courses, or public courses, contain people's thinking about the laws of their thinking and the exploration of society and nature in their lives. The ideological and political theory course is an explicit ideological and political education because of its relatively fixed teaching requirements, teaching content, and teaching resources; The invisible education function under the scene has indispensable vivid education resources. Therefore, under the background of moral education, all teachers have inescapable responsibilities and obligations to take educating people with literature as a mission. Every teacher should pay more attention to the unity between words and deeds, teaching and educating people, constantly improving students' ideological and moral awareness and cultural literacy, guiding students to understand the world correctly, establishing correct values, and helping students grow up healthily.

Due to the misunderstanding of the refinement of the development of majors and disciplines, the separation of knowledge between the humanities and social sciences and the natural sciences has occurred in the development of educational science and technology. Students only focus on the advancement of their specific fields, while they don't know other areas and even despise other disciplines [22]. This results in the lack of mutual understanding between computational thinking and humanistic literacy among art students and engineering students. With the continuous progress of the times, cross-disciplinary research, inter-professional exchanges, and cooperation have become commonplace. Under the existing university curriculum system, public education courses make up for this deficiency, greatly increasing the depth of students' knowledge system and opening the breadth of their learning. Now, general education courses have been regarded as an important way to cultivate talents in university education.

Public education aims to develop the complete person. On the one hand, by helping students absorb knowledge in different fields, comprehend the internal connection between knowledge in various fields, realize the mutual integration between disciplines, and have a complete knowledge structure and solid basic knowledge, on the other hand, focus on improving students' internal humanistic and aesthetic literacy, establish correct values, and promote whole development of their physical and mental health. In terms of nature and content, general education is an important part of higher education, and it is an unprofessional education that should be carried out by colleges. It is a kind of education of basic skills, knowledge, and manner that are wide, no utility, and professional [23].

As a core general education course, public computer courses are similar to the ideological and political theory courses in higher institutions. There is a commonality in teaching objects: they are all taught to all college students, not only one specific skill, nor exclusive to some students or some majors. There is consistency in educational goals: they are all aimed at improving the quality of students and enabling them to develop in an all-around way. There are similarities in course content: take ZJCM as an example, the public computer courses major in teaching digital media content which covers humanities content, and the ideological and political theory courses also cover humanities content. Therefore, by constructing a reasonable curriculum system, public computer courses can play a role in curriculum ideological and political education.

In general education, aesthetic education has played an irreplaceable role. Aesthetics education is a very important part of the Chinese higher education system, and it is also the key to cultivating and improving students' comprehensive quality. It is crucial to perfect human nature. When an educated person feels the existence of beauty, it usually guides his cognition in other fields. From another perspective, many issues suddenly become clear. As a significant part of public education, it can not only help students improve their humanistic quality, innovative awareness, and positive spirit, but also promote the realization of the educational goal of cultivating complete people in public education. The aesthetic education promotion at an appropriate stage is of great significance to the healthy growth of students. In addition, a good aesthetic education is conducive to the improvement of innovative thinking ability, and cultivating educated people to comprehend, discover, create, and appreciate beauty will benefit them for life. As a public computing course in art colleges, it has its particularity to improve the ideological and political ability of the course through aesthetic education. Taking Zhejiang Conservatory of Music as an example, the video or audio editing contents in the curriculum, and even the teaching contents of office software, all have their own aesthetic needs. And this requirement is particularly prominent in video editing learning. Good aesthetics can enhance a person's spiritual temperament, and aesthetics is an indispensable essential quality on the road of art. It is the best and boosts motivation to develop and realize beauty. Therefore, it is particularly important to integrate public computer courses into aesthetic education, which can help them improve their pursuit of beauty, expand their thinking ability, and inspire creativity from the unique perspective of computers.

6   Aesthetic Education Construction

To combine subject knowledge with aesthetic education, public computer courses integrate aesthetics into teaching forms and teaching environments through appropriate teaching modes and methods.

6.1   Integrate into Teaching Content and Guide Students to Perceive Beauty

Marx said that if you want to enjoy beauty, you must first be an artistic person [24]. As a common social phenomenon, people's aesthetic ability is formed through acquired learning and cultivation. The ability to perceive the beauty of natural landscapes and human activities needs to be guided through aesthetic education. Taking the Premiere video editing and production course of our school as an example, in the teaching process, the characteristics of art students and aesthetic education in the course should be considered, so that the course content not only covers the necessary knowledge but also meets the need to cognize beauty. For example, to make original video work, we must start by looking for suitable materials, which requires students to select a video, photo, or sound materials that meet both the theme of the work and the aesthetic education. At the same time, during the editing process, the transition effect in the video, the pick of the background music, the setting of the color and size of the subtitles, and other details can make the students feel a kind of beauty. Through specific case teaching methods, students can have a positive perception of beauty, such as showing and explaining an excellent award-winning work, comparing the differences between two works, and arranging a creative video assignment.

6.2   Utilize Network Media Resources and Guide Students to Discover the Beauty

In the "Internet +" era, public computer courses cannot be taught purely by textbooks but must also make good use of various forms of network media resources. Due to the class in the computer room, appropriate network multimedia resources can be added during class time, which makes the classroom atmosphere more active and makes the course more attract students. When completing the exercises, students can actively search for online resources that match the theme and introduce network resources into the classroom. This method not only extends the teaching ideas but also allows students to learn how to use information technology and network resources, learn network laws and regulations, and gradually cultivate decent network etiquette and network literacy. Taking the study of Audition audio editing software lesson as an example, students can choose their favorite songs, accompaniments, or film and television works to complete the recording learning. This process enables students to be more active in finding beautiful audio materials. As shown in Fig. 1, in an Audition recording lesson, by utilizing internet media resources, students became more focused and active in class. A schoolgirl in the photo is actively using the QQ Music website to get her favorite audio material.

Fig. 1. A student is using the QQ Music website to find audio materials.

6.3 Enlighten Students' Creativity and Guide Students to Create Beauty

Cultivating the ability of art students to create beauty is another important function of aesthetic education. In order to change the world, people need to know the world. In the same way, in order to create beauty and a better life, people need to feel and appreciate beauty. Taking the Audition audio editing course as an example, although many students have sufficient computer literacy and practice ability, they still need to keep learning about the creation of beauty. For example, make sure the sound state is in good condition when recording microphone vocals, make sure the surrounding environment is quiet when recording ambient sound, and make sure the work has added appropriate scene sound effects. All these practices, will add points to the work, make the work more outstanding, and present a more beautiful state. In the teaching process, a relaxed and moderate teaching environment can help students elevate their love, creative inspiration, and creativity in creating novel works with a computer.

6.4 Use Mobile Network Tools and Broaden the Spread of Beauty

Face-to-Face teaching plays a very central role in aesthetic education, but in the time and space dimension of conveying beauty, the time for students to immerse in such a way of thinking of beauty is too short, and the space they get is a bit narrow. In the practice of this course, with the help of Internet tools such as WeChat group, QQ group, Superstar Learning Pass APP, and Rain Classroom WeChat applet, students can also communicate with their classmates and teachers promptly after class, which broadens the time of aesthetic education in subject teaching. Figure 2 shows the SPOC course model based on Rain Classroom. As seen from the figure, before starting the class, we should clarify the learning goals for the students and let them learn with the goal, and all available network resources will be used. During class, online courses will be launched through live broadcast, and online and offline teaching will be carried out simultaneously through SPOC. In the whole teaching process, aesthetic education runs through all links, such as online teaching, course interaction, online testing, and one-to-one teaching. The actual and offline teaching effect is enhanced through feedback from students; that is, students first think through collaborative learning and active learning then give teaching feedback. If 70% of students in a class understand the course contents, one-to-one teaching will begin, and special guidance will be given to students who do not yet understand. If less than 30% of students understand the course contents, we must teach it again. In other cases, communicate and discuss online based on key issues. Two public computer courses of the author were established in the second half of 2021 and the first half of 2022 by relying on the Rain Classroom network smart teaching platform and the SPOC blended teaching method. These two courses offer 4 classes and 5 classes respectively. Taking the public computer course this semester as an example, while the regular average traditional class is taking place, SPOC is used for synchronous online teaching, and the course resources are uploaded to the Internet. Most importantly, through the live streaming this way through the online platform of Rain Classroom, students who are not present because of isolation can participate in online classes. The second benefit is students, who need to review or have not attended the class in time can watch the video playback. The third benefit is students can do some test paper exercises after class, especially for those students who are absent from class. Through information communication and solving problems related to the course, students can enjoy the opportunity of aesthetic education at any time and experience the beauty of vision, perception, and creation.

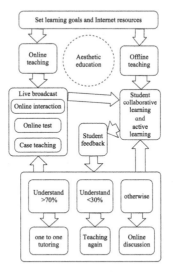

Fig. 2. SPOC course model based on Rain Classroom.

6.5 Do a Good Job in Self-improvement and Improving Aesthetics

As qualified university teachers, we must continue to learn and improve ourselves, so as to promote teaching and research. This is not only for the improvement of the teaching content and methods of the course itself but also for the improvement of the course aesthetic education. The specific practice is as follows:

- Participate in relevant teaching and academic research conferences at home and abroad to broaden academic horizons. For instance, attending the conference held by the Association of Fundamental Computing Education in Chinese Universities (AFCEC) can get a lot of help and enlightenment from it.
- Participate in teaching and training related to this course to improve business ability. For example, attend the Python training in Xi'ning held by the Teaching Guidance Committee of the University Computer Courses of the Ministry of Education of China (Education Advisory Committee).
- Go to observe the teaching methods of other teachers in the course, especially the open courses related to the curriculum ideological and political education, which can be from other majors or online. Like, observe curriculum ideological and political education demonstration courses of our school on-site, or watch live online courses of Tsinghua University through the Rain Classroom software platform. This semester, we observed an open class on traditional Chinese painting held by the Department of Humanities and Social Sciences of our university, as shown in Fig. 3.
- Join the computer virtual teaching and research section of domestic colleges and universities to obtain more teaching resources and get more pertinency aid. For example, both authors of this paper have joined "the Virtual Teaching and Research Office of the University Computer Public Courses Group" of the Beijing Institute of Technology. Facts have proved that self-improvement can be achieved by participating in online seminars, learning knowledge base documents from this teaching and research office, and communicating with other scholars, experts, and teachers in this virtual teaching and research office.

Fig. 3. Observe an open class of traditional Chinese painting in ZJCM.

7 Results

Table 1 shows the final exam scores obtained by students in the second half of 2021. Based on the emphasis on the cultivation of students' daily humanistic quality, the course grades are composed of the usual performance scores and the final paper scores, and the scores account for half of each. It can be seen from the table that there are a total of 4 teaching classes, and classes are divided into 1 to 4 classes in the order, of course, each week. The average score of each class is more than 80 points, and the overall average score is close. We can see that only Class 3 has relatively more scores. Compared with the other three classes, all performance classes, the Musicology major in the third class is a theoretical research major in the Conservatory of Music. So we can see that although the final grade has achieved a satisfactory performance, there are local differences due to different majors. In addition, it can be seen from Table 1 that the fourth class has the smallest number of people, but the lowest ranking. Therefore, it can be concluded that in a class with a gap of more than 40 students and less than 10 students, the effect of the course is not affected by the number of students. Overall, the exam results were satisfactory.

Table 1. Final grades of students after teaching reform.

Class name	Major	Video Shooting and Premiere Clip Course		
		The average score	number of students	ranking
Class 1	Pop music	81.00	56	2
Class 2	Orchestral Instruments	80.04	57	3
Class 3	Musicology and Chinese Traditional Instrument	85.65	51	1
Class 4	Vocal and Opera	80.00	48	4

8 Corresponding Achievement

Through this combination of online teaching mode and aesthetic education, computer public courses have achieved more satisfactory curriculum achievements than ever before. In particular, there has been significant progress in student competitions. In the years after the COVID-19 outbreak, just looking at the courses taken by the author, the achievements of student competition are in the following aspects. It is worth mentioning that in these competitions when we first participated in the competitions, students all won prizes. And the themes of these competitions are related to the curriculum of ideological and political education and aesthetic education, such as expressing the power of youth and showing the century-old struggle and glorious tradition of the Communist Party of China.

In January 2022, two student teams won the second prize, and one student team won the third prize in the final of the 3rd National University Computer Capability Challenge Digital Media Innovation Design Competition (Short Video Category). All the students who participated in this national competition won prizes in the preliminary competition and won the first, third, and excellence awards in the East China Division in December 2021.

The time for the preliminary round and the semi-finals is very tight. Under such a post-COVID-19 epidemic background, our university is full of students' curriculum arrangements. When submitting work in the preliminary round, some students faced the pressure of final exams. In this way, it is not easy for students to participate in the entire competition. However, our students have shown the style of doing everything right, trying to deliver the best work under the premise of tight time. It is worth mentioning that the two teams at the bottom of the ranking both won awards in the finals. These all prove the importance of aesthetic education combined with online education in public computer courses. The picture (Fig. 4) below shows the certificate of one of the student teams who won the second prize in the final of this national university computer capability challenge competition.

In addition, also this year, a student won the Excellence Award in the "Lynk & Co Cup" Tianmu News 3rd Yangtze River Delta College Student Short Video Competition. The student has always maintained a great interest in making videos. And in 2021, a student also won an award in this competition. In the 30 out of 1000 competition, she won the third prize. This student also likes to shoot and make videos. This also verifies that cultivating students' interest in a course can better stimulate their creativity and improve their academic performance.

In addition to student awards, the author also won the title of outstanding instructor in all competitions this year. Especially in the Yangtze River Delta competition, it is not the student who wins the competition; the corresponding instructor can get this honorary title.

Fig. 4. One of the student teams receives a certificate for the second prize.

9 Conclusion

The all-around development of students cannot be without aesthetic education. According to the actual course, combined with the blend teaching method of SPOC plus flipped classroom teaching mode, aiming at the characteristics of students in art colleges and universities, under the thinking of curriculum ideology and political education, this paper designs an aesthetic education construction that forms to the training goals of computer public course talents and integrates this aesthetic education construction into our curriculum system. Finally, the rationality of such an aesthetic education construction of public computer courses combined with online teaching is verified through the corresponding course achievements.

References

1. Wu, J., Hu, H.: Xi Jinping at the national conference on ideological and political work in colleges and universities emphasize putting the ideological and political work through the whole process of education and teaching to create a new higher education situation of development in our country (2016). http://www.xinhuanet.com/politics/2016-12/08/c_1120082577.htm
2. Sun, B., Dong, Y.: Construction and implementation of ideological and political curriculum system for computer science and technology major. In: 2021 16th International Conference on Computer Science & Education (ICCSE), pp. 452–455 (2021)
3. Li, G.J.: Five key links must be firmly grasped in course ideological and political construction. Chinese High. Educ. **Z3**, 28–29 (2017)
4. Mardonov, S.K., Kuttibekova, G.T.: The effectiveness of the innovative art-pedagogical system for the aesthetic education of younger students. Europ. J. Res. Reflection Educ. Sci. **8**(5), 116–121 (2020)
5. Ikhtiyorovna, N.G.: Aesthetic education and methods of aesthetic development in children with disabilities. Middle European Scientific Bulletin, vol. 1, no. 1, June 2020
6. Han, X.: The Importance of Aesthetic Ability in Arts Education: A Case Study of undergraduate students of universities in Chengdu City of Sichuan Province China, Preprints, June 2022
7. Yue, J.P.: Research and practice of blended teaching of aesthetic education course based on multimedia platform. Adv. Soc. Sci. Educ. Humanities Res. **616**, 148–156 (2021)
8. Peng, Y.L., Jemmott, J.B.: Feast for the eyes: effects of food perceptions and computer vision features on food photo popularity. Int. J. Commun.Commun. **12**, 313–336 (2018)
9. Li, N., Fan, Y.F., Jing, Z.: On the aesthetic education of students majoring in information technology. High. Educ. Res. **6**(5), 132–137 (2021)
10. Li, X., Qiu, K.: A research on symbiotic relationship between online and offline aesthetic education curriculum from the perspective of new engineering of 'ICT' in Universities. J. Aesthetic Educ. **12**(5), 8–15 (2021)
11. Rapanta, C., Botturi, L., Goodyear, P., Guàrdia, L., Koole, M.: Online university teaching during and after the covid-19 crisis: refocusing teacher presence and learning activity. Postdigital Sci. Educ. **2**, 923–945 (2020)
12. Gao, L.: Research on online learning behavior in China: stages, models and hotspots. In: 2021 16th International Conference on Computer Science & Education (ICCSE), pp. 92–97 (2021)
13. Basilaia, G., Kvavadze, D.: Transition to online education in schools during a SARS-CoV-2 Coronavirus (COVID-19) Pandemic in Georgia. Pedagogical Res. **5**(4), Article em0060 2020

14. Gamage, K.A.A., Wijesuriya, D.I., Ekanayake, S.Y., Rennie, A.E.W., Lambert, C.G., Gunawardhana, N.: Online delivery of teaching and laboratory practices: continuity of University Programmes during COVID-19 pandemic. Educ. Sci. **10**(10), 291 (2020)
15. Banerjee, G.: Blended environments: learning effectiveness and student satisfaction at a small college in transition. J. Asynchronous Learn. Networks **15**(1), 8–19 (2011)
16. Yang, L.: The teaching design of computer network's flipped classroom based on fanya SPOC teaching platform. Sino-US English Teach. **15**(2), 87–91 (2018)
17. An, S., Li, W., Hu, J., Ma, L., Xu, J.: Research on the reform of flipped classroom in computer science of university based on SPOC. In: 2017 12th International Conference on Computer Science and Education (ICCSE), pp. 621–625 (2017)
18. Li, R.C.: The construction of college aesthetic education information management system under the background of big data. In: Cyber Security Intelligence and Analytics. CSIA 2022. Lecture Notes on Data Engineering and Communications Technologies, vol. 125, pp. 557–563. Springer, Cham, March 2022
19. Parsons, M.: Aesthetic experience and the construction of meanings. J. Aesthetic Educ. **36**(2), 24–37 (2002)
20. Wang, J.: Discussion on construction of aesthetics course system at colleges and problems in its teaching. In: International Conference on Education, Management and Computing Technology (ICEMCT 2014), June 2014
21. Wu, Y.Q.: On the three focus points of colleges and universities to promote 'course ideology and politics.' School Party Build. Ideological Educ. **1**, 67–69 (2018)
22. He, H.J.: The internal logic of the development from 'ideological and political courses' to 'course ideological and political courses' Construction strategy. Res. Ideological Political Educ. **5**, 60–64 (2017)
23. Shi, S.C.: Discussion on the relationship between ideological and political theory courses and general education courses in colleges and universities. High. Educ. China **5**, 21–23 (2011)
24. Fan, Y.K.: A Brief Discussion on Aesthetic Virtue. https://news.gmw.cn/2021-11/15/content_35309628.htm, November 2021

Exploring the Public Space Model of Smart Recreation for Chinese Medicine Cultivation Based on Artificial Intelligence and Blockchain Technology

Qiyan Li[1], Jin Wang[2], and Yiping Zhang[3(✉)]

[1] School of College of Architecture and Urban Planning, Qingdao University of Technology, Qingdao, China
[2] Organization of Technical Quality Department, Qingdao Beiyang Design Group Co., Ltd., Qingdao, China
[3] School of College of Architecture and Urban Planning, Qingdao University of Technology, Qingdao, China
823365011@qq.com

Abstract. Traditional Chinese medicine (TCM) has made great contributions to the national health of China and has gone global, however, the culture of TCM in China has not been well inherited and the TCM industry has not prospered. When the rapid development of digital technology revolution, China is also rapidly entering an aging society, and the elderly play an irreplaceable role in the inheritance of Chinese medicine culture, yet in the digital era, the elderly have difficulties in crossing the "digital divide". Yet how to step into the digital life and how to use the digital era to pass on the Chinese medicine culture provides a feasible solution in this issue.

A pilot smart leisure park for the elderly was established in Qingdao, a city suitable for the elderly. The main approach is to select a public space for renovation, so that nearby elderly people can plant and pick herbal plants together near their homes, get remedies, study, work, make friends, buy and sell, and have fun. On the basis of the activities to protect and pass on their herbal culture. For Chinese herbal plants a combination of online and offline is used, using artificial intelligence and blockchain technology to manage the planting, picking, management and sales of medicinal plants in the offline park as an autonomous virtual agent in the form of a cell phone applet. This is also a gateway to digital education for the elderly.

Keywords: Chinese medicine heritage · digital divide · smart leisure parks · artificial intelligence · blockchain technology · Chinese medicine cultivation · digital education for the elderly

1 Introduction

"During the 14th Five-Year Plan period, China will enter a phase of extremely rapid ageing, with more than 300 million people aged 60 and above, accounting for more than 20% of the total population, and will enter a typical ageing society. It is estimated that

J. Gan et al. (Eds.): CSEI 2023, CCIS 1900, pp. 210–218, 2024.
https://doi.org/10.1007/978-981-99-9492-2_18

by 2050, China will have 380 million people aged 65 and above and will enter a super-ageing society. Therefore, China's 14th Five-Year Plan has included elderly care as a key element, proposing the goal of combining medical and recreational care [1].

Today, China's technological development has entered an era of high speed, with increasingly newer technologies changing the old way of life. On the one hand, the digital technology revolution such as artificial intelligence and 5G is on the rise, and on the other hand, the social process of population ageing is accelerating, and these two historical nodes are coinciding in the third decade of the 21st century in China. While the digital economy has brought convenience to people, it has also created a "digital divide" for the elderly that is difficult to cross. The digital economy has pushed economic development to a new stage and become an important force in creating new international competitive advantages. It is expected that the construction of information infrastructures such as 5G, artificial intelligence and blockchain, as well as the construction of major scientific and technological infrastructures and industrial technology innovation infrastructures, will accelerate, improving the quality and efficiency of the ageing business and providing strong information technology and technological creativity support for the transformation and upgrading of the ageing industry [2]. The initial aim of this study is to provide a technology platform that aims to help older people break the digital divide using logical and easyto-operate applets for the benefit of older people and society as a whole, and to promote social development. Through the platform's applets, knowledge of Chinese herbal medicine is promoted and cultural heritage of Chinese medicine.It also combines online and offline, allowing older people to sell the herbs they grow in their leisure time on the platform, cultivating interest while also providing opportunities for retired seniors to be employed again.

2 Background

The only survivor of the four major ancient traditional medicines lies in the fact that TCM is an open and evolving system; therefore, inheritance and innovation are the foundation of TCM's existence [3]. However, at present, when talking about traditional culture of TCM, people think more about how to seek cures from ancient prescriptions, forgetting that traditional culture of TCM can better treat traditional diseases and better cope with new diseases only through continuous innovation with the development of the times. Therefore, it is necessary to establish an incentive mechanism for the innovation of traditional culture of Chinese medicine to promote the modernization of theories, scientific research, standardization of technology, and objectivity of therapeutic effects of Chinese medicine, so that it can be easily understood and accepted by the modern nation and the people of the world, so that Chinese medicine can be innovated in its inheritance and passed on in its innovation, and eventually become prosperous.

In 2016, the construction of recreational landscapes was rapidly combined with Chinese medicine, forestry, tourism, and agriculture industries to form a new development model [4].

In the context of rapid development of science and technology, a new era of information and technology has been ushered in, and intelligent technology has been progressing and innovating, and the traditional planting methods in the field of Chinese agriculture are undergoing dramatic changes. The traditional production mode of plastic greenhouses can no longer meet the development needs of modern society. Under the digital life, the intelligent greenhouse greenhouse that can effectively improve the survival rate of plants has been gradually known. In addition the new intelligent greenhouse greenhouse planting mode can help people to grasp the growth of herbs in real time and detect the environment, in addition to the professional auxiliary system to achieve watering, fertilization, pesticide spraying and other related processes [5].

3 Research Content

3.1 Create a Multi-level Public Planting Space Landscape

Combine artificial intelligence with urban public space landscapes and use digital landscapes to break the digital divide for the elderly. The needs of older people are universal and have certain similarities. Teaching older people to learn to use small programs through practice allows them to enjoy their digital lives. Combining artificial intelligence and blockchain technology, the "green in four seasons" application is an autonomous virtual agent that manages the planting, harvesting and management of medicinal plants in offline parks and their sale online. On this basis, it provides opportunities for the elderly to re-employ, relieving the excessive burden of old age and the pressure of pension expenditure brought about by ageing, achieving a sense of worthiness in old age and activating the secondary demographic dividend.

3.2 New Leisure Park Model

During the design process of the pilot park, emphasis should be placed on the physiological and psychological characteristics of the elderly. In the construction of traditional parks, it is difficult to fully satisfy this special group of elderly people, and at a time of rapid economic and technological development, technological concepts such as artificial intelligence and blockchain are introduced and a dual online and offline approach is adopted to design a special intelligent recreational and elderly park. The elderly are given a specific feeling in a specific area. The various facilities in the park need to be improved according to the various physical and psychological activities of the elderly. And more activity areas need to be provided for the elderly. Therefore, in the design stage, intelligent physical areas, entertainment and play areas, intelligent planting areas, platform play areas, rest and recreation areas, leisure and recreation areas, planting and rest areas, intelligent care areas and green picking areas are set up. The park includes elements of Chinese medicine and technology, using AI, VR, AR and other technologies to introduce different artificial intelligence devices to increase the opportunities for the elderly to learn about technological activities and to understand and use them in the park, so that they can use the smart greenhouse to grow Chinese medicine and selfregulate, and provide a platform to use blockchain to trade Chinese medicine in the park.

3.3   Establish an Online Chinese Medicine Exchange Platform

Online aspects: The project provides an online platform to increase communication between the elderly and others, forming an organic system. The applet provides a technical exchange platform for the elderly, in which they can view the details of all the plants in the pilot park, a variety of herbal formulas for treating common diseases, the purchase of virtual coins needed for the park in the blockchain system and the purchase of seeds for medicinal plants. See Fig. 1

It provides a technical exchange platform for the elderly to learn and use the many functions of the applet in a way that interests them in the process of understanding, planting and selling Chinese medicine. Through blockchain technology, it realises the online independent virtual agent and transaction management mode to complete the sale of Chinese medicine plants, and also shows their Chinese medicine planting area to other elderly people anytime and anywhere with the help of the applet. The "green in four seasons" application allows the elderly to learn to use artificial intelligence tools and enjoy digital life.

| Plant profile page for the applet | Applet herbal formulas page | Virtual coin purchase page | Chinese herbal seeds purchase page |

Fig. 1. Functional interface of the applet (Image credit: Self drawn by the author)

3.4   Establishment of Offline Herbal Cultivation System

Offline aspects: planting ponds, intelligent greenhouses, structures and landscape vignettes of different scales and shapes are designed according to different functions. See Fig. 2.

The intelligent greenhouse is used to manage and regulate the growth environment of medicinal plants with different attributes. Intelligent displays are set up in the site to introduce the plants to science, provide a selection of Chinese herbal formulas for common diseases and learn about the process of concocting various Chinese medicines. Rational allocation of plants to improve the quality and beautify the park's environment. Through green plants, the air is improved, the temperature is regulated, noise is reduced and the functions of environmental beautification are enhanced, allowing the elderly to nurture their health and regulate their lives in the park environment. A pleasant public space environment is constructed alongside the planting of Chinese herbs to achieve a recreational effect. Enjoy the recreational space while planting, maintaining and picking herbal plants [6].

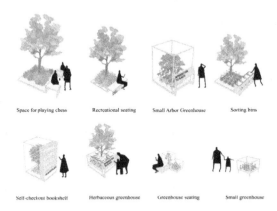

Fig. 2. Rendering of the offline planting pool (photo credit: author's own drawing)

3.5 Transaction Management Model

The "green in four seasons" applet uses the blockchain model to manage all kinds of artificial intelligence technology, making the whole system more secure and efficient, and more convenient for users. The whole project does not require human participation in the unified management, the system has the characteristics of decentralization, traceability and non-tamperability, so that each user can experience a better self-management mechanism in the venue.

4 Technology Applications

4.1 Application of Artificial Intelligence

Artificial intelligence technology is booming and its application in various industries is accelerating in popularity, and the technology is already available to support the functional requirements of this project. With the development of the Chinese herbal medicine industry in China, intelligent greenhouses for growing Chinese herbs have become a new and highly promising field. The intelligent and autonomous virtual agent management of Chinese herbal medicine greenhouses is being strengthened to improve the management of Chinese herbal medicine greenhouses. The intelligent greenhouse management mainly realises the statistical analysis of data information of each greenhouse.

4.2 Intelligent Greenhouse Management System

Smart greenhouses are modern production models that combine sensor technology, communication technology and control technology. The smart greenhouse system simulates the most suitable natural environment for plant growth and enables continuous crop production without external influences. In the cultivation of traditional Chinese medicine, it is very important to master the required climatic conditions. The effects of light, temperature, water and air on medicinal plants are integrated, with a combination and limiting relationship between various factors [7]. The proper use of smart greenhouses can promote the growth and development of medicinal plants and improve the yield and quality of Chinese medicine.

A number of smart greenhouses have been set up in the park's pilot areas, mainly planted in the form of trees, shrubs and herbs, and the medicinal plants are mainly planted in the form of herbs. The intelligent greenhouse monitoring system mainly displays the temperature and humidity, carbon dioxide concentration and light intensity data in the greenhouse in a small program. When the environmental information in the greenhouse exceeds a specific value, it will be fed back to the small program for feedback adjustment to make the greenhouse environment suitable for the growth of Chinese medicine. The system is divided into a greenhouse information collection end, a feedback adjustment end and a remote receiving information end [8]. The intelligent greenhouse is used to intelligently regulate the site and monitor and manage the growth environment and data of Chinese herbs, etc. [9]. See Fig. 3.

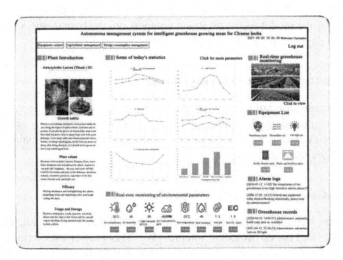

Fig. 3. Intelligent multi-device visual management system (image credit: author's own drawing)

4.3 Blockchain Technology

Blockchain technology can essentially be seen as a shared database that stores data or information and keeps it open and transparent, enabling an online autonomous virtual agent and transaction management model through blockchain technology. It can ensure the openness and transparency of information on Chinese medicine cultivation in the whole park, achieve traceability of information on Chinese medicine cultivation, and the combination with artificial intelligence can make the whole system more secure and efficient. The combination of artificial intelligence and blockchain technology is expressed in the form of the "green in four seasons" applet and in different forms of expression in the project design.

5   Technical Approach

5.1   Technical Approach to the Project Design

Research method: The design site (Qingdao Lao She Park) was visited through literature, and a questionnaire survey was conducted to find out the specific needs of the elderly and other people around the site for the use of urban public space. Through a rich sample size, the potential social value that the model can bring is analysed.

Evidence-based feedback design process: The elderly residents around the design site were invited as volunteers to conduct closed tests and stress tests on the applet, etc. The volunteers collected feedback after using the applet to eliminate problems in the applet and continue to improve it.

Assessing the value of the model from a sociological perspective: As a special disadvantaged group existing in society, the elderly should be given attention and concern by society. Through the status quo of the social benefits that will be generated under the operation of the model for an all round comparison, the humanistic value function is reflected on the basis of scientific and theoretical research.

5.2   Program Development Technology Route

Develop the small program through program design. The specific process is: concept formation → market research, competition analysis → business needs → product design → demand review, application development → preliminary testing → online operation → user feedback, data analysis.

5.3   Human-Computer Interaction Technology

The interaction technology in the era of artificial intelligence is essentially changing the way people and the environment interact [10]. This project uses human-computer interaction technology to realise the needs of the elderly to learn, make friends and display.

The project will place a special interactive device in the selected public space, which will convert some of the users' comments about Chinese medicine knowledge on the "Four Seasons are Green" application into voice message in advance [11]. When more than two users approach, the latest voice messages are randomly played, and users can discuss these voice messages with each other. In addition, users can also leave messages with the device, which will be translated into text in real time to appear in the small program comments, using the elderly's favorite "phonetic entry method" to promote their learning and making friends.

At the same time, the "Four Seasons are Green" application introduces intelligent recognition and scanning modelling technology, which enables users to transform their own Chinese medicine plantation in the project's public space into an online virtual Chinese medicine plantation, and activate VR and AR planting and intelligent management scenarios [10], inviting their neighbors and friends to plant and manage the online virtual Chinese medicine plantation together. This mechanism allows the elderly to create their own personalised online Chinese medicine plantation and allowing some elderly people with limited mobility to enjoy the pleasure of growing Chinese medicine in their friends' online virtual plantation.

6 Limitations

Wechat mini program is developed on the basis of wechat. It has a very wide audience and has become one of the most commonly used mobile phone programs for the elderly due to its convenience and ease of use. Therefore, we choose wechat as the technology platform of "Four Seasons are Green". With the passage of time, wechat will be updated on the existing basis, and the "Four Seasons are Green" mini program will also be updated. We will continue to optimize the application based on user feedback and market demand to achieve a better user experience.

In addition, all of our ideas for the "Four Seasons are Green" project were a "thought experiment". Practicability has not yet been proven. In the future, we will consider the following aspects, such as whether the herbal medicines grown in the smart greenhouse in the pilot park are qualified and usable, and how to effectively promote the technology platform to the elderly community and make them accept it.

7 Conclusion

In summary, in the context of today's digital society developing at a rapid pace, in order to keep the elderly from falling out of step with the times, development is achieved based on artificial intelligence technology and blockchain technology, making full use of artificial intelligence and blockchain technology to provide security for the elderly and seek a better way for them to integrate. Based on Chinese medicine cultivation, it enables the elderly to grow herbs close to their homes, achieving multiple pleasures while alleviating the cost of economic development and making the allocation of resources the optimal solution. It allows the elderly community to easily master artificial intelligence tools while living digitally on the basis of this to better pass on the culture of Chinese medicine.

References

1. Lianghua, D.: Planning and Design of Residential Facilities for the Elderly in Urban Communities. China Construction Industry Press, Beijing (2016)

2. Li, Z.: The situation of actively coping with population aging and national strategic measures in the 14th Five-Year Plan period. Scientific Research on Aging (2020)
3. Xi, L.: Annotating Names and Supplementing Evidence, p. 276. Zhonghua Book Company, Beijing (2008)
4. Lin, S., Yang, Y.: The emergence and development of recreational garden landscape. Beauty and the Times, (7), 79–81 (2020)
5. Wang, X.: Exploration on the application of intelligent greenhouse vegetable planting technology based on Internet of Things technology. Agric. Eng. Technol. 41(36), 55–56 (2021)
6. Yu, F.Y., Li, J., Xing, J.: The creation of indoor and outdoor spatial environment in elderly buildings. Huazhong Architecture (08), 159–163 (2011)
7. Sikai, J.: Design and implementation of visualization management system for planting Chinese herbs in intelligent greenhouse. Southwest University (2020)
8. Rui-Bin, C.: Application of big data visualization technology in intelligent industry. Electron. Technol. Softw. Eng. 01, 133 (2019)
9. Liu, Z., Fan, L., Zhai, T.: Design and implementation of an STM32-based agricultural mini-weather station. J. Nanyang Inst. Technol. 12(06), 69–73 (2020)
10. Jing, C., Tingying, H., Zheng, C.: Landscape Architecture 6(02), 38–40 (2018)
11. Wei, K.: The future of "dynamic" landscape design supported by human-computer interaction technology. Landscape Archit. 02, 17 (2016)

Application of VR and AR Technology in Fish Simulation Teaching

Ran Li⦿, Yuchen Jiang⦿, Jing Tang⦿, Peng Yuan⦿, and Nan He$^{(\boxtimes)}$ ⦿

Dalian Ocean University DLOU, Dalian 10158, China
henan@dlou.edu.cn

Abstract. In view of the shortage of fish teaching experimental objects, the shortage of experimental places, and the shortage of funds, a fish simulation teaching platform is constructed. With the help of AR, VR and AI technology, the multimodal learning mode of VR end, PC end and mobile end is realized, and the repeated virtual operation is realized through VR technology, which comprehensively and clearly shows the anatomical structure of fish, the adjacent internal organs and the spatial position relationship of fish Through AR technology, the knowledge content is displayed on the mobile end, so that learning is not limited by time and space, and the learning content is vivid. The system sets up different teaching links such as simulation demonstration, repeated training, examination evaluation, etc., and integrates the key points and difficulties of knowledge into virtual teaching. The practical application results show that the system can solve the problem of lack of experimental objects, give students easy and fast learning experience, and stimulate students' interest in learning. It can be used for reference to explore the application of AR / VR technology in fish simulation teaching.

Keywords: Virtual reality · augmented reality · Fish simulation · teaching system · dynamic loading technology · VR interactive design

1 Introduction

Ichthyology, hydrobiology, science of fish culture and other courses are important courses in aquaculture and aquatic genetics breeding. However, with the restriction of various problems, such as lack of fish teaching experimental objects, shortage of experimental places, few practical opportunities for students and tight funding, many colleges and universities use maps and fish specimens for teaching, which greatly lowers the quality and effect of practical teaching.

In the process of fish anatomy teaching, the use of live fish is required, and some rare live fish resources are limited, so dissection is difficult to operate repeatedly; when using specimens for teaching, the teaching method lacks realistic three-dimensional sense and interactivity, which reduces the accuracy of students' understanding of knowledge, and it is difficult to stimulate students' interest in learning. In addition, fish specimens are prone to deformation and discoloration after being stored in formaldehyde dilution solution, which is difficult to preserve for a long time, and is easily damaged during use. at the

J. Gan et al. (Eds.): CSEI 2023, CCIS 1900, pp. 219–230, 2024.
https://doi.org/10.1007/978-981-99-9492-2_19

same time, the experiment is limited by the storage location of the specimens and the number of visits [1].

With the continuous development and deepening of information technology, educational informatization has received more and more attention from the state, and informatization education has been developing rapidly as a new education form. since 2013, the ministry of education has launched the construction of the national virtual simulation experimental teaching center nationwide, which has greatly promoted the improvement and sustainable development of the connotation construction of experimental teaching. virtual experiment has the characteristics of low cost, high efficiency, strong scalability, safe operation, high openness and resource sharing.

Virtual simulation experiment teaching is conducive to cultivating students' self-training and innovative consciousness, achieving the teaching effect of "virtual complement, virtually and reality combination, deep interaction and rational integration", and providing a tool with great potential for experimental teaching. therefore, it has become an important development direction of laboratory construction [2].

In this study, VR and AR technologies are applied to fish simulation teaching, to construct virtual fish models and fish organ dissection models, and to integrate relevant teaching points and difficulties into virtual teaching practice. This platform can be operated on a computer, and also on a mobile phone. it enriches the teaching content and means, and surpasses the time and space limitations of experimental teaching. By observing the anatomical structure of fish in an all-round way and repeating virtual operations, we can gain more practice opportunities and experience close to reality, master fish knowledge deeply, and then achieve the teaching effect that cannot be achieved in traditional teaching, and will be based on VR/AR technology are used in practical teaching.

2   Structural Design of Fish Simulation Teaching Platform

The platform is mainly composed of modules such as virtual experiment, popular science garden, teaching resources and database management. As shown in Fig. 1.

We use Photoshop and Premier two image processing software to process the materials required by the page, use HbuilderX to write front-end scripts, and flexibly process html, css, javascript and other languages; use Chrome for page display and debugging; use IntelliJ IDEA to write the back-end Script; use the Spring Boot framework to write interfaces to implement various functions of the website; use MySQL and Navicat visual development tools to design databases and manage website resources; use the FinalShell tool to remotely connect to the server to maintain and update the website in real time.

The system sets up different teaching links, including demonstration learning, VR/AR virtual training, and test evaluation. Students can achieve the teaching effects that cannot be achieved in real teaching through repeated virtual training [3, 4].

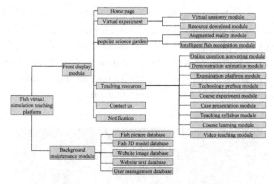

Fig. 1. Structure chart of system.

3 Key Technologies

3.1 Resource Collection

The main data required for modeling includes the appearance and texture map of the fish and the anatomy of its internal organs. When dissecting the live fish in the lab, images of fish's appearance and organs taken from various angles were collected to provide sufficient picture information for subsequent modeling. The process of specimens collection is shown in Fig. 2.

Fig. 2. Specimens collection pross.

3.2 Modeling

First, use Photoshop to draw the side view and top view of the fish, and then draw the shape and internal organs distribution map of the fish according to the photos and skeleton maps of the fish provided by the laboratory. Next, use the side view and top view as a reference to make a white model in blender, and then export the finished white model to obj format and import it into Unfold3D. To conveniently draw maps, in the process of splitting uv, the pictures need to be kept symmetrical and the reserved area of important parts should be as large as possible.

The model of this software uses CYLINDRICAL UNWRAP for multi-faceted design, and this model is suitable for the characteristics of fish's body shape. When drawing model maps, use photos of fish taken in the laboratory to brush onto the model. We can use the painting barrels tool to brush the model blue. Then we can easily observe the missing parts. As shown in Fig. 3, the blue part in the figure is the missing part. Finally, import the model into Unity for optimization.

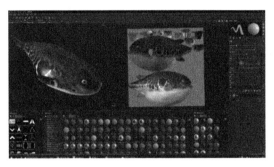

Fig. 3. Model maps.

3.3   Interaction Design

Since it is difficult to implement the operation of clicking on UI in VR environment, the ray method is provided in SteamVR. However, the maintenance of accuracy and control method of the ray is also complicated to implement in the code. This system uses the touch of 3D objects to accomplish interaction. When the handle touches the 3D button, the corresponding function will be realized. The specific method is: Make a button listener to write the monitoring method, and then implement the corresponding function according to the different return value of the listener.

3.4   Dynamic Loading Technology

The development of the simulation platform is a continuous work, and new fish resources will be added in the future. To lighten the workload of future system updates, dynamic loading technology is used. Based on the imported Json file and the current design in the UI part, copying the text and pictures that may be expanded in the future can lighten the workload of programming. Dynamic loading uses the SDK provided by Json for Unity, analyzing added items in singleton pattern, assigning values to various parameters of the base class. The core code is as follows:

```
public class InventoryManager : MonoBehaviour {
   private static InventoryManager _Instance;
   public static InventoryManager Instance
   {get{if (_Instance == null)
   {_Instance
=GameObject.Find("InventoryManager").GetComponent<InventoryManager>();}
   return _Instance; }}
   private void Awake()
   {ParseItemJSON();
   InstantiateFish();}
   private List<Fish> itemList = new List<Fish>();
   private void ParseItemJSON()
   {TextAsset ta = Resources.Load<TextAsset>("Json/fish");
      JSONObject j = new JSONObject(ta.text);
      foreach (JSONObject temp in j.list)
      {int id = (int)temp["id"].n;
         string name = temp["name"].str;
         string jianJie = temp["jianJie"].str;
         string shiPinJianJie = temp["ShiPinJianJie"].str;
         Fish fish = null;
         fish = new Fish(id, name, jianJie, shiPinJianJie);
         itemList.Add(fish); }}
```

3.5   Object Grasping

When designing object grasping, the phenomenon of model piercing often occurs, as shown in Fig. 4. The solution of this system is: Add two collider components and a rigid body component to the grasped object. Rigid body components can make the objects subject to the gravity of engine. One of the two collider components selects the IsTrigger as a listener, and executes the grasping method when the handle hits the listener. The other one is set to prevent the phenomenon of model piercing. When the buttons on both sides of the handle are pressed, the system will detect whether it touches the grasped object and give a returned value. When the returned value is true, the position coordinates of the grasped object will synchronize with the handle, providing an immersive feeling of grasping objects for experimenter, as shown in Fig. 5.

Fig. 4. The phenomenon of model piercing.

Fig. 5. The phenomenon of model no piercing

3.6 System Repair

The development of AR programs requires a lot of work. During the development process, due to hard disk drive damage or other reasons that could occur when Unity engine is going to be started, an error message will pop up as shown in Fig. 6, causing the engine fail to work. If it cannot be effectively recovered, it will cause fatal losses to the development work.

Fig. 6. Error window

This study combined with practice, summed up an effective solution. First, right-click the hard disk of the project, and click the property > tool > check to see whether the file system in the hard disk drive is damaged. Then see the location of the damaged file if the file system is damaged, make sure it is not in the three folders of Assets, Packages and ProjectSettings of the project. Finally, copy these three folders to a new folder, open UnityHub, click add, and select a new folder. Unity will supplement the system file for this new folder, so that the project can be opened with this new folder.

If the file in the Assets folder is damaged, try deleting the file, which causes the missing of the file in Unity's Hierarchy, and the file needs to be recreated in the engine [5].

3.7 Application of AR Technology

Vuforia software is used in the development of AR. In order to make the program lightweight, the 3D model database is deployed to the cloud, and the model is dynamically downloaded and generated from the cloud. After the model is dynamically loaded, the problem of poor interaction between the model and ARcamera often occurs. The solution of this study is: Create a custom function in the DefaultTrackableEventHandler script in the imagetarget under ARcamera and add the following statement:

```
GameObject loadedObject = obj.Result;
whale1 = Instantiate(loadedObject, mTrackableBehaviour.gameObject.transform.position +
            new Vector3(0, 0.15f, 0), Quaternion.identity);
whale1.transform.localScale = new Vector3(0.2f, 0.2f, 0.2f);
whale1.transform.Rotate(-90, 0, 0);
whale1.transform.SetParent(mTrackableBehaviour.gameObject.transform);
whale1.AddComponent<enlarge>();
whale1.AddComponent<playerrotato>();
```

The above problem is well solved by setting the dynamically generated transform as a subclass object of imagetarget.

Vuforia sets the recognition level for the uploaded images labels. Some fish images found by the project cannot meet the system recognition standards. It can be corrected by adding identification points or sharpening image details with Photoshop [6].

3.8 Development of WeChat Applet

We use the WeChat developer tool to develop WeChat applet, use the Mysql database to store the required pictures, and deploy the database in the cloud. Python and Flask are used to form a small web application framework. In order to ensure that the web application can continue to provide service support for the open port even when the cloud DOM window is closed, the Gunicorn server is added, so that the web framework can run persistently on the cloud server.

The SSL certificate is used to ensure the security of data interaction, and Nginx proxy DNS resolves the server domain name to realize the access and interaction of the front-end and back-end data of the WeChat applet. At the same time, we have optimized the code, optimized the random function and the character encoding format of the data packet, so that the applet is lightweight and has a good user experience.

After fully considering the compatibility of the applet on Android/IOS devices of different sizes, in order to ensure that the page is kept proportionally scaled on mobile phones or other mobile devices of different sizes, we set the wxss style and use vw, rpx unit to achieve the same size of physical logic on each model. In element positioning, we use absolute positioning to determine the element position to ensure that the display page is adaptive [7–9]. The core code is as follows:

```
back-container{
  position: absolute;
  top: 52%;
  left: 50%;
  transform: translate(-50%,-50%);
  width: 80%;
  height: 75%;
back-container{
  position: absolute;
  top: 52%;
  left: 50%;
  transform: translate(-50%,-50%);
  width: 80%;
  height: 75%;
  border-radius: 20px;
  padding: 50rpx;
  box-sizing: border-box;
  background-color:#fff;
  color: #DAE1DA;
}
.back-container .choice button{
  display: block;
  height: 90rpx!important;
  width: 100%!important;
  border-radius: 10px;
  font-size: 32rpx;
  letter-spacing:2rpx;
  text-align: left;
  padding-left: 20rpx;
  margin-bottom: 20rpx;
  background: rgb(235, 243, 235);
  color:#312354;
  background-color: #F3F3F3;
}
```

4 System Implementation

The fish simulation teaching platform takes the Fish dismantling as the main line, using AR, VR, AI and some other technologies to implement the multi-modal learning mode. On the platform, knowledge is explained and demonstrated through 3D models, text, audio, video, etc., to comprehensively and clearly display the anatomical structure of fish. Through the display of each anatomical structure, students can fully understand and master the adjacency and spatial relationship between anatomical structures. The teaching mode is rich in interaction, suitable for students' physical and psychological characteristics, and effectively improves the teaching effect and students' learning enthusiasm.

4.1 Virtual Experiment

This module is consisted of the fish virtual anatomy module and resources loading module. In the fish virtual anatomy module, each corresponding knowledge point is equipped with a text introduction, images and 3D models. By scanning the images, the 3D model of the fish anatomy structure can be displayed on the mobile terminal and the angle of the model can be adjusted to meet the needs of 360° repeated viewing, which helps students to understand the anatomical structure of fish, the adjacency of fish's internal organs and the spatial relationship.

Through resources loading, repeated viewing is available for students to grasp the knowledge by using VR helmet and handle on PC, as shown in Fig. 7.

Fig. 7. VR learning scene.

4.2 Popular Science Garden

This module includes an AR learning module and an intelligent fish recognition module. In the AR learning module, the 3D models of the fish can be displayed on the mobile terminal by scanning images. Students can control the angle of the models by touching the screen to achieve 360° repeated viewing, at the same time, use the corresponding text introduction to understand the biological characteristics of different fish such as names, species and habits, as shown in Fig. 8. AR learning has rich interactivity and interestingness, which is more suitable for students 'physiological and psychological characteristics. Text combined with dynamic stereo images enables students to quickly grasp new knowledge and improve learning enthusiasm.

Fig. 8. AR learning scene.

The intelligent fish recognition module is mainly based on the supporting WeChat applet. It uses AI recognition technology to intelligently recognize the photos uploaded by the user, and gives information such as the name, species and habits of the fish. Students can also play the mini game of answering and passing on the applet, which adds pleasure to the teaching of fish knowledge as shown in Fig. 9.

4.3 Teaching Resources

The teaching resource module includes course study, syllabus, video teaching, video animation, knowledge quiz, course experiment, case presentation, technology frontier, online Q&A, course evaluation, etc. Through these modules, the knowledge covered by the platform is sorted out as a whole to meet students' diverse needs in the learning process, and various forms are taken to achieve and improve the quality of teaching. Among them, the knowledge test module can intelligently organize papers according to the knowledge points, difficulty, teaching requirements, scores and other indicators of the topic, and conduct comprehensive and multi-dimensional statistical analysis according to the test situation, provide error information feedback, and let students improve the learning effect independently in the process of knowing and correcting their mistakes. It is worth mentioning that students' evaluation data will also be reported to teachers, so

Fig. 9. AR learning scene.

as to help teachers understand students' mastery in real time, achieve precise guidance, and connect the process of pre-class, while-class, and post-class training evaluation with each other [10]. As shown in Fig. 10.

Fig. 10. Teaching resource module.

5   Promotion and Service of Simulation Platform

The system is first aimed at the promotion of teaching in colleges and universities, focusing on the experimental teaching of professional courses such as Ichthyology, hydrobiology and science of fish culture, and then extended to the experimental teaching of related courses in other professional directions. Through the virtual experiment, it stimulates students' interest in experiment, cultivates students' self-learning ability and practical ability. In addition, for social promotion and continuous service, it is open to domestic enterprises, social school-running institutions and individuals through training, conferences, forums and other forms. Effective resource sharing platform with universities, enterprises and research institutions at home and abroad will be established to open to society and provide online services continuously.

6 Conclusion

This paper introduces the key technology and application of fish simulation teaching platform based on VR/AR technology. VR/AR technology is introduced into virtual practice teaching, and a practical training platform integrating interactive learning, training and evaluation is built, which solved the problems of lack of experimental subjects, shortage of experimental sites and few practical opportunities for students. The teaching effect is improved, and the resource sharing is realized. The high-quality resources based on VR/AR technology are truly used in education and training to expand the application scope of virtual simulation system and the beneficiaries.

References

1. Fan, L., Ma, J., Zhang, K., et al.: Application and development of AR/VR technology in human anatomy teaching and operation training. Sci. Technol. Rev. **38**(22), 31–32 (2020)
2. Liu, M., Han, Z., Xiugang, X.: Construction and application of virtual simulation experimental teaching system in marine earth sciences. Res. Exploration Lab. **39**(01), 245–247 (2020)
3. Liu, T., Zeng, Z.: Design and implementation of website under MVC architecture. Comput. Technol. Dev. **30**(02), 188–191 (2020)
4. Wang, R., Fangchen, X.: Design and implementation of web platform for open and shared lab. Ind. Control Comput. **32**(07), 120–122 (2019)
5. Unity Technologies. Unity case study manual [M]. Beijing: China Railway Publishing House, 2015-04:80-81
6. Wang, M.: Unity game Cloud quick start guide: Cloud resource distribution [EB/OL]. 2020-7-22 [2020.1.18]. https://unity.cn/projects/mstudio_ccd
7. Tencent. Weixin public doc[EB/OL].2012-01-01[2020-12-22]. https://developers.weixin.qq.com/miniprogram/dev/framework/
8. Olsson, M.: CSS3 Quick Syntax Reference, 2nd edn. Finland: Hammarland, 2019:129–130
9. Jackson, W.: JSON Quick Syntax Reference. USA: Lompoc, California, pp. 51–58 (2016)
10. Liu, Z.: JavaScript Development Technology, pp. 75–88. Tsinghua University Press, Beijing (2009)

Educational Informatization and Big Data for Education

Design and Research of STEAM Education Project on Online Learning Space

Jinxian Cai(✉) 🄳, Jinming Jiang, and Lunxi Xie

Guangdong Construction Polytechnic, Guangzhou, China
1258095883@qq.com

Abstract. This study uses literature research to sort out the research status of STEAM education and online learning space, and summarizes and forms the theoretical basis, design basis, core elements and other contents of STEAM education project design based on online learning space. The quasi-experimental study method was adopted to carry out the experimental design of equal groups before and after testing, and to compare and analyze the implementation effects of STEAM education project cases in different environments. In the learning effect analysis stage, test questions and questionnaires are used to analyze the learning effect of STEAM education project. The results show that STEAM education project based on online learning space can enhance students' knowledge construction level, promote the cultivation of problem solving ability, improve and correct learning attitude. This proves that the STEAM educational project design model based on online learning space has theoretical and practical value.

Keywords: STEAM education · online learning space · project design · problem solving ability

1 Research Background

At present, the practical paths of STEAM education are mainly summarized as problem-solve-based STEAM education, engineering-design-based STEAM education and project-based STEAM education. These three practical paths mostly rely on traditional classroom or realistic application environment, in which resources are relatively scarce, which is difficult to meet the needs of realistic teaching. Compared with traditional learning environment, online learning space breaks through the boundaries of time and space. This study will be guided by the relevant theories and take the corresponding projects as the carrier to build a STEAM education project design model based on online learning space, so as to optimize the project design process and develop STEAM education project cases.

2 The Concept and Application of Online Learning Space

2.1 Concept of Online Learning Space

The study on online learning space was first started in 2003. Brown, an American scholar, believed that learning space should include real space and virtual space, including all places where learning occurs, emphasizing the combination of virtual and real in learning

J. Gan et al. (Eds.): CSEI 2023, CCIS 1900, pp. 233–245, 2024.
https://doi.org/10.1007/978-981-99-9492-2_20

space (Brown & Lippincott, 2003). In 2010, when Scott and Benlamri analyzed learning space to build ubiquitous learning system, they believed that learning space should provide more opportunities for formal learning and informal learning, and realize social and intellectual interaction through seamless integration and integration of technologies and services (Scott & Benlamri, 2010). With the continuous rise of the research heat of online learning space, many scholars have put forward different definitions of online learning space, but there is still a lack of unified understanding. However, in April 2018, the Ministry of Education of China issued guidelines on the Construction and Application of Online Learning Spaces, defining online learning Spaces as real-name online learning places that support sharing, interaction and innovation and are recognized by education authorities or schools integrating resources, services and data (Circular of the Ministry of Education, 2018).

2.2 Application Research of Online Learning Space

At present, the application research of online learning space mainly includes three aspects: strategy research, teaching mode and environment design. strategy research refers to various path exploration, application strategy, guidance strategy, guarantee path and so on about online learning space. Based on distributed cognitive theory, Zhang Lixin and Qin Dan proposed effective application strategies of online learning space for building effective social interaction platforms, creating effective paths for knowledge creation and providing learners with immersive learning support systems (Zhang and Qin, 2018). Based on the connotation of online learning space and the development of school education, Guo Shaoqing et al. Put forward policy suggestions to promote the application of online learning space in view of the challenges posed by online learning space at different levels to school education (Guo, et al., 2017). As for the study of teaching mode, Wu Zhongliang and Zhao Lei proposed the flipped classroom teaching mode based on the online learning space (Wu and Zhao, 2014), and Wang Hui constructed the intelligent teaching design mode based on the online learning space on the basis of the wisdom education teaching concept (Wang, 2016). The common ground of both of them is that they integrate new teaching concepts, draw lessons from new learning methods, and pay attention to independent learning, teacher-student interaction and all-round development. The research on environment design mainly aims at the problems existing in the current environment and puts forward the strategies to promote the improvement of online learning space environment. according to the characteristics of virtual learning environment and personal learning environment, Zhu Zhiting et al. Proposed the integration of virtual learning environment and personal learning environment, and took personal learning space as the new focus of digital learning environment design (Zhu, et al., 2013).

Although relevant scholars have carried out in-depth studies on strategies, teaching modes and environmental design respectively, these strategies, teaching modes and environmental design are difficult to be popularized due to the influence of various teaching factors. In view of these deficiencies, this study conducts an in-depth analysis on the supporting role of online learning space for STEAM education projects to ensure that the design model of STEAM education project based on online learning space can be developed and practiced in teaching.

3 Design Basis of STEAM Education Project Based on Online Learning Space

3.1 Analysis of Realistic Needs of STEAM Education

In 2019, the STEM Education Research Center of The Chinese Academy of Education Sciences investigated the current situation of STEAM education through a questionnaire survey. It concludes that the practical needs of STEAM education are to explore the implementation of STEAM education, promote the balanced development of STEAM education, improve the STEAM education evaluation system, promote the training of STEAM teachers and cultivate innovative talents. At the same time, through the investigation of 2021 Computer Making Competition for Primary and Secondary Schools in Guangdong Province, this study finds that most schools in Guangdong province mainly carry out STEAM education through two ways: makers and robots, which are intended to participate in the competition. Currently, schools with high frequency of STEAM education are mostly located in cities with good economic development, while schools with low frequency of STEAM education are mainly due to lack of funds and teachers. Finally, through further understanding, it is found that STEAM education activities are mainly carried out in the form of elective courses and clubs, and the teaching scale has certain limitations.

Therefore, exploring new ways to implement STEAM education, promoting the balanced development of STEAM education and expanding the scale of STEAM education has become an important part of the practical needs of STEAM education. Starting from the realistic needs of STEAM education, it is of certain research significance to explore new implementation methods of STEAM education by using online learning space.

3.2 Supportive Analysis of Online Learning Space

3.2.1 Support of Online Learning Space for Application Environment

There are two main ways to build online learning space. One is to attach to the public service platform of education resources and make a function extension in the platform. For example, the public service platform of Education resources in Guizhou province incorporates online learning space as a function module into the platform. Second, it is independent of the public service platform of education resources, and builds regional education cloud platform, education cloud space and other cloud platforms with the function of online learning space. For example, Zhejiang Province actively promotes the construction and application of online learning space relying on "Zhi Jiang Hui Education Square". Although the presentation form of online learning space is different, it can be seen that the initial construction has been completed, and has also been put into practical use.

3.2.2 Support for Deep Interaction in Online Learning Space

Online learning space has rich functional modules, which make interaction more diversified and broaden the breadth of interaction through network interpersonal interaction, human-computer interaction and other forms. In addition, teachers and students can realize synchronous or asynchronous interaction across classes, schools and regions through online learning space, so that learning activities break through the limitation of time and space (Guo, et al., 2018). In addition to providing support in interpersonal interaction, online learning space can also provide support in the interaction between people and information, deepening the depth of interaction between teachers and students and information. In terms of both breadth and depth, e-learning space provides interactive support for the implementation of STEAM education projects with its unique functional advantages.

3.2.3 Support of Online Learning Space for Project Management

Compared with traditional classroom activities, STEAM education program has the characteristics of rich learning content and long learning cycle. Therefore, recording students' learning progress and managing students' project progress have become an important task for teachers to carry out STEAM education projects. STEAM education project can be carried out in online learning space, through which teachers can know students' learning progress, conduct teaching evaluation and provide learning support, so as to better manage project progress (Zhao, 2020). At the same time, the online learning space can also record students' learning process and provide process data for teachers to evaluate learners' learning outcomes later.

Based on the above construction basis, the practical needs of STEAM education provide necessity for model construction, and the construction of online learning space provides support for model construction.

4   Design of STEAM Education Project Based on Online Learning Space

The design process of STEAM education project based on online learning space should give full play to the advantages of online learning space and attach importance to the inquiry process of students' problem solving. People, technology and activities are interwoven repeatedly in the design process. Integrated STEAM education key link in the process of project design, and the characteristics of the online learning space, web-based learning space of STEAM education project design model should include the project objectives to determine the theme, project design, project design, space environment deployment, project design, project design and project evaluation design seven core elements. These seven core elements complement each other and together build the design model of STEAM education project based on online learning space in the continuous cycle process, as shown in Fig. 1.

This study takes information technology as the main learning content of Grade seven, and develops STEAM education project according to the design model of STEAM education project based on online learning space. Here is an example of how one STEAM education project was developed.

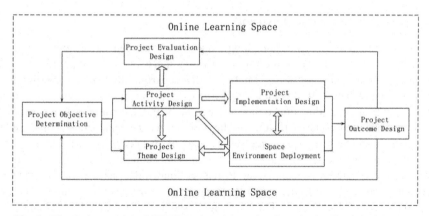

Fig. 1. The design model of STEAM education project based on online learning space

4.1 Determination of Project Objectives

This study preliminarily determined the project goal is to enable students to combine things and phenomena in life to better learn how to use computer to integrate information and understand the principles and methods of information processing technology. Therefore, based on the project objectives as the starting point of STEAM education project design and development, this study sorted and classified the knowledge points of the textbook, and explored the effective connection between the project objectives and interdisciplinary knowledge.

4.2 Project Theme Design

By fully consulting the students' learning intention and referring to the sample questions of PISA 2021 on the evaluation of mathematical problem-solving ability, this study finally decides to develop the STEAM education project "I am a Little Programmer". The case of the project is to integrate information technology with other subject knowledge, integrate interdisciplinary ideas into the project development, and enable students to realize knowledge construction and ability improvement by solving project problems.

4.3 Project Activity Design

The project is based on a group. After the students have learned binary and binary addition, the group members cooperate to design a binary puzzle game. In order to enable students to accurately understand binary and binary addition, teachers can use specific cognitive tools to help them understand. In order to keep students motivated and interested in the project, and to have a high sense of participation, the project creates a realistic project situation.

4.4 Space Environment Deployment

This study intends to select Guangdong Education Financing and Entrepreneurship Smart Sharing Community as the online learning space (website: https://srsc.gdedu. gov.cn/srsc/pub/thepub/index1.do). First of all, the copyright of the platform belongs to the Education Department of Guangdong Province, which conforms to the characteristics recognized by the education authorities. Secondly, the real-name system is adopted for the management of the platform, and the users are teachers and students in the education system of Our province. To register an account, one needs to verify his/her name and affiliation, and the school status information is also connected with the school status management agency of Guangdong Province. Finally, the platform has a variety of innovative courses, case studies and other resources, as well as functional services to support teachers and students in their teaching. Based on the above analysis, Guangdong Education Financing and Entrepreneurship Smart Sharing Community has the implementation conditions of online learning space, which can be regarded as online learning space.

4.5 Project Implementation Design

In order to let the student to understand deeply the binary, this study through the analysis of the connotation of the binary, designed and developed a binary cognitive tool (https:// wapp.gz-cmc.com/html/laocai/index.html). Through the intuitive interface, which can enable students to have a deep understanding of binary expressions. The binary cognitive tool is shown in Fig. 2.

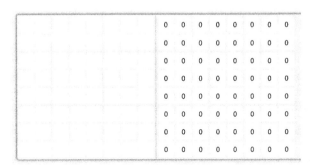

Fig. 2. The binary cognitive tool

In order to let the students can clearly understand the operation process of binary addition, this study based on binary addition algorithm independently designed and developed an understanding of binary addition cognitive tool (https://wapp.gz-cmc.com/ html/laocai/plus.html). Through converting binary numbers into graphs, students can intuitively understand the operation rules of binary addition by adding graphs. The binary addition cognitive tool is shown in Fig. 3.

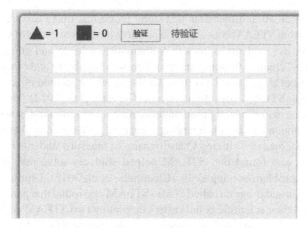

Fig. 3. The binary addition cognitive tool

4.6 Design of Project Results

In the design stage of project results, how to share students' project results is considered. Compared with the traditional learning environment, web-based learning space can not only share the project results in the class, but also share the project results in the learning community, so as to expand the scope of sharing.

4.7 Project Evaluation Design

Project evaluation design mainly includes evaluation content design and evaluation tool design. The evaluation content design summarizes the effectiveness evaluation of STEAM education project into three aspects: knowledge, ability and attitude. The evaluation tool mainly evaluates students' knowledge, ability and attitude comprehensively by compiling test papers and evaluation questionnaires.

5 Practical Effect Analysis of STEAM Education Project Based on Online Learning Space

This study selected Grade seven students from Middle School in Guangzhou as experimental subjects, which were divided into experimental class and control class. The experimental class carries out STEAM education project based on online learning space, while the control class carries out STEAM education project based on traditional environment. In terms of course content, the two classes maintain basically the same knowledge content, but the difference is that the experimental class adopts hybrid teaching method, mainly online teaching. Teachers take online learning space as the main teaching tool, and design offline classroom activities to help students consolidate and flexibly use online learning knowledge. The control class adopts traditional teaching methods, mainly offline classroom activities, and combines multimedia and network technologies as auxiliary teaching tools to help students consolidate and flexibly use classroom knowledge.

In terms of evaluation dimension, this study found that many scholars have proved through practice that STEAM education can promote the improvement of students' learning attitude, improve students' scores in mathematics, science and other subjects, and cultivate students' creative thinking and problem-solving ability and other higher-order abilities. Cervetti et al. proposed a comprehensive teaching method of science and literacy by integrating STEAM education concept (Cervetti, et al, 2012). The study proved that students in the experimental group made significant progress in science understanding, science vocabulary and science writing compared with the control group.Chanthala used the Gilford Creative Thinking Questionnaire to measure students before and after STEAM classes and found that STEAM helped students solve real problems, thus improving their problem-solving skills (Chanthala, et al, 2018). Chittum et al. implemented a design-based program called Studio STEAM and found that participants significantly improved their scientific beliefs after completing two STEAM courses (Chittum et al., 2017). Judging from the above scholars' evaluation of STEAM education results, the evaluation of STEAM education can be measured from three dimensions: knowledge construction, ability and attitude. In terms of ability, researchers believe that STEAM education can cultivate learners' ability to solve problems with interdisciplinary thinking through the implementation of activities or projects. Based on this understanding, this study evaluates the effectiveness of STEAM education program from three dimensions: knowledge construction, problem-solving ability and attitude.

In terms of evaluation methods, this study mainly tested the difference in knowledge construction level between the experimental class and the control class through question questions, and tested the change of problem-solving ability and attitude between the experimental class and the control class through questionnaires.

5.1 Knowledge Dimension

Before the experiment, the knowledge dimension of the experimental class and the control class has been evaluated, which is shown in Table 1. Through the descriptive analysis of the results of the two classes, the standard deviation is 2.79, and the P value is 0.235. Since the P value is greater than 0.05, it is considered that there is no significant difference between the two overall data. So, there is no significant difference in the knowledge ability level between the experimental class and the control class before the experiment. After the experiment, the standard deviation of the experimental class and the control class was 9.729 and 13.323. Through independent sample T test on the data, the p-value corresponding to the homogeneity test of variance is 0.006, which is shown in Table 2. Since 0.006 is less than 0.05, the final P value of the independent sample T-test of the two groups of data in this study is 0.02. It is believed that there is a significant difference between the two aggregate data, which indicates that there is a significant difference in the knowledge ability level between the experimental class and the control class after the experiment.

5.2 Ability and Attitude

Independent sample T test is conducted on the correlation dimensions of problem-solving ability and attitude, and the analysis results are shown in Table 3. Before the experiment,

Table 1. The knowledge dimension pretest analysis

		Levene's variance equality test		T test for whether the mean is equal						
		F	Significant	T	df	Significant	Average difference	Standard error of	95% difference confidence interval	
									Lower limit	Upper limit
Score	Use equal variances	1.514	.223	1.198	68	.235	.857	.716	-.571	2.285
	Equal variances are not used			1.198	66.912	.235	.857	.716	-.571	2.285

Table 2. The knowledge dimension post-test analysis

		Levene's variance equality test		T test for whether the mean is equal						
		F	Significant	T	df	Significant	Average difference	Standard error of	95% difference confidence interval	
									Lower limit	Upper limit
Score	Use equal variances	8.219	.006	-2.398	68	.019	-7.229	3.014	-13.243	-1.214
	Equal variances are not used			-2.398	58.434	.020	-7.229	3.014	-13.261	-1.196

the significant P values of problem-solving ability and attitude between the experimental class and the control class were 0.812 and 0.352 respectively, both greater than 0.05, indicating that there was no significant difference in problem-solving ability and attitude between the experimental class and the control class before the experiment. After the implementation of STEAM education project, the significant values of problem-solving ability and attitude of the experimental class and the control class are 0.006 and 0.019, less than 0.05, indicating that there are significant differences in problem-solving ability and attitude between the experimental class and the control class. It can be concluded that launching STEAM education program based on online learning space can improve students' problem-solving ability and attitude more than launching STEAM education program under traditional learning environment.

Table 4 is obtained by analyzing the changes of various dimensions of problem solving ability of the experimental class and the control class before and after the implementation of STEAM education project. It can be seen that after the implementation of STEAM education project, the significant value P of the attitude toward problems of the experimental class and the control class is 0.001, and the significant value P of the way to deal with problems is 0.152. The significant value of quality of problem solving

Table 3. The Comparative analysis of the dimension of problem solving ability and attitude before and after testing

		Problem solving skills				Attitude			
		Sample size	Average	Standard deviation	P	Sample size	Average	Standard deviation	P
Before	Experimental classes	31	3.007	0.341	0.812	31	2.887	0.338	0.351
	Control class	35	2.985	0.381		35	2.978	0.420	
After	Experimental classes	39	3.648	0.430	0.006	39	3.508	0.415	0.019
	Control class	36	3.356	0.458		36	3.280	0.404	

was 0.027. In these three P value data, in the face of the attitude of the problem and the quality of problem solving P value is less than 0.05, and the way the P value is greater than 0.05, shows that STEAM education after project implementation, the experimental classes and that in comparative classes in the face of the attitude of the problem and the quality of problem solving that there was a significant difference between the no obvious differences in the way to deal with problems. Therefore, online learning space can improve students' attitude towards problems and the quality of problem solving during the implementation of STEAM education project, but it does not play a significant role in improving students' way of dealing with problems.

Table 4. The impact of STEAM education program on problem solving ability before and after implementation

		Attitude towards problems				Ways of approaching problems				Quality of problem solving			
		Sample size	Average	Standard deviation	P	Sample size	Average	Standard deviation	P	Sample size	Average	Standard deviation	P
Before	Experimental classes	31	3.172	0.576	0.737	31	2.838	0.429	0.799	31	3.010	0.567	0.690
	Control class	35	3.123	0.583		35	2.871	0.587		35	2.961	0.418	
After	Experimental classes	39	3.820	0.396	0.001	39	3.525	0.490	0.152	39	3.598	0.680	0.027
	Control class	36	3.425	0.577		36	3.328	0.679		36	3.314	0.364	

Descriptive statistics and independent sample T-test were conducted on the attitudes of the experimental class and control class before and after the implementation of STEAM education project, and the analysis results are shown in Table 5. As can be seen from Table 5, after the implementation of STEAM education project, the significant value P value in the dimension of interest between the experimental class and the control class is 0.048, and the significant value P value in the dimension of self-efficacy is 0.062, indicating that the implementation of STEAM education project based on online learning space has a significant impact on students' interest. However, it has little effect on the self-efficacy dimension. Therefore, STEAM education program based on online learning space can improve students' interest and cultivate students' interest in information technology, mathematics, science and other interdisciplinary subjects.

Table 5. The influence of STEAM education program on attitudes before and after implementation

		Interest				Self-efficacy			
		Sample size	Average	Standard deviation	P	Sample size	Average	Standard deviation	P
Before	Experimental classes	31	2.801	0.520	0.391	31	2.973	0.399	0.553
	Control class	35	2.909	0.498		35	3.042	0.532	
After	Experimental classes	39	3.559	0.655	0.048	39	3.457	0.300	0.062
	Control class	36	3.273	0.569		36	3.287	0.451	

6   Research Summary

Through the analysis of the implementation effect of STEAM education project case, this study found that STEAM education project in online learning space can significantly improve students' knowledge construction, problem solving ability and attitude.

6.1   The Application of Online Learning Space Can Promote the Knowledge Construction of Students

In terms of knowledge construction, through a one-semester STEAM education project before and after the two-group test experiment, it is found that the implementation of STEAM education project based on online learning space can significantly improve the level of knowledge construction of students. Students learn relevant knowledge in a real situation, which is related to the reality, their interest in learning will be greatly enhanced, and their learning efficiency will also be improved. In general, we believe that online learning space, as a place integrating resources, data and services, can create various real project scenarios for STEAM education project of information technology curriculum development, so that students can learn scientific concepts in the created scenarios, which will be conducive to students' understanding and application of scientific concepts.

6.2 The Application of Online Learning Space Can Significantly Improve Students' Problem-Solving Ability

In terms of problem solving ability, through the analysis of questionnaire data, we find that students who use online learning space to carry out STEAM education project have significantly higher problem solving ability than those who do not use online learning space. In the further analysis of the data, it can be found that the online learning space has a significant promotion effect on the attitude and quality of facing problems. We believe that the situational, innovative and cooperative characteristics of online learning space are important factors affecting students' attitude and quality of facing problems. At the same time, as a learning place for collaborative learning and achievement sharing, online learning space gives students the opportunity to cooperate freely with others and show their achievements to more people. All these reasons can inspire students to show more positive attitude and quality when facing problems.

6.3 The Application of Online Learning Space Has a Positive Effect on the Improvement of Students' Attitude

In terms of students' attitudes, the analysis of questionnaire data shows that students who carry out STEAM education project based on online learning space have a significantly higher attitude level than those who carry out STEAM education project in traditional environment. Of two pairs of test results before and after this research data show that STEAM education project can promote the students' interest in learning and self-efficacy has increased, when the data for further analysis of the questionnaire, found that online learning space for students' learning interest has significantly increased, but the level of self-efficacy and should not be used there was no significant difference between students of the online learning space. As a stable emotional state, the formation of self-efficacy is the result of interaction with students' internal psychology and external environment. It is difficult to improve the self-efficacy significantly by relying on only one semester's learning time.

Based on all the above data, the STEAM education project case developed by the STEAM education project design model based on the online learning space is effective and feasible, which further verifies the correctness of the STEAM education project design model based on the online learning space.

In the current process of teaching mode reform, STEAM education can expand the scale of STEAM education by taking advantage of the practical path of online learning space, so that more students can have the opportunity to participate in STEAM education courses. Through the implementation of the curriculum, students are guided to understand the world in the way of discipline integration, to transform the world in the form of comprehensive innovation, and to cultivate their innovative ability to solve problems.

Fund Project.　2021 University-level general research project of Guangdong Construction Polytechnic "Mechanism Research of Vocational College Teachers' Research Activities in Online Learning Space" (JG2021-13); 2023 Guangzhou Youth and the Communist Youth League work project "Virtual reality technology innovation of young students ideological guidance path research" (2023TSW15).

References

Brown, M.B., Lippincott, J.K.: Learning Spaces more than meets the eye (2003)

Scott, K., Benlamri, R.: Context-aware services for smart learning spaces. IEEE Trans. Learn. Technol. **3**(3), 214–227 (2010)

Circular of the Ministry of Education on issuing guidelines on the Construction and Application of Online Learning Space [EB/OL]. http://www.moe.gov.cn/srcsite/A16/s3342/201805/t20180 502-334758.html

Zhang, L., Qin, D.: Research on the path of effective learning in personal online learning space from the perspective of distributed cognition. E-educ. Res. (01), 55–60 (2018). https://doi.org/10.13811/j.cnki.eer.2018.01.008

Guo, S., et al.: Research on the path and policy guarantee of e-learning space transforming school education: study on the connotation of e-learning space and development of school education (7). E-educ. Res. (08), 55–62 (2017). https://doi.org/10.13811/j.cnki.eer.2017.08.009

Wu, Z., Zhao, L.: A preliminary study on flipped classroom teaching model based on online learning space. China Educ. Technol. (04), 121–126 (2014)

Wang, H.: Intelligent teaching design and practice exploration based on online learning space. China Educ. Technol. (11), 87–93 (2016)

Zhu, Z., et al.: Personal learning spaces: a new focus in digital learning environment design. China Educ. Technol. (03), 1–6+11 (2013)

Guo, J., et al.: Interpretation of the guide to construction and application of cyberspace. E-educ. Res. (08), 34–38 (2018). https://doi.org/10.13811/j.cnki.eer.2018.08.005

Zhao, W.: Research on the construction and application of rural teachers' teaching and research model based on online learning space. Master thesis, Northwest Normal University (2020). https://kns.cnki.net/KCMS/detail/detail.aspx?dbname=CMFD202101&filename=102 0977337.nh

Cervetti, G.N., Barber, J., Dorph, R., Pearson, P.D., Goldschmidt, P.G.: The impact of an integrated approach to science and literacy in elementary school classrooms. J. Res. Sci. Teach. **49**(5), 631–658 (2012)

Chanthala, C., Santiboon, T., Ponkham, K.: Instructional designing the STEM education model for fostering creative thinking abilities in physics laboratory environment classes. In: International Conference for Science Educators and Teachers, vol. 1923, p. 030010 (2018)

Chittum, J.R., Jones, B.D., et al.: The effects of an afterschool stem program on students' motivation and engagement. Int. J. STEM Educ. **4**(1), 11 (2017)

Exploration and Design of College Course Examination Scheme Based on Artificial Intelligence

Kun Niu[✉], Qi Liu, Xiao Chen, Hongfeng Gu, Ting Diao, and Jing Li

School of Computer Science (National Pilot Software Engineering School), Beijing University of Posts and Telecommunications, Beijing, China
niukun@bupt.edu.cn

Abstract. With the rise of the global technological revolution, Artificial Intelligence in Education (AIED) has become one of the currently emerging research fields. Integrating Artificial Intelligence into higher education will improve the quality of talent cultivation and promote the development of intelligent education greatly. Focusing on college curriculum examination, this paper analyzes the disadvantages of the traditional mode of examination and puts forward a whole process scheme of examination based on Artificial Intelligence. This scheme divides the process into three parts: before, during, and after the examination, and each part is closely combined with Artificial Intelligence. In addition, the current limitations and trends of AIED are discussed. This scheme can greatly improve the efficiency and quality of examination, and reach the goals of truly personalized and differentiated talent cultivation which provides a reference for curriculum examinations in Chinese colleges.

Keywords: Artificial Intelligence · AIED · Examination Scheme · Higher Education

1 Introduction

With the continuous development of deep learning, Artificial intelligence has had a great impact on business, medicine, industry, and other fields, and has become one of the important technologies to promote the development of society and people's lives. As of 2021, more than 30 countries have included AI in national artificial intelligence policy strategies [1]. However, Artificial Intelligence in Education (AIED) remains relatively unexplored [2]. To meet the new opportunities and challenges brought by new technologies actively, China released the "Artificial Intelligence Development Plan" in 2017, referring to the significance of Intelligent Education and emphasizing the use of AI to accelerate the reform of talent cultivation and teaching modes. In 2018, China issued "Innovative Action Plan for Artificial Intelligence in Colleges and Universities", which proposed the goal of deep integration of Artificial Intelligence and education. Nowadays, AI has become a key solution to many problems in the field of education and plays an important role in Intelligent tutoring systems, evaluation of teaching, personalization, and student profiling.

© The Author(s), under exclusive license to Springer Nature Singapore Pte Ltd. 2024
J. Gan et al. (Eds.): CSEI 2023, CCIS 1900, pp. 246–252, 2024.
https://doi.org/10.1007/978-981-99-9492-2_21

College curriculum examination is not only an effective means to urge students to access knowledge and build capabilities, but also an important way to check the quality of talent training in higher education. Teachers can timely master the students' situation and pay attention to individual development by examination. Schools can also reasonably evaluate the quality of teaching and discipline development planning [3]. The traditional paper-based examination can reflect students' academic performance to some extent, but it has many shortcomings, such as overreliance on manpower, low efficiency, and complex processes. To help teachers perform the tasks of test paper setting, scoring, and invigilation, it is urgent to introduce AI into the examination process.

Nowadays, intelligent technologies such as automatic scoring [4, 5], score prediction [6], personalized feedback [7, 8], and learning attributions [9], have been put into use to improve the efficiency and quality of examinations effectively.

In this paper, we creatively put forward a whole process scheme of college curriculum examination based on AI, which divides the process into three parts: before, during, and after the examination. Combined with the characteristics of each part, it is deeply integrated with Artificial Intelligence. Natural language analysis, computer vision, knowledge graph, and machine learning are employed to cover a full range of scenes such as automatic paper generation, electronic invigilation, intelligent scoring, personalized feedback, and so on. Through the deep integration of AI and traditional examination scenes, we create an intelligent examination process and realize the closed-loop of teaching, examination, and feedback. This scheme will be a useful guideline and have significance in the intelligent development of college curriculum examinations.

2 Disadvantages of Traditional Examination

Considering the limitations of traditional paper-based examination, it is getting hard to fully evaluate students' knowledge level, give personalized feedback and improve teaching materials. To deeply understand the real views of Chinese college students on the drawbacks of the current curriculum examination, we surveyed the students in higher education and designed a questionnaire on the disadvantages of the current examination mode. The questionnaire was distributed to college students in Beijing and lasted for two months. A total of 319 results were received in this survey, including 184 undergraduates, 124 postgraduates, 8 doctoral students, and 3 other degrees, involving students in engineering, science, economics, literature, art, and other majors. The statistical results of the questionnaire are as follows.

According to the results of the questionnaire, we can draw the following conclusions. The main disadvantages of traditional examination can be summarized as inflexibility, lack of feedback, and failure to innovate. More than 70% of the students didn't think they got enough feedback to accurately locate their knowledge defects after the exam. Sixty percent of the students expressed dissatisfaction with the low frequency of updating the test questions and believed that there were too many impersonal questions and a lack of exploration of the comprehensive ability. Half of the students thought the exam failed to investigate innovative thinking and practical ability and didn't recognize the form of *one test determines the score* (Table 1).

Table 1. The Result of The Questionnaire on The Disadvantages of Traditional Examination

Category	Description	Approval Rate
Form	Overemphasis memory ability and uniqueness of the answer	59.84
	Lack of personalization and innovation	47.25
	Students are not allowed to participate in exam design	48.81
	Relative singleness of form	41.73
Content	Lack of updates for long years	65.36
	The content is too focused on teaching materials	37.85
	Lack of test on innovative thinking and practical ability	50.39
Result	Lack of feedback after the exam	74.02
	One paper determines the grade, but the fault is inevitable	52.76
	The score given by teachers is too subjective	27.56

In addition, traditional examinations rely too much on manpower, and teachers need to spend a lot of energy on the entire exam process, which will inevitably lead to various problems under the existing mode. Therefore, the combination of AI and traditional examination provides a breakthrough to solve the above problems. Through the establishment of a knowledge database, automatic marking system, score prediction, and analysis system based on AI, teachers can be liberated from monotonous and repetitive work, effectively improve the efficiency of examination, and promote the development of talent cultivation.

3 Design of AI-Based Examination Scheme

3.1 Overall

This scheme consists of three parts: pre-exam, during-exam, and post-exam. The tasks are split according to the actual scenes in each part, such as paper generation, marking, feedback, etc. The pre-exam part focuses on the task of paper generating and realizes the automatic exam paper generation by combining natural language analysis and knowledge graph. From the perspective of invigilation, the during-exam part uses computer vision and face recognition to verify the identity of students, and monitors the behaviour of students in examinations. The post-exam part is the core part of this scheme, covering tasks such as automatic marking and scoring, data analysis, personalized feedback, intelligent data storage. This scheme truly achieves teaching students according to their aptitude and realizes the automation, intelligence, and personalized cultivation of the examination.

3.2 Pre-exam

Before the exam, we focus on the tasks of question generation, automatic classification, knowledge map, and intelligent exam paper composing. Teachers are supposed to provide curriculum outline, key concepts, and the previous exam papers as core data. The knowledge graph connects knowledge in the form of maps according to the structural relationship and plays an important role in organizing the knowledge points and designing questions. In addition, combined with deep learning, text analysis is carried out on the test questions in the question database, and the questions are classified based on natural language understanding. The scheme also completes the generation of new questions according to intelligent rules and supplements the test question database.

This scheme makes reasonable arrangements for the test questions in combination with the information of the knowledge database and students' knowledge level, to break away from the situation where the questions were set completely according to the textbooks in the past. The test questions are extracted according to the preset rules and AI algorithms from the database, considering the proportion of different knowledge points and the difficulty of the questions. Finally, all the test questions are combined into an exam paper. The pre-exam part will be completed after the administrators review the paper.

3.3 During-Exam

In the traditional examination mode, exam invigilators need to manually complete the tasks of student identity authentication, cheating monitoring, and so on. So, they have to maintain a high degree of concentration, which is time-consuming and labor-consuming. This scheme introduces identity authentication and cheating detection technology based on face recognition and computer vision, which can efficiently complete the above tasks through the camera.

When the students are admitted, the cameras connected to the intelligent system scan them, compare the information in the database through the face recognition algorithm, and pass the authentication after confirmation, allowing the students to enter. In this way, students entering the examination room do not have to wait in line for manual authentication, so as to avoid delays and the risk of forgetting their ID cards. During the examination, the cameras keep detecting the situations of the exam rooms, dynamically capturing the students' expressions and actions through computer vision technology to monitor whether there are cheating and other behaviours. If there is a violation of discipline, the system will immediately locate the student, determine his identity, and remind the invigilator to deal with it, to standardize the examination discipline.

3.4 Post-exam

This scheme introduces increasingly mature AI technologies (e.g., OCR, NLP, and NLU), and focuses on the tasks of intelligent marking, personalized feedback, and failure prediction after the examination. OCR is used to recognize students' test papers and NLU is responsible for analysing the text. The results are uploaded for subsequent review. The neural networks are trained based on the datasets in advance to make it have the ability to understand the answer and score. Then, matching rules and AI algorithms are deployed to complete the scoring task.

After that, this scheme uses data mining and knowledge graph to analyse the students' scores, find the relationship between knowledge points, classify different questions through classification, clustering algorithms, and summarize the course knowledge points. Teachers can easily master different students' knowledge levels, improving teaching content with targets.

In order to give timely feedback to students, AI plays an important role in QA after the exam. Combined with voice transcription, image processing, and cloud storage, it is available for students to have access to subtitle synchronization, cloud live broadcast, intelligence feedback, breaking the space and time constraints. The AI dialogue system is used to answer the questions raised by students in this scheme, and AI virtual teachers can complete automatic answering and teaching tasks. This scheme also adopts deep learning to construct the score and dropout prediction model to help teachers focus on the students who might need help.

4 Advantages and Limitations

4.1 Advantages

- Efficiency and Manpower Saving: The advantages of high efficiency, accuracy and flexibility of AI are fully utilized, which optimizes the examination process and greatly improves efficiency. This scheme greatly lightens the workloads of teachers and liberates them from repeated and complicated work.
- Personalized feedback: The problem of lack of feedback in traditional examinations is well solved. AI can accurately mine individual differences from big data and realize targeted and differentiated feedback according to students' knowledge levels. The learners' enthusiasm and initiative can be stimulated and put into study.
- Focus on the individual and the whole: This scheme fully grasps the macro and individual knowledge levels and makes a comprehensive analysis of the examination results by AI. On the one hand, teachers can help students achieve the generation of individual knowledge. On the other hand, the college can master the teaching effect of all courses.
- Intelligent Data Management: Massive teaching data is efficiently collected, managed, and utilized in this scheme. While reducing the data scale and the pressure of storage, AI extracts implied valuable information and knowledge from teaching data.

4.2 Limitations

There are still some limitations, including technical problems such as accuracy, data storage, and communication, as well as application problems such as policy, public acceptance, and resource investment. Technically, AI has not reached an ideal level in terms of accuracy and efficiency. Training models depend on a large amount of data, time, and computing power. The transmission and storage of massive data is also a big test for the system. From the perspective of the application, how to make the AI-based scheme accepted by teachers, students, and society needs a long-term process and continuous work. The investment in equipment procurement and the cost of system maintenance cannot be ignored. Regional policy differences, curriculum differences, technical personnel and so on all have an impact on the application of AI.

5 Outlook

With the popularity of intelligent terminals and the success of MOOC mode, online-offline education will become the direction of intelligent education. Teaching efficiency can be improved by transferring teaching, homework, and examination to online. Based on the scheme proposed in this paper, the examination will be completed online, the future examination will be conducted online in the form of electronic test papers. The exam strategy will be dynamically adjusted to break the singleness of the traditional paper-based examination, truly achieving the automation and intelligence of the examination process. In the future, the deep integration of AI and education will become an inevitable trend. Combined with 5G technology, cloud computing, big data, and other emerging technologies, it will promote the all-around optimization of the teaching process, break the restrictions of time, space and environment, and promote the construction of intelligent and personalized education system [10].

6 Conclusion

Promoting the development of artificial intelligence meets the needs of national strategy. Using artificial intelligence to promote the development of education in the direction of intelligence is an urgent and huge task, with important research significance. Therefore, aiming at solving the problems of Chinese college curriculum examination, this paper proposes an improvement scheme of the whole examination process based on AI. The new scheme realizes the intelligent tasks of paper generation, invigilation, intelligent marking, personalized feedback, and so on, which greatly improves efficiency and personalized talents cultivation. In the future, the continuous development of AI will provide more possibilities for intelligent examination and intelligent education.

Acknowledgements. This work is supported by the National Natural Science Foundation of China (Grant No. 61971066) and the Beijing Natural Science Foundation (No. L182038), the Fundamental Research Funds for the Central Universities and Beijing University of Posts and Telecommunications 2021 Education and Teaching Reform Project, Beijing University of Posts and Telecommunications Graduate Education and Teaching Reform and Research Project, and ByteDance Feishu.

References

1. Schiff, D.: Education for AI, not AI for education: the role of education and ethics in national AI policy strategies. Int. J. Artif. Intell. Educ. 1–37 (2021)
2. Hinojo-Lucena, F.J., Aznar-Díaz, I., Cáceres-Reche, M.P., et al.: Artificial intelligence in higher education: a bibliometric study on its impact in the scientific literature. Educ. Sci. **9**(1), 51 (2019)
3. Zawacki-Richter, O., Marín, V.I., Bond, M., et al.: Systematic review of research on artificial intelligence applications in higher education–where are the educators. Int. J. Educ. Technol. High. Educ. **16**(1), 1–27 (2019)

4. Xu, S., Sheng, Y.: Discussion on the reform direction of curriculum examination in higher education in China from the perspective of foreign university examination. Contemp. Educ. Sci. **19**, 20–22 (2009). (in Chinese)
5. Westera, W., Dascalu, M., Kurvers, H., et al.: Automated essay scoring in applied games: reducing the teacher bandwidth problem in online training. Comput. Educ. **123**, 212–224 (2018)
6. Beseiso, M., Alzubi, O.A., Rashaideh, H.: A novel automated essay scoring approach for reliable higher educational assessments. J. Comput. High. Educ. **33**(3), 727–746 (2021)
7. Phani Krishna, K.V., Mani Kumar, M., Aruna Sri, P.S.G.: Student information system and performance retrieval through dashboard. Int. J. Eng. Technol. **7**, 682–685 (2018)
8. Kose, U., Arslan, A.: Intelligent e-learning system for improving students' academic achievements in computer programming courses. Int. J. Eng. Educ. **32**(1), 185–198 (2016)
9. Chen, J., Zhang, Y., Wei, Y., et al.: Discrimination of the contextual features of top performers in scientific literacy using a machine learning approach. Res. Sci. Educ. **51**(1), 129–158 (2021)
10. Liu, D., Du, J., Jiang, N., Huang, R.: Trends in reshaping education with artificial intelligence. Open Educ. Res. **24**(04), 33–42 (2018). (in Chinese)

Research of Dialogue Analysis and Questioning Strategies for Classroom Concentration Enhancement

Jian Zhou(iD), Jianxia Ling, Jia Zhu, Changqin Huang$^{(\boxtimes)}$(iD), Jianyang Shi, and Xin Liu

Key Laboratory of Intelligent Education Technology and Application of Zhejiang Province,
Zhejiang Normal University, Jinhua, China
`cqhuang@zju.edu.cn`

Abstract. Classroom concentration is an essential factor affecting classroom teaching, and classroom dialogue is a bridge connecting teachers and students. It is worth studying how dialogue affects classroom concentration and what kind of classroom questions can improve classroom concentration and thus improve the teaching effect. Therefore, this research analyzed concentration and dialogue in the middle school math classroom records, explored the dialogue characteristics with high concentration, compared the differences in dialogue with different concentration degrees, further proposed the question strategies for improving concentration to provide references for better teaching.

Keywords: Classroom Concentration · Classroom Dialogue · Discourse Analysis · Questioning Strategy

1 Introduction

Classroom concentration refers to an individual's ability to select crucial messages and exclude irrelevant distractions from a large number of external messages on time, often showing stillness in their irrelevant external actions, focusing their attention on the learning stimulus, and staying on top of the learning task to achieve learning outcomes [1]. Classroom concentration is a way to provide feedback on the quality of teaching and learning. Teachers can adjust the content and pace of teaching according to students' classroom concentration, build a more scientific classroom teaching system and design more reasonable teaching solutions. At the same time, students can also use it to remind themselves to adjust the state of the class and promote personalized development.

Improving classroom concentration is an effective way to optimize learning outcomes in the teaching and learning process by exploring the factors that influence classroom concentration and adjusting to those that can be artificially moderated to improve classroom concentration. Numerous studies have shown that dialogue is critical to classroom teaching and learning. Effective dialogue is the foundation of a high-quality classroom, developing students' critical thinking skills and increasing their understanding of knowledge, thereby contributing to learning outcomes [2–5]. Teachers often start a

J. Gan et al. (Eds.): CSEI 2023, CCIS 1900, pp. 253–264, 2024.
https://doi.org/10.1007/978-981-99-9492-2_22

dialogue with students by asking questions, and a reasonable question design is of great significance to maintain students' concentration in class and improve teaching effect.

With the in-depth exploration of artificial intelligence technology in face recognition, the existing research mainly focus on the innovation and improvement of concentration recognition technology [6], and the existing literature on the factors affecting concentration pays more attention to the factors of nonverbal behavior [7]. At the same time, there are few studies on the relationship between classroom dialogue and concentration, and the teacher's language in the classroom has an important impact on concentration. Therefore, based on the classroom records, this paper profoundly explores the dialogue rules in the classroom of teachers, explores the influence of the classroom on students' concentration, and proposes corresponding teacher questioning strategies for improving concentration based on the analysis results.

Based on the above background and purpose, this study takes middle school mathematics classes as an example because of their scientificity and systematicness. The research questions are as follows:

Q1: What are the characteristics of high-concentration dialogue in math class?
Q2: What are the similarities and differences between high-concentration and general-concentration dialogue in math class?

2   Methodology

In this section, we mainly introduce the data sources and the methods of data processing and analysis. Firstly, we used a classroom concentration recognition method based on computer vision technology to identify the overall concentration per second for 19 classroom transcripts. Secondly, we transcribed the dialogue texts of 19 classroom videos and checked the text manually. Then, according to different concentration levels, the dialogue text of video clips with two intervals of concentration (high concentration and general concentration) was screened and encoded. Finally, the dialogue text after coding was analyzed to explore its potential rules.

2.1   Data Sources

The videos used in this research came from math classes at a middle school in Zhejiang Province. We filmed the math class of two classes in this middle school for a semester, taking the front and back two camera positions. The videos included teacher and student videos, each lasting 40 min. The classes were taught by the same teacher who has been teaching for about five years and were held in regular multimedia classrooms. The content was the knowledge of the first semester of grade eight, mainly exercises. Teachers and students have approved the filming process.

2.2   Data Processing

Data processing mainly includes concentration rating, screening of different concentration segments, video speech-text conversion, and dialogue text coding. The specific methods are as follows.

Concentration Recognition and Scoring. In this study, we used a class concentration recognition method based on computer vision technology to identify and score students' group concentration, including face recognition, expression recognition, head posture recognition, and class concentration calculation. Figure 1 shows the process in detail. First, the faces in the videos of students were detected, and then the ResMaskingNet emotion recognition model [8] was used to recognize the students' expressions, and the emotional concentration was calculated. Then, the HopeNet model [9] was used to detect the head posture and determine the behavioral concentration state. Finally, the average concentration of the whole class was calculated according to specific weights.

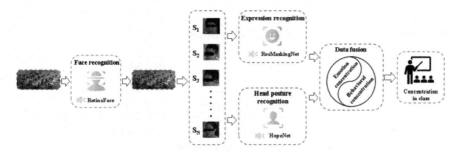

Fig. 1. Classroom Concentration Recognition Framework

Fragment Screening with Different Concentrations. According to the concentration per second value, the video clips of continuous 3 s or more that meet the conditions were screened and recorded. The reason for choosing 3 s was that by observing the classroom record, we found that the teacher usually spoke for about three seconds. The specific screening scheme is as follows.

Step 1: We calculated the average concentration value x and the highest concentration value m of each video.
Step 2: The high concentration group was the segment whose value was in the interval $[m - (m - x) * 0.6, m]$ for three consecutive seconds, and the specific time was recorded.
Step 3: The general concentration group was the segment whose concentration value was located in the interval $[x, x + (m - x) * 0.2]$ for three consecutive seconds, and the time was recorded.

What needs illustration is that the division of high concentration and general concentration in this research is thoughtful. According to the recognition results of concentration, combined with the video recording, we found that when concentration was low, especially lower than the average, the class remained silent in most cases, and the teacher did not speak, or there were no teaching-related activities in the class. Therefore, we chose the fragments whose concentration value was higher than the average to analyze.

Video Speech-Text Conversion and Text Encoding. In this study, iFlytek's interface is used to convert speech to text in videos. After this, the converted text is checked and adjusted manually to improve accuracy. Then, according to the concentration segments of the two sections, the dialogue text of the corresponding video segment is screened out and encoded. There were 444 dialogue statements in the segment of high concentration and 355 in the segment of general concentration.

The coding framework of this research referred to and adapted the classroom dialogue coding tool developed by Song Y [10] and the dialogue coding framework developed by Zhao W [11]. The coding framework is divided into seven categories: prior knowledge, personal information, analysis, coordination, construction, agreement and challenge, instruction and guide. However, in the process of coding, it was found that since the class transcripts recorded in this study were all exercise classes and rarely involved personal information, personal information was deleted in the coding, and only six other types of

Table 1. The coding framework for dialogue

Codes	Descriptions	Examples
prior knowledge	Help students to obtain information, concepts, basic knowledge, and facts, and learn basic methods and basic rules. You can judge the right or wrong answer by referring to the textbook or the knowledge taught by the teacher before	1. T: What is AB? S: Hypotenuse 2. T: What side is BD? S: The direct side
analysis	Abstract separation of a whole into its constituent parts in order to study these parts and their relationships. Guide students to analyze problems deeply, improve deductive ability, and strengthen in-depth understanding	1. So let's see that x should go to the X-axis and look for minus 2, and then go to the Y-axis and look for minus 3, so what point should it be? 2. Because Angle ACD plus Angle BC = Angle BCE, is equal to Angle BCE is equal to 60 degrees, I get Angle ACD + ACB = Angle BCE + Angle ACB
coordination	The process by which general concepts are formed by reasoning about detailed facts. It involves inductive reasoning and the development of thought, aiming at cultivating students' ability to view problems comprehensively and improving their overall thinking	1. Trigonometric function calculation is more complex, and quadratic function is more difficult, especially when we are in the middle school examination, this quadratic function is also a heavy and difficult point 2. 30, 60, and 90 appear, so this particular degree is often tested

(continued)

Table 1. (*continued*)

Codes	Descriptions	Examples
construction	It can be done by asking questions, that is, asking previous responders to expand on what they have said. The extension of the dialogue is a constructive supplement on the basis of the previous dialogue rather than simply repeating the previous speech. It aims to guide students to listen to others and cooperate with others	1. 1500 in 2000 is still 3%, and then the remaining 500 is calculated by who? 2. I can't use the Pythagorean theorem directly. So, what method should I use?
agreement and challenge	"Agreement" indicates explicit agreement and encouragement. "Challenge" means doubt or disagreement	1. Huang Yuehan, is very good, and Zhang Wenzhi is also very good 2. This is the inverse, right? Is this a multiple?
instruction and guide	In the process of classroom teaching, teachers provide targeted support and guidance according to students' learning progress and cognitive level	1. It's an equal right angle, so three pairs, and then let's look at the next question, number seven 2. Just say this and the process of writing is to write diagonally like this and to write vertically and to line up

dialogues were analyzed. Using this framework, two researchers encoded independently, and the inter-rater reliability is 87% (Table 1).

2.3 Data Analysis

In view of the research questions raised, we analyzed the encoded data as follows. Firstly, the proportion of class dialogue types in high-concentration clips was counted to explore the rule of high-concentration clips. Secondly, a t-test (two-tail) was conducted (Via SPSS) to examine the significance level of the differences between high and general concentration fragments. Finally, we analyzed the segments of high concentration in continuous periods to dig into the characteristics and rules of dialogue.

3 Results and Discussion

This research's results are reported in three parts. The first part presents the characteristics of high-concentration segment classroom dialogue and reveals the relationship between dialogue type and concentration. The second part compares the characteristics of general-concentration and high-concentration classroom dialogue. In the last part, case analysis is carried out on the dialogue fragments of high-concentration in a continuous period of time to dig out the characteristics and rules of high-concentration dialogue.

3.1 Characteristics of High-Concentration Segment Dialogue

Figure 2 shows the proportion of different types of dialogue in the high-concentration segment. As can be seen from Fig. 2, the proportion of dialogue types from high to low is analysis (35.1%), prior knowledge (15.1%), agreement and challenge (14.4%), construction (14.2%), instruction and guide (13.3%), coordination (7.9%) respectively.

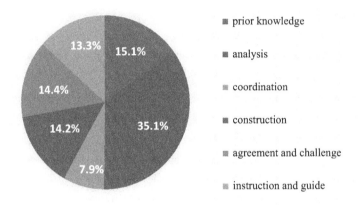

Fig. 2. The distribution of dialogue types in high-concentration segments

From the above proportion, it can be found that the proportion of the analysis dialogue type (35.1%) is the highest when the concentration is high, which may be related to the fact that these courses are exercises. When the teacher explains exercises and carries out analysis, or when the teacher asks analytical questions, the concentration of students is higher, such as "So let's see that x should go to the X-axis and look for minus 2, and then go to the Y-axis and look for minus 3, so what point should it be?".

Prior knowledge (15.1%), agreement and challenge (14.4%), construction (14.2%), instruction and guide (13.3%) are in similar proportion to each other. The nature of mathematics class determines that exercises cannot be separated from knowledge points. Hence, reviewing and explaining prior knowledge is necessary, which can improve the class concentration to a certain extent. In the dialogues of agreement and challenge, most teachers seek students' approval by asking questions, such as "This is the inverse, right? Is this a multiple?" including problem-solving ideas, step results, and recognition or questioning of other students' answers, which helps remind students to listen carefully and stimulate their deep thinking. The discourse of the construction category points to further exploring problems and seeking other solutions to problems. This type of questioning points to higher-order thinking based on knowledge points and is conducive to developing students' higher-order thinking. While coordination (7.9%) accounts for the lowest proportion, indicating that inductive discourse is not very effective in improving students' concentration, which may also be related to the small proportion of inductive discourse in class.

3.2 Differences and Similarities Between High-Concentration and General-Concentration

Figure 3 and Table 2 show the proportion of dialogue types in high-concentration segments and general-concentration segments. And the dialogues between the two concentration intervals exhibit some common characteristics. For example, the types of prior knowledge (15.1% vs. 29.6%) and analysis (35.1% vs. 22.5%) were both heavy, while coordination (7.9% vs. 7.0%) and instruction and guide (13.3% vs. 8.5%) were relatively small. Through the t-test of proportion, it was found that there was a very significant difference between prior knowledge (15.1% vs. 29.6%, $p < 0.01$) and analysis (35.1% vs. 22.5%, $p < 0.01$) in the proportion of dialogues corresponding to different levels of concentration. This means that even in an exercise class, teachers pay more attention to analysis, guide students to in-depth analysis of problems, improve deductive ability, and strengthen in-depth understanding [12], which can effectively improve concentration in class. In contrast, questions and answers directed at prior knowledge were less effective in improving concentration than those directed at analysis, which may be related to the type of course. In exercise class, students have already mastered some basic knowledge, so this kind of dialogue type is not as good as the analysis type for improving concentration.

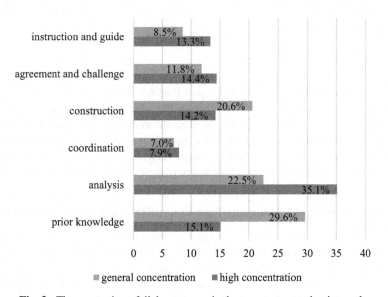

Fig. 3. The proportion of dialogue types in the two concentration intervals

In addition, construction (14.2% vs. 20.6%, $p = 0.017 < 0.05$) and instruction and guide (13.3% vs. 8.5%, $p = 0.031 < 0.05$) also showed a significant difference in two different concentration intervals. From the perspective of proportion, the proportion of construction discourse in the general concentration range is significantly higher than that in the high concentration range, indicating that the construction discourse in the curriculum is not obvious in improving students' concentration. However, according to the research of Song Y [13] and other scholars, constructive dialogues are helpful in expanding students' thinking and improving their reflective ability, so the proportion of such dialogues should be expanded in class. Therefore, it is worth thinking about how to improve the proportion of constructive dialogues in class and use constructive questions to improve students' concentration. As for instruction and guide, it generally refers to teachers offering targeted guidance and help according to students' progress and cognitive level. It is clear and can effectively improve students' concentration and thus improve classroom efficiency.

Table 2. T-test for dialogue code percentages between high and general intervals

Codes	High Concentration (%)	General Concentration (%)	Z statistic	p value
prior knowledge**	15.1	29.6	−4.951	<.001
analysis**	35.1	22.5	3.879	<.001
coordination	7.9	7.0	0.448	0.654
construction*	14.2	20.6	−2.382	0.017
agreement and challenge	14.4	11.8	1.070	0.285
instruction and guide*	13.3	8.5	2.160	0.031

$^*p < 0.05$ $^{**}p < 0.01$

Finally, coordination (7.9% vs. 7.0%, $p = 0.654 > 0.05$), agreement and challenge (14.4% vs. 11.8%, $p = 0.285 > 0.05$) showed no significant difference in the proportions of the two categories of dialogue. But the data showed both were higher in dialogues with high-concentration segments. It shows that it is necessary for teachers to properly coordinate and guide in class, which can help students to concentrate their attention, learn to summarize, listen to others, and improve their critical thinking [14].

3.3 Characteristics of Continuous High-Concentration Snippets of Dialogue

Table 3 presents a collection of dialogues for one continuous segment of high concentration. Numbers represent different coding categories, with 1 representing prior knowledge, 2 representing analysis, 4 representing construction, and 6 representing instruction and guide. This dialogue shows that teachers are good at guiding students and stimulating their thinking by asking questions when explaining exercises. In this high-concentration segment, there are seven dialogue statements, and the sequence is analysis → prior knowledge → construction → analysis → construction → analysis → instruction and guide. It shows that although most teachers use analysis as the central discourse when explaining exercises, there are also a variety of other categories, such as prior knowledge and construction. Especially in the above case of the graph problem, the teacher guides the students to find the equal relation in the problem step by step by asking questions through the construction of class discourse combined with the analysis of class discourse and teaches the students to solve the problem through the step by step. The combination and sequence of such dialogue types can help students maintain a high degree of concentration, indicating that teachers should actively use analytical questions and combine constructional questions to inspire students' thinking.

Table 3. A continuous record of high-concentration snippets of dialogue

Code	Start time	End time	Dialogue
2	8:32	8:36	So, if you want BN to be equal to DM, what do you need to know?
1	8:36	8:38	Midcourt line
4	8:47	8:53	Isn't it? That's right, the middle line, and then what's your second condition? Right Angle
2	8:53	9:00	The right Angle is going to be Angle ABC is equal to 90 degrees
4	9:01	9:13	You see the right Angle guarantee the right Angle guarantees the center line on the hypotenuse, so you get BN is equal to this DN, which is all right equal to? 1/2BC, they're both equal to half of the center line on the hypotenuse
2	9:15	9:21	I'm just going to write it in two parts, and I'm going to write it as if the center line on the hypotenuse is equal to half of the hypotenuse
6	9:21	9:22	All right, let's move on to the next problem

4   Questioning Strategies for Concentration Enhancement

Based on the above analysis, the following strategies are proposed in this research, which can provide references for teachers to improve concentration in classroom questioning and enlighten students' thinking.

4.1   Pay Attention to Analytical Questions, and Train Students' Logical Thinking Ability

Adjust the proportion of basic knowledge questions to avoid too much repetition. From the above analysis, it can be seen that in the clips of high concentration, teachers use more analytical questions to guide students, while in the clips of general concentration, teachers pay more attention to the review of prior knowledge, which may cause some students who have mastered it to lose interest in learning, thus reducing the overall concentration in class. Thus, if teachers could intersperse the questions and answers of prior knowledge in the exercise explanation process, it may improve the teaching effect.

4.2 Pay Attention to the Way of Questioning When Conducting Constructive Questions and Try to Strengthen the Targeted Guidance

Constructive dialogue points to a higher level of thinking and puts forward higher requirements for teachers. Therefore, when conducting constructive dialogues and questions, teachers should proceed step by step according to the actual situation of students and set up particular supports to guide students in the questions of extended questions instead of jumping too much. At the same time, targeted guidance should be strengthened to fit the teaching concept of "teacher-led, student-dominated."

4.3 Combine Appropriate Identification, Questioning, and Summarization of the Knowledge Learned

Teachers cannot do without the affirmation and questioning of students in the class. A proper affirmation can improve students' enthusiasm, and questioning can stimulate students' deep thinking. However, we should pay attention to the tone and method of students' questioning and consider the actual situation of students. Although inductive dialogue does not show significant help in improving students' concentration, teachers still need to coordinate the knowledge learned and students' activities in teaching. In this way, teachers can complete the teaching process, give students positive prompts, integrate scattered content, and help to connect knowledge points and construct knowledge.

5 Conclusion and Limitation

5.1 Conclusion

It can be seen that both analytical dialogue and prior knowledge dialogue occupies a large proportion in both high-concentration and general-concentration segments, but there are significant differences. Prior knowledge dialogue occupies a large proportion in both high-concentration and general-concentration segments, but there are significant differences. Analytical question-and-answer can effectively improve class concentration, while too much basic knowledge question-and-answer may reduce class concentration to some extent. There is also a significant difference in the influence of construction and instruction on concentration. The proportion of construction in general-concentration dialogues is significantly higher than in high-concentration dialogues. However, according to existing studies, construction has a positive impact on expanding students' thinking. Therefore, it is worth considering how to conduct constructivism questions effectively, arouse students' learning enthusiasm, and improve their concentration. Meanwhile, teachers' proper guidance and introduction in the classroom can effectively improve students' concentration and positively impact classroom efficiency. Agreement and challenge dialogues and coordination dialogues do not significantly impact students' concentration. In contrast, these dialogues in high-concentration clips are slightly higher than those in general concentration clips. Therefore, teachers should appropriately use these two dialogues and combine other questions to improve students' concentration.

5.2 Limitation and Further Direction

The limitations of this research are as follows.

Firstly, this research only analyzed the concentration and dialogue text of one subject (mathematics), and the results applied to mathematics and were not universal to other subjects.

Secondly, 19 classroom transcripts were analyzed, but the video sample size needed to be more significant. And all the videos were from two classes in the same school, so the sample range was insufficient.

Finally, in this research, the proportion of dialogue text with different concentration levels, the significance of the difference between each proportion, and individual continuous fragments of high concentration were analyzed, and the analysis method was not innovative enough.

Therefore, given the above limitations, future studies should be expanded to more disciplines for comprehensive analysis. Meanwhile, videos of different schools in different regions should be selected to expand the sample size when selecting analysis samples. As to analyze the more extensive sample data, more methods will be combined to deeply explore the influence of classroom dialogue on concentration in future studies, such as sequence mining, neural network, and other methods to explore how to raise questions to improve concentration in class, so as to promote teaching effect.

Acknowledgements. This work was supported by the National Natural Science Foundation of China under Grant (62077015), the National Key R&D Program of China under Grant(2022YFC3303600), the Key Research and Development Program of Zhejiang Province under Grant (2022C03106, 2021C03141), the Natural Science Foundation of Zhejiang Province under Grant (LY23F020010), and the Key Laboratory of Intelligent Education Technology and Application of Zhejiang Province, Zhejiang Normal University, Zhejiang, China.

References

1. Moore, D.W.: Increasing on-task behavior in students in a regular classroom: effectiveness of a self-management procedure using a tactile prompt. J. Behav. Educ. **22**(4), 302–311 (2013)
2. Mercer, N.: The study of talk between teachers and students, from the 1970s until the 2010s. Oxf. Rev. Educ. **40**(4), 430–445 (2014)
3. Muhonen, H.: Quality of educational dialogue and association with students' academic performance. Learn. Instr. **55**, 67–79 (2018)
4. van der Veen, C.: The effect of productive classroom talk and metacommunication on young children's oral communicative competence and subject matter knowledge: an intervention study in early childhood education. Learn. Instr. **48**, 14–22 (2017)
5. Howe, C.: Teacher–student dialogue during classroom teaching: does it really impact on student outcomes? J. Learn. Sci. **28**(4–5), 462–512 (2019)
6. Hu, M.: Bimodal learning engagement recognition from videos in the classroom. Sensors **22**(16), 5932 (2022)
7. Pi, Z.: All roads lead to Rome: Instructors' pointing and depictive gestures in video lectures promote learning through different patterns of attention allocation. J. Nonverbal Behav. **43**(4), 549–559 (2019)

8. Pham, L.: Facial expression recognition using residual masking network. In: 2020 25th International Conference on Pattern Recognition (ICPR), pp. 4513–4519. IEEE (2021)
9. Ruiz. N.: Fine-grained head pose estimation without keypoints. In: Proceedings of the IEEE Conference on Computer Vision and Pattern Recognition Workshops, pp. 2074–2083 (2018)
10. Song, Y.: Automatic classification of semantic content of classroom dialogue. J. Educ. Comput. Res. **59**(3), 496–521 (2021)
11. Zhao, W.: What is effective classroom dialogue? A comparative study of classroom dialogue in Chinese expert and novice mathematics teachers' classrooms. Front. Psychol. **13**, 964967 (2022)
12. García-Carrión, R.: Implications for social impact of dialogic teaching and learning. Front. Psychol. **11**, 140 (2020)
13. Cheng, B.: Exploring the collective process of classroom dialogue using sequential pattern mining technique. Int. J. Educ. Res. **115**, 102050 (2022)
14. Song, Y.: Exploring two decades of research on classroom dialogue by using bibliometric analysis. Comput. Educ. **137**, 12–31 (2019)

Research on Predictive Analysis of Public Courses and Graduation Grades in Universities Based on GA-BP Neural Network

Jun Wen[1] , Xiaoli Zhang[1(✉)], Guifu Zhu[2], Nuo Xu[1], Can Yang[1], and Jialei Nie[1]

[1] Faculty of Information Engineering and Automation, Kunming University of Science and Technology, Kunming 650000, China
zxl_km@kust.edu.cn
[2] Information Technology Center, Kunming University of Science and Technology, Kunming 650000, China

Abstract. Learning public courses in universities has a significant influence on the learning of professional courses, average graduation credit scores, further education, and going abroad in the later stages of university. It is important to analyse the learning situation of students in public courses and predict their future learning based on these learning data. This article takes the performance data of 12 public courses of all undergraduate students from a university of science and technology from 2010 to 2015 as the research object. Through data processing and establishing a GA-BP neural network model, the average graduation credit score of students is predicted. The results indicate that the overall error between the predicted value and the true value is relatively small, and the prediction is more accurate, proving the importance of university public courses and the feasibility of the GA-BP neural network algorithm. Finally, the article compares this algorithm with multiple linear regression and a BP neural network using two evaluation indicators, RMSE and R Squared, and the results show that this algorithm has the highest accuracy.

Keywords: Public Course Grades · Grade Prediction · GA-BP Neural Network · Average Graduation Credit Score

1 Introduction

In the learning process of universities, regardless of the professional field, it is very important for students to learn basic public courses in universities. The learning situation of public courses in the university exerts a significant influence on the learning of professional courses and the average graduation credit score in the later stage of university. The literature has noted that the phenomenon of college students failing exams is mainly concentrated in the first four semesters [1]. These four semesters are crucial periods for college students' learning careers, and it is also very important to analyse the learning situation of students at this stage and predict their later learning situation based on these learning data. Academic performance is the most intuitive manifestation of students' academic performance. After cleaning and organizing the real data of 12 public course grades and average graduation credit scores of all undergraduate students from a certain University of Science and Technology from 2010 to 2015, the GA-BP neural network prediction model is used to predict students' public course grades. Students can make corresponding adjustments to their learning plans, which can provide educators with scientific and effective management decisions [2].

2   Data Sources

Considering that any university in China must study ideological and political courses, these courses have a significant impact on students' thinking, behaviours, life, and learning [3]. Therefore, in this experiment, the student grades of four ideological and political courses were also used as the raw data for analysis. In this experiment, the authors obtained data from a database of a certain undergraduate university on the scores of students in the first and second parts of public courses from the 2010 to 2015 classes, covering a total of 6 years. These data include grades in 2 math courses, 4 English courses, 2 physics courses, and 4 ideological and political courses. Based on these data, the authors constructed an initial model for predicting the average credit score of students after graduation, as shown in Fig. 1.

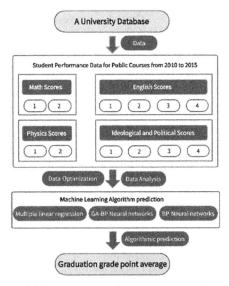

Fig. 1. Initial model diagram for predicting average graduation credit score

3   Data Processing

Because data are obtained directly from the performance management system of the university in the process of screening data, there may be man-made errors that may cause data errors, omissions, etc. To avoid affecting the effectiveness and conclusion of the final prediction model, it is necessary to perform data cleaning on the default values, duplicate values, and abnormal data of the original dataset. The raw data collected in this article mainly include the following four situations that need to be eliminated:

3.1 Eliminate Grades of Nonscience and Engineering Students

In the data sample of this experiment, there are some students majoring in art or law as well as international students. To maintain consistency in the data, the authors use student numbers to determine the students' majors and exclude the scores of students majoring in humanities and international students. Only the public course scores and average graduation credit scores of science and engineering students will be left for research.

3.2 Eliminate Blank Public Course Grades

Among all the public course grades obtained, some students were missing grade data due to special situations such as dropping out or missing exams. By observing the number of students with missing values, the authors found that as only a small portion of each public course grade was missing, we chose to directly exclude the samples with missing values.

3.3 Eliminate Missing Graduation Average Credit Scores

The calculated average graduation credit score results in abnormal graduation average credit scores due to some students' missing or zero course grades. Students with abnormal graduation average credit scores, therefore, will be excluded from the sample.

3.4 Eliminate Duplicate Public Course Student Grades

After obtaining and organizing the student grade data for each public course, due to the failure to obtain the data according to the unique standard of student numbers, when using the MySQL database to connect multiple tables with only student numbers and single public course grades, some tables with duplicate student numbers must be deleted to ensure the independence and authenticity of the samples.

The Pearson correlation coefficient [4] is used to analyse the relationship between the compiled dataset of 12 public course grades and the average graduation credit score. The calculation of the average graduation credit score is shown in Formula (1).

$$Graduation\ average\ credit\ score = (\sum(Total\ evaluation\ score\ of$$
$$completed\ courses * credits\ of\ completed\ courses))$$
$$/(\sum Selected\ course\ credits) \tag{1}$$

The Pearson correlation coefficient can measure the degree of linear correlation. The correlation coefficient between public courses and average graduation credit score is shown in Fig. 2.

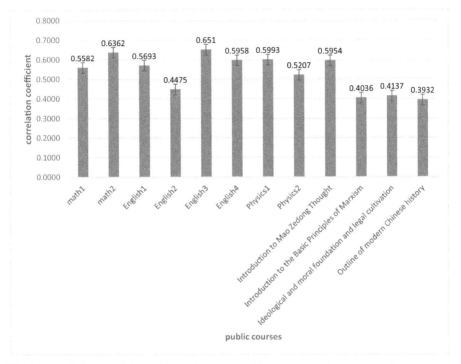

Fig. 2. Correlation coefficient diagram between public courses and average graduation credit score

Through correlation coefficient analysis, it was found that the correlation between public course grades and average graduation credit scores is generally between [0.4,0.6], showing a positive correlation, indicating a moderate degree of correlation.

4 Methodology

4.1 Selection Algorithm

This experiment uses the GA-BP neural network model [5] to predict the average graduation credit score, optimizes the weight of the network structure through a genetic algorithm (GA), and then trains the BP neural network. This model can effectively solve the nonlinear mapping problem of the multiple linear regression model [6] and the slow convergence speed of the traditional BP neural network model [7]. Finally, the model based on its prediction error will be analysed and compared.

4.2 Establishing a BP Neural Network

In the model, the authors first use principal component analysis (PCA) to compress and reduce the dimensionality of the original 12-dimensional data [8]. Retain variable information as shown in Table 1.

Table 1. Reserved Variable Information Table.

Number of principal components	Preserve information about variables
12	1
11	**0.9712**
10	0.9395
9	0.9061
...	...
5	0.7022
4	0.6353

To comply with the requirement of retaining more than 95% of data information, the integrity of the retained data information is 0.9712, reducing the original 12-dimensional data to 11 dimensions. Set the number of neurons in the input layer to 11 and the number of neurons in the output layer to 1.

To achieve better prediction results. It is necessary to select the appropriate number of hidden layer neurons. In this article, the empirical formula for selecting the number of hidden layer nodes is shown in Formula (2).

$$n = \sqrt{m+l} + a \tag{2}$$

In Formula (2), m represents the number of input layers, l represents the number of output layers, and a is a constant between 1 and 10.

In the model, the same learning rate is set first, and after 15000 iterations, it is observed that as the number of nodes increases, the error value of the cost function increases, and the running time also increases. After comprehensive comparison, the value of the first layer node of the hidden layer is set to 6, and the detailed information is shown in Table 2.

After setting the network structure, the authors select the BP activation function [9]. To avoid the gradient disappearing, in this experiment, the two hidden layers in the BP neural network model use the RULE function as the activation function, and the output layer uses the SIGMOID function as the activation function. The common cost functions in the BP neural network are the mean square error and cross entropy cost functions. In this experiment, the mean square error is used as the cost function.

In the selection of initial weights for neural networks, the weights of the network are mainly divided into w and b. The initial value of w is set to the square root of the number of neurons in the upper layer divided by a random number between (0,1). In the model, to prevent the initial value of w from being too large and converging slowly, the initial value of b is uniformly set to 0.

During the learning process of neural networks, if the learning rate is set too low, the training speed will be slow. Model training will proceed very slowly; if the learning rate is set too high, it may directly skip the optimal solution. Ultimately, good results cannot be achieved. In the experiment, the initial value of the training frequency was set to 1000, and the learning rate was set between 0.1 and 0.9, as shown in Table 4.

Table 2. Cost functions and running time corresponding to different node numbers in the first hidden layer.

Number of nodes in the first layer of the hidden layer	Cost function	Running time
4	0.003219	90.01
5	0.003209	106.96
6	**0.003151**	**110.87**
7	0.003155	124.95
8	0.003169	130.43
9	0.003184	172.86
10	0.003168	183.84
12	0.00317	208.15
20	0.003107	323.37

When the number of nodes in the second layer of the hidden layer is 2, the value of the converged cost function is the smallest, as shown in Table 3.

Table 3. Cost functions and running time corresponding to different node numbers in two hidden layers.

The two-layer structure of the hidden layer	Cost function	Running time
[11,6,2,1]	**0.003132**	**123.44**
[11,6,5,1]	0.003141	126.4
[11,6,4,1]	0.003136	130.86
[11,6,5,1]	0.003182	145.05

The final structure of the selected BP neural network is [11,6,2,1], consisting of four layers.

From the above table, it can be observed that when the learning rate is 0.9, the training error of the network is the smallest, so the learning rate used in this experiment is 0.9.

During the model training process, if the training frequency is too low, it can easily lead to the network ending before convergence, resulting in a failure to obtain a better model. However, if the training frequency is too high, it can lead to the network already converging but still running. If it is running for too long, resources will be wasted. It is necessary to choose an appropriate number of training iterations in the model to compromise and achieve the best results. After setting the training frequency to 1500 in this experiment, the model was trained to obtain the network training error curve corresponding to the training frequency, as shown in Fig. 3.

Figure 3 shows that as the number of training sessions increases, the resulting network error decreases. When the number of training sessions reaches 600, the curve stabilizes at approximately 0.00328. Therefore, this experiment will set the training frequency to 1000.

Table 4. Corresponding Network Training Error Table for Different Learning Rates.

Learning rate	Network training error
0.1	0.003201
0.2	0.003175
0.3	0.003161
0.4	0.003143
0.5	0.003123
0.6	0.003106
0.7	0.003094
0.8	0.003086
0.9	**0.003083**

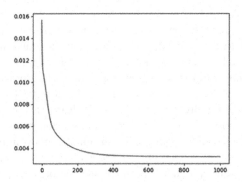

Fig. 3. Error and Training Times

4.3 Optimizing BP Neural Network by Genetic Algorithm

After establishing the BP neural network model, a genetic algorithm was used to optimize the initialization weights and thresholds of BP neural networks, which can improve the network's optimization ability and greatly avoid the possibility of BP neural networks falling into local optima [10].

The important steps in the implementation of the genetic algorithm are population initialization, design of the fitness function, selection, crossover, and mutation.

In this initialization process, the weight values in the BP neural network structure are initialized as the genes of the initial population, and the evolution number, crossover probability, and mutation probability are set to fixed values. By changing the population size, the cost function value and program operation time optimized by the genetic algorithm are observed, as shown in Table 5.

From the above table, it can be seen that the value of the cost function reaches its minimum value when the population is 40, so the weights of 40 randomly initialized

Table 5. The relationship between population size and optimal solution and running time.

Population size	The optimized cost function value	Running time
10	0.01175	7.6228
20	0.0073	12.0001
30	0.00685	17.883
35	0.00616	19.06
40	**0.00425**	**20.5968**
45	0.00532	23.9212
50	0.00469	28.2916

network structures are used as the initial population. In the selection of the fitness function, the reciprocal of the cost function in the BP neural network is taken as the fitness function.

During the model optimization process, the method used for selecting operations is the roulette wheel algorithm. The algorithm first generates random numbers between $(0,1)$ and then selects individuals corresponding to the fitness probability interval pointed by the random value into the next generation population. The cross operation uses single point crossing for operation. Set the mutation probability to 0.01 in the mutation operation. Finally, the first 60 individuals with the largest fitness are selected as the latest population in this iteration. During the model optimization process, as the number of evolutions increases, it tends to stabilize when the number of evolutions reaches 40. Due to the crossover and mutation operations in the evolutionary process, some uncertain factors may arise. Therefore, in this experiment, the number of evolutions will be set to 50.

The training set and testing set were randomly divided 3:1. The BP neural network adopts a network structure of [11,6,2,1], with a learning rate of 0.9. The training frequency is set to a large fixed value before running, and the direct curve trend between the cost function and the training frequency is drawn. Based on the convergence state of the cost function value, the training frequency is finally taken as 20000.

Through the above steps, the training set is used to train the model, and after training, the test set is used for predictive analysis.

5   Experimental. The Results

Due to the large amount of data, it is difficult to observe the predictive effect of the model. Therefore, 200 test data points were randomly selected from the test result set to compare the predicted values with the true values, as shown in Fig. 4.

Figure 4 shows the curve trend between the true value and the predicted value, and in most cases, the predicted value can fit the true value well.

Then, 400 test data points are randomly selected to calculate the absolute error and relative error between the test value and the actual value. In the GA-BP neural network

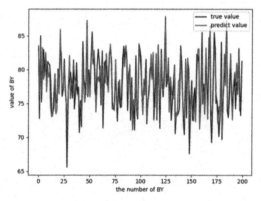

Fig. 4. Comparison between the predicted and true values of 200 random samples using the GA-BP neural network

model, the absolute error is mainly distributed between [−2.5,2.5], while the relative error is mainly distributed between [−0.05,0.05], as shown in Fig. 5 and Fig. 6.

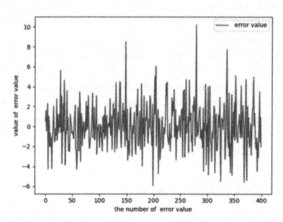

Fig. 5. Absolute error between the predicted value and the true value of 400 random samples in the GA-BP neural network

Figures 4, 5 and 6 shows that there is a small portion of the predicted value error obtained by the model, which is relatively large. The data with large errors mostly show lower true values and higher predicted values. By obtaining these data, it was found that most of the students' public course scores were higher than average. This indicates that these students have good early grades, but their average graduation credit score is lower in the end. The reason for this phenomenon may be due to the continuous changes in learning behaviours, habits, and lifestyle habits of some students from the end of their sophomore year to their graduation from university, resulting in a decrease in learning efficiency in the later stages of university. However, this type of sample accounts for a relatively small proportion of the total sample set, and the majority of samples have

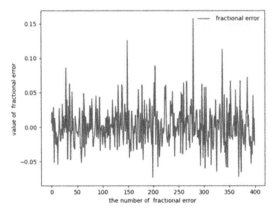

Fig. 6. The relative error between the predicted values and true values of 400 random samples in the GA-BP neural network

a positive correlation between their public course grades and their average graduation credit scores, which is a normal phenomenon.

In this study, multiple linear regression and an unoptimized BP neural network were used as comparative experiments. Finally, root mean square error (RMSE) and R Squared were used to compare and evaluate the three models [11]. RMSE, also known as the fitting standard deviation of regression systems, can measure the deviation between predicted values and true values. In regression prediction models, the smaller the RMSE is, the better the regression effect, and the smaller the average error between the predicted value and the true value. The value range of R Squared is within the [0,1] interval. The closer it is to 1, the stronger the explanatory power of the predicted value of the equation to the true value, and the better the model fits the data. The RMSE and R Squared of the three models are shown in Table 6.

Table 6. RMSE, R Squared for the three models.

	multiple linear regression	BP neural network	GA-BP neural network
RMSE	2.2850	2.2766	**2.1414**
R SQUARED	0.7162	0.7183	**0.7469**

The above table shows that the GA-BP neural network model has the best fitting effect, and the error between the predicted value and the true value is the smallest. The R Squared is as high as 0.7469, and the RMSE is as low as 2.1414, which is superior to the other two prediction models.

6   Conclusion

After analysing and comparing evaluation indicators such as model prediction, RMSE, and R Squared. It can be observed that under the three prediction models, a total of 12 public course performance data in mathematics, physics, English, and ideological and political subjects can effectively predict students' final average graduation credit scores. It has been confirmed that the grades of these public courses have a direct or indirect impact on students' average graduation credit score. This study further demonstrates the importance of public course education in the process of college education. Through this study, students can be urged to develop good learning habits when they first enter university, laying a solid foundation for later learning. Educators can use predictive models to predict the average graduation credit score of students by obtaining their public course grades in the early stages. Based on the predicted average graduation credit score, combined with students' early learning habits and learning situations, targeted adjustments can be made to the teaching plan. By effectively implementing individualized teaching and improving teaching quality, traditional "post-processing" management control can be transformed into a "pre- and during-prevention" guidance service. The results can enable teachers and educational supervisors to tailor their teaching to the time, location, and situation and provide precise guidance to students. At the same time, it effectively guides students to adjust their learning strategies and methods independently, thereby improving learning effectiveness.

Acknowledgements. The work was supported by Yunnan Philosophy and Social Sciences Planning Pedagogy Project (Research on the prediction of College Students' learning results based on online learning behaviour analysis, AC21012), Humanities and Social Sciences Research Project of Yunnan Provincial Institute and Provincial School Education Cooperation (SYSX202008, research on the development countermeasures of intelligent education in Colleges and universities in Yunnan Province), supported by the special project of "Research on Informatization of Higher Education" of China Society of Higher Education in 2020, Analysis and Research on College Students' Learning Behaviour Based on Machine Learning, 2020XXHYB17.

References

1. Wenxian, B., Yongming, Y., Yang, C.: Analysis and research on the related factors of academic problems of university undergraduates from the perspective of Big Data. In: International Conference on Artificial Intelligence and Education 2020. LNCS, pp. 225–228. TianJing (2020)
2. Zhenzhou, Z., Zhenghui, L., Yu, L., et al.: A review of learning early warning research. Mod. Educ. Technol. **30**(06), 39–46 (2020)
3. Yanlin, Z., Zengqiang, R.: Strategies and measures for implementing curriculum ideology and politics: taking the course of "education communication" as an example. China Electron. Educ. **03**, 46–51 (2021)
4. Wiedermann, W., Hagmann, M.: Asymmetric properties of the Pearson correlation coefficient: correlation as the negative association between linear regression residuals. Commun. Stat. Theory Methods **45**(21) (2016)

5. Xiaohan, L., Huading, J., Xue, C.: A stock market volatility prediction method based on improved genetic algorithm and graph neural network. Mod. Comput. Appl. **42**(05), 1624–1633 (2022)
6. Fei, W., Wanling, C., Bahjat, F., et al.: Stock price analysis based on the research of multiple linear regression macroeconomic variables. Appl. Math. Nonlinear Sci. **7**(01) (2021)
7. Jiongen, X.Z., Hongqing, T., Wang, H., et al.: Psychological emotions-based online learning grade prediction via BP neural network. Front. Psychol. **13** (2022)
8. Xiaohua, R., Lanxiang, Z., Jianfeng, Y.: Academic early warning model based on FT_BP neural network. Comput. Appl. Res. **37**(S1), 83–85+97 (2020)
9. Yuqing, L., Tianhao, W., Xu, X.: A new adaptive activation function for deep learning neural networks. J. Jilin Univ. (Sci. Ed.) **57**(04), 857–859 (2019)
10. Xueyan, C., Xupeng, H., Zhenzhen, L., et al.: Using genetic algorithm and particle swarm optimization BP neural network algorithm to improve marine oil spill prediction. Water Air Soil Pollut. **233**(08) (2022)
11. Yi, S., Renyun, L., Song, W., et al.: Evaluation and prediction of exam scores based on multiple linear regression models. J. Jilin Univ. (Inf. Sci. Ed.) **31**(04), 404–408 (2013)

A Summary of Research on China Basic Education Evaluation with the Help of Intelligent Technology

Xiaobo Shi, Ningning Li(✉) ⓘ, Bingying Zhao ⓘ, Weiwei Lian, and Gongli Li

Key Laboratory of Artificial Intelligence and Personalized Learning in Education, Big Data Engineering Lab of Teaching Resources and Assessment of Education Quality, College of Computer and Information Engineering, Henan Normal University, Xinxiang, China
2208283038@stu.htu.edu.cn

Abstract. Under the background of China Education Modernization 2035 and Education 4.0, promoting the integration and innovation of intelligent technology and basic education evaluation is the necessary path for education evaluation reform in the new era. Using visualization tools, interdisciplinary research method and literature research method, this paper systematically analyses the current situation of research on basic education evaluation and systematically describes the various achievements of basic education evaluation based on intelligent technology in China from three stages of rapid, fluctuating and stable rise. It also reveals the problems existing in the practice of basic education evaluation. This paper proposes the development direction of the integration and innovation of intelligent technology and basic education evaluation, breaks through the two bottlenecks of "mechanism" and "technology", gets out of the dilemma of basic education evaluation reform, and provides a reference for exploring the optimization of intelligent technology and deepening basic education evaluation reform.

Keywords: basic education evaluation · intelligent technology · educational evaluation reform

1 Introduction

The idea was initially put out by Bin Liu [1] in April 1987, who stated that "basic education should be the education to cultivate the quality of socialist citizens, with the improvement of the quality of the whole nation as the fundamental value and premise." Preschool, primary, secondary, and literacy education make up the majority of basic education in China. This study's definition of basic education concentrates on elementary and secondary education. Under the supervision of certain educational ideals, based on the defined educational goals, and utilizing specific technology and methodologies, educational assessment refers to the process of scientifically evaluating a variety of educational activities, processes, and outcomes [2]. Researching the effectiveness of basic education enables us to seize the educational reins and guarantee the essential importance of basic education. China has been actively improving educational quality

J. Gan et al. (Eds.): CSEI 2023, CCIS 1900, pp. 277–291, 2024.
https://doi.org/10.1007/978-981-99-9492-2_24

since the turn of the century, and in light of the current circumstances, it is imperative to reverse the pathological education evaluation orientation, establish a new education evaluation "baton," and change the drawbacks of traditional basic education evaluation in order to create a strong nation of talent, science, and education.

Numerous academics have concentrated on the area of educational evaluation in China in recent years, but the current study is mostly concerned with the stage of higher education and does not provide a comprehensive assessment of the current state of basic education evaluation. A lack of original discussion on the evaluation aided by intelligent technology is also present. Instructions on using intelligent technology to enhance Chinese basic education evaluation have been provided in several papers and regulations in the last few years. The General Plan for Deepening Education Evaluation Reform in the New Era [4] proposes for the first time to make full use of information technology to improve the scientificity, specialization, and objectivity of education evaluation. Both plans emphasize the use of intelligent technology to establish an intelligent, quick, and comprehensive education analysis system. All of these show how critical it is to use intelligent technology to support our nation's reform of the basic education evaluation system. The development of intelligent technology and the pressing need for reforming education work well together. It is possible to speed up the reform of basic education assessment through the use of intelligent technology, and the need for reform of basic education evaluation stimulates the development of intelligent technology. Information technology, including the Internet of Things, machine learning, artificial intelligence, big data, natural language processing, virtual reality, and augmented reality, is referred to as intelligent technology.

This paper compiles and analyzes the pertinent literature on the evaluation of basic education in China from 1999 to 2023 using Cite-Space visualization software, interdisciplinary research methods, and literature research methods, displaying the research power and research frontier hot-spots visually.

It has been discovered that "mechanism" and "technology" are the key areas of focus for the issues with China's evaluation of basic education based on intelligent technology. Among them, the "mechanism" primarily refers to the development and implementation of scientific evaluation concepts as well as the continued improvement of specific evaluation mechanisms; the latter mainly refers to the gathering, extraction, and analysis of data-centered intelligent technology for continued innovation and optimization. In order to comply with the request for national reform of educational evaluation. With the aid of intelligent technology, a number of forces break through the development bottleneck and investigate the current state and future course of basic education assessment research in China. This article concludes by defining the current state of research in intelligent technology-assisted basic education evaluation and making recommendations in three areas: "implementing Party policy," "optimizing the evaluation mechanism," and "tamping the technological foundation." And put up recommendations from three angles: "implementing the party's principles and policies," "optimizing the evaluation mechanism," and "tamping the technical foundation," in the hopes of illuminating further study in this area.

2 Research Data and Methods

2.1 Data Sources

The primary source of data for this study is derived from journals obtained from the China Knowledge Network (CNKI) database. Specifically, the theme of "Basic Education Evaluation" was selected on CNKI, and the search was conducted on March 1, 2023, with the selected databases being "Peking University Chinese Core" and "CSSCI". The time frame chosen for the search was "1999–2023". A total of 329 documents were initially retrieved. To ensure the reliability of the data, a rigorous screening process was applied, excluding bidding announcements and other irrelevant documents unrelated to "basic education evaluation". As a result, 299 valid documents were obtained.

2.2 Research Tools and Methods

This study primarily utilizes CiteSpace to visually and analytically examine the annual publication volume of literature, the collaboration network among key authors and institutions, as well as word frequency, co-occurrence, clustering, and the emergence of keywords. Furthermore, by conducting an extensive review of core literature and employing interdisciplinary research methods and literature research techniques, this paper engages in a comprehensive exploration of the research status and cutting-edge trends pertaining to intelligent technology-assisted evaluation in basic education.

3 Research Results and Analysis

3.1 Chronology and Research Power Charts of Basic Education Evaluation Research in China with the Help of Intelligent Technology

299 effective literatures are statistically plotted according to the annual publication volume, and the literature age distribution is finally obtained as showed in Fig. 1.

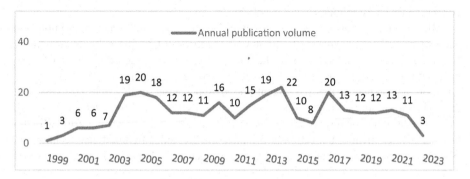

Fig. 1. Chronological distribution diagram of literature

As depicted in Fig. 1, there has been a noticeable upward trend in the number of publications related to intelligent technology-assisted evaluation in basic education research in China over the past twenty-five years. Based on the distribution of article counts across different years, the data can be categorized into three distinct stages, as outlined in Table 1.

Table 1. Analysis of the development cycle

Development period	Number of posts	Percentage
Rapid rise period	62	20.7%
Period of rising volatility	173	57.9%
Stable upward period	64	21.4%

The period from 1999 to 2005 is a period of rapid rise. With the official launch of the eighth curriculum reform in China in 1999, we attach importance to the educational function of evaluation, improve the traditional evaluation methods, and regard learning evaluation as the core content of the reform of educational evaluation. At this time, all kinds of intelligent technologies are put into the construction of educational infrastructure. The basic education evaluation with the help of intelligent technologies such as computer-aided testing and network behavior flow measurement is rapidly becoming known.

The period from 2006 to 2017 is a period of rising volatility. This period is not only the successful conclusion of the 12th five-year Plan and the implementation of the 13th five-year Plan, but also the period of further development or growth of basic education evaluation research. During this period, intelligent technology has been applied on a large scale and gradually formed certain characteristics of the information stage, and the reform of comprehensive evaluation of the quality of basic education has been continuously promoted. International PISA testing, Markov chain and other intelligent technologies help inter-group evaluation, comprehensive quality evaluation and other multiple evaluation methods into the public field of vision, this field is also gradually concerned by many scholars.

2018 to date is a period of steady increase. The average number of articles published each year is about 12. Due to the limitation of retrieval date, the publication volume "3" in 2023 in Fig. 1 is not taken as the final data. Therefore, according to the Chinese basic education evaluation research literature volume curve generated by CNKI visualization, it is expected that the annual publication volume in this field will be stable at 13 (including journal papers and conferences) in 2023 as the final data. This steady trend indicates that the research focus on basic education evaluation is maturing with the gradual advancement of education informatization 2.0, aided by intelligent technology, but this maturity still has the potential to further increase relative to the period of rapid rise.

As can be seen from Fig. 2, the author summary point N and total connected E are 274 and 137, respectively. The number of nodes of the main authors with high research power is 33, the number of connected lines is 19, and the number of nodes with connected lines accounts for 64%. Observing Fig. 2, it can be seen that most of the

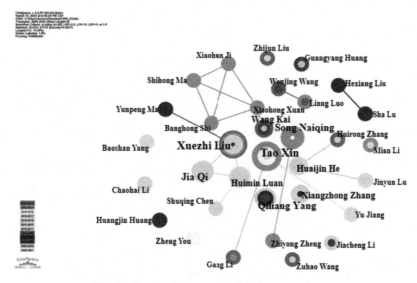

Fig. 2. Cooperative network of major researchers

authors have collaborative research relationships with each other, but there is also a part of isolated nodes, which are judged to be authors of independent research, and on the whole, researchers mainly adopt a collaborative research approach and are supplemented with independent studies. Meanwhile, the size of the nodes determines the number of papers, and Tao Xin, Yuezhi Liu, and Naiqing Song ranked the top three in terms of the number of publications. Different rings represent different publishing time, and the position and size of institutional nodes and the size of name labels can directly reflect the research power of each research institution.

From Fig. 3, it is clear that the core research power comes from famous normal universities in China. Top of the list of publications are Collaborative Innovation Centre of China Basic Education Quality Monitoring, Beijing Normal University, Institute of Curriculum and Teaching etc. In addition, there are 48 nodes N and 16 links E in the main research institutions, indicating that the research units cooperate more frequently, but there is still some room for cooperation. Relying on the students' information obtained by normal colleges, and constantly increasing the collaboration with the professional team of intelligent technology in order to better combine intelligent technology and educational evaluation closely, develop more meaningful evaluation tools, and make intelligent technology play a role in Chinese the evaluation reform of basic education will play its rightful role.

3.2 Cluster Analysis on the Current Status of Basic Education Evaluation Research

To elucidate the relationship among research topics in the field of basic education evaluation in China using intelligent technology, cluster analysis was conducted based on

Fig. 3. Cooperation network of major research institutions

the frequency of keyword occurrence. This analysis resulted in the identification of 11 distinct clusters, as depicted in Fig. 4.

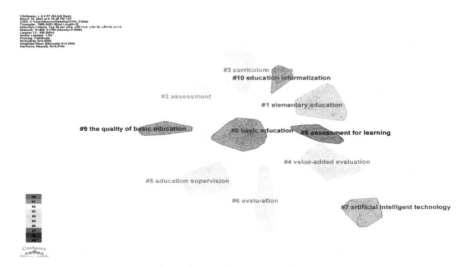

Fig. 4. Keyword clustering picture

Combined with Fig. 4, it can be seen that the modularity of clusters $Q = 0.8552 > 0.3$, which indicates that the structure of clusters is very obvious, and the average profile of clusters $S = 0.9562 > 0.7$, which indicates that the classification results of clusters power. In addition, combined with the cluster labels and SIZE value, the clustering analysis table of basic education evaluation keywords with the help of intelligent technology is derived, as shown in Table 2.

Table 2. Clustering analysis table of key words of basic

Clustering	Cluster label	Size Value
Mechanism-based research	#0basic education	51
	#1elementary education	30
	#2assessment	23
	#3curriculum reform	23
	#4value-added evaluation	22
	#5education supervision	22
	#6evaluation	21
	#8Assessment for learning	14
	#9the quality of basic education	11
Technology-based research	#7artificial intelligent technology	18
	#10education informatization	11

In this paper, the identified clusters are categorized into two main groups: "mechanism-based research" and "technology-based research".

In mechanism-based research, key concepts such as basic education, evaluation, curriculum reform, and assessment are closely related to core vocabulary such as physical education, learning, America, achievement assessment, student performance, high-quality, key competencies, targeted assessment, personalized learning, and more. These concepts represent fundamental elements within the field of basic education evaluation. While the SIZE values of value-added evaluation, educational supervision, and educational quality may be relatively small, they are still significant concerns in the current era of educational evaluation. For instance, the monitoring of Chinese basic education quality started later compared to developed countries, but it has witnessed rapid progress. With the aid of intelligent technology, various provinces, municipalities, and autonomous regions have established institutions dedicated to monitoring basic education quality, and education quality evaluations and academic assessments have gradually been implemented at the compulsory education stage across different regions. In consideration of the broader mechanism-based research, emphasizing value-added evaluation, fostering high-quality education development through intelligent technology, and promoting students' comprehensive and personalized development are fundamental directions for basic education evaluation in the new era.

Technology-based research mainly includes two clusters of artificial intelligence technology and education informatization. Core terms involved are mainly intelligent education evaluation, third-party assessment, evaluation model, and special fund. The SIZE value of the whole technology-based research is small, and the cluster label number is relatively late. The reason for this is that, on the one hand, Chinese technology practice is less than the mechanism theory research, and the intelligent technology is limited and the research is relatively backward. On the other hand, intelligent technology power basic education evaluation is an emerging crossover field, involving many content, itself is included in each basic concept, in view of intelligent technology basic education evaluation has not formed a special mechanism. However, the national financial expenditure on education from 2012 to 2022 remains above 4% of GDP, which is enough to prove the position of intelligent technology in education cannot be ignored.

3.3 Analysis of the Frontier Evolution of Basic Education Evaluation Research in China

To delve into the evolving frontier direction of basic education evaluation research in China with the assistance of intelligent technology, this study employs a mutation detection algorithm to extract and organize prominent keywords from the literature. The urgency value of each keyword indicates the level of attention it received during a particular time period [5]. In this study, the top 25 keywords with the highest urgency values were extracted and sorted by year. The results of this analysis are presented in Fig. 5, showcasing the evolution of these keywords over time.

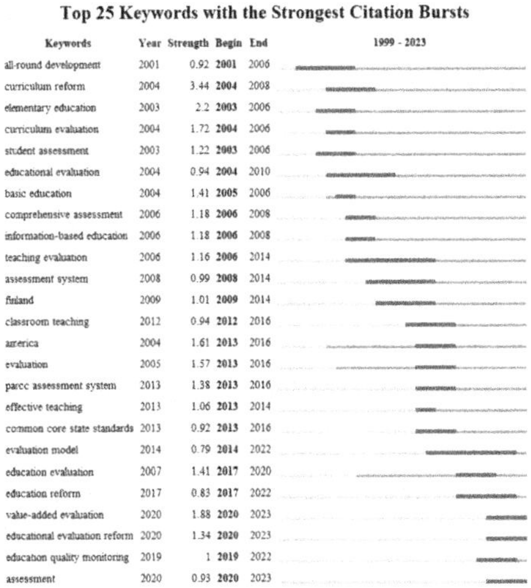

Top 25 Keywords with the Strongest Citation Bursts

Keywords	Year	Strength	Begin	End	1999 - 2023
all-round development	2001	0.92	2001	2006	
curriculum reform	2004	3.44	2004	2008	
elementary education	2003	2.2	2003	2006	
curriculum evaluation	2004	1.72	2004	2006	
student assessment	2003	1.22	2003	2006	
educational evaluation	2004	0.94	2004	2010	
basic education	2004	1.41	2005	2006	
comprehensive assessment	2006	1.18	2006	2008	
information-based education	2006	1.18	2006	2008	
teaching evaluation	2006	1.16	2006	2014	
assessment system	2008	0.99	2008	2014	
finland	2009	1.01	2009	2014	
classroom teaching	2012	0.94	2012	2016	
america	2004	1.61	2013	2016	
evaluation	2005	1.57	2013	2016	
parcc assessment system	2013	1.38	2013	2016	
effective teaching	2013	1.06	2013	2014	
common core state standards	2013	0.92	2013	2016	
evaluation model	2014	0.79	2014	2022	
education evaluation	2007	1.41	2017	2020	
education reform	2017	0.83	2017	2022	
value-added evaluation	2020	1.88	2020	2023	
educational evaluation reform	2020	1.34	2020	2023	
education quality monitoring	2019	1	2019	2022	
assessment	2020	0.93	2020	2023	

Fig. 5. The emergent word map

The analysis of emergent words reveals a strong alignment with the division of development stages outlined in Table 1. Consequently, the evolution of emergent words can be categorized into the same three stages identified in the study.

The First Stage of Rapid Rise (1999–2005)

The term "comprehensive development", which emerged at the earliest time, included "moral", "intellectual", "physical", "aesthetic" and "labor". During this period, the development of information technology in China is in the early stage of steady development, and the technology is not yet mature, so the evaluation of these five aspects mainly depends on the traditional pen-and-paper test and the experience of teachers. However, the focus of basic education evaluation was changed from "score-oriented" to "comprehensive quality" late. Because of the long-time range of "comprehensive development", along with the continuous development of intelligent technology, intelligent technology has been integrated into the quality evaluation of basic education. In 2004, Shavinina [6] applied the concept of intelligence assessment to the assessment of students' intelligence through tests such as "Perfect Computer" and "Concept Integration", and achieved certain results.

The Second Stage of Fluctuating Upward (2006–2017)
This period was an important stage in the reform of basic education evaluation in China, helped by intelligent technology. "Comprehensive evaluation", "information-based education" and "teaching evaluation" all began to appear in 2006, but they lasted for different periods of time. Since entering the information age, computerized education in China has ushered in information-based education. In November 2002, Mr. Guonong Nan, the founder of Chinese computerized education theory, put forward the conceptual formulation of information-based education: "Informational education is a manifestation of the integration of modern information technology and education." This marked the creation of the concept of "information-based education" [7]. Informatization education continues to integrate high-quality resources, optimize the education process, promote the development of traditional teaching methods such as textbooks, blackboards and lectern the direction of information technology. By breaking down the boundaries between learning and evaluation, and by collecting, extracting and analyzing massive amounts of data from teachers and students through various information technology tools, teacher evaluation has shifted from an empirical to a scientific orientation, effectively promoting the rapid development of the evaluation field in basic education. The length of time range (2006–2014) for the emergence of "teaching evaluation" ranks first among the 25 emergent words. Teaching evaluation started from the early educational tests in the West, and then went through the Taylor model, value judgment, and the process of emphasizing the constructs [8]. On the contrary, domestic intelligent technology has continuously helped teaching evaluation to develop in the direction of simplification and quantification, Xiangyong Guo [9], the comprehensive evaluation physical of teaching quality constructed by fuzzy mathematical method makes the evaluation index shift from qualitative to quantitative; The "Guidance on Promoting Comprehensive Evaluation Reform of Primary School Students" was issued in July 2022 from the Department of Education of Zhejiang Province to establish a "student-centred" comprehensive evaluation system for elementary school students for the long-term effectiveness of quality education [10]. With the help of intelligent technology, "comprehensive evaluation" in the field of basic education evaluation is more scientific and more advocated.

Intelligent assessment, such as simulation assessment and game-based assessment, provides students with complete, realistic and open problem situations, allowing students to explore and express themselves freely in task situations [11]. "Assessment systems", "Finland", and "classroom teaching" emerged in 2008–2014, 2009–2014, and 2012–2016, respectively. In 2009, Finland conducted a content analysis of the national curriculum framework and studied the innovation process involved in the technology curriculum [12]. It has some enlightenment for us to solve the problem of curriculum evaluation and promote the reform of technical education. In 2012, Finland showed a backward performance in PISA, and the reason for this was that it did not integrate technology into curriculum teaching [13]. Although Finland has a unique educational evaluation system, the lack of science and technology limits the ability of Finnish education to maintain its peak state, even if there is an excellent concept of classroom teaching-discovering the talents of each student. Maximum personalized and fair teaching. Science and technology and education play an equally important role in improving a country's comprehensive strength, which can be proved by the progress we have made in PISA. Integrating science and technology into the field of education, Tsinghua University's Rain Classroom intelligent guidance system, Tao Xin [14] The automatic evaluation model of the main idea of the essay text, the automatic scoring system of classroom atmosphere built by Kashyap, and Enhong Chen's [15] neurocognitive diagnostic model and etc. all led to the development of intelligent and automated educational assessment systems in China in the past 25 years.

Not only Finland, but also the United States has been a learning object in the process of Chinese education development. This can be verified from the fact that the emergence of "United States", "evaluation", "Parcc assessment system", "effective teaching" and "Common Core State Standards" began in 2013 at the same time, among which the emergence of "effective teaching" ended in 2014, and the other words all ended in 2016. American ACOP Classroom Teaching Quality Assessment Department has led to a consensus on "effective teaching" among interdisciplinary teams [16]. Zhaoge Yao [17] summarized the experience of implementing effective teaching and learning in online learning spaces. The introduction of the Common Core State Standards in 2010 marked a breakthrough in the American "standards-based education reform" movement, which will lead the way in the development of education in the United States. To further promote the development of education, the American government spent $170 million to build the PRACC assessment system, a high-quality basic education evaluation system. Drawing lessons from the experience of the United States and combining the current situation of China, on the one hand, we should carry out further thinking and research on the experience learned, actively carry out field research, based on local characteristics, fully transform the effectiveness of the existing experience and achievements, and give full play to its applicability. On the other hand, continuously improve the level of information, gradually increase investment in intelligent evaluation system, and strive to establish a high-quality, computer technology-supported basic education evaluation system with Chinese characteristics.

The emergence of the "evaluation model" has been going on for 9 years, and the popularity has lasted until last year, which shows that the evaluation model has made great achievements in the past 25 years. Such as MOOCAP learner online learning behavior and effectiveness evaluation model, teaching and research interactive evaluation model, multi-source process data-driven learner comprehensive evaluation model, etc., continue to accelerate the development of basic education evaluation [18–20]. On the basis of fully understanding the characteristics of each evaluation model, it is the development direction of the evaluation model to further optimize the innovative intelligent technology, continuously enhance the generalization ability and interpretability of the evaluation model, enhance the reliability test of the model, continuously dispel the "black box" concerns, lower the threshold of using the model, reduce the technical burden of teachers, and carry out a wider range of expansion.

The year 2017 is an important time node. The release of the 13th Five-Year Plan for the Development of National Education, confirms the re-emergence of "education reform" and "education evaluation". They points out that 2020 education modernization has made important progress, 2030 to achieve the vision of China's education modernization, education quality comprehensive improvement, also confirmed the rationality of "education reform"," education evaluation", "education quality monitoring" respectively appear in 2017–2020, 2017–2022, 2019–2022. The development of China's basic education quality monitoring with the help of intelligent technology is extremely rapid, and in 2013, under the efforts of Ling Li [21] and others, China's cloud computing basic education quality monitoring and evaluation platform was rapidly realized, which provides a scientific reference basis for the social parties to participate in the comprehensive quality assessment of students, accurately monitor and evaluate students' personal development, teach according to their abilities, and improve the quality of education. Later, block-chain and other intelligent technologies took advantage of the national data platform, which was upgraded to achieve concomitant collection, distributed storage and negotiated sharing of data on the whole process of student development [22]. Although the level of quality control is constantly improving with the help of intelligent technology, building a monitoring platform that is more suitable for the overall development of Chinese students still requires both mechanism and technical efforts to further discover and solve problems in a large number of research and communication feedback.

The Third Stage of Steady Rise (2018 to Present)
During this period, the development of basic education evaluation mechanisms and systems in China was relatively stable and in a phase of continuous improvement. The emergence of "assessment", "educational evaluation reform" and "value-added evaluation" all began in 2020 and has continued to this day, among which the emergent value of "value-added evaluation" ranks third. This reflects the frontiers and hot spots of research in the field of basic education evaluation. Value-added evaluation takes into account both development and education, and it is a good medicine to break through the stubborn problems of traditional evaluation and return education to its essence. With the vigorous development of intelligent technology, and value-added evaluation has continuously made breakthroughs. Qingyang District, Chengdu City, in China has comprehensively upgraded the tracking database system, making the resource allocation system based on value-added evaluation more fair. With the support of multi-nested data, it automatically approximates the algorithm function that conforms to the law of the sample data, thus breaking through the linear model for the evaluation of comprehensiveness. Limitations, assist optimal decision-making, and provide an intelligent path for value-added evaluation.

Through the analysis of the above three stages, we can see that the field of basic education evaluation in China is the starting point to promote the orderly reform of education. All-round development, comprehensive evaluation and quality education are the core themes of current Chinese education. However, from the perspective of the whole evolution, the "comprehensive" degree of comprehensive development, the "comprehensiveness" of comprehensive evaluation, the "pertinence" of evaluation model and the "value-added attribute" of value-added evaluation are mostly focused on improving students' academic achievement. With the development of information technology, the degree of differentiation of the four levels of "moral", "physical", "aesthetic" and "labor" has improved, but the degree is still relatively small. With the help of intelligent technology, the accuracy, science and interpretability of basic education evaluation have been guaranteed to a certain extent, but the intelligence, reliability and security of technology itself need to be further studied. Therefore, in order to really force the educational reform with the baton of "evaluation", we must closely revolve around the principles and policies of the Party and the country under the background of Education 4.0. Combined with the actual needs such as "Education Informatization 2.0 Action Plan", "China Education Modernization 2035" and "14th five-year Plan" digital economy development plan, we constantly explore a new mechanism for basic education evaluation. Upgrade and improve big data, NLP, Artificial Intelligence, 5G, Block-chain and other intelligent cutting-edge technologies. While ensuring the safety of student data, we will continue to enhance the coordination and effectiveness of smart technologies, thereby promoting the development of high quality and high level of education.

4   Enlightenment

In the context of the intersection and integration of technology and evaluation, this paper systematically examines the development context and notable accomplishments of China's basic education evaluation over the past 25 years. These developments are analyzed within the framework of three distinct stages: rapid growth, fluctuation, and stability. The aim is to contribute to the advancement of educational evaluation reform in China. The paper also identifies the challenges and issues present in the realms of "mechanism" and "technology". To further explore how intelligent technology can better facilitate the reform of basic education evaluation in the future, the following prospects are presented:

4.1   Carry Out the Party's Policy and Adhere to the Educational Evaluation Orientation of Establishing Morality and Cultivating Talents

The Party's consistent policies on education have paved the way for the advancement of basic education evaluation reform in China. Initiatives such as the General Programme for Deepening Education Evaluation Reform in the New Era, the implementation of the Opinions on Further Reducing the Burden of Homework and Out-of-School Training for Compulsory Education Students, and the convening of the National Education Work Conference have propelled progress in this domain. Emphasizing the fundamental goal of "establishing morality and cultivating talents," we are urged to adopt a scientific perspective on talent development.

As society rapidly evolves, the requirements for talent training in China are continuously evolving as well. Contemporary society demands individuals who possess both competence and moral integrity. Outdated evaluation standards such as prioritizing high scores over actual abilities, focusing solely on test scores, and overemphasizing academic achievements are being challenged. In the new era, schools should prioritize the holistic development of students, strive to identify and nurture the unique talents of each individual, foster their comprehensive qualities, and endeavor to cultivate well-rounded individuals for modern education.

Additionally, it is essential to promote the development of core educational objectives. This entails adopting a multifaceted evaluation approach. The concept of multiple evaluation encompasses diverse evaluation outcomes, comprehensive evaluation content, varied evaluation methods, diverse evaluation purposes, and diverse evaluation subjects. Embracing a pluralistic view of evaluation not only counters the inclination towards utilitarianism and instrumentalism in the field of basic education evaluation but also diminishes the focus on "selection" and "choice" while strengthening the role of "feedback" and "improvement." Such an approach contributes to the vital task of moral education.

Overall, aligning with the Party's educational policies and emphasizing multiple evaluation perspectives, China aims to enhance the reform of basic education evaluation, nurture well-rounded individuals, and cultivate talent in line with the demands of the new era.

4.2 Optimize the Evaluation Mechanism and Construct a High-Quality Basic Education Evaluation System in the New Era of China

First and foremost, it is crucial to establish evaluation standards centered on quality for basic education. Evaluation should be conducted at the county, school, and student levels, in accordance with the requirements of the Compulsory Education Quality Guidelines. Continuous improvement of the quality monitoring system for compulsory education is essential. Schools should collaborate with local governments, third-party institutions, and other stakeholders to develop a multi-level educational quality inspection system that caters to a wider region and exhibits school-based characteristics. Local governments and relevant departments should actively facilitate joint technical training, expedite the construction of a high-level evaluation team, and enhance operational capabilities through comprehensive and systematic training and assessments. Active organization and guidance from higher-level authorities are indispensable for developing a Chinese-style teaching quality evaluation system under the guidance of quality education.

Secondly, it is crucial to prioritize student development throughout the assessment process. Promoting students' all-round development should always be the fundamental starting point of educational assessment. Schools should integrate perception technologies from the Internet of Things, such as ZigBee, intelligent sensors, RFID, and other key technologies. By employing highly integrated micro-sensors, important data pertaining to students' comprehensive development can be comprehensively recorded and retained throughout their educational journey. This data can then be utilized to build a student growth profile platform with distinct school characteristics. Process evaluation should be implemented across the school, and the value-added progress at each stage of student development should be thoroughly analyzed. Value-added evaluation should be effectively combined with process evaluation to drive continuous improvement in students' overall quality.

Lastly, it is essential to understand that the ultimate goal of educational evaluation is not to criticize and punish but to utilize effective evaluation results to their fullest extent. Teachers should maintain the concept of lifelong learning, keeping in mind that "results are based on utility." They should leverage various visualization analysis software, computer graphics and animation, ChatGPT, intelligent teaching platforms, and other tools to scientifically diagnose students' current status, provide fair guidance, care for students' self-esteem, and ensure the security of students' data. Simultaneously, teachers should inspire students to continually adjust themselves in a supportive and convincing manner, fostering improvement and development as the ultimate goals.

4.3 Tamping the Foundation of Technology, Optimizing and Innovating Modern High-Level Information Technology Based on Data

It can be said that the extension of intelligent technologies such as 5G, Artificial Intelligence, Block Chain, Big Data, the Internet of things and Machine Learning in the field of educational evaluation conforms to the development trend of educational evaluation reform in the new era. In the end, in order to promote the intelligent education evaluation system with Chinese characteristics and produce economies of scale in the world, we need to further optimize and innovate modern high-level information technology and consolidate the technological foundation on the basis of data.

First of all, the establishment of data standards, multi-modal data itself has digital barriers. In order to enable the smooth circulation and exchange of multi-modal data, the establishment of a unified data standard platform is an important premise.

By leveraging a standardized data platform and ensuring data security for teachers and students, schools adhere to specific guidelines when handling evaluation information. This facilitates the active exchange of evaluation data among schools in different regions, enhancing the utilization of multimodal data. Additionally, advancements in data collection techniques, such as web crawlers, log data, and code embedding points, are being made to enhance the accuracy of data collection. This enables traceable support for performance evaluation and personalized assessment. Moreover, data integration is being improved by enhancing various technologies including sound, text, images, video, behavior recognition, and tracking. These advancements ensure optimal integration of diverse data, thereby enhancing storage and computation of evaluation data. Finally, advanced technologies like machine learning, knowledge graphs, and natural language processing are being optimized, leading to improved accuracy and interpretability of evaluation data analysis. Consequently, the persuasiveness of evaluation information is significantly enhanced. The application of explanatory representation learning methods in the field of basic education evaluation undoubtedly benefits students in conducting procedural evaluation, outcome evaluation, and value-added assessment.

Acknowledgements. Thanks for the support of the 2022 Ministry of Education Industry-University Cooperation Collaborative Education Project "Artificial Intelligence Boosts Teacher Team Construction, 220604515170027".

References

1. Zhao, C., Wang, R.: Exploring the Essence of Quality Education. China Education News, 2 November 2018
2. Jointly Compiled by 12 Key Normal Universities Across the Country. Foundations of Pedagogy: Educational Science Press (2013)
3. Development Plan for New Generation of Artificial Intelligence. http://www.gov.cn/zhengce/content/2017-07/20/content_5211996.htm. Accessed 5 Feb 2023
4. The General Plan for Deepening Education Evaluation Reform in the New Era. http://www.moe.gov.cn/jyb_xxgk/moe_1777/moe_1778/202010/t20201013_494381.html. Accessed 7 Feb 2023
5. Chen, Y., Chen, C., Hu, Z., et al.: Principles and Applications of Citation Space Analysis Citation Space [A Practical Guide]
6. Qiu, J., Zhang, Q.: Review of Shavinina's intelligence evaluation concept. Psychol. Sci. Adv. **2004**(03), 416–422 (2004)
7. Li, Q.: On information education. Electron. Educ. Res. **2003**(10), 5 (2003)
8. Yu, C.: Cultural and philosophical reflections on teaching evaluation. Educ. Explor. **2011**(03), 20–21 (2011)
9. Guo, X., Fu, G.: Constructing a comprehensive evaluation system of multimedia teaching quality with fuzzy mathematical method. Audio-Visual Educ. Res. **2007**(03), 76–80 (2007)
10. Zhang, F., Ma, H.: Zhejiang: building a school-based comprehensive evaluation system for primary school students. Primary Secondary Sch. Manage. **11**, 13–16 (2022)
11. Cui, Y., Chu, M.W., Chen, F.: Analysing student process data in game-based assessments with Bayesian knowledge tracing and dynamic Bayesian network. J. Educ. Data Min. **11**(1), 80–100 (2019)
12. Wang, G., Kang, Y., Cao, Y.: Finland's unique and stable educational reform and its enlightenment. J. Tianjin Normal Univ. (Soc. Sci. Edn.) **2015**(05), 66–70 (2015)
13. Savolainen, J., Hoveen, A.: The rise and disillusionment of the Finnish educational miracle. Shanghai Educ. **2013**(35) (2013)
14. Zhou, W., Xin, T., Liu, T.: Development of students' personalized learning system under the background of "Internet +": current situation and enlightenment. Tsinghua Univ. Educ. Res. **37**(06), 79–84 (2016)
15. Wang, F., Liu, Q., Chen, E., et al.: Neural cognitive diagnosis for intelligent education systems. Proc. AAAI Conf. Artif. Intell. **34**(04), 6153–6161 2020)
16. Zhou, G., Liu, E.: The pursuit of effective teaching from the American ACOP classroom teaching quality evaluation system. Foreign Educ. Res. **47**(05), 103–118 (2020)
17. Hao, Z., Hou, X., Wang, K.: Experience, restricting factors and optimization suggestions of implementing effective teaching in network learning space—based on in-depth interviews of 11 university teachers. Mod. Distance Educ. **2020**(02), 83–90 (2020)
18. Shen, X., Wu, J., Zhang, Y., et al.: Research on the online learning behavior and learning effect evaluation model of MOOCAP learners. China Distance Educ. **2019**(07), 38–46+93 (2019)
19. Zhou, P., Li, H., Guo, M., et al.: Research on the model and method of interactive evaluation of teaching and research in the network learning space. Electron. Educ. Res. **41**(05), 52–58 (2020)
20. Zhang, B., Chen, Y., Qi, Y., et al.: Research on the comprehensive evaluation model of learners driven by multi-source process data. Inf. Sci. **40**(05), 104–110 (2022)
21. Li, L., He, L., Zhang, H., et al.: Design and implementation of cloud computing basic education quality monitoring and evaluation platform. China Audio-Technol. Educ. **05**, 113–116 (2013)
22. Li, Y., Xu, F., Li, B.: Current situation analysis and improvement suggestions of national data platform for higher education quality monitoring. China Distance Educ. **2022**(04), 65–75 (2022)

Research on Construction Experimental Teaching Model of Artificial Intelligence in High School Based on PBL

Huifeng Zhang[1], Min Xie[1,2(✉)], and Lixian Li[1]

[1] School of Information Science and Technology, Yunnan Normal University,
Kunming 650500, China
294611018@qq.com
[2] Key Laboratory of Education Informatization for Nationalities, Ministry of Education,
Yunnan Normal University, Kunming 650000, China

Abstract. Artificial intelligence is in full swing around the world, and many primary and secondary schools in China also offer AI-related courses, but the teaching practice of AI courses is theoretically oriented, which cannot reflect the comprehensive and practical nature of AI courses. This study applies project learning to high school AI experiments and proposes a project learning-based teaching model for high school AI experiments based on PBL and Bloom's educational goal classification theory to improve students' independent learning ability, innovative thinking and teamwork spirit. The teaching model is consistent with the classification of high school AI experiments, which is subdivided into imitation, design and integrated experimental teaching models. The teaching model is applied in specific experimental cases, and a framework of a high school AI experimental resource system supporting the teaching model is built to provide experimental resources for high school AI courses for teachers and students to use.

Keywords: Project-based Learning · Artificial Intelligence Experiments · Teaching Models · Innovative Thinking

1 Introduction

With the leapfrog development of computer computing speed, artificial intelligence technology has also ushered in a new wave under its impetus, leading the era from traditional informatization to modern artificial intelligence [1]. The Development Plan of New Generation Artificial Intelligence issued by the State Council in July 2017 proposes that by 2030, China's artificial intelligence theory, technology and application should generally reach the world leading level and become the world's major AI innovation center [2]. To achieve this ambitious goal, talent cultivation is the top priority. In this regard, the New Generation Artificial Intelligence Development Plan clearly states that AI-related courses should be set up at the primary and secondary school levels and that universal intelligent education programs should be carried out gradually. Pilot and landing AI courses have been carried out at the primary and secondary school levels

J. Gan et al. (Eds.): CSEI 2023, CCIS 1900, pp. 292–309, 2024.
https://doi.org/10.1007/978-981-99-9492-2_25

across the country, and various AI education programs have been introduced to develop curricula, teaching materials, and various teaching resources to enhance the cognitive level of young people about the current state of AI development and conceptual principles to better adapt to the upcoming comprehensive AI era [3].

Artificial intelligence is a comprehensive course involving knowledge from several disciplines, and high school artificial intelligence experiments are very important in curriculum teaching. Through AI experiments, students can gain an in-depth understanding of the principles and applications of AI and its cross-fertilization with other fields, as well as exercise their practical skills, cultivate their teamwork and problem-solving abilities, and improve their overall quality. At present, most teaching students master AI knowledge mainly by reading textbooks and teachers explaining theoretical knowledge. However, the theoretical approach makes it difficult for students to grasp and understand abstract AI knowledge in depth. Although most of the literature mentions that AI is a highly practical course that requires experimental classes to provide students with an experiential learning environment [4], there is little literature that provides in-depth analysis of experimental classes. In addition, there are some technical and pedagogical difficulties in high school AI experiments; for most high school students, the lack of relevant programming experience may lead to their inability to understand the basic principles and implementation of AI; at the high school level, there is a lack of teaching resources about AI experiments applicable to beginners, which may make it difficult for teachers to find adequate support.

Therefore, in response to the above problems, this study establishes a teaching model that is closer to actual teaching needs, combines PBL with AI experimental teaching, uses projects to start experimental teaching, presents AI experiments in a hierarchical and operable way, stimulates students' interest, cultivates students' practical operation ability, cultivates students' problem-solving ability and innovation ability, and promotes students' learning and application of AI-related theories and technologies.

2 Artificial Intelligence Experiment Classification

In the Artificial Intelligence Development Standards for Primary and Secondary Schools (hereafter referred to as the Standards), around the theme of AI curriculum, the Standards set out six different types of core practices from macroperception experience to microprogramming, which are life perception and investigation practice, simple simulation and reasoning practice, black-box inquiry practice, AI hardware design practice, principle revealing practice and AI programming practice. The Black Box Inquiry Practice and AI Hardware Design Practice allow students to gain a deeper understanding of the underlying technologies and innovative applications of AI and enhance their problem solving and engineering design skills; the Principle Revealing Practice and AI Programming Practice allow students to grasp the core technologies and applications of AI. The principle revealing practice and AI programming practice allow students to master the core technologies and theories in the field of artificial intelligence and develop innovative thinking and programming skills.

2.1 Bloom's Taxonomy of Educational Objectives

Bloom, a famous American educational psychologist and educator, first proposed the "taxonomy of educational objectives" in 1948. Bloom's taxonomy of educational goals includes three goal areas: cognitive, affective and motor skills, each of which contains systematic and complex categories with strong practical orientation and operability and is an important guide for the analysis of the whole curriculum or unit teaching [5]. One of them, closely related to high school AI experiments, is cognitive goal classification theory.

Bloom's cognitive goal classification is based on the law that human cognitive processes move from concrete to abstract and from simple to complex as its basic theoretical basis. The theory assumes that complex problems are often the result of the association of simpler behaviors. According to this view, the cognitive process is divided into the process of transferring from lower to higher levels, and a complete theoretical system of classifying educational objectives in the cognitive domain is constructed: six levels: memory, comprehension, application, analysis, evaluation and creation. Imitation-type experiments correspond to the comprehension level, design-type experiments correspond to the analysis level, and synthesis-type experiments correspond to the creation level.

According to the six core practice types and Bloom's goal classification theory, this study classified AI experiments into three types of experiments: imitation, design and synthesis, whose tasks and awareness difficulties range from simple to complex [6]. The experimental teaching objectives of the three types of experiments, imitation, design and synthesis, point to three levels of basic knowledge, problem solving and innovative thinking, respectively. Among them, basic knowledge is the foundation of course learning, emphasizing the understanding and application of basic AI knowledge; problem solving is the core, emphasizing the ability to synthesize AI knowledge and technology to solve problems; and innovative thinking is the soul, emphasizing the discovery of new problems or the discovery of AI knowledge to solve problems. The relationship between the three types of experiments and the six core types of practice and Bloom's classification objectives is shown in Fig. 1.

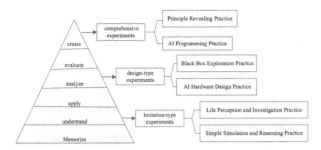

Fig. 1. Diagram of the relationship between experiment type and cognitive goal

2.2 Imitation-Based Experiments

Imitation-based experiments are used to train AI algorithms by imitating existing data or models to achieve a specific task or solve a problem. The role of imitation-based experiments in teaching is to promote students' understanding of basic AI knowledge through experiments that require students to memorize and understand what they have already learned, and the experiments are simple enough for students to complete independently or by imitation. Imitation-based experiments can provide students with the basic knowledge to quickly grasp the experimental steps and principles; at the same time, they can also help students enhance their experimental operation skills and understand the use of experimental equipment and tools. Such experiments should not be too many because they are at the lower order of Bloom's cognitive goals, but there should be enough of them to serve as the basis for higher-level experiments.

2.3 Design-Based Experiments

Design-based experiments are experiments in which students design, develop, and implement projects to gain a deeper understanding and application of artificial intelligence technologies. Design-based experiments are designed to expose students to new knowledge about AI, allow them to learn about new knowledge and learn to apply it in practice, develop their problem-solving skills, and improve their general literacy and practical skills. Such experiments encourage students to explore various aspects of AI technologies, including algorithms, programming, data analysis, and machine learning, through innovation and practice. Design-based experiments go beyond mere knowledge transfer and emphasize students' initiative and creativity in learning AI technologies through hands-on exploration.

2.4 Comprehensive Experiments

Comprehensive experiments refer to the combination of several different knowledge points and skills into one project to develop students' comprehensive application, teamwork and problem-solving skills. Comprehensive experiments are more complex than imitation and design types, mainly for the decomposition of complex problems. In the experiment students all understand the relevant knowledge and learn to apply and decompose knowledge points to solve problems, mainly in the form of group cooperation. In the integrated type of experiments, students need to think and innovate independently, flexibly use the knowledge and skills learned, give full play to their imagination and creativity, and experience the power and potential of artificial intelligence technology in practice. The characteristics of each dimension of the three kinds of experiments of imitation, design and synthesis are shown in Table 1.

Table 1. Characteristics of each dimension of the three kinds of experiments

Dimension	Imitation-based experiments	Design-based experiments	Comprehensive experiments
Purpose of the experiment	Familiarize with the basic knowledge of artificial intelligence, algorithm principles and processes	Cultivate the ability of innovation and problem solving	Cultivate comprehensive application ability and teamwork ability
Experiment Format	Experiment according to a given algorithm flow	Design your own algorithm flow and complete the experiment	Combine several different knowledge and skills into one project
Experimental requirements	Understand the principle and process of algorithm	Be able to design the algorithm process and complete the experiment independently	Strong general quality and teamwork ability
Experimental difficulty	Low	Medium	High
Experimental time	Short	Medium	Long
Experimental results	Simple algorithm implementations	Projects with some creativity and difficulty	Integrated projects in multiple disciplines and skill areas
Experimental evaluation	Correctness and efficiency of algorithm implementation	Creativity and difficulty of the project, problem solving ability	Project integration, teamwork and problem solving skills

3 Construction of the PBL-Based Artificial Intelligence Experimental Teaching Model

3.1 Project-Based Learning

Project-based learning (PBL) sprouted from the theories of the American educator Dewey and continued to develop from the design-based pedagogy of Kebchik [7]. Project-based learning aims to immerse students in the process of meaningful task completion, allowing them to actively learn and autonomously construct knowledge, with student-generated knowledge and developed competencies as the highest achievement goal [8]. Project-based learning focuses on core concepts and principles in the discipline, and it requires students to problem solve and explore some meaningful activity or other learning or work in the real world where students live, work, and learn [9].

Project learning is a kind of teaching method that takes students as the main body and gives full play to the guiding role of teachers. The teaching method has been introduced in China since the introduction of various teaching pilots in primary and secondary schools and colleges and universities and has achieved notable teaching results. This series of teaching practices proves that the project teaching method is fully suitable for all stages of education in China and is a scientific teaching method that is consistent with the construction of teaching theory and promotes students' overall development [10]. At present, there are fewer teaching designs and experimental cases for high school AI experiments, which leads to teachers' shallow understanding of AI experiments and less reflection of students' practical hands-on ability in AI experiments. Compared with traditional experimental teaching and project-based teaching, the former has the advantage of systematic subject knowledge transfer and an obvious teacher-led role and the disadvantage of low student participation [11]. Project-based learning focuses on the team combination of groups to achieve the collective power of brainstorming in the form of groups [12], which is often carried out in AI experimental classes by forming different learning groups with several students as members, and such a teaching format fits well with project-based learning. Therefore, applying project-based learning to high school AI experiments can better stimulate students' interest in learning, help them improve their practical skills, enhance their independent innovation ability, improve their comprehensive application ability, and adapt to the needs of cultivating talent in the digital era.

3.2 High School Artificial Intelligence Experimental Teaching Objectives

The standard mentions that "based on the comprehensive, practical and developmental characteristics of the subject of artificial intelligence, learning tasks and activity scenarios are designed, project-based learning is used as the carrying form, and the acquisition of basic knowledge and important abilities of the subject is permeated in the advancement of learning tasks." Experimental teaching of artificial intelligence in high school should be practice-oriented, combining theory and practice, focusing on students' innovation and inquiry spirit, and encouraging students to actively participate in experimental operations and experimental assessment. This study is the construction of a PBL-based AI experimental teaching mode. The teaching objectives are mainly 3 levels of basic knowledge, problem solving and innovative thinking. The purpose of this teaching mode construction is to allow teachers to better master the teaching process of AI experimental courses. In experimental teaching through group cooperation, task-driven and other teaching methods combined with the project learning approach, students are guided for each project. The experimental tasks are analysed to encourage students to find problems and solve them, to complete the learning of artificial intelligence knowledge, and to cultivate students' innovation ability and practical ability.

3.3 Design of the AI Experimental Teaching Model Based on PBL

Based on Liu Jingfu's project-based learning, this study combines the basic process of project-based learning and the teaching objectives of the high school AI course, referring to the project-based learning model of high school IT subjects constructed by Fan Luyao and He Yangyang, takes Bloom's education goal classification theory and project-based learning theory as the theoretical basis, and then constructs three teaching models according to the experiment types of AI: imitation-based experiment teaching mode (shown in Fig. 2), design-based experimental teaching mode (shown in Fig. 3), and comprehensive experimental teaching mode (shown in Fig. 4). The experimental teaching model consists of five parts: experimental teaching objectives, experimental teaching contents, experimental teaching methods, teaching process and teaching evaluation.

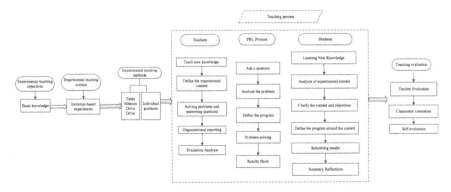

Fig. 2. Imitation-type experimental teaching mode

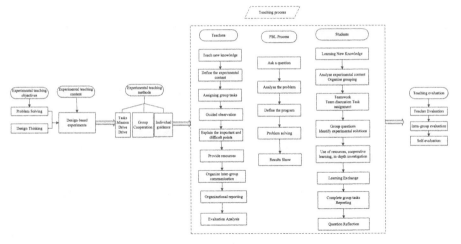

Fig. 3. Design-based experimental teaching model

Imitation-Based Experimental Teaching Mode. The teaching objective of the imitation-type experimental teaching mode points to basic knowledge, promotes students' understanding of the basic knowledge of artificial intelligence through experiments, and enables students to master the knowledge they have learned and learn simple applications in the process of doing experiments. Imitation-type experiments are mainly individual experiments with simple tasks; usually, after the teacher's explanation of theoretical knowledge, students are allowed to conduct experiments to facilitate a better understanding of what they have learned. The teaching method of this experiment is task-driven and individual guidance; task-driven is the teacher through the problem, letting students around the problem to carry out experiments, driven by the problem

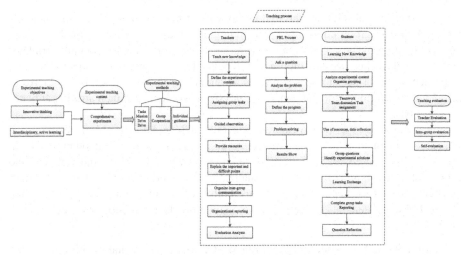

Fig. 4. Comprehensive experimental teaching mode

motivation, students based on experimental resources, the application of theoretical knowledge of artificial intelligence, independent completion of the experimental content, so that students can think independently, problem solving, so that students can experience the process of knowledge formation; individual guidance is students in the experimental operation, the encounter more difficult problems, teachers promptly give individual guidance to students to help them to be able to complete the experiment well.

The teaching process of imitation experiments is consistent with the process of PBL and requires less awareness and ability of students. Before the experimental operation, the teacher will explain the knowledge points involved in the experiment and send the relevant experimental teaching resources to the students. After students complete the experiments, the teacher allows them to demonstrate the experiments to test the learning effect. Finally, the teacher will explain the problems found in the experiments.

Imitation-based experimental resources generally include AI platforms, datasets, programming experimental documents, tools and libraries, teaching videos/lectures, and related literature. The teaching evaluation of the experiments mainly uses multiple evaluation methods, such as teacher evaluation and self-evaluation, to improve teaching efficiency and promote students' active and comprehensive development. It is also easier to implement automated evaluation because there are few parts of students' free development.

Design-Based Experimental Teaching Mode. The goal of the experimental teaching mode of design-based experiments is problem solving and design thinking and cultivating students' ability to analyse and solve problems. In the experiment, the teacher gives the experimental purpose and requirements for students to design and implement their own solutions. Before the experiment is carried out, the teacher will provide experimental resources for students to learn, design experiments will involve some unlearned knowledge, and students need to find and learn their own materials. In the experiments, students need to take the experimental purpose and content as the starting point and create experimental solutions through group work. The experimental teaching methods are task-driven, group cooperation and individual guidance, and individual guidance is mainly the provision of learning resources. The teaching process is mainly student-oriented and teacher-assisted, mobilizing students' learning enthusiasm and giving them sufficient time for peer-to-peer communication and discussion, which is conducive to students' observation, comparison, and analysis of problems and then arriving at better conclusions.

Design-based experiment resources generally include AI platforms, datasets, experiment documentation, tools and libraries, design idea sharing, and other hands-on resources (e.g., APIs for students to develop their own applications and websites and some free libraries and tools for data visualization and interpretation). When performing design-based experimental manipulations, both the instructor and peers give real-time evaluations, and students reimprove them, facilitating the production of excellent work [13].

Comprehensive Experimental Teaching Mode. The experimental teaching objectives of the integrated experimental teaching mode are innovative thinking and interdisciplinary, active learning, focusing on the cultivation of innovative thinking, allowing students to apply theoretical knowledge more flexibly to practical situations, and cultivating students' interdisciplinary integration, in-depth thinking and innovative thinking skills. There are more knowledge points involved in the comprehensive experiments, allowing students to combine the knowledge points they have learned, make full use of the resources released by the teacher, collect information, carry out experimental research in small groups, and then finally complete a report on the experiment. Comprehensive experiments are more difficult, have complex problems and are basically conducted in small groups with a clear division of labor among the members of the group to examine students' teamwork skills.

When conducting integrated AI experiments, because the experiments themselves are more complex and require students to combine knowledge from both imitation and design-based experiments, teachers need to provide more comprehensive experimental resources, including experimental platforms and environments, integrated datasets, programming experiment documentation, experimental case sharing, tools and libraries, experimental projects, and other related resources.

Relationship of the Three Teaching Modes. The imitation-based experimental teaching mode can enable students to have a more concrete understanding of the basic concepts of AI and master the basic skills of AI. The design-based experimental teaching mode can improve students' independent learning and problem-solving ability and enable them to acquire more comprehensive abilities and professional skills in practice so that they can master the basic knowledge of AI more comprehensively. The integrated experimental teaching mode can enhance students' hands-on practice ability, and students will spend much time on practical operations, which can provide an in-depth understanding of the practical applications and problem-solving methods of AI. There are similarities and differences among the three experimental teaching modes (as shown in Table 2).

Table 2. Similarities and differences of the three experimental teaching modes

		Imitation type experimental teaching mode	Design type experimental teaching mode	Comprehensive type experimental teaching mode
Similarities		All three experimental teaching modes require the support of basic knowledge, such as theoretical knowledge and empirical knowledge; all are oriented to the experimental purpose, and the experimental process focuses on improving methods and increasing efficiency; all emphasize visualization of experimental results, which helps developers to verify and observe the results		
Differences	The purpose and significance of the experiment are different	To enable students to quickly grasp the experimental steps and principles, and enhance experimental operation skills	Students develop their creative thinking skills and problem solving abilities	Integrate existing knowledge and skills, enhance teamwork ability and improve overall quality
	The difference of experimental processing	The processing is relatively simple and is learning from big data	Need to design an artificial intelligence system based on the theory, which requires more specific and detailed operation	Need to combine imitation-type experiments and design-type experiments, with more detailed experimental design and experimental operations, more specific and rich in levels and depth

(*continued*)

Table 2. (*continued*)

		Imitation type experimental teaching mode	Design type experimental teaching mode	Comprehensive type experimental teaching mode
The difference in cost and difficulty of experiments		Relatively low cost and difficulty	Requires a lot of experimental experience, ponderous data analysis and processing skills, and is more costly and difficult than imitation-type experiments	Requires a lot of experimental experience, more comprehensive thinking ability and programming skills, and requires continuous experimentation based on the first two experimental methods in order to gradually improve the systematic design
Differences in experimental requirements and design		Students are not required to design the experimental protocol, they only need to follow the experimental steps	Students need to conceive their own experimental protocols and design their own experimental procedures	Students need to integrate the knowledge and skills from both imitation-based and design-based experiments to complete the experiment

There is a strong connection between the three experimental teaching modes. Imitation-based experiments and design-based experimental teaching modes are the basis of AI experiments, while the integrated experimental teaching mode combines the two to further explore the potential of AI systems. The three experimental teaching modes differ in the process and content of experiments, etc., but there are also certain relationships among them.

(1) Each of the three experimental teaching modes can be considered a gradual upgrading process. In imitation experiments, students mainly copy and practice existing experimental operations and principles; in design experiments, students can use their existing knowledge to create new experiments, which increases their thinking ability; and in comprehensive experiments, students need to combine the first two types to better integrate their knowledge and skills.

(2) The three experimental teaching modes promote each other, not only to deepen the understanding and mastery of knowledge but also to enhance the practical application ability of students. Imitation experiments and design experiments can complement each other. Imitation experiments can provide an experimental basis for design experiments, while design experiments can strengthen students' theoretical thinking and creative ability.

(3) Although the three experimental teaching modes are different, they also have something in common, that is, they all focus on the cultivation of students' practical and application skills. From imitation experiments to design experiments to comprehensive experiments, students need to use their knowledge to solve practical problems so that they can complete the experiments in practice and improve their practical application ability.

In summary, in high school AI experiments, imitation-type experiments, design-type experiments and comprehensive experiments are all very important experimental modes, each of which has its own characteristics, and they can all effectively promote the improvement of students' knowledge reserves, experimental operation ability and experimental thinking ability and help students' overall development.

4   Artificial Intelligence Experimental Teaching Mode Application

4.1   Overall Design of High School Artificial Intelligence Experiments

This study was conducted based on the content of the high school version of Fundamentals of Artificial Intelligence, a textbook for high school students, which was prepared by Shang Tang Technology, the world's leading artificial intelligence platform company, in cooperation with the Catechism Center of East China Normal University [14]. According to the constructed teaching model and the determined teaching objectives, the important and difficult points in the teaching contents, the experiments are related to the contents in the Fundamentals of Artificial Intelligence (high school version), and the case materials related to high school AI experiments are collected on domestic and foreign AI websites to write teaching cases of each knowledge point and its related contents. Table 3 gives examples of teaching cases based on the teaching mode of high school AI experiments. Three types of experiments, imitation (27.2% of the total number of experiments), design (36.4% of the total number of experiments) and synthesis (36.4% of the total number of experiments), are discussed.

4.2   Imitation-Based Experimental Example

Taking the perceptron-based binary classification experiment case as an example, the experimental teaching objectives are to master the basic steps of binary classification; to recognize the basic principles of classifiers and the important role of algorithms in the classification process; and to be able to describe the role of loss functions in classifier training. The teacher prepares relevant experimental resources before the class: the openinnolab AI experimental platform used in the class, the Iris-related

Table 3. Overall design of experimental teaching of artificial intelligence in high school

Experimental case name	Experimental case content	Type of experiment
How to determine if a machine has intelligence	1. Tsinghua JiuGe ancient poetry creation system 2. chatgpt	Imitation-based experiments
Iris classification	Classify iris and master the principles and applications of dichotomy	Imitation-based experiments
Handwritten number recognition	Understand the basic principles and applications of machine learning	Imitation-based experiments
Image recognition and classification	Using a deep learning framework such as TensorFlow or Keras, build and train models to detect whether different objects in the test set are correctly classified	Design-based experiments
Sound waveforms and spectral characteristics	1. Observe the waveform graph; 2. Digitize the sound 3. Observe the frequency spectral line; 4. Extract sound features MFCC	Design-based experiments
Voice Recognition	Students can build a speech recognition system using tools such as Python, TensorFlow, and a speech recognition API. This system can recognize human speech and then convert it to text	Design-based experiments
Video Behavior Recognition	Effective feature extraction and representation of spatiotemporal features of videos	Design-based experiments
Clustering of data	Classification of iris using K-means clustering	Comprehensive experiments
Text Sentiment Analysis	Through experiments, you will master the overall process of text analysis and learn about text classification, sentiment analysis, and automatic summarization	Comprehensive experiments

(*continued*)

Table 3. (*continued*)

Experimental case name	Experimental case content	Type of experiment
Face Recognition	The support vector machine algorithm is used to train and learn the extracted image features to derive a face classification model	Comprehensive experiments
Machine learning based image classification and item recognition system	We design and implement a complete image classification and item recognition system by combining image processing, machine learning and deep learning techniques	Comprehensive experiments

dataset, the perceptron-based Iris dichotomous classification programming experimental documentation, and relevant teaching videos.

Experimental teaching process: (1) The teacher determines the experimental content for perceptron-based binary classification. After determining the experimental content, the teacher explains the project steps for perceptron-based iris binary classification: loading the iris dataset; dividing the training set and test set; perceptron training; and model evaluation. The relevant code will be run out so that students will learn to load the iris data, use the perceptron algorithm, train the classifier, and observe the process of classifier training by adjusting the training parameters.

(2) The teacher will send the students the relevant resources for the experiment Iris code examples and the purpose, steps and requirements of the experiment. Students determine the experimental content, clarify the main objectives of the perceptron-based dichotomous classification experimental case, conduct experimental operations and data processing around the experimental content and the experimental steps explained by the teacher; finally, they analyse the experimental data and draw conclusions; when students encounter problems they do not understand, they promptly ask the teacher, who solves the problems and answers them.

(3) Students submit their results, the teacher selects several students to present their experimental works, and the teacher and students summarize the problems and solutions encountered during the experiments and discuss the prospects for the application of machine learning algorithms. The final grading is evaluated by the teacher, peer evaluation and self-evaluation. The teacher should evaluate and guide the students' experimental reports and provide guidance for students to improve their experimental operation ability and experimental thinking level.

4.3 Example of a Design-Based Experiment

The design-based experimental case takes the case of clustering the iris dataset with k-means as an example. The experimental teaching objective is to understand basic unsupervised learning and to experience the use of unsupervised learning in real life to master the principle of the k-means algorithm. The teacher prepares relevant experimental resources before the class: the openinnolab artificial intelligence experiment platform used in the class, the iris dataset, experimental documents and design ideas to share.

Experimental teaching process: (1) The teacher determines the experimental content for clustering the iris dataset with k-means. After determining the content of the experiment, the teacher explains the project steps for clustering the iris dataset with k-means: import the iris dataset iris and BaseML library; define the k-value (number of clusters), maximum number of iterations, and error tolerance; initialize the centroids; perform the following operations until the stopping conditions are met: assign each sample to the cluster with the centroid closest to it; rec-calculate the centroids of each cluster; calculate the distance between the centroids of this iteration and the previous iteration, and determine whether it is less than the error tolerance; and output the final clustering results.

(2) The teacher will distribute the experimental resources: code examples, experimental purpose, steps and requirements and the Iris dataset to the students. Each group will determine the content of the experiment and assign tasks to group members, and each group will discuss and use the resources given online and by the teacher to explore in depth the principle of k-means for clustering the Iris dataset. Finally, each group will come up with its own clustering model. The teacher should observe the completion of each group while the group is discussing and give appropriate help. Finally, the teacher organizes the groups to communicate and report. After the group reports, the teacher evaluates the groups experimentally to check whether they have mastered the basic principles and methods of k-means clustering of iris datasets and whether they can apply what they have learned in practice.

4.4 Examples of Comprehensive Experiments

Comprehensive experiments are more complex and involve more knowledge points, and students work in small groups to start learning. Taking the Chinese word separation principle and text feature representation experiment as an example, the experimental teaching objectives are to master the application process of text feature extraction using the bag-of-words model, to understand latent semantic analysis techniques and to be able to analyse and process small-scale text data using latent semantic analysis techniques. Teachers prepare relevant experimental resources before the class: the openinnolab AI experimental platform and environment used in the class, experimental datasets related to text features, programming experimental documents, and experimental case sharing about the bag-of-words model.

Experimental teaching process: (1) The teacher determines the experimental content of keyword extraction and text feature representation, assigns group tasks, and explains the activities of the experiment: calculating the word count vector and word frequency vector of a text; calculating the word frequency vector after removing stop words; and calculating the word frequency-inverse text frequency feature of a text.

(2) The instructor provides detailed experimental instructions and programming documentation, including basic concepts, algorithm and model descriptions, as well as experimental difficulties, solutions and relevant datasets. After each group determines

the solution based on the principles of keyword extraction and text feature representation, according to the resources provided by the teacher and finding materials and codes on the Internet, the teacher organizes each group to communicate and report the solution, and each group reports their own group's experimental model after students finish, and finally, the teacher and each group evaluate.

5 Framework Design of the High School Artificial Intelligence Experimental Resource System

With the continuous development of artificial intelligence technology, an increasing number of schools are offering artificial intelligence courses. In this paper, we build a framework of a high school AI experimental resource system based on the PBL high school AI experimental teaching model to provide rich experimental resources for students and teachers to use in experimental teaching. The high school AI experimental resource system is composed of three parts: user layer, application layer and data layer, as shown in Fig. 5.

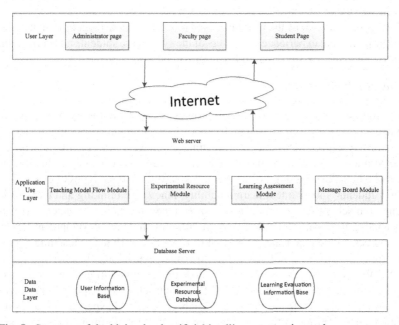

Fig. 5. Structure of the high school artificial intelligence experimental resource system

(1) Data layer. The data layer is the data management part of the system and is responsible for storing and managing the data in the system. The data layer in the high school artificial intelligence experiment resource system includes a user information database, experiment resource database and learning evaluation information

database. The user information database stores information about teachers and students; the experimental resource database stores experimental resources of three types of experiments, including videos, texts, datasets and resources linked to other experimental platforms; and the learning evaluation database stores evaluation scales related to experiments.

(2) Application layer: the application layer is the business logic processing part of the system, responsible for processing user requests and giving the corresponding response to provide effective functional support for users. The application layer of the high school artificial intelligence experiment resource system contains the teaching mode process, experiment resources, learning evaluation and message board. The teaching mode flow module helps teachers prepare and teach experiments step by step according to the steps of the three teaching modes; the experiment resource module has the functions of uploading experiment resources, downloading experiment resources and deleting experiment resources; the learning evaluation module sets test points to evaluate students' knowledge and ability according to the experiment objectives; and the message board allows students to post their learning questions on the message board and teachers or other learners. The message board allows students to post their learning questions on the message board and teachers or other learners to answer them.

(3) User layer. The goal of the user layer is to provide users with a convenient, easy-to-use, and efficient experience. The users of the system are students and corresponding instructors who are studying high school AI courses.

6   Conclusion

Current high school AI teaching has the problem of favoring theory over experiment. This paper constructs a PBL-based high school AI experimental teaching model, which consists of five aspects: experimental teaching objectives, experimental teaching content, experimental teaching methods, teaching process and teaching evaluation. Three experimental teaching modes are constructed according to three types of experiments to improve students' independent learning ability, innovative thinking and teamwork. By dividing high school AI experiments into three types, teachers can match experiments corresponding to cognitive levels based on different students' development levels and find resources on the experimental system to support experimental teaching. However, the creativity of teachers is still needed in experimental teaching. Teachers need to think carefully about how to choose problems, how to design solutions, and how to guide experiments to better apply the ideas of PBL to high school AI experimental teaching.

In subsequent research, the construction of high school AI experimental cases should be strengthened, and the corresponding high school AI experimental resource system should be realized to provide richer resources for high school AI experimental teaching.

Acknowledgements. Project funding: 1. Yunnan Key Laboratory of Smart Education. 2. Project on the cultivation of higher education undergraduate teaching achievements at the provincial and university levels of Yunnan Normal University: the collaborative construction and practice of a double-cycle training system for teacher-training students' teaching ability. Yunnan International Joint R&D Center of China-Laos-Thailand Educational Digitalization, Project No.: 202203AP140006.

References

1. Wang, W.: Exploration of innovative intelligent technology talents cultivation. High Technol. Industrialization **10**, 62–63 (2013)
2. Ministry of Education of the People's Republic of China. Notice of the Ministry of Education on the Issuance of the Education Informatization 2.0 Action Plan [EB/OL], 18 April 2018. http://www.moe.gov.cn/srcsite/A16/s3342/201804/t20180425_334188.html
3. Wang, Z.Q.: Current issues and reflections on artificial intelligence education in primary and secondary schools. China Mod. Educ. Equip. **22**, 1–5 (2019)
4. Wu, J., Yin, C.: Exploring the construction of experimental teaching resources for high school artificial intelligence courses. China Educ. Technol. Equip. **473**(23), 58–60+68 (2019)
5. Hu, H.: Project-based learning: a classroom teaching activity for developing students' core literacy. J. Lanzhou Univ. (Soc. Sci. Edn.) **45**(6), 165–172 (2017)
6. Jin, S.: Research on deep learning evaluation based on Bloom's cognitive process dimension. Huazhong Normal University (2020). https://doi.org/10.27159/d.cnki.ghzsu.2020.002487
7. Pan, C., Xiao, W., Wang, T., et al.: Research on reconstructing the practical teaching system of computer science in local universities under the background of new engineering. J. Hefei Univ. Technol. (Soc. Sci. Edn.) **33**(05), 130–133 (2019)
8. Hou, X.: Research on the application of project-based learning (PBL) in secondary school information technology class. Inner Mongolia Normal University (2007)
9. Zhi, C.: Research on teachers' information technology application and training model. Primary Secondary Sch. e-Learn. **06**, 9–11 (2007)
10. Zhang, W., Yang, Y., Jin, J., Nie, F., Wang, Y.: A comprehensive exploration and practice of robotics practice teaching system. China's Electrochem. Educ. **2022**(07), 115–119 (2022)
11. Bian, S., Wang, J., Cui, X., et al.: Research on the experimental teaching mode of "online teaching + project training." Exp. Technol. Manage. **38**(03), 201–206 (2021). https://doi.org/10.16791/j.cnki.sjg.2021.03.041
12. Chen, H.: Research on the teaching model of project-based learning for the cultivation of computational thinking. Chin. J. Educ. **2023**(S1), 159–160+163 (2023)
13. Lu, X.: Characteristics and implementation path of project-based learning. Educ. Theory Pract. **40**(08), 59–61 (2020)
14. Fundamentals of Artificial Intelligence (High School Edition). Basic Educ. Curriculum **2018**(11), 81 (2018)

A Study and Analysis of Predicting College Students' Final Exam Scores by Integrating Physical Fitness Test Data and Poverty Level Information

Nuo Xu[1] ⓘ, Xiaoli Zhang[1](✉), Guifu Zhu[2], Jun Wen[1], Jialei Nie[1], and Can Yang[1]

[1] Faculty of Information Engineering and Automation, Kunming University of Science and Technology, Kunming, China
zxl_km@kust.edu.cn

[2] Information Technology Center, Kunming University of Science and Technology, Kunming, China

Abstract. To accurately predict the final exam scores of college students, a prediction model based on random forest is constructed by collecting data that may affect the final exam scores from multiplatform databases. The performance of this model is compared with the traditional neural networks and support vector machine model. At the same time, to further optimize the model, a feature selection method based on the random forest is proposed. The number of input parameters was increased or decreased in turn to establish a new model. The contribution of each input parameter to the overall model was calculated through the changes in the accuracy of the models before and after. The parameters required for modelling are selected according to the contribution of each parameter; in this manner, the model is simplified. The results show that the random forest model is better in fitting ability, generalization and fitting accuracy than the traditional neural networks and support vector machine. Feature selection can effectively simplify the model and improve prediction accuracy. Through the verification on the data of students in another grade, the model is universal.

Keywords: Regression Prediction · Educational Data · Physical Fitness Test · Machine Learning · Feature Selection

1 Introduction

With the rapid popularity of online education in China, big data in education has also ushered in a spurt of growth. An increasing number of scholars have focused on the problem of score prediction. An effective prediction model can help teachers make reasonable teaching plans and give accurate and timely feedback on students' learning processes, which has certain theoretical significance and teaching application value. For this reason, scholars at home and abroad have performed much research. In terms of prediction based on offline learning data, Farshid et al. [1, 2] used attendance, class

© The Author(s), under exclusive license to Springer Nature Singapore Pte Ltd. 2024
J. Gan et al. (Eds.): CSEI 2023, CCIS 1900, pp. 310–324, 2024.
https://doi.org/10.1007/978-981-99-9492-2_26

performance, in-class tests and homework as input parameters of the model, and the prediction accuracy was over 81%. Rovira et al. [3, 4] used the grades of prior courses to predict the grades of subsequent courses and found that the model had a good effect. In terms of online learning data prediction, Qian T. et al. [5, 6] found a positive correlation between online learning data and exam grades.

However, in feature selection, the input parameters of most models are selected based on experience or linear analysis methods. Selecting input parameters according to someone's experience is prone to misjudgment due to subjective factors. Considering that the study of college students' learning data and performance is a nonlinear problem, linear analysis tends to produce errors. Therefore, this study compared and analyzed five regression prediction models and selected the machine learning model with the best performance to predict the final exam scores of college students. Furthermore, a feature selection method of input parameters based on random forest is proposed to explore the specific factors that affect college students' performance to provide references for students to develop good learning habits and teachers to develop teaching plans.

2 Experimental Data

2.1 Data Sources

The data used in this paper are from the educational administration system database, the Rain Classroom online education platform and the physical fitness test database of a certain university, and the data have been desensitized. The dataset mainly includes the final exam results, poverty level and physical fitness test data. In addition, since the final exam scores of college students are affected by many factors, this paper adds the attendance rate of Rain Classroom as auxiliary data on the basis of the educational administration system and physical fitness test database in the model construction. The specific information of the experimental data is shown in Table 1.

Poverty Level Data. The data on students' poverty level in each semester used in the paper were collected from the table of students' basic information in the educational administration system. Poverty level data of 17,590 students from the first semester of 2019 to the first semester of 2022 were collected, with a total of 57,416 records. In these records, impoverished students are divided into three grades: general poverty, poverty, and special poverty. In this research, the value 1, 2, and 3 are used to refer to this discrete value.

Attendance Data of Rain Classroom. The attendance rate is collected from the online platform of Rain Classroom. Rain Classroom is an online education platform based in China. It offers a wide range of online courses and educational services, catering to various subjects, exam preparation, and skill development. This research selects the number of classes and attendance of 42,239 students from the first semester of 2021 to the second semester of 2022 to calculate each student's attendance rate per semester.

Final Exam Data. The average scores of the final exam of each semester are from the exam records table of the educational administration system database. In this paper, 11,001 students' 855,496 test results in the grades of 2017 and 2018 are selected to calculate the average final exam score for each student per semester.

Physical Fitness Test Data. The physical test data used in this paper are from the physical fitness test database of the university, and 11055 students' physical fitness test data in the 2020 academic year are selected.

With the above experimental data cleaned and correlated, a dataset consisting of 693 students from grade 2017 and 224 students from grade 2018 was obtained. This paper compared the performance of different models and performed feature extraction on samples of 224 students from grade 2018. A total of 693 students from grade 2017 were taken as extended samples to verify the universality of the feature extraction model.

Table 1. Experimental data and sources.

Data Source	Data Names	Variable Names	Units
Educational administration system database	Poverty level in the first semester	201801PL	N/A
	Poverty level in the second semester	201802PL	N/A
	...	...	...
	Poverty level in the seventh semester	202101PL	N/A
Rain Classroom platform	Rain Classroom attendance rate	YTKAR	N/A
Educational administration system database	Average score in the first semester	201801FES	N/A
	Average score in the second semester	201802FES	N/A
	...	...	...
	Average score in the seventh semester	202101FES	N/A
Physical fitness test database	Height	HEIHGT	cm
	Weight	WEIGHT	kg
	Vital capacity	VITALCAP	ml
	50 m race	50MRACE	s
	Standing long jump	LONGJUMP	cm
	Sit-and-reach	SITREACH	cm

2.2 Data Partitioning and Processing

To reduce the number of experiments, the training set should be used with as little data as possible while ensuring the accuracy of the model. According to the ubiquity and uniformity principle of neural network sample partitioning, the training set samples should include all student samples as much as possible. In this study, 80% of the uniformly distributed data are randomly split as training data and 20% as testing data.

It is easy to slow down the model fitting and increase the prediction error due to the large difference in the variability range of each parameter. It is necessary to normalize the model data to eliminate errors due to inconsistent parameter ranges. Among the various normalization methods, the normalization treatment is chosen, and its specific formulation is as follows:

$$V_{norm} = \frac{V_i - V_{min}}{V_{max} - V_{min}}(V_h - V_l) + V_l \tag{1}$$

In Eq. (1), V_i is the data to be processed; V_{norm} is the normalized result of V_i; V_{max} is the maximum value in the data; V_{min} is the minimum value in the data; V_h is the upper limit of the normalized result; and V_l is the lower limit of the normalized result.

In this study, $V_h = 1$, $V_l = 0$, so that the processed data are distributed between [0,1]. After the above treatment, the values of each indicator are at the same quantitative level, which is beneficial for model building. When looking at the model output, denormalization is applied to obtain realistic scale predictions.

3 Design and Establishment of Model

Due to the stochastic nature of the machine learning model's own fitting, its model prediction accuracy can fluctuate significantly. As a result, in practical applications, the prediction accuracy of the model cannot be guaranteed when the experimental results are unknown, which has a large impact on the performance evaluation of the model. To overcome this drawback of a single neural network, K-fold cross-validation is used to make full use of limited data, reduce the bias introduced by unreasonable data partitioning, and improve the accuracy of model evaluation.

3.1 Algorithm

Random forest (RF) is an integrated learning method that integrates multiple decision tree models and improves the accuracy of the model by synthesizing the prediction results of each model [7]. Its basic structure is shown in Fig. 1

In RF regression, many decision trees are first generated by randomly selecting some subset of the data from the training data. Then, each decision tree is applied to the test data, and their predictions $h_i(x)$ are computed. Finally, the average of the predictions of all decision trees $H(x)$ is taken as the final prediction of RF regression, and the specific formula is shown in Eq. (2).

$$H(x) = \frac{1}{n}\sum_{i=1}^{n} h_i(x) \tag{2}$$

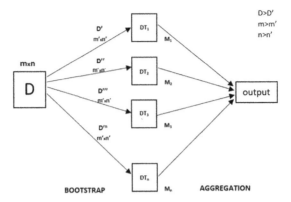

Fig. 1. Schematic diagram of the random forest model structure

3.2 Model Evaluation Methods

To accurately compare the pros and cons of the models' prediction effect, this paper uses the root mean square error (RMSE), the mean absolute error (MAE), the mean deviation error (MBE) and the determination coefficient (R^2) to represent the accuracy of the models.

RMSE is the most commonly used indicator to evaluate the prediction accuracy of a regression model, which measures the degree of deviation between the actual observed value and the predicted value.

MAE is also an indicator used to evaluate the prediction accuracy of the regression model. It is similar to the calculation method of RMSE, but MAE pays more attention to the absolute deviation between the actual observed value and the predicted value.

MBE is used to measure the vector average prediction error of the model.

R^2 is used to measure how well the predicted value fits the real value [8]. The specific formulas for calculation are as follows:

$$RMSE = \sqrt{\frac{\sum_{i=1}^{n}(y_i - \hat{y}_i)^2}{n}} \tag{3}$$

$$MAE = \frac{\sum_{i=1}^{n}|y_i - \hat{y}_i|}{n} \tag{4}$$

$$MBE = \frac{\sum_{i=1}^{n}(y_i - \hat{y}_i)}{n} \tag{5}$$

$$R^2 = 1 - \frac{\sum_{i=1}^{n}(y_i - \hat{y}_i)^2}{\sum_{i=1}^{n}(y_i - \overline{y})^2} \tag{6}$$

Equations (3)–(6): $\hat{y}_i$ is the prediction result of the i-th student's score; y_i is the real value of the i-th student's score; $\overline{y}$ is the average of the real values.

3.3 Modelling

To address the nonlinear nature of the relationship between learning process data and test scores, a comprehensive selection of machine learning models has been made, including support vector machine (SVM), random forest (RF), back propagation network (BP), genetic algorithm back propagation network (GA-BP), and long short-term memory network (LSTM). These models have been chosen due to their robust fitting capabilities and generalization abilities. By leveraging the strengths of each model, they collectively offer improved performance in handling sample noise and achieving a high-quality nonlinear approximation effect.

The number of nodes in the hidden layer of a neural network is very important in model building. If the number of nodes is too small, the fitting ability of the neural network will be insufficient, resulting in "underfitting"; if the number of nodes is too large, the model learning time will be significantly increased. At the same time, it is prone to the problem of "overfitting" [8].

Based on previous empirical formulations and modeling experiments, a structure with 10 nodes in the hidden layer is chosen for the BP neural network model. To monitor the training progress, the Mean Squared Error (MSE) of the training set data is tracked as the number of training epochs increases. If the MSE does not decrease for six consecutive epochs, the training process is halted. The hyperparameters associated with the highest accuracy value on the training set are then identified, and the corresponding model is selected as the final model for making predictions on the testing set. This approach ensures that the model achieves optimal performance and avoids overfitting.

3.4 K-Fold Cross-Validation

When there are multiple models with different structures to choose from, K-fold cross-validation is usually used to select the best model for a specific dataset.

K-fold cross-validation proceeds as follows: a dataset with N samples is divided into K parts, each of which contains N/K samples. One of them is chosen as the testing set, and the other K-1 is used as the training set; thus, there are K cases in the validation set. In each case, the model is trained on the training set and tested on the testing set, and the generalization error of the model is calculated. The cross-validation is repeated K times, and the average of the K-fold results is used as the final generalization error of the model. The value of K is generally between [2,10]. The advantage of K-fold cross-validation is that it repeatedly uses randomly generated subsamples for training and validation at the same time. Considering the computational simplification and accuracy of the prediction performance, 5-fold cross-validation is used in this study.

The number of samples in the training set for K-fold cross-validation should be large enough, generally at least 50% of the total number of samples. The training and validation sets must be uniformly sampled from the full dataset. The purpose of uniform sampling is to reduce the bias between the training, validation, and original datasets. When the number of samples is large enough, the effect of uniform sampling can be achieved by random sampling.

3.5 The Results

The five prediction models described above were used to predict the average final exam scores of 224 impoverished students in the first semester of their senior year of 2018 class. The predictions are shown in Table 2. In particular, the R^2 of the RF model fitted to the training samples reached 0.826, while the R^2 of the RF model fitted to the testing set data reached 0.524. The comparison between the predicted values and the true values of the training set is shown in Fig. 2 and Fig. 3.

Table 2. Comparison of the prediction results of the five models

Dataset	Model	RMSE	MAE	MBE	R^2
Training Set	SVM	**1.067**	**0.590**	0.030	**0.954**
	RF	2.101	1.568	0.005	0.826
	BP	2.976	2.292	0.201	0.648
	GA-BP	2.934	2.241	−0.011	0.648
	LSTM	2.498	2.000	**−0.002**	0.749
Testing Set	SVM	4.304	3.351	0.048	0.140
	RF	**3.287**	**2.591**	**0.002**	**0.524**
	BP	3.783	2.881	−0.045	0.328
	GA-BP	3.982	3.11	−0.240	0.280
	LSTM	3.402	2.674	−0.025	0.443

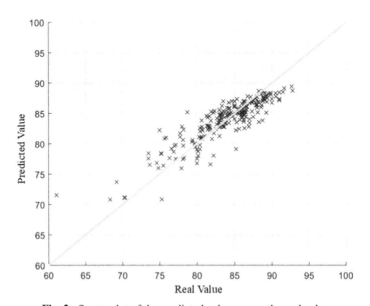

Fig. 2. Scatterplot of the predicted value versus the real value

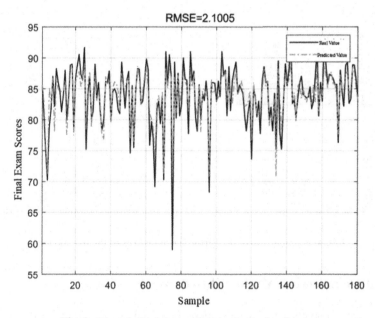

Fig. 3. Line chart of the predicted value and real value

3.6 Analysis of Model Comparison

To compare and analyze the performance, five machine learning models were established using the same training set and testing set. The prediction effects of each model are shown in Table 2, including the prediction and fitting accuracy of each model. From the fitting effect on the training set, SVM performs better on the training samples, and the three evaluation indexes of RMSE, MAE and R^2 are all optimal. From the fitting effect on the testing set, as shown in Fig. 4, the RF regression model performs the best, and the four evaluation indicators of RMSE, MAE, MBE, and R^2 are all best.

The prediction samples contain a series of interpolation points and expansion points, which reflect the fitting performance and generalization performance of the model. From the prediction results, both RF and LSTM have better prediction results, but in comparison, RF has a higher prediction accuracy for the testing set samples. Experimental data show that SVM has poor generalization ability on the problem of score prediction, while RF has strong generalization ability and good fitting ability on both the training set and testing sets.

Overall, compared with the other four methods, the comprehensive ability of the RF model is better, which is reflected in its strong fitting ability, strong generalization ability, high prediction accuracy, and ability to predict the final exam scores of college students well.

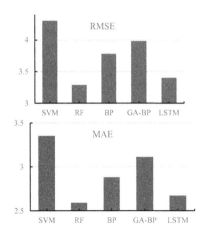
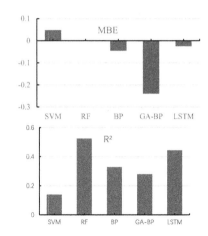

Fig. 4. Comparison of the performance indexes of the five models

4 Feature Selection Method Based on RF

Feature selection involves the identification of relevant features from raw data that possess predictive power for the target variable and are used as input parameters in the model. The contribution of each feature to the model serves as a measure of its importance in predicting the outcome. Selecting inadequate or insufficient input parameters can lead to the model's inability to capture all the crucial features in the data, resulting in oversimplification or overcomplication of the model.

Oversimplified models may overlook essential factors, leading to prediction errors. Conversely, overly complex models can overfit the training data, leading to poor performance when applied to new data.

In the context of scores prediction models, there exists a plethora of data that affect and constrain each other. The selection of input parameters certainly impacts the accuracy of the model. A good model should incorporate the most representative and relevant input parameters, aiming to minimize model errors and enhance prediction capabilities. The structure of the feature selection method used in this research is shown in Fig. 5.

4.1 Feature Selection Method

Due to the high degree of autocorrelation observed among certain parameters in the students' learning process, there is a potential risk of underestimating the true value of the autocorrelation parameter in the feature selection analysis. To ensure the integrity of the analysis results, it is imperative to initially assess the autocorrelation between the input parameters. In this study, the Pearson linear correlation analysis method has been chosen as the preferred approach. To facilitate the distinction, p^2 is used to represent the correlation coefficient. The formula for the calculation is shown in Eq. (7):

$$p^2 = \frac{(n \sum x_i y_i - \sum x_i \sum y_i)^2}{\left[n \sum x_i^2 - (\sum x_i)^2 \right] \left[n \sum y_i^2 - (\sum y_i)^2 \right]} \tag{7}$$

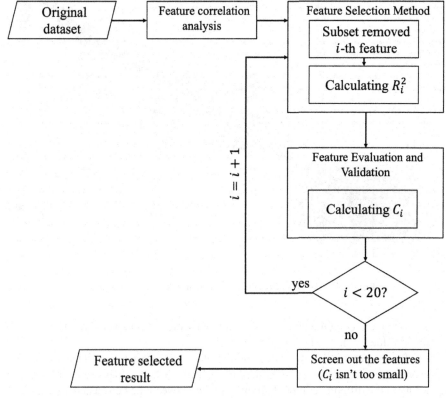

Fig. 5. The flowchart of the feature selection method

where x_i is the value of an input parameter; y_i is the value of another input parameter; n is the number of samples; and p^2 is the correlation coefficient.

The two parameters whose correlation coefficient p^2 is greater than 0.9 are considered autocorrelation parameters. The Pearson correlation among the 21 parameters in this paper is shown in Fig. 6.

After conducting the Pearson correlation analysis, the remaining parameters are utilized to construct the RF regression prediction model. The determination coefficient R_0^2, which measures the correlation between the model's predicted results and the actual exam scores, is calculated.

To assess the individual contributions of each input parameter, the model is then retrained while sequentially excluding the i-th parameter. The resulting prediction accuracy is measured by calculating R_i^2. By comparing the differences in prediction accuracy before and after removing the i-th parameter, the model contribution C_i of that specific parameter is determined. The calculation formula for C_i is provided in Eq. (8).

$$C_i = R_0^2 - R_i^2 \tag{8}$$

A positive value means that the parameter has a positive effect on the prediction of the final scores of impoverished students, while a negative value means that the parameter

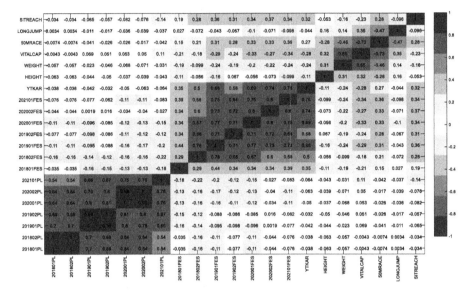

Fig. 6. Pearson correlation coefficient among the 21 parameters

has a negative effect on the prediction of the final scores of impoverished students. The larger the value is, the stronger the effect.

Finally, the previously eliminated autocorrelation parameters are added one by one. Autocorrelation parameters are measured to determine whether they are worth selecting according to the difference in prediction accuracy between the before and after models. If the accuracy of the model does not increase, it means that the key information of this parameter has been included in its autocorrelation parameters. When its autocorrelation parameters exist in the input data, the increase in this parameter has no more effect on the model.

4.2 Feature Selection and Verification

The feature selection of impoverished students' data is carried out. The analysis results of the 20 input parameters are shown in Fig. 7.

From the experimental results, except for the poverty level data in the second semester of the junior year, the contribution of the poverty level data in the other six semesters to the model is negative; that is, these six features interfere with the prediction model. Considering the prediction accuracy and calculation time, 7 parameters with negative contributions and 1 parameter with an excessively small contribution are discarded.

In the problem of predicting the average final scores of impoverished students in the first semester of the senior year, 12 parameters that certainly contribute to the model are selected as the feature extraction results. The average scores of final exams in the first and second semesters of the junior year play a decisive role in the model. The average scores of the final exams in the first semester of freshman, the second semester of freshman, the first semester of sophomore, and the second semester of sophomore and the attendance rate of Rain Classroom have made great contributions to the model. Data on students'

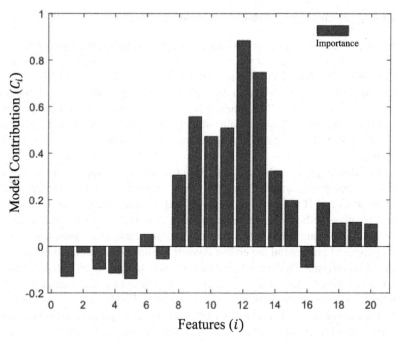

Fig. 7. Model contribution of the 20 input parameters

height, vital capacity, 50 m race, standing long jump and sit-and-reach complement the model.

To verify the correctness of the analysis results, the parameters after feature extraction are selected to establish a new RF regression prediction model. In this way, the calculation time of the model is reduced, and R^2 of the prediction results and real scores reaches 53.39% better than before model's 52.40%. Table 3 shows the comparison results between the prediction accuracy of the model before and after feature selection. After feature selection, the invalid data in the inputs of the model are greatly reduced, which proves that the feature extraction method is effective.

Table 3. Accuracy comparison of the model before and after feature selection

Dataset	Model	RMSE	MAE	MBE	R^2
Training Set	Original	**2.094**	**1.568**	**0.005**	**0.826**
	Feature Selected	2.128	1.575	0.014	0.820
Testing Set	Original	3.287	2.591	0.002	0.524
	Feature Selected	**3.244**	**2.554**	−0.002	**0.534**

4.3   Analysis of the Feature Selection Results

Poverty issues may cause students to lack necessary resources and support in terms of food, accommodation, transportation, medical care, etc., which may affect their physical health and learning effects. With China's overall victory in poverty alleviation in 2021 as scheduled, the impact of poverty on the academic performance of college students has been decreasing year by year. The Chinese government has eased the financial pressure on impoverished college students by issuing student origin loans, national encouragement grants, and work-study programs, giving them more opportunities to focus on learning and development.

The attendance rate calculated by the Rain Classroom platform is directly proportional to the final grade, which shows that class attendance can help college students obtain higher scores. However, some college students can obtain high scores through self-study or other methods. However, the content explained by the teacher in the classroom is one of the main sources of students' learning. First, class attendance can help students grasp and understand the course content, while absenteeism would make them miss important information. Second, attendance can help students establish a good relationship with teachers, help students better understand course goals and expectations, and make it easier to obtain feedback and suggestions. Finally, class attendance could help students develop self-discipline and self-management skills. Especially when students are faced with a large number of courses and learning tasks, attendance can help them plan well and allocate time.

In terms of the correlation between physical fitness test data and final scores, students with high vital capacity and good performance in the 50 m race likely tend to have lower scores than other students. This shows that students who are good at sprinting need to pay more attention to their academic performance. Correspondingly, students with high final exam scores should strengthen physical exercise to improve their physical fitness.

More interestingly, in this sample of 224 students, sit-and-reach, a common test of body flexibility, has a 0.3 Pearson correlation with the average final exam scores. Although this conclusion indicates that there is a certain degree of positive correlation between sit-and-reach test and final exam scores, it does not mean that sit-and-reach directly leads to the improvement of final exam scores. However, college physical education should consider increasing the training of students' body flexibility, such as yoga, Pilates, dance, Tai Chi, etc. These forms of exercise focus on relaxing the body, increasing energy, improving concentration and relaxing the mind through slow movements and deep breathing. Several studies have shown that flexibility exercises can reduce physical tension and emotional problems such as anxiety and depression and improve sleep quality and physical shape.

Although this method is data-driven, it is affected by the range and distribution of different parameters, but the factors that affect the average scores of college students' final exams obtained by this method are basically consistent with the concepts of quality education. This method also provides guidance for theoretical research on college education. Feature selection plays a significant role in the simplification of the model.

4.4 A Subsection Sample

The poverty level data are screened out by the feature extraction algorithm as an invalid input parameter. The model now extends to a sample of 693 students in the 2017 class. The data of this sample also include the poverty level of each semester, the average scores of each semester, attendance data and physical fitness test data. The analysis results of feature extraction are verified again on this sample. Some features of the extension sample are shown in Table 4.

Table 4. Some features of the extension sample

STUNO	YKTAR	201701FES	HEIGHT (cm)	50MRACE (s)	SITREACH (cm)
2017***5	0	80.25	173	7.3	9
2017***1	80%	70.26	173	6.9	16
2017***4	100%	82.17	164	6.9	8.5
2017***1	50%	77.95	164	7.7	10
2017***9	100%	78.20	154	8.9	19

Using the same sample division method and modelling parameters, two models with parameters before and after feature selection are established. The universality of feature selection results is judged by the difference between models' accuracy. The accuracy of the two models is shown in Table 5.

Table 5. Accuracy comparison of the model on the extension sample

Dataset	Model	RMSE	MAE	MBE	R^2
Training Set	Original	2.445	**1.737**	0.003	0.827
	Feature Selected	**2.435**	1.739	−0.003	**0.828**
Testing Set	Original	3.914	2.897	−0.043	0.552
	Feature Selected	**3.910**	**2.878**	**−0.042**	**0.553**

Table 5 shows that the evaluation indicators of the model established by using the parameters after feature selection have slightly improved. The results of feature selection are also applicable to the students in the 2017 class. The verification results are in line with the previous analysis conclusions, which proves that the feature selection method is universal and reliable.

5   Conclusion

1. The prediction accuracy and generalization ability of the RF regression model in this study are superior to those of the traditional neural network models and SVM model.
2. Using the RF regression model can effectively predict the final average scores of college students in the first semester of the senior year. The determination coefficient R^2 of the testing set reaches 0.534, and the correlation coefficient reaches 0.888. The RF regression prediction model leads to a high-precision prediction result for the average scores of college students in the first semester of the senior year.
3. Some average scores of the final exams play a decisive role in the model, while the other average scores of the final exams and the attendance rate of Rain Classrooms made great contributions to the model. Students' height, vital capacity, 50 m race, standing long jump and sit-and-reach supplement the model and can be used as input parameters in the pursuit of high precision.
4. The contribution of poverty level in the model is negative, which reduces the model fitting performance. To a certain extent, this proves that the poverty level of college students has no significant impact on their academic performance.
5. The analysis results obtained by feature selection can slightly improve the accuracy of the model and simplify the model, which has certain guidance.

Acknowledgements. The work was supported by Yunnan Philosophy and Social Sciences Planning Pedagogy Project (Research on the prediction of College Students' learning results based on online learning behavior analysis, AC21012), Humanities and Social Sciences Research Project of Yunnan Provincial Institute and Provincial School Education Cooperation (SYSX202008, research on the development countermeasures of intelligent education in Colleges and universities in Yunnan Province), supported by the special project of "Research on Informatization of Higher Education" of China Society of Higher Education in 2020, Analysis and Research on College Students' Learning Behavior Based on Machine Learning, 2020XXHYB17.

References

1. Farshid, M., Heidi, A., Krishna, M.: Models for early prediction of at-risk students in a course using standards-based grading. Comput. Educ. **103**, 1–15 (2016)
2. Tao, G., Yong, W., Jie, X.: Research on the application of PSO-BP neural network predictive model in smart classroom. Comput. Era **03**, 52–56 (2021)
3. Rovira, S., Puertas, E., Igual, L.: Data-driven system to predict academic grades and dropout. PLoS ONE **12**(2), 1–21 (2017)
4. Mengnan, L., Jinhui, L.: Student achievement grade prediction model based on neural network optimized by adaptive differential evolution. Mod. Electron. Technol. **45**(03), 130–134 (2022)
5. Qian, T.: Construction of student portrait and prediction analysis of learning situation based on educational data mining. Mod. Inf. Technol. **7**(04), 193–198 (2023)
6. Xiaoyi, W., Haishen, L., Crow, T., et al.: A reduced latency regional gap-filling method for SMAP using random forest regression. iScience **26**(1), 1–24 (2023)
7. Sanchez, J.: The inadequate use of the determination coefficient in analytical calibrations: how other parameters can assess the goodness-of-fit more adequately. J. Sep. Sci. **44**(24), 99–110 (2021)
8. Zufiria, P.J.: On the discrete-time dynamics of the basic Hebbian neural network node. J. Sep. Sci. **13**(06), 1342–1352 (2002)

Design of a Decision Support and Service System for Academic Big Data in Universities

Yingqi Du and Yuan Yuan[(⊠)]

Library, Wuhan University of Technology, Wuhan, China
yuancelia@whut.edu.cn

Abstract. Based on university academic big data, the design idea of a decision support and service system to meet the academic data needs in universities is studied. The method of integrating discrete, heterogeneous and multi-source academic data through the datafication of all activities related to academics is proposed. It achieves data collaboration among researchers, research teams, academic papers, academic publications, subject areas and institutions. It is oriented towards academic data to build different application scenarios such as resource evaluation, talent construction, innovation leading and performance improvement, and establish a decision support system to promote knowledge innovation of university researchers.

Keywords: Library · Academic Service · Academic Data · Decision Support System · Big Data

1 Introduction

At present, data governance and utilisation has become a strategic issue of high priority for universities and colleges worldwide. Among them, the governance and utilisation of research data and academic data is an important way to realise the scientific and technological development of universities and even the country. Compared with the statistics and utilisation of academic data under the traditional business model, an intelligent academic data decision support and service system under the big data environment can grasp the development status and guide the development direction of the university in a more accurate and timely manner, thus enabling researchers to create better research results.

With the promotion of "double first-class" construction, facing the challenges of the big data environment and changes in user needs, the academic services of university libraries have also changed, with more diversified service contents, more refined service granularity, more intelligent service means and more personalised service applications. The construction of first-class disciplines in universities requires libraries to provide deep, multi-level and precise academic services. This kind of academic precision service is an advanced stage in the development of academic services, which is user-centred and emphasises the precision of services for different levels and different individual users. New technologies and methods in the field of big data and artificial

© The Author(s), under exclusive license to Springer Nature Singapore Pte Ltd. 2024
J. Gan et al. (Eds.): CSEI 2023, CCIS 1900, pp. 325–332, 2024.
https://doi.org/10.1007/978-981-99-9492-2_27

intelligence, such as user profiling, semantic learning, academic network analysis and precise recommendation, offer the possibility of precise academic services in libraries [3].

In recent years a number of scholars have carried out some relevant research in this area. Qin Zhong-Yun constructed a model for assessing the maturity of data governance in libraries [1]. Song Su-Xuan explored the data governance system in university management, but its focus was not on academic-related data [2]. Zhang Zhi-Wu studied the progress of the application of academic big data in university academic services from three aspects: academic impact evaluation, academic recommendation and talent discovery [3]. Zhu Weiqun conducted a more comprehensive analysis of the academic functions of libraries, but did not build an information-based service system [4]. Hu, Qingyun used visualization methods to study the application of academic data in university libraries in China and Germany in terms of user research, information search, and subject service platforms [5]. Islam, AYM Atiquil used an empirical research method to collect data from 211 librarians working in Pakistani universities to understand the performance of university libraries through data processing. Their findings also suggest that when linked to big data analytics, the components of academic libraries lead to effective organisational performance [6]. Xia, Feng proposed the emerging topics of access, storage, management and processing of academic big data as important issues for the research community [7]. Khan, Samiya investigated the demand for collaborator discovery, expert discovery and research recommendation in digital libraries [8]. Yang, Chao proposed a PARs-based topic analysis method and verified that topic analysis can be performed using small datasets, giving a way to implement some of the applications in the academic big data decision support service system [9].

We focus on the academic data needs of researchers, managers and decision makers in the context of academic big data in universities and the design of an accurate decision support and service system to meet the needs. We establish the role concept model and the related metadata concept system, data the scientific research behaviors and academic activities of researchers, and build the demand model of application scenarios for the data; establish the mapping relationship between role and demand, data and application, realize the intelligent decision support of universities for applications such as resource evaluation, talent construction, innovation leading and performance improvement, and accurately and timely meet the needs of academic data at all levels of universities. It also establishes the mapping relationship between role and demand and data and application to realize intelligent decision support for applications such as resource evaluation, talent construction, innovation and leadership, performance improvement, etc., so as to accurately and timely meet the demand for academic data utilization at all levels of universities and promote the knowledge innovation of university researchers and high-quality development of universities.

2 Methodology

This academic big data-based decision support and service system should integrate discrete, heterogeneous and multi-source academic-related data, and apply the metadata standard element design method to realise data standardisation and integration among researchers, research teams, academic papers, academic publications, subject areas, schools and secondary units. Through the analysis of the integrated standardised and high-quality data, the academic big data storage system is constructed, from which information related to the needs of each application scenario can be extracted for further utilisation. Establish a demand model for application scenarios and a mechanism for matching demand with data. Realise intelligent academic big data applications by researching a cross-disciplinary, cross-type and cross-resource academic big data decision support system.

Therefore, we believe that the system could be designed in three ways:

Data Systems Related to Academic Activities in a Big Data Environment. Analyse the characteristics of academic-related activities in the big data environment, mine and analyse all academic information that can accurately describe researchers, research teams, academic papers, academic publications, subject areas, schools and secondary units, and establish a more complete, comprehensive and standardised academic data system. At the same time, research on the security and evaluation feedback mechanisms in the whole life cycle of academic big data.

Demand Discovery and Management Mechanisms Related to Academic Data in a Big Data Environment. Establish a demand model for academic data-oriented application scenarios, identify and discover the demands of each role and level, analyse and reveal the connotative characteristics of the demands, and standardise and unify them to provide a basis for data extraction and matching.

Decision Support and Service Models for Academic Big Data. By studying the cross-disciplinary, cross-type and cross-resource academic big data decision support system, establishing the matching mechanism between resource needs, research needs and decision-making needs, etc. and the big data system, and studying the specific services and visual expression of this data decision support system to maximise the efficiency of using academic data in universities.

Based on the above design ideas, the university academic big data decision support and service system will face two difficulties: the integration and analysis of academic data and the description and matching of academic data application requirements, and we propose the following solutions:

Integration and Analysis of Academic Data. The first difficult issue is to realise the integration between academic related data across disciplines, types and resources. Here the means of metadata standard element design can be introduced and used to realise data standardisation collaboration and integration. By analysing the integrated standardised high quality data, an academic big data warehousing system is constructed, from which information relevant to the needs of each application scenario can be extracted for further integration and utilisation.

Description and Matching of Academic Data Application Requirements. The description and matching of academic data application requirements is another technical difficulty. Various structured and unstructured information and statistics related to researchers can be collected from the actual business environment of managers and decision-makers, and through systematic combing and in-depth research, a unified model of application scenario requirements can be established and matched with academic data warehousing that has completed metadata normalisation.

3   Results

3.1   Design of the System Architecture

For academic big data, we use the logical order of collection, processing, application and disclosure, so the academic big data decision support and service system we designed has a five layers architecture (see Fig. 1). They are "Raw Data Layer", "Data Management Layer", "Application Scenario Layer", "Expression Layer" and "User Layer". In the raw data layer, there are data from school functions, libraries, database providers, including researcher data, research team data, academic resource data, academic paper data, academic publication data, academic field data, institutional data, and so on. The data management layer plans, manages assets, integrates, mines and analyses raw data. The application scenario layer includes all applications provided to users based on requirements description and matching, such as "Resource Performance Evaluation", "Subject Resource Analysis", "Discipline Competitiveness Analysis", "First-class Subject Analysis", "Academic Impact Evaluation", "Academic Impact Evaluation", "Talent Team Evaluation", "Tracking the hot spots and frontiers of the discipline", "Institutional Development Potential Analysis", "Institutional High Quality Achievement Tracking", "Decision Support for Publishing Academic Achievements", "Decision Support for Publishing Academic Achievements", etc. The presentation layer is the part of the system that is directly seen and used by end users, including "Data Release", "Retrieval System", "Visualization Display" and "Communication and Interaction". The user layer is where the roles of the system end-users are set, including "General users", "Researchers", "Managers", "Decision makers", etc. "Data Security Assurance" and "Standardised Management and Evaluation" are always required throughout the five layers of the system to provide data standardisation and security for the normal operation of the system.

3.2   Two Examples of Applications

Although the university academic big data decision support and service system is still in the design stage, we have already carried out effective service practices for some of these applications. Two examples are given here:

Institutional Quality Results Tracking: By extracting and collating data on the institution's highly cited papers, it provides the university with a disciplinary classification analysis of high-quality scholarship (see Table 1 and Fig. 2) and updates the data every two months to provide the necessary support for the university's discipline building decisions, realising some of the functions of the "Tracking the hot spots and frontiers of the discipline" service mentioned in the system.

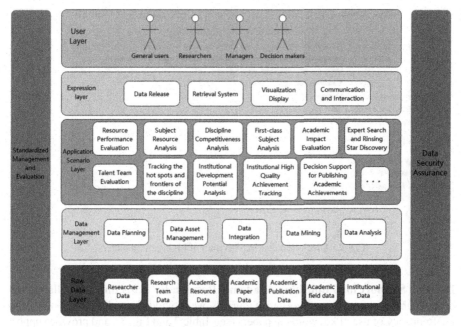

Fig. 1. Design of the system architecture

Table 1. Number of highly cited papers by discipline

Research Field	Number of highly cited papers
Economics & Business	1
Molecular Biology & Genetics	1
Psychiatry/Psychology	1
Biology & Biochemistry	2
Geosciences	7
Mathematics	8
Social Sciences, General	9
Computer Science	14
Environment/Ecology	22
Physics	38
Engineering	103
Chemistry	190
Materials Science	199

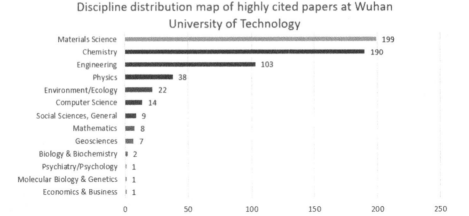

Fig. 2. Discipline distribution map of highly cited papers

Decision Support for Publishing Academic Results: By extracting and collating the data of published papers in authoritative journals, we provide researchers with analysis of the frequency of use of keywords in papers (see Table 2 and Fig. 3), and provide support for researchers in tracking research hotspots and making decisions on research directions, realising some of the functions of the "Decision Support for Publishing Academic Achievements" service mentioned in the system.

For example, the total number of papers published in an authoritative journal in a certain year was 1044, and a total of 11,866 author keywords were used, with 4,900 after de-duplication. Of these, 33 keywords were used 40 times or more as shown in Table 2.

Table 2. List of most frequently used keywords

Keyword	Number of uses	Keyword	Number of uses
resource management	138	Relays	52
optimization	137	sensors	52
noma	126	estimation	51
wireless communication	111	throughput	51
interference	111	trajectory	51
delays	92	security	49
vehicle dynamics	89	reliability	49
task analysis	81	mathematical model	49

(continued)

Table 2. (*continued*)

Keyword	Number of uses	Keyword	Number of uses
signal to noise ratio	74	massive	48
receivers	67	channel estimation	47
array signal processing	66	wireless sensor networks	45
servers	65	training	45
computational modeling	65	protocols	44
unmanned aerial vehicles	59	heuristic algorithms	43
roads	55	radio frequency	41
downlink	54	batteries	40
uplink	53		

Figure 3 shows a cloud of 178 keywords used 10 times or more in the publication. The font size and thickness show the level of frequency of use, the more frequently used, the more prominent the text.

Fig. 3. Keywords cloud

4 Conclusion

The university academic big data decision support and service system designed here can integrate and unify all relevant discrete, heterogeneous and multi-source academic data into an open data system that is richer and more comprehensive than the data in a traditional institutional results repository.

In addition, it realises the association and matching between the needs of all levels of universities for resource evaluation, talent team building, university research and overall development and academic big data by constructing a unified model of academic data application scenario needs, and then makes assisted decision support possible through the mapping of data and needs.。

As the basic conditions of each university library vary, each library can implement the system in steps according to its specific situation. In the first step, the data structure and architecture can be determined and initial data construction and utilisation can be carried out, at which point the system can be called "disciplinary data intelligence service platform". With the comprehensive construction and accumulation of academic data and the continuous upgrading of computer network technology, the system can realize intelligent decision support and human-machine barrier-free interaction, at which time, the "Academic Big Data Decision Support and Service System" will be truly realised.

References

1. Qin, Z.-Y.: Research on data governance and maturity model of university libraries in big data environment. New Cent. Lib. **11**, 62–67 (2019)
2. Song, S.-X., Yang, X.-M., Song, Z.-Q.: Composition and practice path of data governance integrated management system in higher education. China Dist. Educ. **11**, 58–67 (2021)
3. Zang, Z.-W., Xue, J.J., Do, H.: Research on the application of academic big data to help academic services in universities. J. Univ. Libr. Inf. **40**(02), 100–108 (2022)
4. Zhu, W.: Exploring the academic function positioning of university libraries in the new era. Libr. J. **39**(06), 50–55 (2020)
5. Hu, Q.: The quantitative analysis of difference between Chinese and German libraries subject services. Library Hi Tech **38**(2), 334–349 (2020)
6. Islam, A.Y.M.A., Ahmad, K., Rafi, M.: Performance-based evaluation of academic libraries in the big data era. J. Inf. Sci. **47**(4), 458–471 (2021)
7. Xia, F., Giles, C.L., Liu, H.: Guest editorial: scholarly big data. IEEE Trans. Emerg. Top. Comput. **9**(1), 200–203 (2021)
8. Khan, S., Liu, X., Shakil, K.A.: A survey on scholarly data: from big data perspective. Inf. Process. Manage. **53**(4), 923–944 (2017)
9. Yang, C., Huang, C., Su, J.: Topic analysis of academic disciplines based on prolific and authoritative researchers. Library Hi Tech **39**(4), 1043–1062 (2021)

Public English Teaching Strategies in Higher Vocational Colleges Based on Big Data Analysis of Students' English Test Scores

Huaqiao Zhou[✉]

Sanya Aviation and Tourism College, Hainan, China
290280052@qq.com

Abstract. In order to solve the common problem of English learning difficulties among vocational college students, the advantages of big data analysis are used to analyze the characteristics of vocational college students' English scores in a deeper level, providing reference for teachers to flexibly adopt diversified teaching strategies. In the teaching preparation, we will sort out and analyze the students' English sores of college entrance examination and Level A's scores, and actively improve the teaching strategies in combination with the teaching situation to meet the diversified learning needs of students.

Keywords: big data analysis · higher vocational education · English · teaching strategies · scores

1 Introduction

Higher vocational English teaching based on students' learning situation and adopting appropriate teaching strategies will help students improve their English learning effect. Especially for students in higher vocational colleges, due to their weak foundation of English learning and poor autonomy in learning, teachers need to pay more attention to the learning situation of students in the teaching process, adjust teaching strategies in time, and adopt targeted teaching methods to meet the English learning needs of students in higher vocational colleges. Students in higher vocational colleges have generally participated in the college entrance examination English test, and they will also participate in the Practical English Test for Colleges level A (hereinafter referred to as English level A) during college. Both of these tests have the characteristics of many reference students and wide coverage, and the test is held for a long time with good authority, which can better reflect the students' English learning situation, Therefore, it is necessary to strengthen the analysis of the big data of students' achievements and make timely adjustments to teaching strategies.

This paper is one of the research results of the 2021 school-level project "Research on teaching strategies based on the analysis of students' English achievement data" of Sanya Aviation and Tourism College (project number: SATC2021002).

2   Research Assumptions

Higher vocational students' English scores in the college entrance examination and their English learning effects in school have the characteristics of normal distribution, that is, students with good English scores in the college entrance examination are more likely to pass the English Level A test, and reference to the college entrance examination results can provide necessary reference for the implementation of English teaching strategies.

English teaching in higher vocational colleges cannot simply prepare for teaching on knowledge points. It is necessary to strengthen teaching design and implementation from the cultivation of learning interest and learning behavior in combination with the learning characteristics of higher vocational students, so as to comprehensively promote students' comprehensive English learning ability.

3   Research Methods

Sores data sorting method. Taking the enrollment of Grade 19 in a vocational college in Sanya as an example, the college entrance examination English scores and grade A English scores (60 points and above) during the school period were counted, and the characteristics and rules of the scores were summarized by means of data induction.

Student interview method. According to the results of data analysis, select representative students to conduct face-to-face interviews and make interview outlines, so as to obtain more objective theoretical conclusions; Combined with the research conclusion, the teaching implementation is adjusted pertinently to verify the effectiveness of the conclusion.

Teaching status survey method. Investigate the objective teaching evaluation and self-subjective evaluation of English teachers in higher vocational colleges, summarize the current situation of English teaching, and see whether it meets the current needs of English teaching.

4   Results of the Research

4.1   Statistical Results of English Scores of a Vocational College (Including College Entrance Examination English Scores and Level a Scores)

The college has 1555 students enrolled in the 19th grade (excluding the source of Hainan students), and 498 students passed the A grade during the college life, with a passing rate of about 33% (Fig. 1).

According to the statistics, we can draw two conclusions. First, the students who have passed the A-level examination have higher scores in the college entrance examination; The higher the score of the college entrance examination, the better the foundation of English learning, and the better the chance to pass the A-level examination.; Second, some students with poor college entrance examination scores also passed the A-level exam (the score just passed the 60 mark pass line), which shows that students with low starting point in English learning also have the opportunity to pass the Level A exam through their efforts in school. The above data analysis provides the necessary evidence

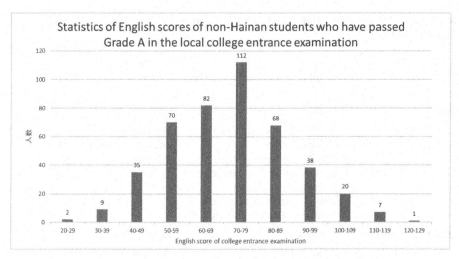

Fig. 1. Distribution of English scores in the national college entrance examination for students who have passed Grade A (excluding places of origin in Hainan)

for the follow-up teachers to teach according to their aptitude. By sorting out the first impression of the students' learning situation given by the students' performance meeting at the first time, actively mastering the situation of students in the class can effectively pave the way for the implementation of effective teaching measures.

4.2 Interview Results

Student Interview Results

In order to ensure the effectiveness of the interview, two students were selected from each score segment, and the same question outline was used for the interview. In the interview, the guiding questions were not carried out as far as possible, and the students responded freely. The questioner only played the role of recording and tried to get more objective interview results.

Interview ideas: Higher vocational students generally have weak learning foundation, learning self-confidence, and learning self-discipline is uneven. Therefore, the focus of the interview is mainly divided into three aspects, namely, learning driving force, learning behavior, and learning effect. In the past, English teachers tended to focus on learning interest as a measure, and attributed the poor learning state of many students to the lack of learning interest. The summary of students' subjective reasons was relatively rough and not comprehensive. Therefore, this interview used "learning driving force" to make a summary, focusing on more learning motivation factors as much as possible, so as to provide reliable thinking conditions for the follow-up implementation of teaching students according to their aptitude. Learning behavior mainly focuses on students' overall learning quality and daily learning habits in order to find out whether students have enough cognition to cope with English learning. The learning effect is mainly to examine the self-evaluation effect of students in order to verify the effectiveness of learning (Table 1).

Table 1. Outline of interview questions

Items	Questions	Purposes
drive of learning	1. Are you interested in English learning? Why? 2. Why do you want to learn English? Discipline requirements or employment pressure? 3. What do you think of the role of teachers in English learning?	Learn about the internal and external causes of English learning
Learning behavior	1. Can you concentrate on your study in class? Why? 2. Can you preview before class and review in time after class? Why? 3. Is there frequency and duration of daily English learning? Why? 4. Do you have learning habits such as reading aloud and copying vocabulary? Why?	Learn about class status, daily learning status and habits
learning effect	1. Can you keep up with the pace of English learning? Why? 2. Can you remember English words for a long time? Why? 3. Can you read words accurately? Why?	Learn about the initial effect and sustainability of English learning

The interview was carried out in a relaxed state. Through continuous guidance, the real ideas of the students interviewed were obtained at the first time. From the interview results, the students mainly showed that they were not particularly confident about their own learning, mainly in two aspects.

On the one hand, students generally fail to have a good view of learning. The main performance is that most of the students mentioned that their English learning was not very good in the past, and the understanding of the lack of learning was often biased simply towards results, and the attribution was often not scientifically summarized, which reflected from the side that students did not form a more comprehensive evaluation of their own English learning, leading to the formation of an inherent one-sided understanding of "poor English learning" to some extent, This one-sided subjective consciousness mostly leads to students' lack of active learning awareness, serious lack of learning behavior, and lack of strong objective evidence related to their learning ability.

On the other hand, the lack of English learning behavior is also a common phenomenon. From the interview with students, most of the students' learning behaviors are mainly based on English classroom teaching. They are not effectively connected before and after class. At the same time, they fail to adopt more effective learning strategies for English learning. The relatively simple learning mode is also a special concern in the interview. The reason why students cannot form an effective learning loop is, one is the inevitable consequence that learners' learning behavior cannot support the learning progress. At the same time, students lack the way to understand the future English needs of the industry, teachers' guidance on students' future English ability needs and corresponding English learning literacy is not enough, and daily teachers' urging is not enough to form a comprehensive learning motivation.

Results of the Survey of Teachers' Teaching Status

In order to fully grasp the current situation of English teaching, the front-line in-service English teachers were also investigated. The survey of the current situation of teachers' teaching is mainly based on three aspects. First, the results of the regular student evaluation organized by the school to understand the overall evaluation of students on English teachers; secondly, observe the advantages and disadvantages of English teachers in actual teaching by listening in class; at the same time, we can understand the current teaching situation through face-to-face communication with English teachers.

Taking Sanya Aviation and Tourism College as an example (Fig. 2), there are 15 in-service English teachers, and the school's educational administration department organizes students to conduct teaching evaluation activities for teachers at the middle and end of each semester. By screening and comparing the teaching evaluation scores of English teachers, they are generally above 90 points, which is excellent. To some extent, it shows that English teachers are recognized by students when teaching. In combination with student evaluation, young teachers in the department are welcomed, The scores are all above 95, while the relatively strict male teachers are relatively behind, which is also worthy of attention.

According to the results of the supervision and grading, nearly half of the 14 teachers have scored above 90 points in the past two semesters, which is excellent; At the same time, only 2 new teachers scored below 85; From the perspective of the supervisor's evaluation of English teachers, the overall evaluation of the performance of English teachers' classroom implementation is on the high side, reflecting the high level of the overall teaching of English teachers' team. Through randomly entering the classroom to listen, it is found that English teachers pay too much attention to the explanation of knowledge points, lack of mobilization for students' classroom participation, and students' learning is relatively passive.

Through after-class communication, English teachers generally reflect two problems: first, the number of students in English classes is large, which is not conducive to personalized language teaching; On the other hand, students' learning performance tends to be helpless. Students' learning enthusiasm is not good enough to match the teaching strength of teachers. At the same time, there are few guidance and management measures for students, and the main focus is on the interpretation of language knowledge points. The teaching effect is poor, and fails to meet good teaching expectations.

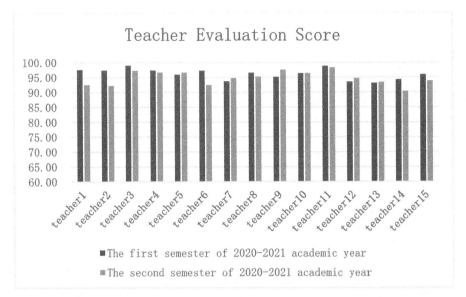

Fig. 2. Teaching evaluation results of students of college English course in grade 19 (2019–2020 academic year)

5   Conclusions of the Research

In the learning stage of higher vocational education, no matter how the students' basic English achievements are, there is an opportunity to improve the English learning effect through necessary actions and efforts. There will be individual differences in the learning cycle, but good learning habits and lasting learning strength play a key role in the positive learning effect output. While English teachers are at a high level in terms of professional knowledge analysis and classroom knowledge interpretation, but the implementation of teaching lacks attention to the students' main body. The space-time dimension of teaching processing is mainly maintained in the classroom, and the cultivation of students' learning behavior and learning habits still need to be continued. As an English teaching worker in higher vocational colleges, it is necessary to do more research on the students' learning mentality, strengthen the cultivation of students' learning self-confidence in teaching work, and cultivate students' good learning behavior in different ways, guide students to change from passive to active, have a more comprehensive understanding of English learning and overcome learning barriers.

6   Reflections on Teaching Strategies

6.1   The Setting of Teaching Objectives Should be Combined in the Long Run

At present, English teachers in higher vocational colleges set teaching objectives too narrowly when implementing English classroom teaching, which needs to be set in combination with students' current characteristics and future development trends. In the short term, it is a common phenomenon for students to have a weak foundation of English knowledge. However, we should pay attention to the characteristics of students' lack of necessary learning habits. Therefore, if we can help students establish a good learning view during their follow-up period, and thus cultivate a better learning quality, it is necessary and scientific to set teaching objectives from this perspective. The setting of long-term goals determines the implementation of short-term goals. The combination of long-term goals makes it easier for students to accept teaching arrangements, so that they can overcome the necessary learning obstacles.

6.2 Carry Out Scientific Research Work of Students' Learning Situation

At present, English teachers in higher vocational colleges mostly rely on textbooks to implement classroom teaching when carrying out English teaching. They have not set up a teaching link to find out the students' English foundation and learning situation, and almost do not grasp the students' basic learning situation. Empiricism is still the mainstream, so they have not formed the necessary conditions for teaching students according to their aptitude. Through investigation and research, by sorting out the students' English scores and total scores in the college entrance examination at the first time before entering school, it can provide necessary reference for the specific implementation of English teaching. According to the different learning basis of students, it can adopt diversified teaching design and learning task arrangement, and gradually guide students to improve their learning basis and skills in an orderly manner. In combination with the previous A-level achievements, timely sort out the necessary learning plans for students; In daily teaching, combined with the students' learning situation, we will arrange a phased investigation to verify the students' learning effect.

6.3 Implement Ladder Task-Based Teaching Arrangement

At present, higher vocational students still have large class size, uneven foundation and other conditions that restrict teaching according to their aptitude, especially for the accurate teaching of English, which has caused a lot of problems. The ladder task-based teaching method can be used, and teachers and students can participate in the teaching process. Three stages can be set for the English course, namely, the introductory stage (basic practice). For students who meet the requirements of zero foundation, teaching tasks are mainly set from the aspects of pronunciation learning, word memory, grammar learning, etc. In the consolidation stage (skill upgrading), more oral interaction and audio-visual assignments should be arranged to further expand students' learning dimension and release learning vitality; In the application stage (competition and examination), to meet the needs of students with good English skills, more students are encouraged to participate in various English competitions and examinations. Through a series of competition mechanisms, students are motivated to learn, and they are transformed to "I want to learn". More school competitions are arranged, such as English speaking skills competition, English writing skills competition, and so on. Volunteers are encouraged to participate in various events to exercise their English communication skills.

6.4 Visual Reconstruction of Teaching Resources

English learning needs a lot of repeated practice to consolidate long-term memory, and the existing teaching resources rely too much on the teacher's explanation, far from meeting the needs of students' diversified learning mode. Therefore, on the basis of the existing, combined with the actual learning needs, multi-dimensional expansion of teaching resources, such as the use of micro-class production and online course production; At the same time, in order to meet the needs of online teaching, online teaching videos are produced. The online video is mainly based on the reinforcement of course teaching, with "English pronunciation", "English grammar", "spoken English", and "English writing" as the main production direction, which visualizes part of the classroom teaching content, so that students can practice repeatedly according to their needs at any time, so as to meet the learning needs of students at different levels. In the later stage, the interactive teaching content is further reshaped. Students can not only follow the practice, but also carry out self-evaluation to test the learning effect from time to time.

6.5 The Course Adopts Comprehensive Evaluation

From the aspect of learning evaluation, change the evaluation mode of "one volume is determined to win or lose" in the final exam, increase the proportion of process evaluation, evaluate students' learning tasks in three aspects: "completion degree", "completion quality" and "completion effect", pay more attention to the test of students' immediate learning effect, strive for qualitative change through quantitative change, and effectively improve students' learning basis. Optimize the assessment method and score proportion, and focus on the learning process. Gradually change students from "don't like learning, passive learning" to "active learning, love learning", so that students can abandon the thinking pattern of "don't want to learn, can't learn well", and can achieve the more active goal of "understand, speak openly".

7 Conclusion

There are subjective and objective reasons for the difficulty of English learning of higher vocational students. Therefore, English teachers should avoid rigid teaching and change the stereotyped teaching mode; the investigation of students' learning situation in teaching is an essential link in teaching preparation. Based on authoritative English scores, students should actively master their learning status. In teaching, diversified teaching methods should be adopted to gradually promote the sense of participation and achievement of students at different levels.

References

1. Cheng, L.: Analysis and discussion on English learning strategies and guidance for students in higher vocational colleges. J. Guangdong Norm. Univ. Technol. **05**, 128–131 (2006)

2. Huang, X.Y.: The construction of student-centered English classroom—"task-based" teaching in public English education in higher vocational colleges. China Sc. Educ. Innov. Guide **20**, 65 (1999)
3. Lin, H.Y., Wu, S.R., Liu, M., Lin, F.: Research on the correlation between English learning strategies and learning achievements of vocational college students. Educ. Teach. Forum **37**, 225–227 (2017)

Research on the Pair Programming Partner Recommendation Method Based on Personalized Learning Features

Yali Wang[1,2(✉)] [iD] and Rong Zhang[1]

[1] School of Computer and Information Engineering, Henan Normal University, Xinxiang, Henan, China
yaliwan_g@163.com
[2] Engineering Lab of Intelligence Business and Internet of Things, Xinxiang 453007, Henan, China

Abstract. Computational thinking is becoming a hot topic of research in education and pair programming is an effective strategy for developing learners' computational thinking. How to provide suitable pairing partners is a key issue to enhance the effectiveness of pair programming learning. This study analyzed the common factors that affect the effectiveness of pair programming, a five-dimensional learner personality learning feature vector model is constructed. A pair programming homogeneous and heterogeneous partner recommendation method combining multiple distance algorithms is proposed. The method collects student questionnaire data to extract student personality learning feature information for experimental analysis. The results show that the proposed method can effectively improve the learning efficiency of pair programming learners.

Keywords: Pair Programming · Distance · Pair Partner Recommendation

1 Introduction

With the rapid development of science and technology represented by artificial intelligence, the cultivation of computational thinking has attracted widespread attention from experts and scholars from all over the world. Programming, as an essential way to cultivate computational thinking, is becoming a hot research topic in the current education field. However, programming learning is relatively boring, and learners are prone to feelings of loneliness and helplessness, as well as psychological obstacles such as fear and reluctance to learn. To enhance learners' self-confidence and sense of achievement and to increase their motivation and initiative in learning programming, pair programming can be introduced into teaching practice. Pair programming, originating from extreme programming (XP), refers to two people sitting side by side and sharing the same operating tools, such as computer monitors, hosts, keyboards and mouse, to jointly explore problems, design algorithms, write programs, conduct testing, and collaboratively solve the same problem or complete the same task. In actual implementation, one person acts as the "motorist" who mainly writes the program, and the other person acts as the "observer/navigator" who reviews and supervises the "driver's" work in real time, provides opinions and suggestions, and exchanges roles at specific times.

Numerous studies have shown that pair programming can help to enhance learners' interest in learning, increase their confidence and sense of achievement, facilitate the cultivation of their learning thinking [1–6], promote knowledge transfer [7], and reduce confirmation bias [8]. However, the key issue is how to pair learners to better play the role of pair programming. Literature [2, 9–15] investigated the impact of gender as a pairing criterion on pair programming. Most of these studies analysed the effectiveness of pair programming based on group compatibility or harmony as indicators. Literature [2, 16, 17] examined the impact of pairing approaches based on different learning styles on the cultivation of computational thinking in pair programming. Literature [2, 18] studied the pairing method based on learners' personality traits. Literature [2, 10, 11, 13] investigated the impact of programming ability on paired programming. The above studies consider the impact of different pair programming approaches when applying pair programming, but the consideration of the factors affecting the pairing approach is more one-sided, which leads to the lack of choice of pair formation and sometimes even depends on teachers' subjective allocation or learners' independent pairing, which greatly affects the utility of pair programming. In addition, in practice, it has been found that differences in members' personalities, learning styles, and programming abilities can result in low pairing fusion between members, leading to problems such as "low pairing efficiency" and too many "irrelevant behaviours" in the classroom.

In this paper, we first analyse the factors affecting the effectiveness of pair programming in pair learning, construct a model of personality learning characteristics by taking the data collected by the questionnaire as input, select a suitable similarity algorithm based on the data type, and then recommend homogeneous and heterogeneous peers for learners automatically based on the distance calculation. Finally, the effectiveness of the model and method is verified through experimental analysis.

2 Pairing Methods in Pair Programming

Differences in personality traits, social factors, and knowledge and ability levels between partners in pair programming can affect knowledge transfer and communication during the learning process and subsequently affect the effectiveness of pair programming.

Gender is an issue that needs to be considered in pair programming. Demir and Seferoglu experimented with university students in pair programming, paired by gender, setting up three groups: female–female, female–male, and male–male. They found no significant differences between homogeneous and heterogeneous genders in group compatibility, flow experience, or coding quality [2]. McDowell et al. also found that there was no significant difference in programming scores between male and female college students [14]. Chen Jie found that gender did not significantly affect pairing harmony in primary school research [9]. However, some studies have put forward different opinions. Choi (2015) found in a study targeting college students that there was no significant gender difference in the coding output of pair programming in quantitative analysis, but in qualitative analysis, it was found that same-gender pairs were more harmonious in terms of pairing harmony [12]. The above study shows that the most discussed indicator for gender is group compatibility or pairing harmony, but there is no clear definition of which gender is most conducive to pairing harmony or other indicators. The most discussed indicator of gender is group compatibility or pairing rapport, but there is no clear definition of what gender is best for pairing rapport or other indicators, and there is some disagreement even within the same grade. Therefore, it can be seen that gender is still an issue when considering pair compatibility and intra-pair communication, and is best considered in conjunction with other factors, on a case-by-case basis.

Learning style refers to the preferences and ways of learners in the process of learning and thinking [19]. Li Tongtong used the active/reflective dimension of the Felder and Silverman scale for primary schools to classify learners' learning styles and found that homogeneous pairs outperformed heterogeneous pairs in terms of computational thinking performance and that homogeneous learning styles were more tacit and harmonious during collaboration [17]. Demir and Seferoglu found no significant differences in compatibility and encoding performance between homogeneous and heterogeneous gender groups in terms of learning styles, but homogeneous learning styles showed significant differences in flow experience [2]. However, Gu Feier also used the active/reflection dimension in the Felder and Silverman scale to classify the learning styles of middle school student and explored the impact of pairing based on learning styles on overall computational thinking and the integration of computational concepts, practices, and ideas. The study found no significant differences in computational concepts between homogeneous and heterogeneous groups; the computational practices, ideas, and integration degree of homogeneous groups were significantly higher than those of heterogeneous groups, and there was no difference in the overall level of computational thinking among learners with different learning styles [16]. People with the same learning style approach problems in a similar way, which can make it easier for them to understand and work with each other, and for both parties to be more fully engaged in the task. But heterogeneous pairs are not useless; different preferences provide the team with more expertise than each member of the team has individually, potentially opening up new possibilities.

Regarding the influence of personality traits on paired programming, Chao and Atli found no evidence that personality trait pairing would affect the quality of generated code, and there was no correlation between personality traits and compatibility or enjoyment with peers [18]. Demir and Seferoglu found no difference in group compatibility in terms of conscientiousness, but homogeneous groups were more conducive to a flow experience, while heterogeneous groups were more conducive to coding performance [2]. It is worth noting that in homogeneous groups, if two individuals with low conscientiousness are paired, there may be problems of free-riding and inaction; in heterogeneous pairs, learners with high conscientiousness may demand more effort from those with low conscientiousness [20].

Regarding the influence of programming ability on paired programming, Demir and Seferoglu found that pairing based on programming prior knowledge, whether homogeneous or heterogeneous, does not affect group compatibility, flow experience, and coding performance [2]. Huang Qiongmei found that partners with similar programming abilities have higher compatibility [10]. Zeng Yuqian (2022) found that paired programming with different levels of knowledge significantly improves the computational thinking development of learners in low-level knowledge pairing groups [21]. Similar programming abilities may lead to better compatibility, but there is a risk of "the blind leading the blind" when two novices pair up [22]. According to Vygotsky's theory of the zone of proximal development, individuals with weaker abilities can achieve more with the help of those with stronger abilities than they could alone, and maximum knowledge transfer can be achieved through heterogeneous pairing [23]. However, heterogeneous pairing also has drawbacks, such as novices affecting the speed of proficient partners and even causing dissatisfaction among them, which can lower the confidence of the former.

Communication is a crucial part of paired programming [24], and it is an important factor that affects the efficiency and effectiveness of paired learning. Demir and Seferoglu found that in terms of friendship, homogeneous pairing was more conducive to a flow experience, while heterogeneous pairing was more conducive to coding performance [2]. Li Tongtong (2022) found for primary schools that partner-based pairing has a significant impact on the overall level of computational concepts and concepts of primary school learners and has a significant impact on the level of computational concepts of medium students, while good partnership and average partnership are not good for excellent students [17].

In summary, there is no unified consensus on the factors and indicators that affect pairing, and the situation varies across different educational levels. Pairing grouping strategies should start from understanding the learning situation and comprehensively considering teaching content, teaching objectives, and learning tasks. The factors to consider when pairing should vary for different classes and when facing different tasks. This paper establishes a five-dimensional personalized learning characteristic model for learners based on their gender, learning style, programming attitude, programming experience, cooperative attitude, and programming skills. Using gender as a distinction and other personalized learning characteristics as the main line, multiple algorithms are combined to calculate the similarity of learners and recommend similar or complementary partners.

3   A Paired Peer Recommendation Method Based on Individual Learning Features

3.1   Overall Framework

The overall framework of the paired-partner recommendation method under the paired programming learning method proposed in this study is shown in Fig. 1. First, we established a dataset of personalized learning features for learners and recorded information on student attributes, learning styles, emotional attitudes, and programming abilities. Based on this dataset, we establish a personalized learning characteristic model for each student and evaluate their individual model. Then, we calculated the distance between the individual learning models of students to obtain a distance matrix. Based on this distance, we recommended a list of homogeneous and heterogeneous pairing partners for students to choose from and form a pairing group that suits them best.

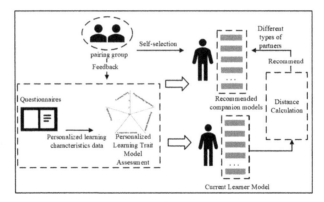

Fig. 1. Pairing peer recommendation framework based on personalized learning features

3.2 Establishing a Dataset of Learner Features

To make pair peer recommendations more effectively in a pair programming environment, in addition to considering personal attributes and learning styles, it is also necessary to consider students' programming knowledge and abilities. This article uses students' perceived skills to evaluate their programming abilities. To avoid being too subjective, it is also necessary to consider students' programming experiences and attitudes. In addition, cooperative attitudes are also important factors affecting collaboration efficiency. Therefore, this study considers building a five-dimensional personalized learning characteristic vector model for learners from five aspects: learning style, programming attitude, programming experience, cooperation attitude, and actual skill level. We collected data on learners' gender and personalized learning characteristics through a survey questionnaire and used the collected data as input for the algorithm.

Personal Attributes. Collect questions related to personal information, such as gender, etc. The data type is classified as a Boolean value, such as male 1 and female 0.

Learning Styles. This study uses the example of active or reflective learning styles and sets up two items concerning the active or reflective questions on the Felder and Silverman scales. This includes how I typically solve a programming problem, with the following two options: "start solving the problem immediately" and "try to fully understand the problem first", representing active learning styles and reflective approaches, respectively.

Programming Attitudes. Learners are asked to answer two simple programming attitude questions, ranging from very nonconforming to fully conforming. These included "I like programming" and "I can believe I can learn to program well". The score ranges from 1 to 5.

Programming Experience. Participants are required to answer two questions about their programming experience. They included "Have you studied programming before (1 = Yes, 0 = No)" and "Have you participated in programming competitions and achieved good results (1 = Strongly disagree to 5 = Strongly agree)".

Cooperative Attitude. Participants answered two questions about their attitude towards cooperation, ranging from strongly disagree to strongly agree. The questions were adapted from Barron, Gomez, Martin, and Pinkard [25], including "I am happier when working with others" and "When more than one person is involved in a project, we have better ideas and make better things". The score ranges from 1 to 5.

Programming Skill Level. Students are required to rate themselves on a scale of 1 to 5 based on their programming skills. This scale is adapted from CTS [26]. Including questions such as "I understand the principles of common algorithms such as recursion, backtracking, and greedy algorithms," "I can choose appropriate algorithms for different types of problems", "I can write programs that can be executed by a computer based on the solutions to problems" and so on. These 9 items are rated on a 5-point scale, ranging from strongly agree to strongly disagree (a = 0.956). Based on the above questions, we collected personalized learning feature data from students and conducted a preliminary statistical analysis. Based on the analysis results, we created a personalized learning feature model evaluation form.

Table 1 define five dimensions for assessing personalized learning characteristics. Each dimension consists of two or more questions, and the dimension value is calculated by computing the attribute values of the questions. Each dimension is divided into five levels, corresponding to scores of 1 to 5. The level division for each dimension differs and is evaluated based on the sum of attribute values for all questions in that dimension. For example, the programming attitude dimension has two questions. The maximum attribute value for each question item is 5, and the minimum attribute value is 1. Therefore, the minimum and maximum values for the programming attitude dimension are 2 and 10, respectively. When the sum of attribute values is 2, the level is set to 1, and when the sum is greater than 2 but less than or equal to 4, the level is set to 2, and so on, until the sum of attribute values is 10, which corresponds to level 5. For instance, if a student selects "General" for the first question and "Very Suitable" for the second question in the programming attitude dimension, their attribute values are 3 and 5, respectively. The programming attitude dimension value for this student would be 8, which corresponds to level 4. Using the evaluation method in Table 1, the six-dimensional values for each learner's learning feature can be calculated.

Table 1. Assessment table for personalized learning feature models

Item	1	2	3	4	5
Learning style	≤ 0	/	≤ 1	/	≤ 2
Programming experience	≤ 3	≤ 5	≤ 7	≤ 9	≤ 12
Programming attitude	≤ 2	≤ 4	≤ 6	≤ 8	≤ 10
Collaborative attitude	≤ 2	≤ 4	≤ 6	≤ 8	≤ 10
Programming skills	≤ 9	≤ 18	≤ 27	≤ 36	≤ 45

Note: The above is an assessment based on the sum of all values for each dimension

3.3   Algorithm Design and Model Definition

This article considers the influence of five dimensions, learning style, programming attitude, programming experience, cooperative attitude, and programming skills, on pair
programming recommendation and uses the vector method to represent the model of
learners' personalized learning characteristics. To measure the similarity between learners' personalized learning characteristic models, we chose three distance algorithms,
Euclidean distance, Jaccard distance, and Pearson correlation distance, and determined
which distance algorithm to use based on the collected data attributes. Specifically,
Euclidean distance is suitable for measuring low-dimensional data, such as programming attitude and cooperative attitude; Pearson correlation distance is more suitable for
measuring high-dimensional data, such as programming skills; and Jaccard distance is
suitable for sparse data, such as gender, and is particularly suitable for evaluating two
sets of data that have common attributes, where attribute values are Boolean data. The
specific Formulas (1) are as follows:

$$
R_K = \begin{bmatrix}
r_{11}^K & r_{12}^K & \cdots & r_{1j}^K \\
r_{21}^K & r_{22}^K & \cdots & r_{2j}^K \\
\vdots & \vdots & \vdots & \vdots \\
r_{i1}^K & r_{i2}^K & \cdots & r_{ij}^K
\end{bmatrix}
\tag{1}
$$

The personalized learning characteristic model of learners can be represented by the
above matrix R_K, R_K where each element r_{ij}^K in the matrix represents the distance between
the i-th learner and j-th learner in the k-th dimension attribute, where $K \in \{1, 2, 3, 4, 5\}$
represents learning style, programming experience, programming attitude, cooperative
attitude, and programming skills, respectively. The calculation formula for r_{ij}^K is shown
in Formula (2):

$$
r_{ij}^K = \alpha P_K + \beta E_K + \gamma D_K
\tag{2}
$$

where P_K represents the Pearson correlation distance formula in this article, as shown
in Formula (3).

$$
P_K = 1 - \frac{\sum\limits_{k=1}^{n} \left(Y_{ik} - \overline{Y}_i\right)\left(Y_{jk} - \overline{Y}_j\right)}{\sqrt{\sum\limits_{k=1}^{n} \left(Y_{ik} - \overline{Y}_i\right)^2} \sqrt{\sum\limits_{k=1}^{n} \left(Y_{jk} - \overline{Y}_j\right)^2}}
\tag{3}
$$

P_K is the distance between learners Y_i and Y_j, where $Y_i, Y_j \in S$ and n is the dimensionality. Y_{ik} is the k-th attribute value of learner Y_i, and Y_{ik} is the k-th attribute value of
learner Y_j. $\overline{Y}_i$ is the attribute mean value of learner Y_i, and $\overline{Y}$ is the attribute mean value
of learner Y_j.

E_k in this article represents the Euclidean distance, which is formulated as Eq. (4).

$$
E_k = \sqrt{\sum_{k=1}^{n} \left(Y_{ik} - Y_{jk}\right)^2}
\tag{4}
$$

D_k is represented as the Jaccard distance in this article, which is formulated as Eq. (5).

$$D_k = 1 - \frac{\left|Y_{ik} \cap Y_{jk}\right|}{\left|Y_{ik} \cup Y_{jk}\right|} \tag{5}$$

In contrast, "α", "β", and "γ" represent the weights of their algorithms, and their distance coefficients are calculated by the weight of the algorithm in the dimension. For example, in the calculation of the distance of programming experience, the Pearson correlation distance is not applicable to the calculation of the coefficient for this problem, so the weight taken in this paper is 0. Instead, the statistical use of the Euclidean distance and the Jaccard distance, with weights of 0.2 and 0.8, respectively. Therefore, the calculation formula is as follows.

$$r_{ij}^K = 0 \times P_K + 0.2 \times E_K + 0.8 \times D_K \tag{6}$$

The distances of all learners, except for the current learner Y_i, are ranked, and the distance is extracted nearest to the homogeneous model and the farthest distance to the heterogeneous model.

3.4 Generate a List of Recommendations

After calculating the distance between the personalized learning feature models of the learners, we differentiate by gender and use other features as the main criteria to compare the distance between the students who need to be recommended and the other male and female students in the student list. Then, we recommend same-sex homogeneous, same-sex heterogeneous, opposite-sex homogeneous, and opposite-sex heterogeneous paired companions for students and generate a list of paired companion recommendations. Specifically, same-sex homogeneous refers to same-sex students with similar personalized learning feature models as the student, opposite-sex homogeneous refers to opposite-sex students with similar personalized learning feature models as the student, same-sex heterogeneous refers to same-sex students with different but complementary personalized learning feature models as the student, and opposite-sex heterogeneous refers to opposite-sex students with different but complementary personalized learning feature models as the student. Through this approach, we can provide students with different types of paired companion recommendations to meet different needs and preferences. Students can freely choose their paired companions, which can improve group compatibility and harmony to a certain extent, thereby enhancing collaboration efficiency and learning effectiveness.

This article uses male student as an example to recommend paired partners for him based on individual learning characteristics and gender. First, the individual learning characteristic data of student are extracted from the dataset, and their individual learning characteristic model is evaluated. Using the formula, the distance between the student's individual learning characteristic model and that of all male students (excluding himself) is calculated, and the closest and farthest distances are selected as same-gender homogeneous and same-gender heterogeneous partners, respectively. Similarly, the distance between the student's individual learning characteristic model and that of all female students is calculated, and the closest and farthest distances are selected as opposite-gender homogeneous and opposite-gender heterogeneous partners, respectively. The feature and distance values of student and their recommended partners in each dimension in Table 2 (This paper normalizes the evaluated data to make different indicators more comparable and to present the results more clearly and aesthetically.

Table 2. Assessment data of personality learning characteristic models for learner and four recommended peers

Item	S_1	Homogenous male	Heterogenous male	Homogenous female	Heterogenous male
Serial number	1	46	4	68	79
Gender	0	0	0	1	1
Learning style	1.00	1.00	3.00	1.00	5.00
Programming experience	2.71	2.43	2.14	2.43	1.00
Programming attitude	4.00	4.00	1.00	4.50	1.00
Collaborative attitude	3.50	4.00	1.00	3.00	1.00
Programming skills	3.22	3.67	1.00	2.89	1.00
Distance value from S_1		1.27	4.96	1.36	4.92

Based on the table, we can depict the individual learning characteristic models of the learner and the four types of recommended paired partners, as well as the distances between these four recommended partners and, as shown in Fig. 2.

In the figure, male students are represented by solid lines, and female students are represented by dotted lines. The recommended same-gender homogeneous and heterogeneous partners for S_1 are students S_{46} and S_4, respectively, while the recommended opposite-gender homogeneous and heterogeneous partners are S_{68} and S_{79}, respectively. With this recommendation method, students can choose suitable paired partners according to their own situation, giving them more space for choice.

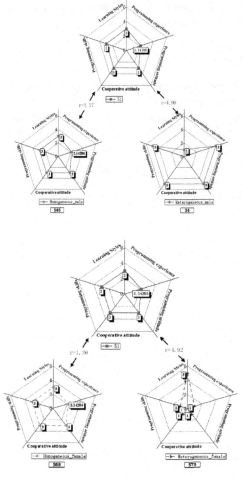

Fig. 2. Personality learning characteristic models and distance map for learner S1 and four recommended peers

4 Results

4.1 Experimental Design

To verify the effectiveness of the paired peer recommendation method based on personality learning characteristics, first-year mobile development students who were taking an introductory programming course at Henan Normal University were selected as the subjects for this study. The control group consisted of 64 students who performed individual programming. In contrast, for the 86 students in the experimental group, we used a pair peer recommendation method based on individual learning characteristics to recommend a list of suitable peers for the students to choose on their own. When programming, one person wrote the programme and the other supervised it, swapping roles at certain intervals or when there were problems. At the same time, the teacher observed the students' collaboration during the programme.

4.2 Analysis of Effects

Satisfaction Survey. The most important aspect of this study was to investigate the effectiveness of a pairing peer recommendation method for pair programming based on personality learning characteristics, so a satisfaction questionnaire was released to the experimental group. The questionnaire asked students to answer four questions to analyse their preferred type of peers, their satisfaction with their peers and their feelings about learning. These included "What is your preferred type of peer?", "How satisfied are you with the recommended peers?", "Would you like to continue learning with this peer" and "How do you feel about learning with this peer in a programming pair?

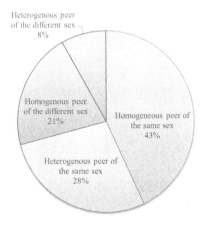

Fig. 3. Analysis of peer type preferences

Analysis of Peer Type Preferences. Figure 3 shows that 43% of students prefer to be paired with same-sex homogeneous peers, 28% choose same-sex heterogeneous peers, 21% choose opposite-sex homogeneous peers and only 8% choose opposite-sex heterogeneous peers. This indicates that students preferred to pair with same-sex peers and were less likely to choose opposite-sex heterogeneous peers. During the observation of students' paired programming learning process, communication between peers of the same gender and similar characteristics is more harmonious, especially among male students who tend to discuss task-related content, while female students tend to discuss other topics. When working together between heterosexuals, communication between students was less intense than that between same-sex peers, but students talked while operating, which may be related to their learning styles. However, among heterosexual heterogeneous peers, a small proportion of them performed most of the tasks mainly by one person and did not exchange roles promptly. Therefore, partner factors and role swapping also need to be considered when using personality learning traits for matching in future studies.

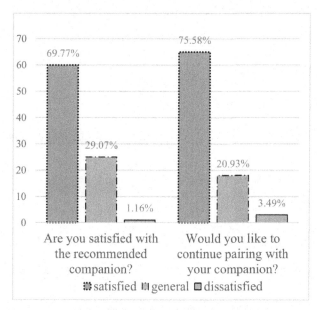

Fig. 4. Peer Satisfaction

Student Feedback on Paired Programming Experience Based on Personalized Learning Characteristics. Figure 5 shows that 92.31% of students said that with the help of their peers, they learned more methods and ideas for completing tasks. A total of 52.75% of students felt that paired programming under this method reduced their fear of programming, and 87.91% of students reported that they rarely slack off under their peers' supervision. A total of 71.43% of students felt very happy and efficient in problem solving. In summary, the majority of students felt good about their pair programming experience under the personality-based learning characteristics of the pair peer recommendation method, and the method was highly beneficial to their programming learning.

Peer Satisfaction Analysis. From Fig. 4, it can be seen that 69.77% of students are very satisfied with the recommended peers, 29.07% of students consider the recommended peers to be average, but 75.58% of students expressed their willingness to continue pairing with the recommended peers, 20.93% remained neutral, and only 3.49% were unwilling. From these data, it can be seen that most students are relatively satisfied with the recommended peers and are willing to continue pairing with them. Therefore, teachers need to maintain the stability of these paired groups. For students who are unwilling to pair with the recommended peers, teachers will gain a deeper understanding of their reasons and thoughts and make timely small-scale adjustments. This is because frequent changes in peers can affect learners' flow and the effectiveness of paired programming [27].

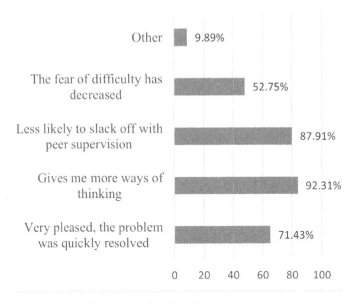

Fig. 5. Benefits of pairing programming

Analysis of the Computational Thinking Skills Test. To assess the effectiveness of paired programming in teaching university courses, we used the Computational Thinking Skills Scale to compare the differences in computational thinking skills between the control and experimental groups. This scale was adapted from the Computational Thinking Scale (CTS) [26] based on actual situations, containing 17 questions covering five aspects of computational thinking ability: abstraction, decomposition, algorithmic thinking, assessment, and summarization (a = 0.93). We collected 64 questionnaires from the control group and 86 questionnaires from the experimental group and analysed the collected questionnaire data using SPSS. The specific analysis results are presented below.

We used the Computational Thinking Ability Scale to test students' computational thinking ability and analysed it from five dimensions. Table 3 shows the results of independent sample t tests on the computational thinking of the experimental and control group students. According to the chart, there were significant differences ($p = 0.00 < 0.05$) between the control and experimental groups in terms of overall computational thinking ability and each dimension. This indicates that, compared to the control group, the computational thinking ability of students in the experimental group improved.

Table 3. Summary of computational thinking ability test results

group		Number	Mean	Standard deviation	Sig.
Overall	Experimental group	86	4.19	0.54	0.000
	Control group	64	3.56	0.67	
Summarizing skills	Experimental group	86	4.21	0.61	0.003
	Control group	64	3.69	0.82	
Decomposition skills	Experimental group	86	4.20	0.62	0.000
	Control group	64	3.54	0.90	
Abstraction skills	Experimental group	86	4.18	0.64	0.000
	Control group	64	3.55	0.89	
Assessment skill	Experimental group	86	4.18	0.60	0.003
	Control group	64	3.54	0.84	
Algorithmic thinking	Experimental group	86	4.17	0.61	0.005
	Control group	64	3.50	0.79	

5 Conclusion

The pairing method is an important issue in the research on paired programming teaching. This study extracted personalized characteristic data of learners based on survey questionnaire data and proposed a definition and paired partner recommendation method based on personalized characteristic models. This model and method not only comprehensively consider the personalized differences in learners' programming learning but also give learners a certain degree of autonomy in pairing and, to a certain extent, respect the students' wishes in pairing, further solving the problem of "difficult pairing" and achieving automated recommendation of paired partners in the pairing programming environment.

References

1. Cliburn, D.C.: Experiences with pair programming at a small college. J. Comput. Sci. Coll. **19**(19), 20–29 (2003)
2. Demir, M., Seferoglu, S.S.: The effect of determining pair programming groups according to various individual difference variables on group compatibility, flow, and coding performance. J. Educ. Comput. Res. **59**(1), 41–70 (2021)

3. Lejeune, N.F.: Teaching software engineering practices with extreme programming. J. Comput. Sci. Coll. **21**(3), 107–117 (2006)

4. Mcchesney, I.: Three years of student pair programming: action research insights and outcomes. In: Proceedings of the 47th ACM Technical Symposium on Computing Science Education (SIGCSE 2016), pp. 84–89 (2016)

5. Preston, D.: PAIR programming as a model of collaborative learning: a review of the research. J. Comput. Sci. Coll. **20**(4), 39–45 (2005)

6. Zhen, L., Plaue, C., Kraemer, E.: A spirit of camaraderie: the impact of pair programming on retention. In: 2013 26th International Conference on Software Engineering Education and Training (CSEE&T), pp. 209–218 (2013)

7. Vanhanen, J., Lassenius, C.: Effects of pair programming at the development team level: an experiment. In: 2005 International Symposium on Empirical Software Engineering, pp. 336–345 (2005)

8. Nawahdah, M., Taji, D.: Investigating students' behavior and code quality when applying pair-programming as a teaching technique. In: 2016 IEEE Global Engineering Education Conference (EDUCON), pp. 32–39 (2016)

9. Chen, J.: Research on teaching strategies of paired programming for elementary school students. MA thesis, Nanjing Normal University (2016)

10. Huang, Q.: A quasi experimental study of different pair programming strategies on the programming learning effect of primary school student. MA thesis, Shanghai Normal University, 2022

11. Zhang, Y., Yang, Y., Yang, Y., et al.: Research on pair learning methods and patterns based on paired programming. Comput. Knowl. Technol. **5X**, 114–116 (2017)

12. Choi, K.S.: A comparative analysis of different gender pair combinations in pair programming. Behav. Inf. Technol. **34**(7–9), 825–837 (2015)

13. Katira, N., Williams, L., Osborne, J.: Towards increasing the compatibility of student pair programmers. In: Proceedings of the 27th International Conference on Software Engineering (ICSE 2005), pp. 625–626 (2005)

14. Mcdowell, C., Werner, L., Bullock, H.E., et al.: Pair programming improves student retention, confidence, and program quality. Commun. ACM **49**(8), 90–95 (2006)

15. Werner, L.L., Campe, S., Denner, J.: Middle school girls + games programming = information technology fluency. In: Proceedings of the 6th Conference on Information Technology Education (SIGITE 2005), pp. 301–305. Association for Computing Machinery (2005)

16. Gu, F.: The impact of pair programming learning on middle school students' computational thinking based on differences in learning style. MA thesis, Central China Normal University (2022)

17. Li, T.T., Hao, Q., Wen, Y.S., et al.: Research on the influence of pair-programming on elementary school students' computational thinking based on learning style and partnership. J. Dist. Educ. **40**(3), 105–112 (2022)

18. Chao, J., Atli, G.: Critical personality traits in successful pair programming. AGILE 2006 (AGILE 2006), pp. 89–93 (2006)

19. Kolb, D.: Experiential Learning: Experience as the Source of Learning and Development, pp. 16–17 (1983)

20. Williams, L., Kessler, R.: Pair Programming Illuminated. Addison-Wesley Professional Press (2002)

21. Zeng, Y.Q.: Research on paired programming strategies for cultivating computational thinking for junior high school students. MA thesis, Guangzhou University (2022)

22. Ally, M.A., Darroch, F., Toleman, M.: A framework for understanding the factors influencing pair programming success. In: Extreme Programming and Agile Processes in Software Engineering (XP 2005), pp. 82–91 (2005)

23. Plonka, L., Van der Linden, H., Dittrich, J., Yvonne: knowledge transfer in pair programming: an in-depth analysis. Int. J. Hum. Comput. Stud. **73**, 66–78(2015)
24. Cockburn, A., Williams, L.: The Costs and Benefits of Pair Programming, pp.223–243. Addison-Wesley Longman Publishing Co., Inc. (2001)
25. Barron, B., Gomez, K., Pinkard, N., et al.: The digital youth network: cultivating digital media citizenship in urban communities. MIT Press (2014)
26. Korkmaz, O., Cakir, R., Ozden, M.Y.: A validity and reliability study of the computational thinking scales (CTS). Comput. Hum. Behav. **72**, 558–569 (2017)
27. Belshee, A.: Promiscuous pairing and beginner's mind: embrace inexperience. In: Agile Development Conference (ADC 2005), pp. 125–131 (2005)

Predicting Student Performance in Higher Education Based on Dynamic Graph Neural Networks with Consideration of Grading Habits

Xing Qi[1] 📧, Yueshu Yu[2], and Yan Chen[2(✉)]

[1] Anhui University, Hefei, China
[2] Anhui Taohuadao Inc., Hefei, China
370442797@qq.com

Abstract. Accurately predicting student performance in higher education is crucial for educators and institutions to evaluate and improve teaching and learning outcomes. Traditional methods for predicting student performance often use machine learning algorithms that rely on the student learning behaviours, such as students' performances of the past years or students' attendance data, whereas the teacher grading habits are usually not considered yet. In this paper, we propose a new approach for predicting student performance in higher education based on dynamic graphical neural networks that consider not only the students behaviour but also teachers' grading habits. We evaluate the proposed approach on a real-world dataset and show that our approach outperforms existing methods in terms of accuracy and F1-score.

Keywords: dynamic graphical neural networks · machine learning · student performance prediction · teacher grading habits

1 Introduction

Accurately predicting student performance in higher education has important implications for educators and institutions in evaluating and improving teaching and learning outcomes. By identifying at-risk students early, educators can provide targeted support and resources to improve student outcomes and retention rates [1]. Accurate predictions of student performance can also help educators identify areas for improvement in their teaching practices and adjust their methods to better support student learning [2].

Traditional methods for predicting student performance often rely on static features such as student scores from past years, attendance rates from previous courses, and other behavioural data [3]. While these features can be informative, they often ignore the dynamic and complex relationships between students and teachers that can have a significant impact on student performance. If the dynamic and complex relationships between students and teachers are ignored, traditional methods for predicting student performance may overlook important factors that contribute to student performance. For example, a student who has consistently performed well on standardized tests and has a high attendance rate in their courses may still struggle in a course with a teacher who grades more strictly or provides minimal feedback. Similarly, a student who has struggled in the past may excel in a course with a teacher who provides targeted support and feedback.

In this paper, we propose a method for predicting student performance based on dynamic graphical neural networks, that takes into account both the students' performance data and the teachers' grading habits. By modelling the relationships between students and teachers in a dynamic and adaptive way, our model can capture the pattern of how different teachers grade, and use this information to improve the accuracy of performance predictions. Meanwhile, our model provides a more comprehensive understanding of the factors that contribute to student success, which can inform the development of new teaching methods and practices that better support student learning and achievement.

The rest of the paper is organized as follows. Section 2 provides an overview of the related work in student performance prediction and dynamic graphical neural networks. Section 3 presents the proposed approach for predicting student performance in higher education based on dynamic graphical neural networks that consider teacher marking habits. In Sect. 4, we describe the experimental setup and evaluation metrics, as well as the results of the evaluation. Section 5 presents an ablation study to investigate the impact of incorporating teacher marking habits in predicting student performance. Finally, Sect. 6 concludes the paper and discusses future research directions.

2   Related Works

In recent years, there has been a growing interest in predicting student performance in higher education using various methods. These methods can be broadly categorized into two groups: classical machine learning-based methods and deep learning-based methods.

Classical machine learning-based methods often use naive bayes [4], decision trees [5], or random forests [6] to predict student performance. For example, Huynh-Cam et al. used a decision trees and random forest algorithms to predict student performance based on their father occupations, living expenses admission status [7]. Ayanet et al. used liner and logistic model to predict student performance based on Grades in basic courses [8].

Deep learning-based methods, such as deep neural networks [9] and deep convolutional neural networks [10], have been widely used in predicting student performance. For example, Nabil et al. proposed a deep neural network model to predict student performance in online courses based on their clickstream data [11]. Kooris et al. proposed a recurrent neural network to predict student performance in MOOCs based on their behaviour data [12].

Although these methods have achieved promising results, they often ignore the important factors such as the dynamic nature of student behaviour data and teacher grading habits. To address these limitations, we propose a new approach for predicting student performance based on dynamic graphical neural networks that consider teacher marking habits.

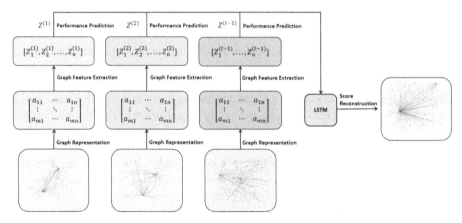

Fig. 1. Overview of the proposed dynamic graph neural networks

Dynamic graphical neural networks have recently gained popularity in various fields such as social network analysis [13], biology [14], and recommender systems [15]. These models are capable of capturing the temporal dependencies and interactions between entities in a dynamic graph. For example, Diao et al. proposed a dynamic spatio-temporal GCNN to track the spatial dependencies among traffic data for accurate traffic forecasting [16]. Wu et al. proposed a dynamic graph convolutional network to solve the inherent class imbalance problem of video summarization task [17]. Our proposed approach is inspired by these works, and extends the dynamic graphical neural network model to predict student performance in higher education.

3 Methodology

3.1 Overview

The overview of our proposed method is demonstrated in Fig. 1, which involves the following four components: 1, **graph representation**: the students' performance data over the past few years and the corresponding teachers who given the such performance data are used to establish the graph structure, and the node feature matrices of such graph is calculated; 2, **graph feature extraction**: taking the node feature matrices as the input, the convolutional network to extract the graph-level features; 3, **performance prediction**: a long-short-term-memory (LSTM) network is used to predict the above graph-level features in a time-series way, so that the students' future performance can be predicted adaptively; 4, **score reconstruction**: as the predicted performance are demonstrated in form of a high-level feature vectors, in practice such high-level vectors should be reconstructed into the actual score values.

3.2 Graph Representation

The relationship between the student performance and the teacher grading habits is represented as a graph structure $\mathcal{G}$, as shown in Fig. 2. In $\mathcal{G}$, the entities of the students and the teachers are taken as the nodes, and the student performance given by the teachers are taken as edges. Suppose $\mathcal{G} = \{\sqsubseteq\}$, where $\sqsubseteq = \{v_1, ..., v_N\}$ is the set of nodes of size N. The nodes in the graph $\mathcal{G}$ should be transformed into a vector form. To realize this, the nodes $v_i \in V$ ($I = 1, ..., N$) is firstly mapped from the graph domain to the embedding domain, and the mapped value is denoted as x_i.

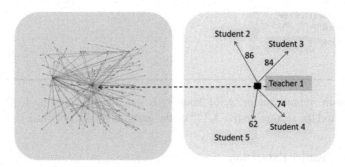

Fig. 2. Graphical representation model of teacher and student performance

The mapping function f is written as:

$$x_i = f(\sqsubseteq_i) = \mathbf{W}^T e_i \tag{1}$$

where $e_i \in [0, 1]$ denotes the one-hot encoding of the node v_i, which means in e_i there exists only one element of 1, and the rest elements are 0. After the one-hot encoding, a random walk algorithm, denoted by $RW(\cdot)$, is used to extract the key information, which is:

$$\mathcal{W} = \mathrm{RW}(\mathcal{G}, \sqsubseteq^{(0)}, K) \tag{2}$$

where $\mathcal{W} = v^{(0)}, ... , v^{(k-1)}$ denotes the generated random walk sequence; $v^{(0)}$ denotes the starting node; and K denotes the length of the random walk. To achieve the random walk algorithm, we generate random walk sequence firstly, the algorithm is demonstrated in Algorithm 1. Then we need extract the key information of random walk sequence in form of the node co-occurrence, the algorithm is demonstrated in Algorithm 2.

Algorithm 1. The algorithm of random walk

Algorithm.1: Random walk

Input: $\mathcal{G} = \{V$ Input: $\mathcal{G} = \{V$ Input $\{\mathcal{G}, v, T, \gamma\}$//$T$ is the length of random walk sequences, γ is the number of random walk sequences.

Output: $\mathcal{R}$ // $\mathcal{R}$ is the set of random walk.

Initialize: $\mathcal{R} \leftarrow \square$

1: **for** i in range(γ) **do**

2:     **for** $v \in V$ **do**

3:         $\mathcal{W} \leftarrow \mathrm{RW}(\mathcal{G}, v^{(0)}, T)$

4:         $\mathcal{R} \leftarrow \mathcal{R} \cup \{\mathcal{W}\}$

5:     **end**

6: **end**

Algorithm 2. The algorithm of random walk

Algorithm 2: Extract node co-occurrence

Input: $\mathcal{R}, w$

Output: $\mathcal{I}$ // $\mathcal{I}$ is the list of co-occurrence tuple.

Initialize: $\mathcal{I} \leftarrow [\,]$

1: **for** $\mathcal{W}$ in $\mathcal{R}$ **do**

2:   **for** $v^{(i)} \in \mathcal{W}$ **do**

3:     **for** j in range $(1, w)$ **do**

4:       $\mathcal{I}$. append$((v^{(i-j)}, v^{(i)}))$

5:       $\mathcal{I}$. append$((v^{(i+j)}, v^{(i)}))$

6:     **end**

5:   **end**

6: **end**

The feature representation x_i of node v_i is calculated according to the optimal parameters, and the feature matrix $\mathbf{X}^{N \times d}$ of the graph is finally obtained.

3.3 Graph Feature Extraction

This subsection aims to extract the graph-level feature. Let $\mathbf{A} \in \{0,1\}^{N \times N}$ be the adjacency matrix of graph $\mathcal{G}$. The i-th row and j-th column elements of $\mathbf{A}$, denoted by $\mathbf{A}_{ij}$, represents the relationship between node v_i and node v_j. If v_i and v_j are adjacent, $\mathbf{A}_{ij} = 1$, otherwise, $\mathbf{A}_{ij} = 0$. $\mathbf{D} \in \mathbb{R}^{N \times N}$ is the degree matrix [18] of graph $\mathcal{G}$, denoted by:

$$\mathbf{D}_{ii} = \sum_{j=1}^{N} \mathbf{A}_{ij} \tag{3}$$

Then we construct the graph convolutional network (GCN) to calculate the graph-level feature. Taking the adjacency matrix $\mathbf{A}$ and the graph feature matrix $\mathbf{X}^{N \times d}$ as input, the feature vector $\mathbf{Z}$ can be calculated as:

$$\mathbf{Z} = GCN(\mathbf{A}, \mathbf{X}) = \widetilde{\mathbf{A}} \, [\text{ReLU}(\widetilde{\mathbf{A}} \, \mathbf{X} \mathbf{W}_0)] \mathbf{W}_1 \tag{4}$$

$$\widetilde{\mathbf{A}} = \mathbf{D}^{-\frac{1}{2}} \mathbf{A} \mathbf{D}^{-\frac{1}{2}} \tag{5}$$

where $\mathbf{W}_0$ and $\mathbf{W}_1$ are the parameters to be learned, $\mathbf{Z}$ is an $N \times k$-dimensional vector consisting of 0, and 1 and $ReLU()$ is the activation function:

$$ReLU(\mathbf{Z}) = \max\{0, \mathbf{Z}\} \tag{6}$$

3.4 Performance Prediction

This subsection aims to predict the student's performance according to the feature vector $\mathbf{Z}$. To realize this, the historical student performance should be first divided according to different semesters, and then the student performance graphs in each semester should be constructed, at last the feature vector **Z** calculated from Sect. 3.3 is input to a LSTM network for performance prediction. The LSTM model is constructed as:

$$f_t = \sigma\left(W_f \cdot Z^{(t)} + U_f \cdot h^{(t-1)} + b_f\right) \tag{7}$$

$$i_t = \sigma\left(W_i \cdot Z^{(t)} + U_i \cdot h^{(t-1)} + b_i\right) \tag{8}$$

$$o_t = \sigma\left(W_o \cdot Z^{(t)} + U_o \cdot h^{(t-1)} + b_o\right) \tag{9}$$

$$\tilde{C}^{(t)} = tanh\left(W_c \cdot Z^{(t)} + U_c \cdot h^{(t-1)} + b_c\right) \tag{10}$$

$$C^{(t)} = f_t \odot C^{(t-1)} + i_t \odot \tilde{C}^{(t)}) \tag{11}$$

$$h^{(t)} = o_t \odot tanh\left(C^{(t)}\right) \tag{12}$$

where $Z^{(t)}$ is the feature vector in t-th semester, and f_t, i_t, o_t are the forgetting gate, input gate, and output gate in the LSTM, respectively, as shown in Fig. 3.

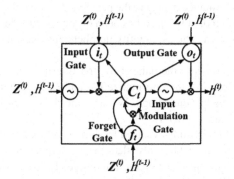

Fig. 3. Schematic diagram of LSTM module

Where W_f, U_f, b_f, W_i, U_i, b_i, W_o, U_o, b_o, W_c, U_c, b_c are the parameters to be learned by the model, and *tanh* is the activation function, written as:

$$tanh(Z) = 2 \cdot \sigma(2Z) - 1 \tag{13}$$

where σ is the sigmoid activation function:

$$\sigma(Z) = \frac{1}{1 + e^{-Z}} \tag{14}$$

Finally, the output of the LSTM, denoted by **Z'**, is the predicted performance in form of the graph feature vector.

3.5 Scores Reconstruction

Since the output of LSTM is in form of graph feature vector, in practice it should be reconstructed into actual score values. To do this, the prediction graph matrix **A'** should firstly be calculated according to the following equation:

$$\mathbf{A}\prime = \sigma\left(\mathbf{Z}\mathbf{Z}\prime\right) \tag{15}$$

The edges of the adjacency matrix **A'** are taken as the students' course grades, where the element **A'** in the i-th row and j-th column of **A' ij** denotes the course grade of the teacher course node v_j corresponding to the student node v_i.

4 Experiments

In this section, we describe the experimental setup and evaluation metrics for our proposed approach.

4.1 Experiment Setup

Dataset: We use a real-world dataset collected from a university in China. The dataset consists of student performance data over the past few years and the teacher grading data. It should be noted that all data we used has been desensitized, which means all privacy-related information, such as names, identity numbers and ages, have been removed for privacy protection.

Preprocessing: We preprocess the dataset by first filtering out irrelevant features and removing missing values. We then normalize the numerical features and convert categorical features into one-hot encodings. We split the dataset into training, validation, and testing sets with a ratio of 8:1:1.

Evaluation Metrics: In this study, we used freshman and sophomore data from a major as training data and junior data as test data. The tolerance for prediction is plus or minus 10 points, which means that a prediction is considered successful if the difference between the predicted score and the ground truth score does not exceed 10 points. To evaluate the performance of the proposed method, we use the accuracy and F1-score as evaluation metrics. The accuracy measures the proportion of correctly classified samples, while the F1-score is the harmonic mean of precision and recall.

Implementation Details: We implement the proposed approach using *Python*、*Keras* and the *Networkx*. We set the number of layers in the dynamic graphical neural network to be 4, and the number of hidden units to be 3,162. We train the model using the Adam optimizer with a learning rate of 0.0001 for 800 epochs.

4.2 Experiment Results

In this section, we present the experimental results of our proposed approach for predicting student performance in higher education based on dynamic graphical neural networks that consider teacher marking habits.

Table 1. Performance comparison of different methods for predicting student performance

Method	Accuracy	F1-score
Linear regression	0.67	0.63
Random forest	0.72	0.70
Deep neural network	0.86	0.82
Proposed approach	**0.91**	**0.87**

Table 1 shows the performance comparison of our proposed approach with traditional statistical or machine learning-based methods and deep learning-based methods. Our proposed approach achieves the highest accuracy and F1-score, demonstrating the effectiveness of incorporating teacher marking habits in predicting student performance.

Our method achieves such promising results by taking into account the grading habits of teachers. In comparison to previous methods such as random forest and LSTM, which only utilize student data as training data, our method considers the influence of teachers' grading habits, as shown in Fig. 4. It is widely known that different teachers may assign different score ratings even for the same course, which is a crucial factor in the accuracy of performance prediction. Therefore, our approach involves constructing a graphical model to accurately capture this significant factor in the teacher's grading habits, which results in improved prediction accuracy. In conclusion, the incorporation of teacher grading habits into our model enhances its accuracy and reflects the importance of considering the complex factors that can affect the prediction of grades.

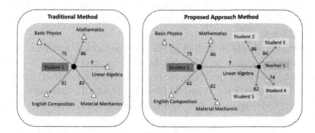

Fig. 4. Schematic diagram of the model considering the grading habits of teachers

5 Conclusion

In this paper, we proposed a novel approach for predicting student performance in higher education based on dynamic graphical neural networks that consider teacher grading habits. We constructed a dynamic graphical that integrates student performance data and teacher grading habits and used a dynamic graphical neural network to predict student performance. Our experimental results demonstrated the effectiveness of our proposed approach in predicting student performance and the importance of considering teacher marking habits. In future work, we plan to further investigate the impact of other factors, such as social network analysis, on predicting student performance.

References

1. Jokhan, A., Sharma, B., Singh, S.: Early warning system as a predictor for student performance in higher education blended courses. Stud. High. Educ. **44**(11), 1900–1911 (2019)
2. Alyahyan, E., Düştegör, D.: Predicting academic success in higher education: literature review and best practices. Int. J. Educ. Technol. High. Educ. **17**, 1–21 (2020)
3. Lukkarinen, A., Koivukangas, P., Seppala, T.: Relationship between class attendance and student performance. Procedia Soc. Behav. Sci. **228**, 341–347 (2016)
4. Tripathi, A., Yadav, S., Rajan, R.: Naive Bayes classification model for the student performance prediction. In: 2019 2nd International Conference on Intelligent Computing, Instrumentation and Control Technologies (ICICICT), vol. 1. IEEE (2019)
5. Kabra, R.R., Bichkar, R.S.: Performance prediction of engineering students using decision trees. Int. J. Comput. Appl. **36**(11), 8–12 (2011)
6. Jayaprakash, S., Krishnan, S., Jaiganesh, V.: Predicting student academic performance using an improved random forest classifier. In: 2020 International Conference on Emerging Smart Computing and Informatics (ESCI). IEEE (2020)
7. Huynh-Cam, T.-T., Chen, L.-S., Le, H.: Using decision trees and random forest algorithms to predict and determine factors contributing to first-year university students' learning performance. Algorithms **14**(11), 318 (2021)
8. Ayán, M.N.R., García, M.T.C.: Prediction of university students' academic achievement by linear and logistic models. Spanish J. Psychol. **11**(1), 275–288 (2008)
9. Kim, B.-H., Vizitei, E., Ganapathi, V.: GritNet: student performance prediction with deep learning. arXiv preprint arXiv:1804.07405 (2018)
10. Ma, Y., Zong, J., Cui, C., Zhang, C., Yang, Q., Yin, Y.: Dual path convolutional neural network for student performance prediction. In: Cheng, R., Mamoulis, N., Sun, Y., Huang, X. (eds.) WISE 2020. LNCS, vol. 11881, pp. 133–146. Springer, Cham (2019). https://doi.org/10.1007/978-3-030-34223-4_9
11. Nabil, A., Seyam, M., Abou-Elfetouh, A.: Prediction of students' academic performance based on courses' grades using deep neural networks. IEEE Access **9**, 140731–140746 (2021)
12. Kőrösi, G., Farkas, R.: MOOC performance prediction by deep learning from raw clickstream data. In: Singh, M., Gupta, P.K., Tyagi, V., Flusser, J., Ören, T., Valentino, G. (eds.) ICACDS 2020. CCIS, vol. 1244, pp. 474–485. Springer, Singapore (2020). https://doi.org/10.1007/978-981-15-6634-9_43
13. Held, P., et al.: Advanced analysis of dynamic graphs in social and neural networks. In: Towards Advanced Data Analysis by Combining Soft Computing and Statistics, pp. 205–222. Springer, Heidelberg (2013). https://doi.org/10.1007/978-3-642-30278-7_17
14. Kriegeskorte, N.: Deep neural networks: a new framework for modeling biological vision and brain information processing. Annu. Rev. Vis. Sci. **1**, 417–446 (2015)
15. Wu, S., et al.: Graph neural networks in recommender systems: a survey. ACM Comput. Surv. **55**(5), 1–37 (2022)
16. Diao, Z., et al.: Dynamic spatial-temporal graph convolutional neural networks for traffic forecasting. In: Proceedings of the AAAI Conference on Artificial Intelligence, vol. 33, no. 01 (2019)
17. Wu, J., Zhong, S.-H., Liu, Y.: Dynamic graph convolutional network for multi-video summarization. Pattern Recogn. **107**, 107382 (2020)
18. Yang, H., Ma, K., Cheng, J.: Rethinking graph regularization for graph neural networks. In: Proceedings of the AAAI Conference on Artificial Intelligence, vol. 35, no. 5 (2021)

Research on Personalized Learning Recommendation Based on Subject Knowledge Graphs and Learner Portraits

Shoujian Duan[1,2], Ken Chen[1(✉)], Yanli Yang[2], and Shunchao Shi[2]

[1] Key Laboratory of Education Informatization for Nationalities, Ministry of Education, Yunnan Normal University, Kunming, China
35701741@qq.com
[2] School of Big Data, Baoshan University, Baoshan, China

Abstract. In the context of the digital transformation of education, large-scale online learning has become the new normal of learning. The deep integration of artificial intelligence technology and education provides an effective path for achieving the organic combination of large-scale education and personalized training. This article reviews relevant research on subject knowledge graphs and learner portraits based on a large number of studies and proposes a personalized recommendation framework. The framework is composed of a subject knowledge graph, learner portrait based on xAPI, personalized recommendation and feedback. Focusing on learners' individual characteristics and learning feedback reflects the "learner-centered" concept and enables the use of dynamically growing educational resources to support personalized learning for learners.

Keywords: Digitalization of education · Subject knowledge graphs · Learner portraits · Personalized learning

1 Introduction

Digitalization of education is a new stage in the development of educational informatization, and the development of digital education is an important component of building a digital China. At present, the "Internet plus Education" platform relies on the national education resources public service system and the education resources sharing plan to provide high-quality educational resources for learners and teachers. The "Modernization of Education in China 2035" [1] proposes to use modern technology to accelerate the reform of talent cultivation models and achieve an organic combination of large-scale education and personalized training. It can be seen that in the context of digital education, large-scale online learning has become the New Normal of learning. Personalized learning, as a key measure to solve the problem of large-scale personalized education, has attracted much attention. Relevant core concepts and core technologies have become the focus of research on smart education.

The continuous development of artificial intelligence technology has made knowledge-based computing possible, enabling recommendations based on content and

J. Gan et al. (Eds.): CSEI 2023, CCIS 1900, pp. 367–374, 2024.
https://doi.org/10.1007/978-981-99-9492-2_31

learner portraits, and providing high-quality personalized learning services for learners. As a new hot topic in the development of artificial intelligence technology, knowledge graphs have a strong expressive ability. It can establish nonlinear semantic connections between different knowledge points, and solve personalized learning support problems such as recommendation, monitoring, evaluation, and feedback in online learning. It can help learners efficiently construct knowledge systems and optimize learning decisions, providing a new perspective for personalized learning support research [2]. The development of modern education methods such as online education has promoted the construction of information technology education resources. The educational needs in different scenarios have made educational information resources massive and diverse. The rapid growth of data and the increasing personalized demand for service requirements from learners have brought new problems in the organization and management of educational information resources, namely how to process and use educational resources within a unified framework and how to utilize dynamically growing educational resources to support personalized learning for learners.

2   Review of Relevant Key Technologies

2.1   Subject Knowledge Graphs

The knowledge graph is a technology launched by Google in 2012 based on the concepts and principles of the semantic web. It is a graph-based data structure consisting of nodes and edges. It represents the things and concepts in the real world as entities, and the relationships between entities as relationships, expressed in the form of triplets (head entity, relationship, tail entity). In the field of education, there have been many applications and expressions of knowledge graph, such as the subject knowledge graphs and educational knowledge graphs, which are used to model knowledge in the field of education. Liu Y. et al. [3] established an open knowledge graph to expand subject knowledge, facilitating students to review textbook knowledge in a targeted manner. Li Z. et al. [4] explored key technologies for constructing an educational knowledge graph from multidimensional perspectives such as knowledge modelling, resource management, knowledge navigation, learning cognition, and knowledge base. Numerous studies have shown that adaptive learning and personalized recommendations driven by knowledge graphs can effectively promote the implementation of precision teaching. For example, Zhao L. et al. [5] constructed a learner portrait model based on a knowledge graph, which is beneficial for the meaning construction and ability cultivation of learners' knowledge system. Zhong Z. et al. [6] constructed an educational knowledge graph model framework for mapping the relationship between knowledge, problems, and abilities. Li Y. et al. [7] believe that subject knowledge graphs can enhance the interpretability of artificial intelligence and assist in the construction of a framework for smart education systems.

At present, the subject knowledge graph, as an important supporting technology of the intelligent education environment, has gradually become a research hotspot in the field of intelligent education. However, there are still problems in the construction and application of knowledge graphs at present. The first reason is that the construction method requires not only a large number of manual annotations but also a high-quality corpus for automatic knowledge extraction algorithms. The current knowledge extraction algorithms still have problems of low performance and weak generalization ability, and knowledge extraction technology and knowledge fusion technology suitable for subject knowledge graphs need further exploration.

2.2 Learner Portraits

Learner portraits should be able to capture, represent, store, and modify learners' features and states, including their basic characteristics such as age and gender, and their learning and emotional states. Mayo M. et al. [8] established a learner model based on student performance and optimized learning behavior using the Bayesian network and decision theory. Triantafillou E. et al. [9] established a system to adapt to learners' learning styles and cognitive styles to conduct experiments. Weber G. [10] established a learner model ELM based on domain knowledge, which can capture the growth of learner knowledge. To better describe learners' learning experiences and achieve data exchange between different systems, platforms, and devices, the ADL project team in the United States proposed the interface specification xAPI (Experience API) based on the SCORM standard in 2013. It can store and retrieve any scalable learning records, learner information, and learning experience archives without considering specific learning platforms [11]. With the increasing demand for personalized learning services, Chen L. et al. [12] proposed the establishment of a learner model based on physiological, experiential, and psychological dimensions, aiming to explore personalized learning solutions for distance learners. Huang H. [13] proposed an emotion-based student model in the e-Learning learning environment. Wu F. et al. [14] proposed a scenario-aware learner model, that incorporates dimensions such as social networks and situational states into the learner model, making the model more refined. Tang Y. et al. [15] designed a precise personalized learning path planning framework based on learner portraits. The framework consists of four elements: learning objectives, learning content, learning activities, and learning evaluation, as well as six major components: learners, knowledge graph, mainstream learning paths, learner big data, learner portrait, and personalized learning paths. Yu M. et al. [16] adopted a data-level fusion method and constructed a research learning multisource data fusion architecture based on the xAPI specification. They developed a research learning behavior record library and achieved the fusion of multisource research learning experience data.

By analysing the relevant research on learner models both domestically and internationally, it is not difficult to find the following problems in the study of learner models. First, most models simply complete the data collection work and do not directly process the data in the models. Second, domestic researchers generally do not adopt the same general modelling method but focus on analysing the various factors that affect learners' learning, while foreign researchers focus on modelling a certain aspect of learning activities. Third, the operability of the learner model is not strong enough. Although the model has been established, the requirements for frontline teachers are too high, and it is still not convenient to use the model for personalized teaching.

2.3   Personalized Recommendation Technology

The idea of personalized learning can be traced back to the famous Chinese educator Confuciu's proposal of "teaching according to one's aptitude", which adopts different approaches, measures, and methods for individual teaching of different learners. Learners have differences in their learning backgrounds, knowledge levels, and learning methods, making it challenging to recommend suitable learning resources to specific learners. Even if two learners have similar academic performances, they also need different learning content due to their different learning characteristics. Therefore, personalized recommendation systems must consider the specific needs of learners.

The key to building a personalized learning environment is the recommendation system. The core purpose of recommendation systems is to solve the problem of information overload, and finding the content that users are interested in from massive data is the core focus of recommendation system research. After Resnick [17] proposed the first recommendation system in 1997, scholars designed various recommendation system models based on this to help users find information of interest in the vast amount of information. Recommendation algorithms can be divided into content-based recommendation, collaborative filtering-based recommendation, and hybrid recommendation. The theoretical basis of content-based recommendation algorithms comes from information retrieval and filtering, which filter recommendations by calculating user interests and similarity of information content. The collaboration of recommendation algorithms based on collaborative filtering refers to finding items that may be of interest to users in the item set through online means, and filtering refers to filtering out some data with low scores through offline means. The hybrid recommendation algorithm is a combination of multiple recommendation algorithms. Due to its unique advantages of multisource heterogeneous data fusion and fusion of multiple recommendation technologies, it can effectively alleviate the common problems of data sparsity and "cold start" in traditional recommendation systems. However, due to the multimodal, heterogeneous, large-scale, sparse, and uneven distribution of auxiliary information, research on hybrid recommendation methods that fuse multisource heterogeneous data still faces many challenges [18].

In recent years, research on personalized learning recommendation systems based on deep learning has received increasing attention from researchers. A recommendation system based on deep learning can take user and project-related data as model inputs, use deep learning algorithms to learn implicit representations of users and projects, and generate personalized recommendations based on these using traditional recommendation algorithms. The personalized recommendation method based on knowledge graphs and deep learning provides a new approach to constructing interpretable recommendation systems. Introducing the rich information contained in knowledge graphs into educational resource recommendation algorithms plays a crucial role in enhancing algorithm performance and improving personalized learning quality; Deep learning has the ability of autonomous learning and information filtering. It can learn the essential features of datasets from samples through deep nonlinear network structures, thereby obtaining deep feature representations of learners and learning resources, bringing new opportunities for personalized learning research.

3   A Personalized Learning Recommendation Framework

Based on the above analysis, this study designed a personalized learning recommendation framework based on a subject knowledge graph and learner portrait, as shown in Fig. 1. This framework explores the construction of personalized learning support mechanisms from a learner-oriented perspective, where learners consciously choose or actively explore their own learning situations during the learning process, thereby effectively engaging in personalized learning.

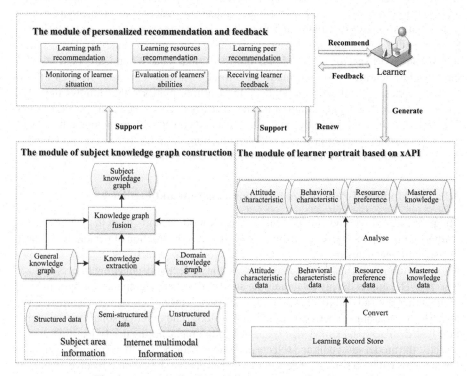

Fig. 1. A personalized learning recommendation framework

3.1   The Module of Subject Knowledge Graph Construction

On the basis of entity recognition and attribute extraction of authoritative information in the discipline field and related massive internet data resources, focusing on the issue of semantic diversity of educational information resources, technologies such as neural network matching models, deep graph calculations, and deep reinforcement learning are adopted to construct a more fine-grained discipline knowledge graphs by integrating existing general knowledge graphs and domain expert knowledge graph, achieving the integration of educational resources and knowledge expansion and mining. This module associates and combines knowledge obtained from different data sources to construct an updated knowledge graph, where the data can be structured, semistructured, or even unstructured. Third-party generic knowledge graphs such as CN-DBpedia, Wikidata, and domain expert knowledge graphs are used as knowledge bases or existing data sources to participate in the fusion process.

3.2 The Module of Learner Portrait Based on xAPI

Build a learner portrait module based on xAPI to achieve real-time tracking of learners' current learning records, learning attitudes, behavioral preferences, and knowledge mastery, thereby improving the performance of learning resource recommendation algorithms and optimizing the quality of personalized learning services. This module achieves learner profiling through data storage, data conversion, and data analysis. Data storage follows the xAPI specification and uses unified format data. When learners access different online learning resource platforms through various terminals, such as PCs or mobile phones, the collection module of the learning platform that follows the xAPI specification will generate a unified format of learner record data and store it in LRS. The collected data will be analyzed through Watershed LRS. By modelling data in various xAPI formats, learner portraits covering learning attitudes, behavioral preferences, resource preferences, and mastered knowledge can be generated.

3.3 The Module of Personalized Recommendation and Feedback

The personalized recommendation and feedback module starts from the perspective of learner-oriented personalized learning, exploring the construction of personalized learning support mechanisms. Learners consciously choose or actively explore their own learning situation during the learning process, thus effectively engaging in personalized learning. The model deeply integrates the subject knowledge graph as a supporting tool with learner portrait and records and tracks learners' basic information, cognitive level, ability level, learning experience, emotional attitude, and other personality characteristics. Based on personal knowledge status, learning time, learning needs, learning scenarios, etc., the model sets goals and selects paths to provide personalized recommendations for learning paths, resources, peers, and other aspects. The module receives feedback from learners, monitors learning status, evaluates learners' abilities, and updates user portrait to more accurately and effectively support personalized learning activities for learners.

4   Conclusion

Education is the interaction between humans, and education cannot be separated from humans. Only by integrating humans and machines, achieving human-machine interaction and collaboration can the function of educational digitization be truly realized, which is the essence of educational digitization [19]. This article reviews relevant research on subject knowledge graphs and learner portraits based on a large number of studies and proposes a personalized recommendation framework. The framework is composed of subject knowledge graph construction, learner portrait based on xAPI, personalized recommendation and feedback modules, focusing on learners' personality characteristics and learning feedback, reflecting the idea of "learner-centered" learning. However, the lack of research lies in the fact that this framework still has "one-sided" intelligent diagnosis, "programmatic" educational intervention, "feed-in" service supply, and "machine-driven" educational decision-making issues [20]. The application and practice of the framework are the key directions of future research work, and more attention should be given to teachers in the learning process and guidance of learners.

Acknowledgements. This research work was supported by following projects: Scientific Research Fund Project of the Education Department of Yunnan Province (2020J0705),Key Laboratory of Education Informatization for Nationalities, Ministry of Education, Yunnan Normal University(EIN202114),Yunnan Key Laboratory of Smart Education and Yunnan International Joint R&D Center of China-Laos-Thailand Educational Digitalization (202203AP140006).

References

1. Modernization of Education in China 2035. http://www.gov.cn/xinwen/2019-02/23/content_5 367987.htm, (Accessed 1 May 2023)
2. Liu, F., Zho, W., Jiang, Q., Wang L.: Research on personalized learning model and support mechanism based on knowledge graph. China Educ. Technol. (05), 75–81+90 (2022)
3. Liu, Y., Lou, L.: Research on extraction of subject single knowledge points based on knowledge map. Appli. Res. Comput. **26**(06) , 1693–1695+1699 (2019)
4. Li, Z., Zhou, D., Wang, Y.: Research of educational knowledge graph from the perspective of artificial intelligence+: connotation technical framework and application. J. Dis. Educ. **37**(04), 42–53 (2019)
5. Zhao, L., Fan, J., Zhao, Y., Tang, Y., Zhong, S.: The Design and application of the learners' portrait model based on knowledge mapping –taking the high school physics course as an example. Mod. Educ. Technol. **21**(02), 95–101 (2021)
6. Zhong, Z., Tang, Y., Zhong, S., Zhao, Y.: Research on constructing model of educational knowledge map supported by artificial intelligence. e-Educ. Res. **41**(04), 62–70 (2020)
7. Li, Y., Zhang, X., Li, X., Du, J: Construction and innovative application of discipline knowledge graph oriented to smart education. e-Educ. Res. **40**(08), 60–69 (2019)
8. Mayo, M., Mitrovic, A.: Optimising ITS behaviour with Bayesian networks and decision theory. Int. J. Artif. Intell. Educ. **12**, 124–153 (2001)
9. Triantafillou, E., Pomportsis, A., Demetriadis, S.: The value of adaptivity based on cognitive style: an empirical study. Br. J. Edu. Technol. **35**(1), 95–106 (2004)
10. Weber, G.: Episodic learner modeling. Cogn. Sci. **20**(2), 195–236 (2010)
11. Huang, J., Tang, Y., Fan, J., Zhong, S.: Research on the construction of precision teacher training portrait in online learning environment based on xAPI. China Educ. Technol. **399**(04), 102–108 (2020)
12. Chen, L., Zhang, W., Hao, D.: The three-dimensional model of Chinese distance learners' learning style. Open Educ. Res. **02**, 48–52 (2005)
13. Huan, H.: Research on Learner's Emotion Modelling and its Application in e-Learning, PhD Thesis, Central China Normal University (2014)
14. Wu, F., Huang, S., Ying, B.: Research on learner modelling based on context-awareness. e-Educ. Res. **40**(03), 68–74 (2019)
15. Tang, Y., Ru, L., Fan, J.: Research on planning of personalized learning path based on learner portrait modelling. e-Educ. Res. **40**(10), 53–60 (2019)

16. Yu, M., Zhang, Z., Liu, X.: Research on multi-source data fusion of research-based learning based on xAPI. Mod. Dis. Educ. **201**(03), 63–69 (2022)
17. Resnick, P., Varian, H.R.: Recommender systems. Commun. ACM. **40**(3), 56–58 (1997)
18. Huang, L., Jiang, B., Lv, S.: Survey on deep learning based recommender systems. Chinese J. Comput. **41**(07), 1619–1647 (2018)
19. Yuan, Z.: Educational governance in the perspective of Digital transformation. J. Chin. Soc. Educ. (08), 1–6+18 (2022)
20. Wang, Y., Zheng, Y.: Intelligent learning intervention: realistic dilemma original clarification proper form. Open Educ. Res. **44**(3), 28–35 (2023)

University Learning Situation Data Governance Model Based on Blockchain

Xiaomeng Pan[1] and Lingyun Yuan[1,2(✉)]

[1] Key Laboratory of Educational, Information for Nationalities, Ministry of Education, Yunnan Normal University, Kunming, China
blues520@sina.com

[2] School of Information Science and Technology, Yunnan Normal University, Kunming, China

Abstract. In view of the current problems of difficult sharing, privacy leakage and confusion in the management of learning situation data in universities, this paper analyses the feasibility of blockchain technology, which is used to enable the governance of learning situation data in colleges and universities, and constructs a learning situation data governance model based on blockchain. In addition, the architecture of the learning situation data governance model is built, and the "on-chain + off-chain" collaborative storage mode is designed. Hash addresses of learning situation data are stored on the chain, while IPFS is used to store actual learning situation data off the chain. Moreover, blockchain networks are built based on Fabric, and smart contracts are also well designed. Security analysis and experimental verification show that our model can realize the secure storage and controllable access of learning situation data, and it can solve some problems that exist in the data governance process of universities.

Keywords: Blockchain · Learning Situation Data · Data Governance · Storage Mode · Smart Contract

1 Introduction

As the intersection of education governance and data governance, education data governance is a collection of actions taken by education authorities or educational institutions around education data to make full use of the value of data. Yu Peng argues that education data governance is a solution to the "low quality of data, confusing data flow, insufficient sharing and missing historical data" [1]. Xu et al. argue that data governance is necessary to improve the quality of university education, scientific decision-making and management efficiency and that its efficient, accountable and transparent features meet the requirements of higher education governance [2].

However, with the continuous development of big data, the process of education data governance has also given rise to a number of problems. In various stages of education data collection, transmission, storage and processing, the owners and users are often different, and there is a separation of data ownership and usage rights, which can easily lead to data misuse and unclear data ownership; unscrupulous elements take advantage of information system loopholes and hacking techniques to steal personal information, resulting in personal information, and the leakage of personal information is seriously further exacerbated; the complexity of education data statistics means that it requires the coordinated accommodation of multiple subjects to ensure the comprehensiveness, authenticity and accuracy of education data.

On October 24, 2019, the 18th collective study of the Central Political Bureau mentioned blockchain as an important breakthrough in the independent innovation of core technologies, exploring the application of "blockchain + " in the field of people's livelihood and actively promoting the application of blockchain technology in education and other fields. "Blockchain + education" has gradually become a new research hotspot in the field of education informatization after "Internet + education" [3]. In May 2020, the Ministry of Education issued the "Action Plan for Blockchain Technology Innovation in Higher Education", which stated: "Build a blockchain-based education governance and application innovation platform, and support the development and application of innovative technologies in such fields as authentic and trustworthy digital file storage and tracking, sensitive information circulation control and privacy protection [4]. "The integration of blockchain technology with higher education academic data governance can solve the problems of student privacy leakage, education data sharing and data intractability arising from university education data governance.

Therefore, this paper intends to integrate blockchain technology to build a decentralized, secure and traceable model for the governance of university learning situation data, to achieve privacy protection of learning situation data through encryption and decryption technology, to solve the problem of storing massive learning situation data through on-chain and off-chain learning situation data storage, to achieve tamper-proof and traceable learning situation data through data on-chain, and to provide a reference model for education data management, especially learning situation data management, especially school situation data management.

2   Problems Facing the Governance of Learning Situation Data in Universities

2.1   Difficulties in Sharing Learning Situation Data

Most universities do not have a very clear information construction plan at the early stage of digital campus construction. The diversity of the system underlying design leads to various interface problems in the sharing process of each method with the data centre. Business departments store and manage data around the needs of their current business, lack management of data that they consider unimportant or irrelevant, and even modify the resulting data arbitrarily for the convenience of work [5]. Some businesses require multiple departments to collaborate. Due to poor collaboration mechanisms, data maintenance responsibilities are not clear, process data are easily missing, and the result leads to multiple sources of data and data conflicts, data incompleteness, and sharing is also relatively singular.

2.2 Learning Situation Data Privacy Leakage

In terms of information collection, there are chaotic situations such as forcibly taking information and stealing information; in terms of data storage, there are hidden dangers such as loopholes, hackers, web crawlers and data hacking; and in terms of data use, universities do not pay enough attention to the protection of students' privacy. Students' ID numbers, mobile phone numbers and home addresses are sensitive information that may be unconsciously leaked out by the personnel of the school management bodies, and the privacy supervision of data is not perfect, resulting in the leakage of education data privacy.

2.3 Confusion Management of Learning Situation Data

The confusion in the management of learning situation data in colleges and universities is reflected in the management system of data and the life cycle management of data [6]. The shared data centre built based on the concept of digital campus data sharing lacks a data coordination and management department. The data management of business departments is fragmented, with the shared data centre passively acquiring the data provided by business departments. The scattering of data management authority leads to confusion in data management authority and responsibility, slow progress in the data construction of university management institutions, and the management of data becoming disorganized, further leading to a decline in data quality, which is not conducive to the realization of the value of data itself and the development of universities.

3 Blockchain Technology Enables Learning Situation Data Governance in Universities

3.1 Multiple Parties Participate

The university includes different types of participants, including students, teachers, administrators, etc., who all have an impact on the decision-making and management of universities. Each governance subject and stakeholder on the data chain can become a node in the provision, use and decision-making of data, which fundamentally forms a transformation from a single subject to a plurality and can realize multiparty governance in the decision-making of university affairs [7]. Blockchain can effectively improve the interoperability and mutual trust between different nodes in the region, promote the flow of multisource learning situation data in an orderly, secure, credible and transparent way for sharing and open application, and thus crack the problem of siloed university learning situation data.

3.2 Building Security Mechanism

Blockchain can make learning situation data records more secure. Using blockchain technology, it can trace the source and ensure that the whole process of data from collection to calculation and analysis can be stored so that data quality can be backed by strong trust and trust can be established between relevant entities. Blockchain adopts the same trust mechanism between different data nodes and protects data information security through algorithms, and all blocks jointly participate in maintaining the whole data chain; the privacy of blockchain lays down the security of learning situation data sharing. The main difficulty and challenge of open data sharing is how to open data while protecting the privacy of individuals. The consensus-based encryption algorithm adopted by blockchain technology can guarantee the privacy of learning situation data, and the use of blockchain data desensitization technology can meet the need for privacy protection during the sharing of data [8].

3.3 Reaching Educational Consensus

The consensus mechanism of the blockchain can ensure the validity of information between nodes, avoid anomalies in any node and make the data governance business run safely and stably. Through the consensus mechanism, an education governance community of school management bodies, teachers and students in the region is built. The consensus mechanism supports "collective decision making" by all nodes on the chain and facilitates fast transactions between nodes on the chain by establishing a trustworthy network, ensuring openness and transparency of transaction data in the blockchain system [9].

4 Building a Blockchain-Based Model for Learning Situation Data Governance in Universities

4.1 Blockchain-Based Governance Model Architecture for University Learning Situation Data

The "learning situation" is a relatively broad concept, including not only the knowledge structure, ability level and learning interest of students before learning a certain professional course but also the learning habits, learning status, learning atmosphere and other learning process conditions, as well as postlearning feedback and other information. Through the analysis of the components, governance processes and system levels of learning situation data governance under blockchain technology, a blockchain-based model of learning situation data governance for university students is proposed, as shown in Fig. 1:

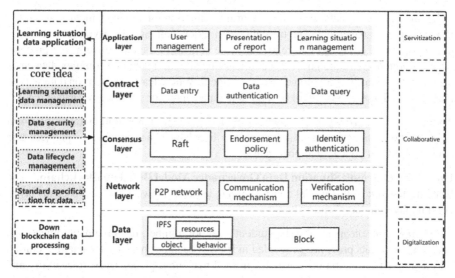

Fig. 1. Blockchain-based governance model architecture for university learning situation data

Based on the Blockchain Learning Situation Data Governance Framework. *Down Blockchain Data Processing*: Once the learning situation data are on the blockchain, it is difficult to modify and delete them. Therefore, to ensure the authenticity and high value of the data on the blockchain, the governors must carry out preliminary governance at the stage of collecting and uploading the learning situation data and screen the uploaded data to exclude duplicate data and wrong data to reduce the possibility of errors in the data on the chain and ensure the quality of the uploaded data.

The Core of Learning Situation Data Governance includes the Following: (1)Standard specification for data. On the one hand, data standards provide a unified data standard definition and platform logic model for university data platforms; on the other hand, data standards are the basis and foundation for the data governance of university data platforms, which can formulate the standard of learning situation data and use smart contracts for storage on the blockchain. (2) Data lifecycle management. This represents the process of data acquisition, upchaining, normalized processing, governance, and value output. Most managers of business systems in higher education institutions are focused on their own business and have little awareness of data lifecycle management, and there are few complete data lifecycle management processes from the business system authorities to the school level. Using blockchain, business participants can perform the full lifecycle management process of application, review, integration and distribution of learning situation data through the learning situation data management system; (3) Data security management. The traceability of blockchain and the asymmetric encryption algorithm it possesses can realize flexible control of the data governance process, which is conducive to the governance of learning situation data in a complex data environment; (4) Learning situation data management. Where learning situation data will be managed so that each node will be a reliable data center for storing governance data;

Application of Learning Data: By building a blockchain-based collaborative platform for learning management and services, it will enhance the autonomy, openness and controllability of educational governance.

University Learning Situation Data Governance Model Based on Blockchain. The basic framework of this model consists of a data layer, network layer, consensus layer, contract layer and application layer.

Data Layer, encapsulating the student's school number, resource data, object data and behaviour data previously recorded in IPFS. The nodes perform the chain operation on the above transaction data, which can facilitate subsequent access, traceability and downloading while ensuring data storage security. The data structure of blockchain includes two parts: the block header and the block body. The chain structure of blockchain realizes the data storage function by linking the hash values of the front and back block records, combined with the Merkle tree and chain structure.

Network Layer, covers the P2P networking mechanism, data communication mechanism and data verification mechanism. To achieve the synchronization and verification of block data between different nodes, the node settings include the university administration, students and teachers. The nodes in the system network synchronize and distribute data through the Gossip protocol, which is a P2P system protocol used to distribute data or exchange information between multiple nodes in the network.

Consensus Layer, using the Raft consensus mechanism, the Raft algorithm is a consistency algorithm to manage replication logs. To improve comprehensibility, Raft breaks down the consistency algorithm into several key modules, such as leader election, log replication and security. The use of the consensus algorithm is to implement a replication state machine that keeps the sequence of commands consistent, thus keeping the consistent state of their state simplified. At any given moment, each server node is in one of the three states of leader, follower and candidate, and the server nodes use RPC to communicate with each other.

Contract Layer, including script code, algorithm virtual machine and smart contract. After the data layer completes the encapsulation of the block data, the smart contract layer further sub encapsulates the block data through smart contracts. This includes smart contracts for learning situation data entry, data addition, and data query, which can ensure that the results of these data are not tampered with or deleted, greatly simplifying the process of supervising learning situation data.

Application Layer, is used to provide various operations based on blockchain externally, including user management, data upload, report display, etc. The data layer also provides support for the application layer, and the data generated by the application layer will be stored in the data layer.

4.2 Design of the Storage Mode

The data to be stored in the blockchain-based learning situation data governance model are generally divided into two types: learning information data and user information data, which are multisourced and complex. In view of the data characteristics, the mode is designed with an on-chain and off-chain collaborative storage model, as shown in Fig. 2. The user information, data summary, data information and data address (hash) are stored on the blockchain, and the detailed learning situation data are stored under the chain (IPFS). IPFS uses a directed acyclic graph based on Merkle trees to store a database stored in IPFS that is split into blocks of data. Only the IPFS distributed hash table (DHT) is retained on the blockchain for data file addressing operations. Learning situation data are divided into three different types: resource data, object data and behavioral data. Resource data mainly store student work data such as student award-winning work and outstanding work on homework. Object data mainly store student management data and basic situation data information, such as student course selection information and student registration information. Behavioural data mainly store student learning behavioural data (student participation data, student interaction data, student experience data, etc.).

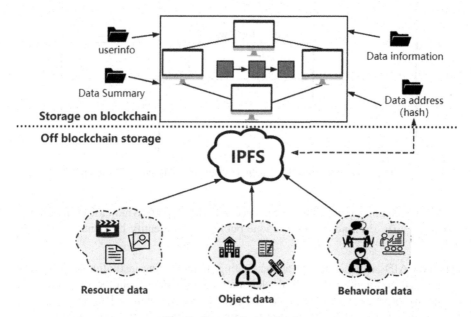

Fig. 2. Storage Pattern Design

4.3 Learning Situation Data up to Chain and Sharing Process Design

The organizations involved in the sharing of learning situation data store their own relevant learning situation data on the blockchain, which can be accessed and used by other relevant organizations. The management body will send a storage request, and the data will be stored in the learning situation data chain for student/teacher to access after passing the audit and verification of identity authentication and consensus mechanism, as shown in Fig. 3.

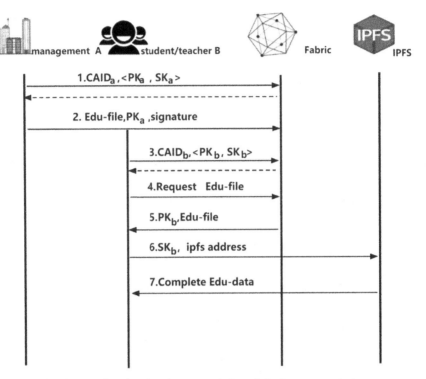

Fig. 3. Learning situation data up to chain and sharing process design

In blockchain, authentication is achieved with the help of asymmetric cryptographic principles [10]. Each node uses a unique public key to identify its identity across the network.

(1) The $CAID_a$ is generated by authenticating the managing institution A. The institutional unit applying to join the learning situation data chain locally generates a public–private key pair based on the elliptic curve algorithm $< PK_a, SK_a >$.

(2) Institution A uses PK_a to encrypt the stored learning situation data (Edu-file) and SK_a to digitally sign it (signature). When all nodes in the network receive the storage request, the request is confirmed by the consensus mechanism, the complete learning situation data resource will be stored on the IPFS, and the main information of the learning situation data will be stored on the learning situation data chain in the form of data blocks.

(3) When student/teacher B wants to access the student's learning situation data uploaded by institution A, the user's identity will first be verified, generating $CAID_b$ and $< PK_b, SK_b >$.

(4) Once authenticated, the request for sharing the learning profile data sent by student/teacher B and the private key corresponding to the requested learning situation data will be sent to the master node of the learning situation data chain. The master node first checks the received information and decrypts the learning situation data with institution A's SK_a through a smart contract and then encrypts the learning situation data with student/teacher B's PK_b.

(5) The master node sends the asymmetrically encrypted learning situation data (Edu-file) to student/teacher B. When student/teacher B receives the encrypted learning situation data (Edu-file), it decrypts it with its SK_b, enabling sharing from A to B.

(6) Teacher/student B accesses the IPFS with the obtained ipfs address.

(7) Teacher/student obtains complete Edu data.

4.4 Design of Smart Contract

Smart contracts, also known as chaincodes in Fabric, are programmable protocols that enable user-customisable functionality and are written in the Go language in Fabric. The initEdu() contracts up chain student information through the school administration, mainly by initializing basic student information such as name, student number, college, address, etc. The addEdu() contract stores student information such as student resource data, object data, behavioral data, etc. The administration, teachers and students have the right to add student data. The queryEdu() contract provides access to student data based on the student's student number. The delEdu() contract is used by the school administration to delete student data.

Table 1. Smart contract design

Smart contract	Specific function
initEdu	Learning situation information on the chain
addEdu	Add learning situation information
queryEdu	Query learning situation information
delEdu	Delete learning situation information

Taking the example of the learning data on the chain stage, the smart contract part of the algorithm is:

Table 2. Smart contract algorithms for data on the chain

algorithm initEdu

Input: Name, Gender, StuID, EntityID, College, Address, Mob, Major, Length
Output: txID

1. EduinitAsBytes = Stub.GetState(StuID)//Whether a StuID record exists
2. if eduinitAsBytes! = nil
return exists
3. EduinitObj ← &eduinitObj{Name, Gender, StuID, EntityID, College, Address, Mob, Major, Length}//Encapsulate the upper-chain data structure
4. EduinitJSONasBytes = json.Marshal(eduinit)//serialization
5. Err ← PutState(StuID,initEduJSONasBytes)//Blockchain up operation
6. if err! = nil
7. Return Error
10. Else
11. Return txID‖Successful, return transaction hash

5 Experimental Validation and Analysis

5.1 Model Security Analysis

The security of this model is analysed and explained in terms of the security of data storage, the security of private data and the security of data sharing.

Security of Data Storage. In the model, the data storage adopts the "blockchain + IPFS" storage method, in which the complete data of the learning situation is stored in IPFS, and the hash value generated by IPFS is saved in the blockchain, which can solve the security threat of centralized storage by adopting the decentralized method of IPFS to store the learning situation data, and the data are not easily lost. The data are chained through the blockchain, and the transaction hash value is generated. According to the decentralized and tamper-proof characteristics of the blockchain, the security of the school information data can be ensured.

Security of Privacy Data. In the model, considering that the basic information data of students in the school learning situation data involves privacy, the student situation data are graded according to the degree of data privacy, and the level is set to 0 (public) and 1 (private). The three organizations use admin, student and teacher to represent the user roles in the abovementioned school situation data chain entity, and the school situation data with level 1 can only be level 1. Level 1 data can only be accessed by the authoritative admin in the school, and students and teachers cannot directly access the private data of others to ensure the security of the private data in the learning situation data.

Security of Data Sharing. The security of data sharing is an important indicator to measure the security of the model. In the model, if a user wants to join the learning situation data chain and share the data therein, first, the identity will be verified to determine whether the user has authority, and if the user has access authority, then the data in the learning situation data chain can be shared. The key is only available to those who have permission to access the private data.

5.2   Experimental Tests

The test development environment was Intel(R)Core(TM)i7-7500UCPU@2.70 GHz. A virtual machine was built using VMware Workstation20 to simulate a real node. In this case, the environment was built based on the Fabric project, and the go language was chosen as the main programming language for the test. The specific environment configuration for the experiment is shown in Table 3. The blockchain network contains three organizations (governing bodies, teachers, students), six peer nodes, one orderer node, and three CA nodes, and all use the draft consensus sorting service.

Table 3.   Test environment

Name	Configuration
CPU	Intel(R)Core(TM)i7-7500UCPU@2.70 GHz
Operating system	Ubuntu20.4
Memory	16G
Fabric version	2.2.0
Language	GO

Table 4.   Example of data grading for the learning situation data chain

Level	Description	Data
0	public	Name、StuID、Acatype、Hash
1	private	Gender、EntityID、College、Address、Mob、Major、Length

Table 5.   The relationship between roles and data hierarchy access rights

Role	Level = 0	Level = 1
admin	√	√
student	√	×
teacher	√	×

Data Chaining Test.   The data are tested for chaining using Fabric Explorer for visualization.

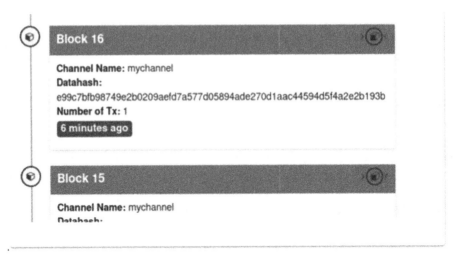

Fig. 4. Learning situation data on the chain

Figure 4 represents the number of blocks currently on the blockchain, and it can be seen that there are currently 16 blocks in the blockchain that have completed their upload on the mychannel channel. The blockchain uses the SHA-256 encryption algorithm to encrypt the data on the chain, which converts an input of any length into a hexadecimal string of length 64 (Data Hash).

🗊 **Block Details**	
Channel name:	mychannel
Block Number	16
Created at	2023-04-04T11:29:50.040Z
Number of Transactions	1
Block Hash	27586bacdd616857688b8cae5140319303eac529fb7b0265ea9bcceb090f0f37
Data Hash	e99c7bfb98749e2b0209aefd7a577d05894ade270d1aac44594d5f4a2e2b193b
Prehash	3da9564466567df6b57e15d17d76c031d6e078791ad8123daa6515f9583bc016

Fig. 5. Learning situation data chain block details

Figure 5 shows the details of the current block, which was created on 4 April 23 and has a transaction count of 1. The data on learning transactions are verified and successfully added to the blockchain by the nodes across the network and are difficult to change or delete at will, while the blockchain uses a chained data structure, so each block has the hash value (prehash) of the previous block, which ensures data traceability (Fig. 6).

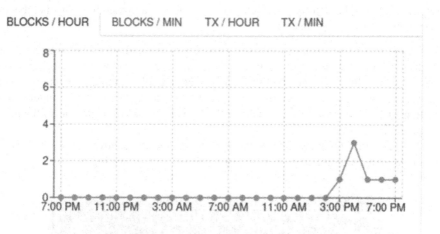

Fig. 6. Correspondence between time and blocks

The horizontal axis of the coordinate chart shows the time, and the vertical axis shows the number of blocks, giving a visual indication of how many blocks have been created at a given time. Approximately 3 blocks are generated at 5 pm (Fig. 7).

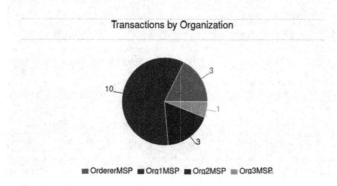

Fig. 7. Distribution of the number of transactions by organization

The pie chart shows the number of transactions for each organization, and it can be seen that org1, as the school governing body, has the bulk of the transactions.

Data Hierarchical Access Control Test. The blockchain network contains three organizations (Org1, Org2 and Org3) that use admin, student and teacher to represent the user roles in the abovementioned learning situation data chain entity. Three roles correspond to the common nodes of each of the 3 organizations, and the learning situation data are graded according to the degree of data privacy with multiple sources and varying degrees of importance. The lowest level is set to 0, which is public data. The lowest level is set to 0, which is public data. All members of the chain can access it, while the lowest and highest levels of privacy are set to 1, which is private data, and private data require higher requirements for the sharing of subjects and can only be accessed by some members to ensure the security of private data.

At the same time, each learning situation data owner and management agency user determines the correspondence between roles and data hierarchy and their access permissions according to the needs of the scenario. For the role of admin, she represents the administration of the university and has the highest authority to view basic student information such as address, college, etc. For the role student/teacher, only level 0 student data can be accessed.

Based on the above design, the data hierarchical access control test was conducted on the learning situation data, and the test result graph is shown Fig. 8:

Fig. 8. Data hierarchical access control test results

In Fig. 8, after a series of data chaining processes to access the learning situation information of the person whose name is Li Si, if the access is done for the node of organization 1 (admin), it can be seen that a series of private data such as Li Si's gender, ID number, phone number are displayed, if the access is done for the node of organization 2 (student)/organization 3 (teacher), only the academic data with level 0 is displayed, if the access is done for the private data with level 1, it will report an error and display the response: status: 500.

Data Security Storage Test. A query on the IPFS address of the learning situation data accessed by the role as teacher shows that the complete information on the learning situation is stored in IPFS, enabling decentralized storage (Fig. 9).

Fig. 9. IPFS for complete learning situation data

The experiment was tested from three aspects: data on the chain, data hierarchical access control, data security storage, and data on the chain. The data cannot be modified by data security storage. By storing the complete data to IPFS, to solve the centralized storage security problems, the "on-chain + of-chain" storage method greatly reduces the storage space of the blockchain. Through data hierarchical access control, for learning situation data transactions of private data, role administrators can access all data, and role students and teachers can only access the public data at level 0. Different roles have different access rights to graded data to ensure privacy data security. The experimental results prove the feasibility and effectiveness of the blockchain's learning situation data security protection mechanism at the specific application level.

Acknowledgements. This work was supported by the Yunnan Key Laboratory of Smart Education and Yunnan Innovation Team of Education Informatization for Nationalities, the National Natural Science Foundation of China (62262073 No.), the Yunnan Provincial Applied Basic Research Program (202101AT070098 No.), the Yunnan Provincial Ten Thousand People Program (YNWR-QNBJ-2019–237 No.) and the Yunnan Normal University Graduate Student Innovation Fund Grant (YJSJJ23-B175 No.).

I am extremely grateful to my supervisor, who has been very generous with her time in helping me. Her valuable suggestions, rigorous supervision and constant encouragement have contributed greatly to the completion of this thesis.

References

1. Yu, P., Li, Y.: Research on data governance scheme of universities under the perspective of big data. Mod. Educ. Technol. **28**(06), 60–66 (2018)
2. Xu, X., Wang, J., Bian, L., et al.: A study on data governance in higher education. Res. High. Eng. Educ. **154**(05), 25–30 (2015)
3. China Blockchain Technology and Industry Development Forum. Chinablockchain technology and application development white paper (2016). https://wenku.baidu.com/view/15bf5d 5d85c24028915f804d2b160b4e767f81f3?bfetype=new, (Accessed 28 March 2023)
4. Ministry of Education. Notice of the Ministry of Education on the Issuance of the Action Plan for Blockchain Technology Innovation in Higher Education. http://jszx_cau.edu.cn/art/2020/ 5/17/art_30570_679761.html, (Accessed 28 March 2023)

5. Dong, X., Zheng, X., Peng, Y.: Framework design and implementation of big data governance in higher education. China's Electrifi. Educ. **391**(08), 63–71 (2019)
6. Zheng, Y., Liang, Z.: Research on data governance in universities in the context of education informatization. China Educ. Inform. **17**, 50–54 (2020)
7. Li, Y., Liu, Y.: Research on blockchain integration in the field of higher education data governance. China Educ. Informat. **500**(17), 60–66 (2021)
8. Zhang, Z.: The utility of blockchain for educational data governance and the field of innovation. Educ. Rev. (12), 37–46 (2021)
9. Xudong, Z., Xuan, D., Tingyan, Y.: Blockchain-enabled regional education governance: logic, framework and path. Mod. Dis. Educ. Res. **34**(01), 31–39 (2022)
10. Dongxian, Y., Xiaoyan, W., Junlei, D.: A study on the requirements of a blockchain-based online course federation certification platform. Elect. Compon. Inform. Technol. **5**(05), 129–130 (2021)
11. Wang, L.: Research on building a blockchain-based food emergency intelligence system. J. Intell., 1–8 (4 July 2023)
12. Yu, H., Li, J., Liu, W., et al.: A blockchain-based access control scheme for energy data sharing. Inform. Sec. Res. **9**(03), 220–227 (2023)
13. Tian, X., Yang, M.: Smart contract-based access control mechanism in home Internet of Things. Comput. Eng. **49**(03), 18–28 (2023)
14. Ding, B., Wang, B., Feng, D., et al.: Trusted circulation of federated data based on blockchain supervision. Comput. Eng. Sci. **44**(10), 1771–1780 (2022)
15. Wu, Y.H., Cheng, G.X., Chen, Y., et al.: Current status, hotspot analysis and development thinking of "blockchain+education" at home and abroad. J. Dis. Educ. **38**(01), 38–49 (2020)
16. Javed, M.U., et al.: Blockchain-based secure data storage for distributed vehicular networks. Appli. Sci. **10**(6) (2020)
17. Wang, S.W.: Application analysis of blockchain technology in the field of emergency management. Adv Appli. Sci. **5**(2), 49 (2020)
18. Nizamuddin, N., et al.: Decentralized document version control using ethereum blockchain and IPFS. Comput. Electr. Eng.. Electr. Eng. **76**, 183–197 (2019)
19. Li, F., He, Y., Qi, Y.: Research on MOOC learner identity authentication model - based on two-factor fuzzy authentication and blockchain technology. J. Dist. Educ. **35**(04), 49–57 (2017)
20. Jin, Y.: Demand analysis and technical framework of blockchain+education. China's e-Learning **368**(09), 62–68 (2017)

Automatic Teaching Plan Grading with Distilled Multimodal Education Knowledge

Qing Wang ⬤, Hanwen Zhu ⬤, Yilong Ji, Jianyang Shi, Xiaodong Ma,
and Jia Zhu^(✉) ⬤

Key Laboratory of Intelligent Education Technology and Application of Zhejiang Province,
Zhejiang Normal University, Jinhua, China
`jiazhu@zjnu.edu.cn`

Abstract. With the development of artificial intelligence, more and more technologies are used in teaching design. The teaching plan is the direct guidance
document of teaching design. Through the teaching plan, teachers can effectively
evaluate their teaching design level to improve teaching methods and promote
improving students' core literacy. Current qualitative research and manual coding
are challenging to analyze for the teaching plan grading. There are factors such as
subjectivity and time-consuming in manual grading. Hence, the manual grading
of teaching plans is irrational to some extent. The evaluation process of manual
grading needs to be further strengthened and improved. This study adopts the
deep learning method and proposes a multimodal education knowledge distillation model (MEKD) to analyze multimodal data to solve the above problems. In
this study, the experimental analysis of more than 50,000 teaching plans verifies
the MEKD's effectiveness in helping alleviate the problem of automatic teaching
plan grading.

Keywords: Teaching plan · Auto grading · Knowledge distillation · Intelligent
system · Educational technology

1 Introduction

This section consists of three parts. The first part is the research background. The second
part introduces the definition of teaching plans, and the third part focuses on applying
artificial intelligence technology to teaching plans.

1.1 Research Background

Teaching plans are critical in optimizing classroom quality and bridging teaching theory and practice. Teaching plans are practical documents teachers formulate according
to curriculum standards to carry out teaching activities smoothly and effectively. The

---

Q. Wang and H. Zhu—These authors contributed equally to this work and should be considered
co-first authors.

teacher's teaching program directly results from teaching plans, guiding teachers in all aspects of education and teaching. In April 2022, the Ministry of Education issued the "Compulsory Education Curriculum Plan and Curriculum Standards (2022 Edition)", which is dominated by Jinping Xi's socialist ideology with Chinese characteristics in the new era, and highlights the specific requirements for the cultivation of newcomers in the stage of compulsory education, emphasizing the cultivation of the core literacy required for students' lifelong development and adaptation to social development [1]. Teaching plans usually contain objectives, essential and challenging points, and activities. The teaching objectives directly point to cultivating students' core literacy. Designing reasonable teaching plans helps implement students' core literacy and guides students from different teaching objectives.

1.2 Teaching Plan Definition

Teaching plans are part of teaching design, and teaching plans centered on students are conducive to cultivating students' core literacy and developing higher-order thinking. Teaching plans are practical teaching instruments designed before the teaching activities are carried out with a specific design and arrangement of teaching content, teaching steps, teaching methods, etc., by teachers in units of class hours or topics according to curriculum standards, syllabus, textbook, and the actual situation of students [2]. Literature has proved that student-centered instructional design can help improve teachers' teaching effect [3], but there needs to be more systematic research on evaluating and considering the effect of teachers' teaching plan design. The teaching plan design of different courses has different characteristics. The teaching design of science and engineering courses pays more attention to the concepts of problem exploration and logical reasoning, while the teaching design of language courses pays more attention to the setting of divergent thinking and open questions. Most of the research on instructional design is qualitative research, which only analyzes a particular class in a subject or uses a new method, which needs more universality and scientificity. It is not easy to quantify the level of instructional design of all teachers.

1.3 Application of Artificial Intelligence Technology

In the era of educational informatization 2.0, many artificial intelligence technologies have been applied to all teaching activities to improve teaching and learning. Researchers use face recognition technology to judge students' emotional changes in many classroom videos, such as Xiaohua Yu's "How Much Do You Know About Teachers' Comments? - Exploring the Emotional Value Behind the Text" [4], and some researchers use AR, VR, and other mixed reality technologies to enable students to learn in virtual classrooms, such as Joey's "Enhancing learning and retention with distinctive virtual reality environments and mental context reinstatement" helps students restore memory through VR using context [5]. In terms of educational evaluation, most artificial intelligence technologies are applied to evaluate students' learning effects, but there are few studies for teachers in the lesson preparation process. Universities, middle schools, and primary schools are building resource-rich innovative education network platforms, and a large amount of data is growing exponentially on the education management platform.

For example, on the Zhejiang Teachers Smart Education Platform, the content includes teacher teaching video data and teaching plan data. Based on artificial intelligence technologies such as knowledge distillation and multi-modal analysis, this research analyzes more than 50,000 novice teacher data from various schools in Zhejiang Province. Through the proposed model, namely MEKD, the automatic grading of teaching plans is realized.

2 Methodology

This section first introduces the origin of the dataset, then introduces the structure of the model and related knowledge, and finally describes the training process in detail.

2.1 Datasets

The teaching plans used in this research were extracted from Zhejiang Normal University's innovative education platform (http://www.smtedu.cn). The platform collects teaching plans from novice teachers from multiple subjects and periods. The periods include junior high school, primary school, kindergarten, etc. Subjects include Chinese, English, mathematics, art, music, physical education, science, information technology, history, geography, chemistry, biology, physics, politics, and special education. Each teaching plan is a 'docx' file containing multimodal information such as text images and tables. The number of available data is 52,827 after removing missing scores, missing files, and low-quality teaching plan designs. It contains 35,054 samples with incomplete modalities (missing images or texts) and 17,773 high-quality multimodal samples. According to the statistics of the data set, it can be found that the average score of the multimodal text is higher. That is, the quality is higher. This experiment uses these 17,773 high-quality data for training and testing. The original score of the teaching plan is 0–100 points, scored by the trainee teacher and the college teacher, respectively. The original scores of the lesson plan in this experiment were re-divided into five grades, including 'A, B, C, D, and E,' corresponding to 100–95 points, respectively. 90–94 points, 89–80 points, 79–70 points, 69–0 points. Table 1 shows the details of the dataset.

Table 1. Details of the dataset.

	Original dataset	Multi-modal dataset
A(100–95)	8196(15.51%)	3615(20.34%)
B(90–94)	22058(41.76%)	7485(42.11%)
C(89–80)	21102(39.95%)	6404(36.03%)
D(79–70)	1181(2.24%)	211(1.19%)
E(69–0)	290(0.55%)	58(0.33%)
Total	52827	17773

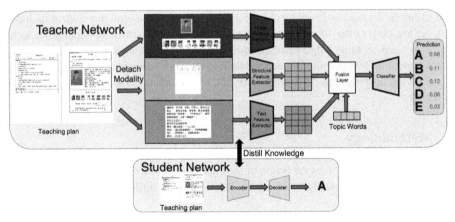

Fig. 1. The framework of MEKD.

2.2 The MEKD

In recent years, artificial intelligence has played an increasingly important role in education [6]. We use deep-learning methods to realize automating multimodal teaching plan grading. Knowledge distillation [7, 8] is an emerging deep learning technique that induces the training of student networks by introducing soft targets related to the teacher network as a part of the total loss to achieve knowledge transfer. Knowledge distillation uses a Teacher-Student model, where the teacher outputs the "knowledge," and the student receives it. The process of knowledge distillation consists of two phases: the training of the original model, or the "Teacher model," referred to as Net-T, which is characterized by its relatively complex model and superior prediction accuracy and can be composed of multiple models trained separately. The second phase is training the simplified model or the "Student model," referred to as Net-S, which has a smaller parameter quantity, a relatively simple model structure, and is more suitable for inference deployment as a single model.

Typically, research on multimodal multi-label classification [9] is based on deep neural networks, focusing on constructing neural network models and the fusion of multimodal data. Topic models are a helpful tool for extracting topic words and keyword information. In topic models, a topic is a probability distribution supported by all the characters in the text, representing the frequency of occurrence of the character in the topic, i.e., characters with a high degree of association with the topic are more likely to appear. When a text has multiple topics, the probability distribution of each topic includes all characters, but the value of a character in the probability distribution of different topics is different. A topic model attempts to represent this characteristic of documents mathematically. The topic model automatically analyzes each document, counts the words in the document, and determines which topics are present in the current document and what proportion each topic occupies based on the statistical information. M3L-Contrast [10] is a topic word extraction model with multimodal knowledge. We combine the M3L-Contrast model to extract topic words to enhance knowledge in the education domain.

Our model is mainly based on knowledge distillation and driven by education knowledge and incorporates topic words to enhance education knowledge, called the multi-modal education knowledge distillation model(MEKD). The model can be divided into a complex teacher network and a simple student network. The teacher network consists of five parts: image feature extractor, structure feature extractor, text feature extractor, fusion layer, and classifier. The student network only includes an encoder and a decoder. The image feature extractor combines ResNet-50 to extract image features. The structure feature extractor combines GCNN to extract structural features. The text feature extractor combines BERT to extract text features. The fusion layer contains a cross-attention multimodal fusion layer for feature fusion and a bottleneck layer to effectively reduce the output feature space. The classifier contains a fully connected layer and a softmax function for classification. The encoder in the student network adopts the encoder of the Transformer, while the decoder uses the decoder of the Transformer and combines it with a classifier that shares weights with the classifier in the teacher network. The structure of the model is shown in Fig. 1.

The final classification loss is the binary cross-entropy (BCE) loss which can be expressed as follows:

$$L_{class}\left(y, y^{'}\right) = \sum_{i=1}^{n}\sum_{j=1}^{L} -y_{ij}log\left(y_{ij}^{'}\right) - (1 - y_{ij})log(1 - y_{ij}^{'}),$$

where y_i is the ground truth, and $y_i{}'$ is the labels predicted by text information. They are both L-dimensional one-hot vectors.

2.3 Training Process

We perform experiments on Linux (Ubuntu 20.04.1). The experiments use four Nvidia GeForce RTX 3090 GPUs with Intel(R) Xeon(R) Gold 6254 CPU @ 3.10 GHz to do calculations in parallel, every GPU memory is 24 GB. The software part uses pycharm and is programmed based on the pytorch package.

Before starting training, we noticed that out of the available 52,827 data samples, there were 17,773 high-quality multi-modal teaching materials, while the remaining 35,054 samples lacked either text or image modalities. The high-quality multi-modal teaching plans be used as training and testing datasets, while other 35054 low-quality samples be used to pre-train the teacher network. Pretraining allowed the network model to capture more comprehensive educational knowledge, thereby improving the model's ability to rate teaching plans.

Training used five-fold cross-validation. The first step of five-fold cross-validation is randomly dividing the original dataset into five non-overlapping subsets. The second step is to select one subset as the test set and the remaining four subsets as the training set to train the model. The third step is to repeat the second step five times so that each subset has one chance to be the test set and the remaining chances to be the training set. After training on each training set, a model is obtained and used to test on the corresponding test set to calculate and save the model's evaluation metrics. The fourth step is calculating the average of the five test results to estimate the model accuracy and as a performance indicator for the current five-fold cross-validation. In this experiment, the number of samples in each subset is 3554, 3554, 3555, 3555, and 3555, respectively.

Each teaching plan contains multiple modalities of information. Therefore, the first step is to separate the modalities. Specially, we treat structural features as a modality. Because for any lesson, the structure is essential and is the basis for expert grading. For structural features, we consider not only basic structural information such as paragraphs, tables, and frames but also extract standard structural information from educational theories, including "textbook analysis," "student analysis," "teaching objectives," "teaching difficulties," "teaching methods," "teaching tools," "teaching process," and "teaching reflection." After separating this information, we input the contents of each modality into their corresponding feature extractors. After feature extraction, we obtain high-dimensional feature vectors for each modality. The extraction of multi-modal topic word feature vectors will be done using the M3L-Contrast model. The feature vectors of each modality and the topic word features are then input into the bottleneck layer in the fusion layer to compress the dimensions. They are then fully integrated using a cross-attention layer and input together into the classifier to obtain the 'teacher predictions.' At the same time, the multi-modal data of the samples are also input into the student network. The student network generates the 'soft' and the 'hard predictions.' The 'soft prediction' calculates a distillation loss with the 'teacher prediction,' while the 'hard prediction' calculates a student loss with the ground truth. Finally, the two losses are summed and backpropagated to optimize the model. After multiple epochs of iteration and updates, the model is trained, and professional education knowledge from the education domain is distilled from the teacher network to the student network. The lightweight and straightforward student network makes it more convenient for application and deployment.

3 Experiments and Analysis

3.1 Results and Fundamental Analysis

The personnel in this study included several students majoring in education, tutors in universities, and tutors in internship schools. Manual grading is based on the completeness of teaching plan design elements, the relevance of teaching content, and the achievement of teaching goals. The grading process takes about five months in total, and the teaching plans of each class have passed the consistency test (Kappa = 0.88). Moreover, inconsistent content has been verified. Among them, in the grading part of the education majors, the teaching plans of each stage are assigned by different personnel, and every three students score the teaching plans of a stage.

We take the evaluations of our practice school instructors as our standard and consider their ratings to be entirely correct. Moreover, the evaluation of college instructors is used as a reference value. The experimental results show that our model is better than the average of students in the School of Education regarding the scoring accuracy of teaching plans of all levels. Since the knowledge distillation method is used to train the model, the teacher and student networks are obtained, respectively. The complex teacher network has higher prediction accuracy than the simple student network. Refer to Table 2 for specific results.

Table 2. Comparison of different methods on accuracy. The results are the average of three experiments, where TDMG-S represents the prediction accuracy of the student network, and TDMG-T represents the prediction accuracy of the teacher network.

Method Grade	Students in education departments	TDMG-S	TDMG-T	Tutors in universities	Tutors in internship schools
A	55.3%	68.3%	72.2%	98.7%	100%
B	63.1%	78.7%	81.7%	98.9%	100%
C	64.7%	76.8%	81.0%	99.8%	100%
D	73.0%	79.6%	89.1%	98.6%	100%
E	81.0%	96.6%	96.6%	100%	100%
Average	62.3%	76.0%	79.7%	99.2%	100%

3.2 Similarity Analysis of Topic Words

In order to further verify the validity of the model, we use the similarity comparison of the topic words to analyze. This study uses Word2Vec for similarity analysis. First, use all the teaching plan texts to train the word2vec model to obtain the teaching plan word vector space. Then three outstanding students (grading accuracy rate of 91%, 94% and 93%, surpassing the machine) combined with the curriculum standard respectively for the three main courses (Chinese, mathematics, English) from 8 dimensions, namely subject core literacy, teaching objectives, Key and challenging points in teaching, student analysis, teaching method, Teaching activities, Topic words of structure, Topic words of Content, to design the subject word extraction framework. Several representative topic words are extracted in each dimension. Tables 3, 4, and 5 show the specific topic words extracted from the three courses. Different weights are used for the topic words evaluated in each dimension to calculate the semantic vector through word2vec.

Our model extracts and trains eight topic words for the three courses respectively and compares them for semantic similarity. The heat maps of the semantic similarity comparison of topic words in Chinese, Mathematics, and English classes are shown in Figs. 2, 3, and 4, respectively. For the three heat maps, note that the vertical axis represents the subject word categories selected by excellent students in combination with the curriculum instead of words, and the horizontal axis represents the topic words selected by the model. Some of the topic word classes are abbreviated ('core literacy' means Subject core literacy, 'objectives' mean Teaching objectives, 'Key&difficult' means Key and difficult points in teaching, 'stu analysis' means student analysis, 'method' means teaching method, 'activities' means teaching activities, 'tp structure' means Topic words of structure, 'tp Content' means Topic words of Content). Add the semantic similarity of all 64 topic words of each course to the average to get the semantic similarity probability of topic words of each course: Math: 0.64, Chinese: 0.58, English: 0.56 are all greater than 0.5, from a statistical view that the topic words selected by excellent students in combination with the curriculum standard match the topic words selected by the model.

Table 3. An example of topic words in a Chinese teaching plan.

	Topic words of structure	Topic words of content
Subject core literacy	comprehension、reading	article context、main topic、main idea
Teaching objectives	read and write、comprehension、organization、reading、feeling	burst、flag、parade、uniform、tank、distance、congregation、founding ceremony、narrative method
Key and difficult points in teaching	comprehension、generalization、feeling	article context、grand scene
Student analysis	teaching object、learning style、cognitive features、emotional features	junior high school students
Teaching method	/	lecture、discussion、case study
Teaching activities	introduction phase、new lesson lecture、homework summary	article context、main topic、main idea、outbreak、flag、parade、uniform、tank、distance、congregation、founding ceremony、narrative method

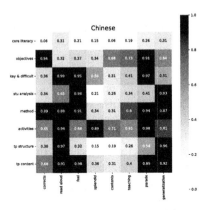

Fig. 2. The semantic similarity heat map in a Chinese teaching plan.

3.3 Quantitive Analysis of Topic Words

We randomly sample the teaching plan examples of Chinese, Mathematics, and English and analyze them by topic words to verify the effectiveness of the classroom automatic grading model. Three students majoring in pedagogy extracted topic words according to the curriculum standards of the Ministry of Education and the format of teaching plans, and then our model extracted topic words for semantic similarity comparison.

Table 4. An example of topic words in a Math teaching plan.

	Topic words of structure	Topic words of content
Subject core literacy	identification、mastery	propositional concept、logical ability
Teaching objectives	comprehension 、identification、mastery 、analysis、generalization	propositions、converse propositions、negative propositions、converse negative propositions、propositional relations
Key and difficult points in teaching	mastery、comprehension 、identification	proposition concept 、relationship between four propositions
Student analysis	teaching object、learning style、cognitive features 、emotional features	high school students、mastery of proposition concepts
Teaching method	/	lecture、discussion 、demonstration、practice
Teaching activities	introduction phase、new lesson lecture、homework summary	proposition concept、converse proposition、negation proposition、contra negation proposition、propositional relation

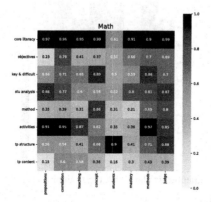

Fig. 3. The semantic similarity heat map in a Math teaching plan.

3.3.1 Chinese

This teaching plan relates to the Chinese text "Founding Ceremony" of the sixth-grade volume one, edited by the Education Ministry. Three students majoring in Chinese selected the topic words shown in Table 3 according to the compulsory education Chinese curriculum standards and the teaching plan style, including structure topic words

Table 5. An example of topic words in a English teaching plan.

	Topic words of structure	Topic words of content
Subject core literacy	generalization 、 comprehension 、 feeling	keyword 、 main topic 、 main idea
Teaching objectives	knowing 、 understanding 、 identification 、 feeling	keyword 、 main topic 、 main idea 、 article structure 、 antelope 、 laughing 、 rhino 、 endangered 、 nature foundation
Key and difficult points in teaching	comprehension 、 generalization	main idea 、 article structure
Student analysis	teaching object 、 learning style 、 cognitive features 、 emotional features	high school students
Teaching method	/	PWP model
Teaching activities	introduction phase 、 new lesson lecture 、 homework summary	keyword 、 main topic 、 main idea 、 article structure 、 antelope 、 laughing 、 rhino 、 endangered 、 nature foundation

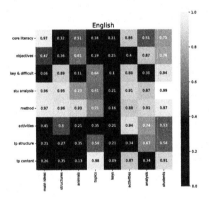

Fig. 4. The semantic similarity heat map in an English teaching plan.

and content topic words. "Chinese Curriculum Standards for Compulsory Education (2022 Edition)" pointed out: "The Chinese curriculum structure of compulsory education follows the internal logic of students' physical and mental development and the formation of core literacy, is based on life, takes practice activities as the main line, takes learning themes as the guide, and take learning tasks as the carrier, elements such as learning content, situations, methods, and resources are integrated, and learning task groups are designed [11]."

Topic Words from Students: At the core literacy level of the subject, "comprehension," "reading," "article context," "main topic," and "main idea" were selected to help students understand the content of the text as a whole. At the level of teaching objectives, topic words such as "read and write," "comprehension," "feeling," "burst," "flag," and "parade" was selected to visualize the three-dimensional objectives of the course and provide a teaching implementation path. On the essential and challenging points of teaching, choose "article context," "grand scene," "comprehension," "generalization," and "feeling," which summarize the main points of teaching objectives. In terms of teaching methods, "lecture," "case study," and "discussion" are selected to practice the language learning tasks better. In the teaching activities, words such as "article context" and "main topic" were selected to show the critical words.

Topic Words from MEKD: The different similarity comparisons of the topic words extracted from the TDMG model in different teaching design elements are displayed in the heat map. The invisible relationship of the topic words in various teaching structures is reflected through the different distribution of colors. It can be seen that among the important and difficult points in teaching, the similarity between "read aloud," "feel," and "parade" and the corresponding elements is as high as 90%, indicating that these three topic words are the core knowledge points in teaching, while "corrects," "read aloud," "feel," "splendid," "contents," "teaching," "parade," and "generalization" are all more than 50% similarity with teaching activities, which reflects that the topic words generated by the model are consistent with those in the teaching plans. The content of teaching activities has a high degree of matching.

3.3.2 Math

This teaching plan relates to the first section of chapter 1 of the B edition of elective 2–1 of the "High School Curriculum Standard Experimental Textbook" published by the PEP. Three students majoring in mathematics selected the following subject words according to the high school mathematics curriculum standards and the teaching plan style, including format keywords and content keywords. The curriculum objectives in the "General High School Mathematics Curriculum Standards (2017 Edition)" embody the core literacy of mathematics. The core literacy of mathematics is a comprehensive reflection of the quality of thinking, essential abilities, emotions, attitudes, and values that have the essential characteristics of mathematics. It is gradually formed and developed in learning and applying mathematics. For teachers, understanding curriculum objectives is the primary link in curriculum implementation [12].

Topic Words from Students: At the core literacy level of the subject, "identification," "mastery," "propositional concept," and "logical ability" are selected to help students understand the propositional relationship as a whole. At the level of teaching objectives, "comprehension," "mastery," "analysis," "analysis," etc., are selected, and the implementation of the three-dimensional objectives of the course is carried out step by step. In terms of teaching objectives, topic words such as "propositions," "converse propositions," and "negative propositions" were selected. In terms of teaching difficulties, select "proposition concept," "relationship between four propositions," "mastery," "comprehension," and "identification," which put forward higher requirements for teaching objectives. In terms of teaching methods, "discussion," "demonstration," "practice," etc., are selected to train students' mathematical thinking quality better. In the teaching activities, words such as "proposition concept," "converse propositions," and "negative propositions" were selected to show the important words.

Topic words from MEKD: "Propositions," "correlation," "teaching," "concept," "mastery," "methods," and "judge" are all similar to the core literacy of the subject by more than 90%, indicating that these keywords belong to our quality education The core knowledge points in the teaching activities, among which "propositions," "correlation," "teaching," "concept," "methods" and "judge" have a similarity of more than 60% in teaching activities, and "students" and "mastery" are only About 30%, indicating that teachers pay more attention to the teaching of knowledge points and methods in the specific implementation of teaching interaction, but pay less attention to students and their learning ability requirements.

3.3.3 English

This teaching plan relates to the Zhejiang Education Edition "Ordinary Senior High School English Textbook." According to the public high school English curriculum standards and the teaching plan style, three students majoring in English selected the structure and content topic words shown in Table 5. "Ordinary Senior High School English Curriculum Standards (2017 Edition, 2020 Revision)" has made specific requirements for the educational function of senior high school English teaching. It divides the core English literacy that high school students should achieve after learning English into four parts: language ability[13], culture Consciousness, thinking quality, and learning ability.

Topic Words from Students: From the core literacy level, topic words such as "generalization," "comprehension," "feeling," "keyword," "main topic," "main idea," etc. are selected to help students understand the content of the text as a whole. At the level of teaching objectives, "knowing," "understanding," "feeling," "identification," "antelope," and "laughing" were selected, showing the three-dimensional objectives of the course from the shallower to the deeper. In terms of essential and complex teaching points, choose "comprehension," "generalization," "main idea," and "article structure" to summarize the main points of the three-dimensional goal. Regarding teaching methods, the 'PWP model' was selected to show the teaching situation better and strengthen students' English expression ability. In the teaching activities, words such as "keyword," "main topic," "main idea," "article structure," "laughing," and "rhino" were selected to show the essential words.

Topic Words from MEKD: The "main ideas," "structures," "activities," "analysis," and "students" are more than 90% similar to student analysis, reflecting the critical requirements for learners. For the teaching method, the similarities between "main ideas," "structures," "animals," "topics," "activities," "analysis," "students" and are as high as 70%, indicating that these keywords are in the teaching method played a key role. Generally speaking, the topic words generated by the MEKD model can succinctly and clearly reflect the core knowledge points of teaching plans so that education and teaching personnel can judge the quality of teaching plans more scientifically and promote the professional development of teachers.

4 Conclusion

This study designed an automatic teaching plans grading system (MEKD) based on knowledge distillation and multimodal mining. The experiments verify the MEKD's effectiveness which outperforms students' abilities in teaching plan grading. For the interpretability of deep learning, three examples from different subjects were selected and qualitatively analyzed topic words. The teaching plan is essential to teaching design and is the standard of teaching and learning. This study uses the model to automatically grade teaching plans effectively, avoiding subjectivity and other uncertain factors caused by manual grading. Moreover, it better evaluates the teaching ability of novice teachers in teaching plan design which can improve teaching methods and promote students' core literacy.

Acknowledgements. This work was supported by the National Natural Science Foundation of China under Grant (62077015), the National Key R\&D Program of China under Grant (2022YFC3303600), the Key Research and Development Program of Zhejiang Province under Grant (2022C03106, 2021C03141), the Natural Science Foundation of Zhejiang Province under Grant (LY23F020010), the Education Science Planning Project of Zhejiang Province under Grant(GH2023585) and the Key Laboratory of Intelligent Education Technology and Application of Zhejiang Province, Zhejiang Normal University, Zhejiang, China.

References

1. Ministry of Education Homepage. http://www.moe.gov.cn, (Accessed 1 Sep 2022)
2. Shi, Y., Fu, N.: Design, writing and use of teaching plans in the new era. Contemporary Educ. Culture **11**(6), 96–100 (2019)
3. He, K.: Constructivist teaching mode, teaching method and teaching design. J. Beijing Normal Univ. (Soc. Sci. Edn.) (05), 74–81 (1997)
4. Yu, X., Zhan, X.: How much do you know about teacher reviews?. E-Education Res. **43**(07), 97–105 (2022)
5. Essoe, J.KY., Reggente, N., Ohno, A.A. et al.: Enhancing learning and retention with distinctive virtual reality environments and mental context reinstatement. npj Sci. Learn. **7**, 31 (2022)
6. Reddy, T., Williams, R., Breazeal, C.: Text Classification for AI Education. In: SIGCSE (2021)
7. Hinton, G., Vinyals, O., Dean, J.: Distilling the knowledge in a neural network. arXiv preprint arXiv:1503.02531.(2015)
8. Zhang, S., Jiang, L., Tan, J.: Cross-domain knowledge distillation for text classification. Neurocomputing **509**, 11–20 (2022)
9. Wu, Y., Zhan, P., Zhang, Y., Wang, L., Xu, Z.: Multimodal fusion with co-attention networks for fake news detection. In: Findings of the Association for Computational Linguistics: ACL-IJCNLP 2021, pp. 2560–2569 (2021)
10. Zosa, E., Pivovarova, L.: Multilingual and Multimodal Topic Modelling with Pretrained Embeddings. arXiv preprint arXiv:2211.08057.(2022)

11. Ministry of Education: Standards for Compulsory Education Chinese Curriculum (2022 Edition), China (2022)
12. Ministry of Education: Mathematics Curriculum Standards for General High Schools (2017 Edition), China (2017)
13. Ministry of Education: English Curriculum Standards for General High Schools (2017 Edition, 2020 Revision), China (2020)

Personalized Markov Learning Model in Knowledge Map Space

Mengnan Xu[1], Guosheng Hao[1,2(✉)], Xiaohan Yang[1], Minjian Sun[1], and Yi Zhu[1]

[1] School of Computer Science and Technology, Jiangsu Normal University, Xuzhou, China
hgskd@jsnu.edu.cn

[2] Jiangsu Wisdom-Driven Research Institute Co., Ltd, Xuzhou, China

Abstract. The personalized learning model is the primary basis for selecting educational resources and the foundation of customized education. Currently, the research on personalized learning models is mainly qualitative, with less quantitative analysis. In addition, there is also little research on the dynamics of personalized learning models. In this study, a personalized Markov learning model is constructed in the Knowledge Map space of the educational resource. Firstly, the dynamic, personalized learning state is characterized using the edges in the Knowledge Map. Secondly, the personalized learning state transition is described based on the Markov chain. Finally, the personalized Markov learning model is established based on the personalized learning state and the learning state transition matrix. This model provides a basis for personalized recommendation of educational resources and helps to improve the accuracy and quality of resource recommendation in the network space of educational resources.

Keywords: Markov Chain · State-Transition Matrix · Knowledge Map · Knowledge Points Sub-interface

1 Introduction

With the rapid development of Internet technology, educational resources have grown exponentially. Teachers present carefully designed educational resources to students, but providing the same educational resources to all students ignores individual differences in their knowledge levels. Educational resources that do not meet students' personalized needs lead to suboptimal learning outcomes and have yet to improve the quality of education [1] significantly. Therefore, it is necessary to establish personalized learning models for students to provide learning resources that meet their needs.

The personalized learning model refers to a learning model that provides personalized learning resources and learning paths based on the personalized learning characteristics of the learners. This model can recommend the most appropriate learning resources and paths for the learners based on their characteristics, such as interests, knowledge level, learning style, and learning goals. By modelling and analyzing the personalized characteristics and learning the history of the learners, the personalized learning model provides personalized learning services, which can improve learning outcomes, enhance learners' interest and motivation, and optimize the utilization efficiency of educational resources [2].

The personalized learning model aims to provide more appropriate personalized learning for learners. In recent years, many scholars at home and abroad have researched personalized learning models extensively. Zhu [3] designed an intelligent mobile learning system that can automatically establish a personalized learning model based on the effectiveness of learning, the order and emphasis of knowledge, and the student's learning interests, and push the knowledge points that students can continue to learn and choose independently. Peng [4] et al. constructed a personalized adaptive learning implementation strategy and personalized adaptive learning framework for precision teaching. Xie [5] et al. proposed a personalized knowledge point recommendation based on constructivist learning theory. The model expresses the knowledge system as a knowledge network, introduces a candidate knowledge selection strategy based on the nearest neighbours' priority, and recommends top-k unlearned knowledge based on the maximum learnable support priority. Liu [6] et al. constructed a personalized learning model based on a knowledge graph from the learner-oriented perspective, based on four dimensions of motivation, knowledge construction, willpower enhancement, and ability enhancement. The dynamic and changing learning state is an essential personalized feature of students [7]. However, when constructing personalized learning models, there is little consideration for students' dynamic and changing learning states. There is a lack of quantitative analysis and characterization of the dynamic, personalized features of students, and the properties of the personalized learning models are not fully explored. There is still insufficient theoretical support for studying dynamic and changing learning states in personalized learning model research. Therefore, this article focuses more on students' dynamic and changing learning states and profoundly explores the properties of personalized learning models to improve their accuracy and practicality to better serve students' learning needs.

There are still many issues in the current construction of personalized learning models, mainly reflected in the following two aspects:

(1) Little consideration is given to the dynamic and changing learning states when constructing personalized learning model.

Students' learning states are intangible and dynamically changing. Traditional personalized learning models usually only consider students' characteristics, while the critical data of dynamic and changing learning states is not well utilized. Therefore, fully utilizing dynamic and changing learning states is vital in constructing personalized learning model.

(2) Little consideration is given to the Markovian nature inherent in personalized learning model when constructing them.

Personalized learning models provide precise guidance and recommend the next most suitable knowledge point. To achieve accurate knowledge point recommendations, it is necessary to fully utilize the relationships between knowledge points, such as linear relationships, hierarchical nonlinear relationships, and so on. These relationships make personalized learning models inherently Markovian. Therefore, how to deeply explore the Markovian nature of personalized learning models is another critical issue in constructing them.

This paper proposes a personalized Markov learning model based on Knowledge Map from the perspective of learning state transitions to address the two issues above. (1) subject domain knowledge is mapped onto a Knowledge Map, which clarifies the relationships between knowledge points and constructs a subject-oriented Knowledge Map; (2) the BKT model [8–10] is used to evaluate students' mastery of knowledge points, and the concept of knowledge point boundaries is proposed to quantitatively characterize students' dynamic and changing learning states; (3) the Bayesian network [11] is introduced into the Knowledge Map to quantitatively represent the dependence and degree of dependence between knowledge points based on the learning state transition matrix; (4) the learning state transition matrix is used to determine the mastery level of the upcoming knowledge points, and the knowledge point with the highest mastery level is selected for recommendation.

The main contributions of this paper are as follows:

(1) Quantitatively characterize the dynamic changes in students' learning states;
(2) Introduce Bayesian networks into the Knowledge Map, fully utilize the relationships between knowledge points, and quantitatively characterize the transition of students' learning states based on the transition probability matrix;
(3) Build a personalized learning model based on Markov chains and apply it to dynamic recommendations.

2 Prearrangement Knowledge

The personalized learning model constructed in this paper is based on the Markov chain [12] and Knowledge Map. The relevant concepts and fundamental knowledge will be introduced below.

2.1 Markov Chain

Definition of Markov Chain. An important class of stochastic processes exists in which the conditional probability distribution of future states depends only on the current state, given a state space $S = \{s_1, s_2, s_3, \cdots, s_m\}$. In other words, the occurrence of a state in a stochastic process depends solely on its previous state, independent of time. Such a process is said to possess the Markov property and is called a Markov process.

A Markov process where both time and state are discrete is called a Markov chain. Suppose X_t represents the system's state variable at time t. In that case, the probability of the Markov chain from state s_i to state s_j is independent of the current time t, only related to the state s_i at the previous time. Such a Markov chain is called homogeneous Markov chain [13]. Its mathematical description is as follows:

$$P(X_t = s_j | X_{t-1} = s_i, X_{t-2} = s_k, \cdots) = P(X_t = s_j | X_{t-1} = s_i) \qquad (1)$$

Markov Transition Matrix. The one-step transition probability of a homogeneous Markov chain can be represented as p_{ij},

$$p_{ij} = P(X_t = s_j | X_{t-1} = s_i) \qquad (2)$$

The probability p_{ij} must satisfy the following two conditions:

$$(1)p_{ij} \geq 0, i, j = 0, 1, 2, \cdots (2) \sum_{j=0}^{\infty} p_{ij} = 1, i = 0, 1, 2, \cdots$$

Denote all one-step transition probabilities p_{ij} in matrix form, then the one-step transition probability matrix of the resulting homogeneous Markov chain, denoted as **P**, thus:

$$\mathbf{P} = \begin{bmatrix} p_{00} & p_{01} & \cdots & p_{0j} & \cdots \\ p_{10} & p_{11} & \cdots & p_{1j} & \cdots \\ \vdots & \vdots & \ddots & \vdots & \vdots \\ p_{i0} & p_{i1} & \cdots & p_{ij} & \cdots \\ \vdots & \vdots & \vdots & \vdots & \vdots \end{bmatrix}$$

Homogeneous Markov chain state at time t from s_i, after n steps at time $t + n$ status to s_j probability, is called Markov chain step n transition probability. It is denoted as:

$$p_{ij}^{(n)} = P\left(X_{t+n} = s_j | X_t = s_i\right) \tag{3}$$

All the n-step transition probabilities $p_{ij}^{(n)}$ are expressed in matrix form; thus, the n-step transition probability matrix of the Markov chain is obtained, which is denoted as $\mathbf{P^{(n)}}$, thus:

$$\mathbf{P^{(n)}} = \begin{bmatrix} p_{00}^{(n)} & p_{01}^{(n)} & \cdots & p_{0j}^{(n)} & \cdots \\ p_{10}^{(n)} & p_{11}^{(n)} & \cdots & p_{1j}^{(n)} & \cdots \\ \vdots & \vdots & \ddots & \vdots & \vdots \\ p_{i0}^{(n)} & p_{i1}^{(n)} & \cdots & p_{ij}^{(n)} & \cdots \\ \vdots & \vdots & \vdots & \vdots & \vdots \end{bmatrix}$$

Generally, the n-step transition probability matrix $\mathbf{P^{(n)}}$ can be calculated from its one-step transition probability matrix; that is, the multi-step transition probability matrix generally satisfies the C-K equation [14], and its mathematical expression is as follows:

Theorem 1 The C-K equation (Chapman-Kolmogorov equation) for any integer m, $n \geq 0$, has

$$\begin{aligned} p_{ij}^{(n+m)} &= P\{X_{n+m} = s_j | X_0 = s_i\} \\ &= \sum_{k \in S} P\{X_{n+m} = s_j, X_n = s_k | X_0 = s_i\} \\ &= \sum_{k \in S} P\{X_{n+m} = s_j | X_n = s_k, X_0 = s_i\} P\{X_n = s_k | X_0 = s_i\} \\ &= \sum_{k \in S} P_{ik}^{(n)} P_{kj}^{(m)} \end{aligned}$$

For any time $n,m \geq 0$ and any state $s_i, s_j \in S$, if we denote $p^{(n)}$ as a matrix of n-step transition probabilities $p_{ij}^{(n)}$, then the C-K equation states that:

$$p^{(m+n)} = p^{(m)} p^{(n)} \tag{4}$$

The Markov chain has three main characteristics:

- Randomness means that the transition from one state to another is random.
- No memory property, which means that the probability of the system being in the nth state depends only on the $(n\text{-}1)$th state and is independent of any state prior to that.
- Stability means that the stochastic process gradually approaches a stable state.

2.2 Knowledge Map Theory

Knowledge Map Concept. Knowledge Map is a network that displays knowledge relationships in a tree or network structure, emphasizes the hierarchy and association of knowledge points, and has functions such as knowledge point management and learning navigation [15].

The application of Knowledge Map to the field of education can be described as follows:

(1) Knowledge Map are static educational resource network spaces.

In education, a cognitive map formed by connecting knowledge concepts based on their potential relationships is called a Knowledge Map. The components of a Knowledge Map include a set of nodes K and a set of relationships R between the nodes. R is composed of relationships such as predecessor, successor, and parallel. The nodes and relationships form a static educational resource network space [16].

(2) Knowledge Map have learning navigation functions.

Knowledge Map can organize scattered knowledge points in a subject into an organically connected knowledge system, which helps students to grasp and understand knowledge as a whole. The close relationship between knowledge points gives Knowledge Map a navigation function. The organizational relationships of the predecessor, successor, or parallel knowledge points directly affect the order in which learners acquire knowledge points.

Knowledge Map Construction. To build a Knowledge Map, knowledge points need to be collected and organised, and then analysed for relevance, and the Knowledge Map is built through the three-step method of extracting points - connecting lines - forming a network. The subject knowledge points are mainly marked and extracted by domain experts.

In particular, the Knowledge Map constructed in this article can be seen as a small-scale, homogeneous network of knowledge points [17]. All nodes are of the same type and have the exact attributes. Moreover, the network's association is based only on five types of relationships between knowledge points: precursor, successor, generalized precursor, generalized successor, and parallel.

To better construct a personalized Markov learning model, the Knowledge Map used in this paper is designed as a directed acyclic graph (DAG), which includes two virtual super nodes, a super predecessor node, and a super successor node, as shown in Fig. 1. This design ensures that the Knowledge Map has only one starting point and one ending point, making it more convenient for probability calculation and model construction.

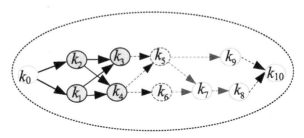

Fig. 1. Knowledge Map

In the Knowledge Map, all nodes that point to node k_i are called the predecessor nodes of k_i, and k_i is called the successor node of these nodes. Let $pre(k_i)$ denote the set of predecessor nodes of node k_i, and let P_c denote the conditional probability corresponding to each knowledge point. For each node k_i with a non-empty predecessor set, its conditional probability is denoted by $P_c(k_i|pre(k_i))$. The conditional probability of a node with an empty predecessor set is the prior probability. For a Knowledge Map with n nodes, its joint probability distribution [18] is represented as:

$$P_c(k_1, k_2, k_3, \cdots, k_n) = \prod_{i=1}^{n} P_c(k_i|pre(k_i)) \tag{5}$$

3 Personalized Markov Learning Model Based on Knowledge Map

In order to construct a personalized Markov learning model, we first quantitatively characterize the dynamic learning states on which the model depends, then determine the Markov state transition process, and finally, apply the personalized Markov learning model to knowledge point recommendation. In order to construct a personalized Markov learning model, two key sub-problems need to be solved: (1) How to quantitatively characterize the dynamic learning state? (2) How to further mine the Markov property contained in the personalized learning model?

3.1 Markov State Space

Learning States Based on the Sub-interface of Knowledge Points. In the Knowledge Map, for a learner, there is a set of edges that divide the knowledge points set K into the mastered knowledge point set K_m and the un-mastered knowledge points set K_u. The set of these edges is called the personalized knowledge points sub-interface, denoted as R_k, and its mathematical expression is as follows:

$$R_k = f(k_m, k_u, pre_i) = \left\{ r_{ij} | i \in K_m, j \in K_u, pre_i \in K_m, r_{ij} \in R \right\} \tag{6}$$

Here, pre_i represents the set of predecessor nodes of knowledge point k_i. R_{ij} denotes the directed edge connecting knowledge point k_i and knowledge point k_j.

In the Knowledge Map, we default to a virtual super-predecessor $k_0 \in K_m$ and a virtual super-successor knowledge point $k_{|K|+1} \in K_u$. For example, the corresponding mathematical representation of the sub-interface shown in Fig. 2 is as follows:

$$R_k = \{ r_{02}, r_{01}, r_{23}, r_{24}, r_{13}, r_{14}, r_{35}, r_{45}, r_{46} \}$$

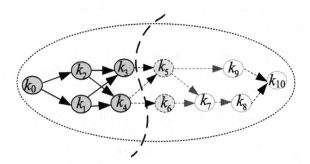

Fig. 2. The sub-interface R_K of knowledge points

The Knowledge Map is stored using a two-dimensional matrix, where 0 represents no edges and 1 represents edges, as shown in Table 1 The sub-interface of personalized knowledge points and their adjacent nodes are subgraphs of the whole Knowledge Map, a directed acyclic graph. The shaded part shows the matrix representation corresponding to Fig. 2 The matrix corresponding to R_K is a subset of the corresponding matrix of the Knowledge Map.

The Determination of the Learning State Space. The set of knowledge points sub-interfaces, which is the student learning state space, is a non-empty subset of the power set of edges in the knowledge map. It can be seen from Table 1 above that there are 15 directed edges in this knowledge map, and the number of non-empty subsets of its power set is $2^{15}-1$. However, based on the definition of the knowledge point sub-interface in 3.1 above, it is clear that there are subsets and redundant subsets in the non-empty subset that do not meet the definition requirements, so the following three steps need to be performed on the subset:

1. The number of learning state spaces is initially determined.

   The number of learned state spaces is equal to the non-empty subset of the power set of edges in the knowledge point graph.

2. Delete the learning states that do not conform to the definition of the knowledge points sub-interfaces.

Table 1. Two-dimensional array storage of Knowledge Map

	k_0	k_1	k_2	k_3	k_4	k_5	k_6	k_7	k_8	k_9	k_{10}
k_0	0	1	1	0	0	0	0	0	0	0	0
k_1	0	0	0	1	1	0	0	0	0	0	0
k_2	0	0	0	1	1	0	0	0	0	0	0
k_3	0	0	0	0	0	1	0	0	0	0	0
k_4	0	0	0	0	0	1	1	0	0	0	0
k_5	0	0	0	0	0	0	0	1	0	1	0
k_6	0	0	0	0	0	0	0	1	0	0	0
k_7	0	0	0	0	0	0	0	0	1	0	0
k_8	0	0	0	0	0	0	0	0	0	0	1
k_9	0	0	0	0	0	0	0	0	0	0	1
k_{10}	0	0	0	0	0	0	0	0	0	0	0

By traversing the state space, the knowledge point is deleted if the last grasp of the knowledge point is unknown; that is, the $pre_i \in K_m$ is not satisfied.

3. Merge the redundant knowledge points sub-interfaces.

According to the definition of the knowledge point sub-interface $R_k = f\left(K_m, K_u, pre_i\right) = \{r_{ij}|i \in K_m, j \in K_u, pre_i \in K_m, r_{ij} \in R\}$, if a successor knowledge point k_1 exists, and $i \in K_m, l \neq j$, then r_{il} is added to R_K.

4. Determine the final learning state space.

3.2 Markov State Transition Matrix

At time t, the sub-interface of the knowledge points where the student is located in the Knowledge Map is denoted as $R_k^{(t)}$, and the sub-interface changes with the learning progress. As shown in Fig. 3, $R_k^{(t)} = \{r_{01}, r_{02}, r_{23}, r_{13}, r_{14}, r_{24}\}$, $R_k^{(t+1)} = \{r_{01}, r_{02}, r_{23}, r_{13}, r_{14}, r_{24}, r_{35}\}$, The change process of the knowledge points sub-interfaces of students is the process of transferring students' learning state.

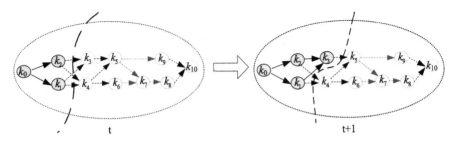

Fig. 3. Schematic diagram of student learning state transition in the Knowledge Map

The dynamic learning state of the student can be abstractly represented as $\{stu, R_k^{(1)}, R_k^{(2)}, \cdots, R_k^{(t)}, \cdots, R_k^{(n)}\}$, where stu represents the student and n represents the number of knowledge points boundaries. As stated in 2.1, the transition of the students' learning state satisfies the homogeneous Markov property, which means that the probability of the student transitioning from $R_k^{(t)}$ to $R_k^{(t+1)}$ is independent of time t and only depends on the current location of the knowledge points boundary. Therefore, the Markov process of the student's dynamic learning in the Knowledge Map can be represented as:

$$P\left(stu, R_k^{(t+1)} | R_k^{(t)}, R_k^{(t-1)}, \cdots, R_k^{(1)}\right) = P\left(stu, R_k^{(t+1)} | R_k^{(t)}\right) \tag{7}$$

In this paper, the personalized Markov learning model is described by a directed graph. Consider that in knowledge point recommendation, and learners learn knowledge point k_i after the knowledge points sub-interface R_K, which may represent a transfer of learning state. Therefore, a learning state transition of the personalized Markov learning model is regarded as an event representing the deviation of the student's learning state.

Figure 4 is a diagram of the student learning state transition, where R_K is the student learning state, in the knowledge point recommendation, the learning state R_K refers to the knowledge points sub-interface if the learner is in the learning state $R_k^{(t)}$, that is, the knowledge points sub-interface is $R_k^{(t)}$, all the precursor knowledge points of the knowledge points sub-interface have been mastered. All subsequent knowledge points constitute the set of knowledge points to be recommended. E is the edge set, which records all the learning state transitions in the learner's learning process. e_{12} represents the transition of the learner's learning behaviour from the learning state $R_k^{(1)}$ to the learning state $R_k^{(2)}$. PE is the learning state transition matrix composed of $n \times n$ (n represents the number of knowledge points sub-interfaces). For example, p_{12} in Fig. 4 is the conditional transition probability of the learner from the learning state $R_k^{(1)}$ to the learning state $R_k^{(2)}$.

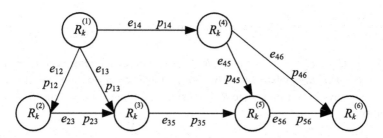

Fig. 4. Schematic diagram of student learning state transition

From this, the learning state transition matrix **P** can be determined, where each element represents the probability of transition from the learning state $R_k^{(i)}$ to the learning state $R_k^{(j)}$.

$$\mathbf{P} = \begin{bmatrix} p_{11} & p_{12} & \cdots & p_{1j} & p_{1n} \\ p_{21} & p_{22} & \cdots & p_{2j} & p_{2n} \\ \vdots & \vdots & \ddots & \vdots & \vdots \\ p_{i1} & p_{i2} & \cdots & p_{ij} & p_{in} \\ p_{n1} & p_{n2} & \cdots & p_{nj} & p_{nn} \end{bmatrix}$$

Suppose the probability $P_c(k_1, k_2, \cdots, k_s) = \prod_{i=1}^{s} P_c(k_i|pre(k_i))$ in the learning state $R_k^{(i)}$, then the probability of one-step transition to learning state $R_k^{(j)}$ can be obtained according to Formula (5):

$$p_{ij} = P_c(k_1, k_2, \cdots, k_s, k_u) = \prod_{i=1}^{u} P_c(k_i|pre(k_i)) \tag{8}$$

It is worth noting that the above transition matrix is sparse because some learning states cannot be reached within one step. The transition of the learning state occurs if the knowledge point mastered by the student within one step belongs to the successor knowledge points of the sub-interface of the current knowledge point. Therefore, the nonzero elements of the transition matrix only exist in the position of the sub-interface of the current knowledge point and the sub-interface after its new successor knowledge point. These constraints make the personalized Markov learning model more reliable and accurate, which can better describe students' learning processes and behaviour.

3.3 A Formal Description of Personalized Markov Learning Model

Based on the above, the personalized Markov learning model can be formally described as:

$$G = (R_k, E, PE) \tag{9}$$

Here, $R_k = \{R_k^{(1)}, R_k^{(2)}, \cdots, R_k^{(t)}, \cdots, R_k^{(n)}\}$ is a state of learning sets, $E = \{e_{ij}|i \in R_k, j \in R_k\}$ is edge sets, edge is used to represent learning state transition; $PE \in [0, 1]$ is a function, says by learning state $R_k^{(i)}$ transferred to the learning state $R_k^{(j)}$ transition probability.

3.4 A Framework of Personalized Markov Learning Model

In this paper, a framework for applying a personalized Markov learning model to knowledge point recommendation is designed, as shown in Fig. 5. The processing steps of the framework are divided into three stages. The first stage is the static Knowledge Map construction stage. Firstly, the data is collected based on the "*Data Structure*" course in the personalized education system, which mainly includes a knowledge point set, exercise set, student exercise record set and learner set. Then, a Knowledge Map of knowledge point dependencies is constructed based on the collected knowledge point set and the exercise set, and then the Bayesian network is introduced into the Knowledge Map. In the second stage, the students' personalized learning characteristics were modelled in the Knowledge Map. Firstly, according to the student test record set and the learner set collected in the first stage, the Bayesian Knowledge Tracing (BKT) model was used to locate the students' personalized knowledge points sub-interface [19]. Secondly, the Conditional Probability Table (CPT) of the Knowledge Map was calculated based on statistics [20]. Finally, the learning state transition matrix was calculated according to the conditional probability table. The knowledge point recommendation is carried out in the third stage based on the personalized Markov learning model. According to the knowledge points sub-interface and learning state transition matrix determined in the second stage, the next moment knowledge point recommendation is completed, and the personalized knowledge point recommendation for the current user is obtained.

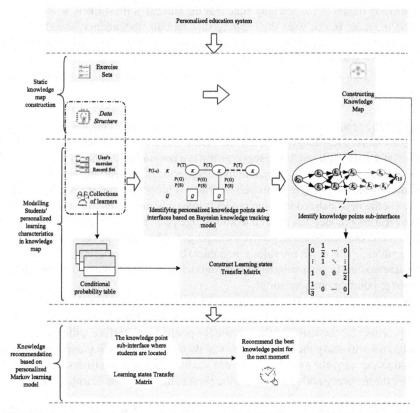

Fig. 5. Knowledge point recommendation framework based on personalized Markov learning model

In the personalized Markov learning model, according to the learning state transition matrix, the learning state that each student will most likely to transfer to at the next moment can be calculated to achieve knowledge point recommendation. The recommendation diagram is shown in Fig. 6.

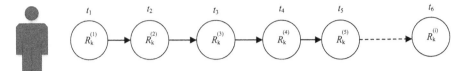

Fig. 6. Recommendation diagram

Suppose that the student is in the learning state $R_k^{(5)}$ at time t_5, According to the transition matrix, the learning state with high transition probability can be calculated from the learning state $R_k^{(5)}$ to other learning states at time t_6. The learning state that the student has transferred $(R_k^{(1)}, R_k^{(2)}, R_k^{(3)}, R_k^{(4)}, R_k^{(5)})$ is excluded, so the learning state with the highest transition probability from the learning state $R_k^{(5)}$ to other learning states in the transition matrix is the learning state that the student is most likely to transfer to in the next moment. In this way, the learning state that all students may transfer to at the next moment can be calculated, and the personalized knowledge point recommendation for the current student can be realized.

4 Conclusion

Aiming at the problem that the dynamic learning state is rarely considered in constructing a personalized learning model, and the Markovian property of personalized learning need to be deeply explored, this paper constructs a personalized Markov learning model based on a Knowledge Map. A quantitative description of the learning state based on the dynamics of the knowledge points sub-interface is proposed, and the Markov property implied in the personalized learning model is intensely mined. Finally, the personalized Markov learning model was applied to knowledge point recommendation, and a knowledge point recommendation framework was proposed based on the personalized Markov learning model. This paper provides a theoretical basis for characterizing dynamic learning characteristics in personalized learning model, which helps improve the accuracy of knowledge point recommendations.

The personalized Markov learning model training loss function will be studied in the future. How to map and characterize the personalized knowledge structure and cognitive process characteristics in the knowledge points sub-interface will be explored. In addition, we will study the characteristics of dynamically changing understanding and absorption capacity, the switching between studiousness and weariness, etc., to further improve the accuracy and reliability of the personalized Markov learning model.

Acknowledgement. G.S. Hao acknowledges the support from National Natural Science Foundation of China under Grants 62277030, 62077029.

References

1. Weiliang, K., Shuyun, H., Zhaoli, Z.: Adaptive learning path construction with artificial intelligence support. Mod. Distance Educ. Res. **32**(3), 94–103 (2020)

2. Li, W., Zhang, L.: Personalized learning path generation based on network embedding and learning effects. In: 2019 IEEE 10th International Conference on Software Engineering and Service Science (ICSESS), Beijing, China, pp. 316–319 (2019). https://doi.org/10.1109/ICS ESS47205.2019.9040721

3. Yiwei, Z.: Design thinking of an intelligent mobile learning system. Mod. Vocat. Educ. **292**(14), 82–84 (2022)

4. Hongchao, P., Zhiting, Z.: Exploration of personalized adaptive learning strategies supported by human-computer collaborative decision making. Electrochem. Educ. Res. **40**(2), 12–20 (2019). https://doi.org/10.13811/j.cnki.eer.2019.02.002

5. Fengjuan, L., Wei, Z., Qiang, J., et al.: Research on personalized learning models and sup-port mechanisms based on knowledge graphs. China's E-learning **424**(5), 75–81 (2022)

6. Zhenping, X., Chen, J., Yuan, L., et al.: A personalized knowledge recommendation model based on constructivist learning theory. Comput. Res. Dev. **55**(1), 125–138 (2018)

7. Qiang, J., Wei, Z., Pengjiao, W., et al.: Personalized adaptive online learning analytics model and implementation based on big data. E-learning China **336**(1), 85–92 (2015)

8. Shiwen, H., Zhaohui, L., Lingyun, L., et al.: A study on Bayesian knowledge tracking model incorporating behavioral and forgetting factors. Comput. Appl. Res. **38**(7), 1993–1997 (2021). https://doi.org/10.19734/j.issn.1001-3695.2020.10.0356

9. Jipeng, L.: Research and application of Bayesian networks in knowledge maps. Master's thesis, University of Electronic Science and Technology (2016)

10. Jianming, H.: Application of Bayesian networks in student performance prediction. Comput. Sci. **39**(S3), 280–282 (2012)

11. Chundi, M., Jianbin, D., Jun, Y.: Bayesian networks for data mining. J. Softw. **5**, 660–666 (2000). https://doi.org/10.13328/j.cnki.jos.2000.05.012

12. Qu, P., Zhiming, D., Limin, G.: Markov chain-based trajectory prediction. Comput. Sci. **37**(8), 189–193 (2010)

13. Caizhi, S., Yi, Z., Xueyu, L.: Application of weighted Markov models to the prediction of precipitation abundance and depletion conditions. Syst. Eng. Theory Pract. **4**, 100–105 (2003)

14. Perera, S, Bell, M.G.H., Kurauchi, F., et al.: Absorbing markov chain approach to modelling disruptions in supply chain networks. In: 2019 Moratuwa Engineering Research Conference, Moratuwa, Sri Lanka, pp. 515–520 (2019). https://doi.org/10.1109/MERCon.2019.8818809

15. Yunxia, F.: Design and implementation of a personalized learning system based on knowledge Map, Master's thesis, Hunan Normal University (2018)

16. Guosheng, H., Tingting, Z., Xia, W., et al.: Description of personalized learning characteristics in education oriented knowledge graph. In: 4th International Conference on Information Systems and Computer Aided Education. Association for Computing Machinery, Dalian, China, September, 2021, pp. 2495–2498 (2021). https://doi.org/10.1145/3482632.3487457

17. Jiping, G., Kun, D., Yuntao, P., et al.: Analysis of the current situation of knowledge network research at home and abroad. Intell. Theory Pract. **38**(9), 120–125 (2015). https://doi.org/10.16353/j.cnki.1000-7490.2015.09.024

18. Jianwei, L., Haien, L., Xionglin, L.: Probabilistic graph model representation theory. Comput. Sci. **41**(9), 1–17 (2014)

19. Käser, T., Klingler, S., Schwing, A.G., et al.: Dynamic Bayesian networks for student modeling. IEEE Trans. Learn. Technol. **10**, 450–462 (2017). https://doi.org/10.1109/TLT.2017.268 9017

20. Changxin, H.: A Bayesian network-based algorithm for social network link prediction. Master's thesis, Xidian University (2018)

The Curriculum Design of College Spoken English Based on AI Spoken English Evaluation System

Yi Cheng, Haoyun Wang, and Yu Wang[✉]

Department of English Languages, NingboTech University, Ningbo, China
bluefish1978@126.com

Abstract. At present, an increasing number of universities have applied language service products of artificial intelligence which brings new opportunities to spoken English teaching and promotes the innovation of teaching mode. Based on the Evaluation System of Spoken English under artificial intelligence, this thesis explores the blended instruction model of college spoken English with the assistance of AI and discusses the overall design of the curriculum. It proves that the combination of AI-assisted spoken English learning with blended instructive teaching modes online and offline meets the personalized learning needs of college students. Meanwhile, it boots the precise teaching of spoken English.

Keywords: The Evaluation System of AI Spoken English · College Spoken English · Blended Instruction Mode

1 Introduction

With the rapid development of artificial intelligence, it grows increasingly mature in machine learning and human-computer interaction technologies and is gradually applied to the field of education. Blended Instruction Mode combines the advantages of traditional and web-based teaching, providing students with a digital learning platform for independent learning. Meantime, through offline face-to-face teaching based on the integration of teacher and students, teachers help students solve problems to develop students language ability. In 2019, the CPC Central Committee issued the China Education Modernization 2035. [1] Quality in blended learning Exploring the relationships between online and face-to-face teaching and learning, proposing to accelerate educational reform and the reform of the talent cultivation model with modern technology. Under the guidance of the policy, some areas and schools have begun to explore the integration of artificial intelligence and education.

Artificial intelligence is changing the teaching mode and educational ecology of college English. As an essential part of college English teaching, Spoken English teaching needs the help of artificial intelligence to carry out individualized and precise teaching reform. Therefore, teachers can improve students' language expression ability more effectively. The Evaluation System of Spoken English, as the application tool of the blended instruction model, not only promotes the reform of the teaching model of spoken English but also is the practice of "Chinese educational modernization 2035".

© The Author(s), under exclusive license to Springer Nature Singapore Pte Ltd. 2024
J. Gan et al. (Eds.): CSEI 2023, CCIS 1900, pp. 418–425, 2024.
https://doi.org/10.1007/978-981-99-9492-2_35

2 The Spoken English Evaluation System Applied in Spoken English Learning

2.1 Requirements for College Spoken English Teaching

In 2017, the Chinese government released the development plan for the new generation of artificial intelligence [2], proposing accelerating the training of high-end artificial intelligence talents and developing intelligence education. In 2020, the requirements for the college English curriculum issued by the Ministry of Education put forward that "colleges and universities should pay more attention to the cultivation of students' listening and speaking ability." [3] Therefore, college-spoken English education should grasp the opportunity brought by the development of network technology and adopt a new teaching mode supported by artificial intelligence. The new teaching model should be interactive, realizable, and easy to operate in technology.

2.2 Problems in College Spoken English Teaching

College spoken English teaching has achieved specific results after the long-time reformation, but it still cannot meet the operational needs of the Society for college students' spoken expression ability. At present, the problems in spoken English teaching are mainly manifested in the following aspects:

Firstly, traditional English class lacks a good language environment. English, as a language, is bound to require a good language environment to get twice the result with half the effort. However, in in-school English learning classes or off-campus spoken English training institutions, teachers do not ultimately create an English language environment to facilitate learners to understand the learning content; they usually adopt the classroom teaching mode in Both Chinese and English. Although learners will also use English to answer class questions, they generally cannot fully express their answers in English and need the help of Chinese.

Secondly, traditional English teaching methods weaken the enthusiasm for oral English learning. In a 45-min English class, teachers cannot reserve enough time for learners to practice oral English to complete the teaching content and transfer English theoretical knowledge within the limited time. The teacher method in the classroom is straightforward and old usually the mode of teacher lecturing, students listen, and the teacher asks students to answer. This traditional teaching mode is challenging to arouse students' enthusiasm and interest in learning. Moreover, in English teaching, the teacher's knowledge reserves ambitious students obviously, this virtually amplified voice and the initiative of the teachers in the teaching process, students in spoken English is poor and without confidence, cannot talk with teacher regular oral communication, and choose to be "information receivers," "Dumb English teaching," "spoon-feeding and full teaching" has been criticized.

Thirdly, In traditional college oral tests, teacher scoring and student testing must be carried out simultaneously, so collecting the test data of students' oral test output is inefficient. What is more, the particularity of the oral test determines that the expression of students in the test is irreversible, and the teacher can not listen to the content the second time. Last but not least, when teachers comment on students' strengths and weaknesses, they stay on paper, and students cannot review their expressions to make better improvements. Since data processing and analysis rely only on the teacher's memory and overall impression, achieving objective data analysis of the examination content data is difficult.

2.3 Use AI to Improve Spoken English Ability

Based on the English pronunciation level evaluation requirement, C/B-S architecture is adopted to design the system. Learners can use mobile phone clients and computers to browse the web; Teachers and system administrators use web pages to realize data interaction. ThinkPHP framework of MVC architecture is used to realize the network server development of the system. The network server is used to realize the pre-processing of the system voice signal, evaluate the English oral level, and store related data [4].

According to the problems mentioned above, with the help of artificial intelligence, not only can students realize the immersive one-on-one spoken English dialogue after class, but they also make scientific spoken English training time according to their study schedule, which avoids the problem of insufficient atmosphere and time for spoken English training in class.

During the speaking test, students output the spoken language to the spoken language evaluation system and transfer the data to the system's database within the specified time; then, the system analyzes and processes the output content of the students. The spoken language data collected through the AI system allows students to perform reversible operations, allowing students to target and accurately detect a specific mispronunciation and language use. [5] In addition, the system terminal will keep the test results of students' spoken English each time, which is convenient for students to track and record the changes in their spoken English ability in the background of the system. Also, it is conducive for teachers to propose specific oral English solutions for students and help students improve the weak links in spoken English in a targeted way to achieve more accurate spoken English improvement.

3 The Blended Instruction Mode Design in Spoken English Teaching

3.1 The Basis of the Teaching Model Proposed

In the context of artificial intelligence, and spoken English evaluation system has emerged. The Spoken English evaluation system aims to develop a small ETL tool independently for the college English test data warehouse system to build a data mart easily and quickly for learning contents, learning methods, and learning evaluation. [6] In the process of learning English oral evaluation, the completion of students' oral preview tasks, the selection and use of oral English evaluation resources, the quality of personal oral expression in oral communication activities, and the completion of after-school review tasks are tracked, recorded, and evaluated by the artificial intelligence technology platform to form corresponding intelligent analysis results. This adapts to the learning needs of modern college students for oral language, and in the case of a sharp rise in the number of modern college students and the lack of excellent teacher resources, blended education has pointed out a new direction for us.

This tool imports the critical data from the database into the data warehouse database, and the conversion part will be completed in the data pre-processing of data mining. The flow chart of the spoken English evaluation system ETL is shown in Fig. 1.

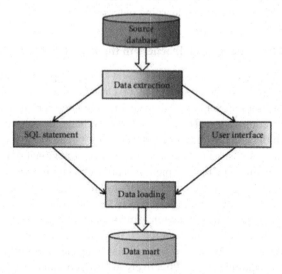

Fig. 1. Shows data extraction and data loading. SQL statement refers to extracting data by manually writing SQL statement, and user interface refers to automatically generating SQL statement to extract data through the user interface.

3.2 Specific Practice of Blended Teaching

Blended teaching is divided into three stages according to the teaching process: the presentation, practice, and extension. In the first stage, the new language is presented to students in an environment that at least allows students to understand the main idea. In the second stage, students repeat and use what they have learned, first mechanically and then more creatively, using AI for feedback on accuracy and fluency. In the final stage, language skills are used in a real communicative context. Students can learn spoken English in many interesting real-world situations and interviews and even play a role in conversations. In such a pleasant learning process, the interest and enthusiasm of students are greatly stimulated. The blended learning approach has three main elements: first, self-study using interactive multimedia. This includes a wide range of activities, followed by group and personal learning. This provides extended reading and listening exercises, additional vocabulary, and communicative activities; and finally, teachers conduct classroom sessions to practice and expand students' knowledge. At many universities, blended learning combines online learning and face-to-face teaching. Therefore, in the blended English speaking course, the first is in the multimedia language laboratory, with the help of computers for computer-based independent learning, so that students are immersed in the authentic English world and receive entirely comprehensible input. Students should then meet their teachers in class, where real-life situations create meaningful outputs for them and communicate with each other. Instructors will provide guidance and feedback to check students' online learning quality. In addition, students are encouraged to participate in various extracurricular activities. The formation of peer learning groups within the class increases the value of teacher-student interaction and produces a variety of beneficial learning outcomes [7].

3.3 The Necessity of the Role of Teachers in the Era of Artificial Intelligence

Teachers are no longer the only source of knowledge of spoken English evaluation; they are also the guide to the organization of classroom activities. Teachers should assign teaching tasks to students and help them complete them through independent learning and group cooperation. Track, record, and evaluate the completion of students' oral skills through the artificial intelligence technology platform, the selection and use of English-speaking assessment resources, the quality of personal oral pressure in oral communication activities, and the completion of after-class review tasks in the process of learning English speaking assessment. Teachers use this tool to assess student learning, focus on individual differences, tailor remedies to the situation, and teach students based on their abilities. Teachers can display relevant vocabulary and sentence patterns on the online learning platform before the Theoretical English Assessment so that students can preview and mark the problems they encounter during the learning process. Teachers and students can communicate more effectively in class, continue speaking lessons from class to after class, and ensure students have time to practice their speaking. On the other hand, this can also effectively save teachers' time and be genuinely efficient.

Blended Instruction Mode [8] combines online learning with offline teaching to meet students' personalized learning needs and improve the quality of spoken English teaching. As a kind of digital teaching platform, the Spoken English Evaluation System brilliantly connects the results of online autonomous learning with offline teaching. Online learning and offline teaching complement and promote each other, exerting students' subjective initiative of online learning and improving the quality of offline teaching.

After Blended Instruction Mode was put forward, teachers in colleges and universities introduced this mode into college spoken English teaching, hoping to address the problems in oral English. According to the analysis of VPN and CNKI, the national hot spots of the research on the mode include the blending of teaching theory, teaching design, teaching resources, and teaching environment. The thesis attempts to introduce the Spoken English Evaluation System into college spoken English teaching to stimulate students' enthusiasm for participation and improve the quality of oral English teaching.

3.4 The Benefits of Spoken English Evaluation System in College Spoken Teaching with Blended Instruction Mode

To realize the individuation of spoken assessment. Analyzing students' task completion and the quality of oral expression, the Spoken English Evaluation System will form the corresponding analysis results. Based on the status, teachers make a formative assessment of students' learning and then teach following students' abilities. With the support of Big Data, teaching assessment is transformed from teachers' subjective experience to objective data. The system can get the students' characteristics from the objective analysis of students' learning information. With the help of the assessment system, students can make spoken English learning plans to learn more effectively. What is more, teachers can design special classroom teaching activities in class, improving students spoken expression ability.

To realize authentic human-computer interaction teaching. When learning spoken English, students are no longer graded only by teachers' personal experience but by the Spoken English Evaluation System in a more impartial way. For example, before the class, the teacher displays the words, phrases, and sentences on the Spoken English Evaluation System that the students may use in the oral practice. As for the students, they are requested to self- evaluate these materials before class and consult with teachers according to their problems whenever necessary, through which is to continue the oral class from class to after class and to extend the time of students' oral practice. Making full use of the Spoken English Evaluation System, students can actively participate in various oral learning activities, such as film dubbing, role-playing, speech, and debate, which is profitable to enhance their communication ability with people.

4 The Design of Blended Instruction Mode of College English Spoken Based on Spoken English Evaluation System

In this thesis, the technology of the Spoken English Evaluation System is applied to college spoken English blended teaching. The implementation process can be divided into three stages: driving before class, promoting in class, and expanding after class.

4.1 Construction of the Spoken English Evaluation System

Driving before class. It is a critical segment in the construction of Blended Instruction Mode at college spoken English teaching, which aims at enabling students to make the utmost of their pre-class time for autonomous learning and laying a foundation for teachers to interact in class. A week before the class, the teachers should publish the materials of the class oral topic on the Spoken English Evaluation System and set up the relevant oral tasks, including topic-related vocabulary reading, sentence follow- up reading, and man-machine conversation. Students can choose to finish according to their preferences and levels and then be evaluated by the Spoken English Evaluation System to correct their pronunciation and sentence expression errors. The pre-class driving module not only fully guarantees the quality and efficiency of Oral English autonomous learning before class but also makes students participate in oral English teaching with confidence and ability.

Promoting in class. It is the most crucial for teachers to achieve offline teaching. Teachers must base their online learning status on the online teaching process to guide. During the classroom promotion, the teaching's key points manifest mainly in the following several aspects:

- The wrong sound correction. "correct pronunciation" is essential in oral English training. In offline teaching, teachers give students specific guidance according to the feedback from the Spoken English Evaluation System.

- The guidance of skills and methods. Concerning the guidance of oral English presentation skills and methods, teachers can use the group teaching model to divide students into different groups for discussion. After the discussion, students will be given sufficient time for group work, and the form of performance can be varied into situational dialogues, interviews, and debates.

Teachers can employ the Spoken English Evaluation as an auxiliary to the training on these topics. In classroom training, teachers can design various activities, such as role reading and interesting dubbing, to interest students in oral communication and expression.

Expanding after class. After the classroom teaching, the teacher publishes the oral test on the Spoken English Evaluation System, giving the stipulated time to test the students' grasping situation in the spoken language learning.

After the individualized evaluation, the teacher sets the targeted oral work to those who need to be strengthened compared with the previous learning data. In this process, students must exploit the learning system to strengthen their weaknesses, further consolidate the classroom oral topic learning, and achieve the set teaching goals. With the support of Blended Instruction Mode, "expanding after class" is not only consolidation but also expansion and extension.

4.2   Experiment in Higher Education at Guangdong Arts and Culture Vocational College

The experimental and control groups selected two parallel teaching classes of non-English majors in higher education at Guangdong Arts and Culture Vocational College. The number of students in the experimental group was 52, and the number in the control group was 54. Before the experiment, the students' English scores and speaking levels in the two classes were statistically analyzed, and it was found that there was no significant difference, and a control analysis could be conducted.

The experiment on smart classroom teaching lasted two months and was conducted by the same English teacher. The same English teacher taught the experimental class. The students in the control group were taught by the traditional English speaking method, i.e., the teacher assigned the teaching tasks and requirements verbally.

At the end of the experiment, we studied the changes in students' English speaking ability in both classes. The study indicators included verbal communication ability, ability to use information-based learning resources, and interest in learning English. The average scores of the three indicators were 8.65, 7.68, and 9.22 for the experimental group and 4.31, 4.74, and 6.59 for the control group, respectively. In conclusion, the advantages of AI-based English-speaking intelligent classroom education are apparent, and it is worth being widely promoted in education [9].

5   Conclusion

The rapid development of educational information has brought new opportunities and challenges for teachers. Network learning, mobile learning, and other means make students' classroom activities present rich and diverse characteristics. Excellent teachers need to keep pace with the times, strengthen education and maintenance, strive to create a good learning atmosphere for everyone, and enhance everyone's learning effect. The Design of Blended Instruction Mode college spoken English provides a reference for public classroom education. When designing online or offline classroom forms, you can fully consider the use of high-level thinking activities such as analysis, evaluation, and innovation to promote students' deep learning and further improve the effectiveness of learning. Through the data labeled into the train, the error is transmitted from top to bottom to fine-tune the network. Based on Spoken English Evaluation System, teachers guide students more accurately about online and offline spoken training, so as to effectively improve students' foreign language competence.

References

1. Ginns, P., Ellis, R.: Quality in blended learning: exploring the relationships between on-line and face-to-face teaching and learning. Internet High. Educ. **10**(01), 53–64 (2007)
2. Walker, M.A.: Can we talk? Methods for evaluation and training of spoken dialogue systems. Lang. Resour. Eval. **39**, 65–75 (2005)
3. Department of Higher Education, Ministry of Education, College English Curriculum Requirements (2019)
4. Ping, Y.: Modular construction of cruise English curriculum under the guidance of competency-based education. Commer. Econ. Res. **18**, 180–182 (2007)
5. Bersin, J.: The Blended Learning Book: Best Practices, Proven Methodologies, and Lessons Learned. Wiley, San Francisco (2004)
6. Yu, Y., Lu, H., Du, X., Yu, J.: An oral English evaluation model using artificial intelligence method. Mobile Inf. Syst. **2022**, 1–8 (2022). https://doi.org/10.1155/2022/3998886
7. Gong, W.: A Study of Blended Learning Theory Applied to College Spoken English Teaching (2008)
8. Xu, Y.: Design of blended instruction mode for college English based on ADDIE mode. Sci. Tribune **20** (2021)
9. Yu, S.: Research on the construction of intelligent classroom for higher vocational English speaking course based on big data and artificial intelligence. J. Yuzhang Normal College **35**(05), 113–116 (2020)

A Tiered Homework Model Designing with Learning Style Under Double Reduction

Chunhong Liu[1]([⊠]) [iD], Zhengling Zhang[2], Wenfeng Li[1], Fuzhen Hu[3], and Dong Liu[1]

[1] Henan Key Laboratory of Educational Artificial Intelligence and Personalized Learning, Xinxiang, Henan, China
lch@htu.edu.cn

[2] Henan Normal University, Xinxiang, Henan, China

[3] Affiliated High School of Henan Normal University, Xinxiang, Henan, China

Abstract. Under the background of the Double Reduction policy in K12 education, how to improve the actual effect of homework training in teaching activities without increasing the total amount and duration has become an urgent problem to be solved. To address this issue, a tiered homework model considering learning style and learning emotion is proposed in this paper. The paper first constructs a student portrait system from the two dimensions of learning style and learning ability. According to the established portrait model, student groups are divided, and tiered homework content is designed. Then, the actual effect of the homework mentioned in the paper is tested by using the microexpression experimental platform. Taking the middle school Information Technology course as an example, with the support of data from 181 students (7th grade) in the middle school attached to our university, we have found that this model can improve students' homework completion rate. Furthermore, the results also indicate that nonintellectual factors such as learning style and learning emotion have a partial impact on students' learning outcomes. Finally, the proposed model can help teachers grasp the classroom learning situation and realize students' personality development.

Keywords: Learning Style · Learning Emotion · Student Portrait · Tiered Homework · Double Reduction

1 Introduction

In July 2021, the General Office of the State Council issued the Opinions on Further Reducing the Homework Burden and Off-Campus Training Burden of Students in Compulsory Education [1]. The document pointed out that basic education should effectively reduce the excessive burden of homework for students in compulsory education on the premise of ensuring instructional quality. While decreasing the total amount and duration, improving the quality and structure of homework can promote the personalized growth of students. In this context, how to improve homework efficiency and achieve precise teaching has become a hot topic of research in K12 education.

To guarantee the smooth implementation of Double Reduction, some studies have proposed that the design wisdom of school assignments should improve the quality while ensuring the reduction of quantity and burden [2]. Therefore, we want to design different levels of homework to meet the individual needs of each student. Tiered homework is an effective measure to reduce students' schoolwork burden and comprehensively improve the quality of basic education. In addition, it also performs well in cultivating personalized talent and supporting the Double Reduction policy. However, research on layered homework is still in its infancy.

After reading the extensive literature, it can be found that a reasonable design of tiered homework structure would effectively improve the completion rate and enhance the quality of basic education. To discover a breaking point for lessening the academic burden and rationally designing layered homework [3], a new educational infrastructure was drawn to help the Double Reduction policy, and a new structure was built for sharing high-quality resources [4]. However, due to the lack of instructional facilities and teacher resources, the current assignments are mainly low-quality and high-quantity mechanical training [5], making it difficult to assign homework for each student in a targeted manner.

Accurate analysis of students' learning conditions and focusing on the intermediary role of homework in education are conducive to increasing the effectiveness of the practical role of assignments and relieving students' academic burden [6]. In this environment, some researchers have seen that learning emotion can be an important factor influencing learners' cognitive processing and learning outcomes [7]. Thus, emotional engagement is a factor that cannot be ignored for the precise design of layered assignments. Learning emotion is a nonintellectual factor that can affect learners' attitude, motivation and interest in learning [8], generally occurring in a specific place and mainly reflected in facial expressions [9]. The accurate identification of students' emotions is the basis of building a smart learning environment and is a crucial means of judging the practicality of tiered homework.

Based on the existing studies, there are still two problems with tiered assignments. First, the content and structure design of the current layered homework failed to focus on the way students have or prefer to learn, which may lead to inaccurate positioning of students' real conditions and make it difficult to achieve exact teaching. Second, most of the current homework pattern effect tests were often verified using learning behaviors, questionnaires and other methods. These methods were incapable of simulating students' real performance in finishing assignments and ignored the influence of nonintellectual factors such as learning emotion on students' thinking styles and learning effects.

To solve these problems, we try to integrate learning emotion into intelligent instruction and introduce learning style as the design index of layered homework. First, we establish student portraits in terms of students' learning style and learning ability. According to the constructed portraits, student groups are divided, and tiered homework content is designed. Subsequently, we actively introduce a microexpression experiment platform to help teachers master students' emotional changes in learning in a timely manner and examine the practical effect of this model.

2 Methodology

2.1 Hypothetical Model

A Student Portrait Model Based on Learning Style. As a nonintellectual factor affecting students' learning outcomes and cognition, learning style has been widely studied in recent years. In addition, many models have been proposed successively, such as Kolb [10], Felder-Silverman [11], and Vark [12]. However, the Vark model involves new concepts such as transformation and apprehension, which are selected for the subsequent design in this paper. The Vark scale is a learning style survey scale proposed by Neil Fleming in 1920 that can classify learning styles into visual, auditory, literacy and kinaesthetic categories. After considering students' preferences, we created a student portrait model based on learning style. The specific labels are shown in Table 1.

Table 1. Student labelling system based on learning style.

Primary label	Secondary label	Label description
Learning style	Visual	Pictures and tables
	Auditory	Discussion and speech
	Literacy	Lists and learning materials
	Kinesthetic	Experiments and activities
Learning ability	Basic	Conceptual and knowledge
	Promoted	Analogical and ability
	Raised	Comprehensive and analysis

A Tiered Homework Mode Based on Student Portrait. Students like to learn and discuss with their peers whenever they have the opportunity [13], so it is necessary to divide the student groups before rationally designing the content of the layered assignments. From the perspective of learning style, students are classified into visual, auditory, literacy, and kinaesthetic groups with the help of the Vark scale. Based on their learning ability, students are divided into basic, promoted and raised categories by online learning behaviour. By fusing the two indexes, 12 groups of students with different learning styles and abilities could be obtained.

After correctly dividing the student groups, considering the various characteristics and abilities of every group, the paper has designed 12 kinds of assignments with different types and difficulties corresponding to them. The aim is to reshape the homework connotation [14] and enhance the awareness of cross-indicator integration in homework design [15], which elevates the completion rate of homework. Table 2 shows the index design. (In the table below, V stands for visual, A for auditory, L for literacy, K for kinaesthetic, B for basic, P for promoted, and R for raised.)

Table 2. Characterization of layered homework.

Primary label	Feature description
V-B	Picture and chart homework about basic knowledge points and textbook examples
V-P	Picture and chart homework about chapter interconnection and comprehensive understanding
V-R	The structure map production homework about knowledge of connections and transformations
A-B	Discussion and debate homework about basic knowledge points and textbook examples
A-P	Discussion and debate homework about chapter interconnection and knowledge understanding
A-R	Debate and lecture questions about subject knowledge transfer and mutual relationship
L-B	Learning material recitation homework about basic knowledge points and textbook examples
L-P	Copywriting and study materials reading homework about comprehensive knowledge
L-R	The learning list preparation homework about the transfer of discipline and chapter knowledge
K-B	Experimental and simulated homework about basic knowledge points and textbook examples
K-P	Experimental homework and hands-on activities about chapter interconnection knowledge points
K-R	The field homework about knowledge transfer and mutual interconnection knowledge points

Experimental Verification of Microexpression Based on Learning Emotion. For the successful use of appropriate technologies to test the quality of homework, students' personal disposition to be able to embrace digital learning is critical in the long run [16]. Learning emotion, as a nonintellectual factor that influences the learning effect, is visualized as indicators of text content [17], facial expressions [18], voice intonation and body language [19], which provide real feedback on students' satisfaction with instructional content. Combined with reality, when assignments conform to individual preference, students usually show happiness, smiling and other positive emotions; when homework is not in line, they show negative emotions such as pain and giving up. Hence, to realistically simulate students' satisfaction with homework, we need to focus on their facial expressions when doing homework.

Facial expression capture requires the support of intelligent technologies. The microexpression experimental platform of our school adopts the PAD three-dimensional emotion model [20], which can timely grasp students' microexpressions and obtain relevant expression data. Through dynamically analysing the acquired expression data, we can effectively track the emotional changes and obtain the time of students' homework completion to verify the actual effect of layered homework.

Therefore, starting from the two dimensions of learning style and learning ability, the paper comprehensively considers the way students process information and have preferences to construct a label system for student portraits. Accordingly, we divided student groups and reasonably designed the types and difficulties of tiered homework. With the aid of a learning emotion recognition tool, facial expressions were introduced into the validation experiment. The above advances the implementation of personalized instruction. Concrete designs are shown in Fig. 1.

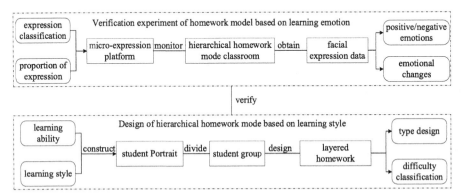

Fig. 1. Design and validation experiments of a layered homework model based on learning style.

2.2 Participants

The participants in the experiment were 181 junior 1 students (taking into account the academic pressure of senior classes) from the Affiliated High School of our university, of whom 46.8% were male and 53.2% were female. Students in each class were randomly assigned to experimental groups, with 78 students engaging in the first group and 103 students participating in the second and third groups. All of the above students were informed before the experiment, and they agreed to collect the corresponding expression data.

2.3 Instantiation Design

Using Facial Expression Indicators to Measure Homework Effectiveness. In this paper, we investigated three microexpression datasets, SMIC-HS [21], CASMEII [22] and SAMM [23], which are commonly used in current research. Among them, the negative emotions included negative, disgust, fear, sadness, depression, contempt, and anger labels, the positive categories contained active and happy labels, and the surprise types had only surprise labels. Based on the above studies, six kinds of expressions were extracted to establish a connection with the microexpression experimental platform. Table 3 shows the relationship between them.

Table 3. Microexpression indicator settings.

Microexpression data	Microexpression platform	Remarks	
		Type	Difficulty
Happy/Positive	Smile/Surprise	Pleased	Simple
Surprise/Anger	Sadness/Anger	Not	Medium
Fear/Disgust	Fear/Disgust	Not	Difficult

Designing Student Portrait Label Based on Learning Style. We would like to utilize the data of 181 junior 1 students to build a portrait model. First, the Vark scale was used to classify students into visual, auditory, literacy and kinaesthetic types. Then, we divided students into basic, promoted and raised categories with the support of student grades, homework and class participation. Eventually, a label system based on learning style was constructed.

2.4 Experimental Environment and Indicator Settings

Before conducting the experiment, we mainly control the environment, content and index settings. First, the environment was the microexpression platform laboratory of our school, which could master students' emotional changes through tracking their expressions in real time. Afterwards, the content was set as follows: taking the information technology course of the middle school attached to our university as a case study, the microexpression data of 181 junior 1 students were investigated. In the end, three evaluation indicators were set: completion time, completion situations and students' facial expressions.

2.5 Data Collection and Research Methods

Data Collection. In view of the design process of tiered assignments roundly, we need to collect two aspects of student portrait data and facial expression data, where the portrait data are employed to establish a labelling system and the expression data are used to test the validity of the proposed model. On the one hand, we obtained the first category of learning ability data through the preprocessing of outliers and repetitive behavior by exporting the learning data of the information technology course. Subsequently, the Vark scale was adopted to classify the learning preferences for Grade 1 students. After removing invalid data, the second category of learning style data was obtained. Finally, we obtained the portrait data of 181 junior 1 students from the affiliated High School of our school by the integration of upper data.

On the other hand, with the microexpression experimental platform, we can accurately recognize and classify students' learning emotions and give the corresponding expression percentage values. By monitoring students' completion of assignments in the laboratory, the facial expression data and personal emotion change trend chart of 181 students were acquired. After exporting through the background, the first group harvested 78 expression data points, and 103 expression data points were received for the second and third groups.

Experimental Content Design. The experiment needs to verify the validity of homework type and homework difficulty. According to the idea of the controlled variable method, the difficulty level should be the same when verifying the homework type. Similarly, we wanted to test homework difficulty by ensuring the same type. Therefore, 5 test papers are set in the paper for verification, as shown in Table 4.

Table 4. Design content of the experimental test papers.

Experimental settings	Difficulty	Type	Remarks
Test paper 1	Basic	Multiple	Learning style
Test paper 2	Basic	Auditory	Contrast
Test paper 3	Basic	Fixed	Learning ability
Test paper 4	Medium	Fixed	Contrast
Test paper 5	Difficulty	Fixed	Verification

Experimental Group Design. According to the content design of 5 test papers, 3 experimental groups have been set up in the paper. Among them, group 1 is the 1st and 2nd test papers, which are applied to verify the type of assignments. Group 2 is test papers 3 and 4, which are used to test the difficulty of homework. Finally, experimental group 3 is test paper 5 to inspect the effect of high difficulty assignments on students' learning, as shown in Table 5.

Table 5. Design content of the experimental groups.

Groups settings	Contrast	Control variable		
		Situation	Time	Expression
Group 1	Test paper 1 and 2	Control	Record	Record
Group 2	Test paper 3 and 4	Control	Record	Record
Group 3	Test paper 5	Record	Control	Record

3   Results

3.1   Experimental Data

By analysing the three experimental groups, assigning one-size-fits-all homework may lessen students' subjective initiative and enthusiasm when learning style is not considered in the long term. Similarly, assigning highly difficult assignments without considering learning ability for a long time will decrease the completion rate and realistic effects. The specific results of the three groups are shown below.

Verifying the Effect of Learning Style on Proposed Mode in the 1st Experiment. The first group of 78 junior school students was selected to ensure that they completed the first and second test papers. At the same time, we recorded the completion time and facial expressions. The first paper is basic and varied and aimed to adopt a learning style index to classify students into visual, auditory, literacy, and kinaesthetic categories. Accordingly, the second paper is basic and auditory, taking data from 4 visual students as an example, as shown in Table 6.

Table 6. Comparison results of test papers 1 and 2.

Subjects	Time (min)		Facial expression (%)	
	Test 1	Test 2	Test 1	Test 2
Vision 1	8.89	22.10	Surprise 85.4/Smile 35.5	Sad 41.5/Anger 3.0
Vision 2	8.26	19.15	Smile 54.0/Surprise 50.1	Anger 7.8/Sad 4.2
Vision 9	25.39	16.17	Smile 17.0/Surprise 65.0	Sad 81.0/Anger 6.3
Vision 13	22.01	14.57	Surprise 99.8	Anger 93.7

According to the above data, when completing the first test paper, students demonstrated positive emotions of surprise and smile and spent an average of 16.14 min. However, when they finished the second test paper, students of the visual type took on the negative emotions of sadness and anger and spent 18.00 min on average. In summary, the other kinds of students took longer to finish the auditory test paper, and their expressions changed from positive to negative emotions. Therefore, we inferred that learning style for students has an impact on layered homework patterns.

Testing the Impact of Learning Ability on Layered Mode in the 2nd Experiment. In the second group, we selected a total of 103 junior school students, and they were guaranteed to accomplish both papers 3 and 4. Moreover, the completion time and facial expressions were recorded. Set the third paper content as the basic and fixed problems, whose purpose is to examine learning ability indicators to divide students into basic, promoted and raised types. Then, the fourth test paper is a medium and fixed question, with data from 4 basic students, as shown in Table 7.

As above, in the third paper, a high percentage of smiling and surprised emotions was shown, and the average completion time was 9.24 min. In the fourth paper, a moderate level of sad and angry emotions was revealed, and the average time was 21.19 min. Comparing the results of two test papers, students took longer for students to complete assignments above their abilities, and their expressions transformed from positive to negative emotions. The comparative result implied that learning ability plays an important role in the content design of layered homework.

Table 7. Comparison results of test papers 3 and 4.

Subjects	Time(min)		Facial expression (%)	
	Test 3	Test 4	Test 1	Test 2
Raised 15	8.99	18.52	Surprise 90.8/Smile 1.2	Sad 65.1/Anger 29.4
Raised 22	9.79	22.05	Smile 7.1/Surprise 82.6	Anger 25.1/Sad 30.43
Raised 34	8.69	22.55	Smile 3.3/Surprise 79.8	Sad 80.95/Anger 6.33
Raised 69	9.49	21.63	Smile 9.7/Surprise 89.8	Anger 51.0/Sad 4.2

Examining the Relationship Between Highly Difficult Homework and Learning Emotion in the 3rd Experiment. The 103 students in the second group were taken as experimental subjects, and the completion time was controlled for 16 and 24 min. Meanwhile, the completion situation and facial expression were recorded. The fifth test paper is a high difficulty and fixed problem, with data from 13 students, as shown in Table 8.

Table 8. Experimental results of test paper 5.

Category	Results		
	Situation (min)		Facial expression (%)
	16	24	
Raised 28	Yes	—	Sad 50.8/Anger 31.2
Raised 34	No	No	Sad 53.1/Fear 20.9
Raised 35	No	Yes	Sad 40.0/Anger 37.5
Promoted 27	No	No	Disgust 61.0/Fear 16.9
Promoted 30	No	No	Disgust 56.0/Sad 19.6
Promoted 29	No	No	Disgust 65.1/Sad 11.5
Promoted 31	No	No	Fear 60.1/Sad 55.7
Promoted 36	No	No	Disgust 68.3/Fear9.6
Basic 18	No	No	Disgust 95.1/Sad 2.1
Basic 32	No	No	Disgust 88.5/Fear 16.1
Basic 33	No	No	Disgust 14.5/Fear 74.7

Among the 11 students listed, both basic and promoted types failed to complete homework in the required 16 and 24 min, while only 2 raised students finished. On the whole, raised students presented a low percentage of passive emotions such as sadness and fear, while promoted students presented a medium proportion. Analogously, the basic type showed a greater percentage of negative emotions such as disgust. With the support of facial data, we found that students' long-term exposure to highly difficult homework led to low emotions, low self-efficacy and weak learning motivation.

3.2 Result Discussion

In the context of double reduction, tiered homework can decrease the academic burden in basic education. However, the traditional homework mode, regardless of the individual learning situation of students, assigned homework with a fixed format and the same topic for the whole class with reference to the progress of the curriculum, which weakened the function of after-class homework. The current ideas of layered homework took into account the study situation, but they ignored students' learning preferences, and the design plan was still in the initial stage. To accurately locate each student's progress and note their uniqueness, we began to establish a student portrait from the two dimensions of learning style and learning ability. Based on a presented label system, we designed 12 kinds of homework with different types and levels to meet student personalized needs.

It has been found that behavioural motivation will be stimulated when students perform positive emotions for content arrangement and contextual presentation; when students have passive emotions, their enthusiasm will be lessened to continue to participate in learning [24]. Learning emotion is a nonintellectual factor that influences students' thinking and learning outcomes. From this, the study attempted to use the learning emotion index to examine students' satisfaction with tiered assignments. With the aid of a microexpression experimental platform, expression data can be captured in real time, emotional changes of students are closely concerned, and actual results can be tested.

Focus on Student Learning Style and Advance Personality Development. The microexpression experiment explained that when the homework type was in line with the learning preference style, students mostly generated positive expressions such as happiness and smiling, which may be related to increasing the homework completion rate. Learning style is a method with personal characteristics reflected by students in different situations. The new curriculum standard points out that teachers should keep a watchful eye on cultivating innovative thinking and practical skills for students in the process of instruction and give full play to their subjectivity and creativity. The rapid development of science and technology requires teachers to care about students' learning styles and establish a good atmosphere of respecting and developing personalities. Doing so will train innovative talent for the new era.

Measure Students' Ability and Refuse to Pluck up a Crop to Help it Grow. Studies have indicated that when student completes assignments that are higher than their abilities, most of them experience negative emotions such as fear and abandonment, which lowers the function of tiered homework. Learning ability is a psychological feature that students have when they are engaged in learning activities. The sequential nature of physical and mental development demands instruction to conform to the law of growth from lower to higher levels, and the cultivation of students' abilities should be gradual and not imposed on them. The new era advises teachers to emphasize ability and avoid the one-size-fits-all traditional homework mode. To a large extent, the measures will further promote personalized development in education.

Master Students' Emotional Changes and Create a Positive Learning Atmosphere. In response to an inverted U-shaped relationship between stimulus intensity and the rate of habit formation, it was implied that individuals at moderate levels of motivation achieve optimal academic performance [25]. Facts have proven that academic emotions are significantly related to students' motivation, learning strategies, cognitive resources, self-regulation, and academic achievement, as well as personality and classroom antecedents [26]. Learning emotion is a key element affecting learning status and outcomes and is sensibly different from learning motivation [27]. Facial data from the experiment have shown that students who are exposed to high levels of homework exceed their abilities for a long time to develop persistent learned helplessness. Furthermore, it may be detrimental to students' physical and mental health development and cause a lack of willpower and behavioural motivation, affecting the generation of learning motivation. To a large extent, high difficulty assignments affect the generation of learning motivation and reduce learning efficiency.

To sum up, accurate portrayal of students' learning conditions is a premise for teachers to carry out personalized instruction. The introduction of nonintellectual factors provides feedback on students' real performance in completing homework and changes the drawbacks of traditional models. With the support of emotional visualization tools, teachers capture emotional data in real time, use it to adjust the structure design of tiered homework to meet hierarchical and gradient needs for students and help students shift their learning status from negative to positive. As a result, students' behavioural motivation and subjective initiative will be stimulated.

4   Conclusion

Under the condition of controlling the total amount and duration, the experimental results illustrated that the tiered homework mode proposed in this paper could improve the completion rate and practical effects. Considering students' unique learning styles and learning situations, we construct a label system with the help of portrait technology. According to the portraits, we reasonably divide student groups and intelligently design the types and difficulties of layered assignments. Focusing on the influence of nonintellectual factors on students' learning outcomes, it is of great practical value to try to integrate learning emotion into a verification experiment of the proposed model. By means of the microexpression experiment platform, we discovered that layered homework can reduce the academic burden of primary and secondary school students to a certain extent. Therefore, it is vital to consider the learning styles and actual abilities of students when designing the content of layered homework. In addition, one of the findings in the paper was that students who choose to perform highly difficult assignments for a long time produced negative emotions such as disgust and giving up, developing learned helplessness in the learning process. The consequences will weaken students' learning motivation and homework completion rate, which is consistent with the results of previous studies. Nevertheless, the extent to which the process affects students remains to be explored. And future research on the impact of the negative emotion will help teachers adjust their teaching strategies.

Acknowledgements. This work was supported by the Henan Provincial Higher Education Teaching Reform Research and Practice Project Foundation [No. 2021SJGLX355], the 2021 special research project of Wisdom Teaching in General Undergraduate College and University of Henan Province, Tracking of Group Intelligent Learning Knowledge Integrated with Learning Emotion, Personalized Guidance and Effectiveness Research.

References

1. Opinions on Further Reducing the Burden of Students' Homework and off Campus Training in Compulsory Education. http://www.moe.gov.cn/jyb_xxgk/moe_1777/moe_1778/202107/t20210724_546576.html. Accessed 24 July 2021
2. Ke, Q.C., Bao, T.T., Li, J.: The supply and service innovation of digital education resources under the background of Double Reduction. China Educ. Technol. **1**, 17–23 (2022)
3. Long, B.X.: The mechanism of the growth of school burden in primary and secondary schools and the way to cure it also on the limitation and enhancement of the Double Reduction policy. Nanjing Soc. Sci. **10**, 146–155 (2022)
4. Fu, W.D., Liu, H.M., Chen, A.N., et al.: New education infrastructure helps implement the Double Reduction policy: needs, advantages and challenges. Mod. Educ. Technol. **32**(1), 27–34 (2022)
5. Galloway, M., Conner, J., Pope, D.: Nonacademic effects of homework in privileged, high-performing high schools. J. Exp. Educ. **81**(4), 490–510 (2013)
6. Huang, X.: An adaptive framework of learner model using learner characteristics for intelligent tutoring systems. J. Educ. Hum. Soc. Sci. **2**, 365–369 (2022)
7. Zhou, J., Ye, J.M., Li, C.: Affective computing in multimodal learning: motivation, framework and suggestions. E-educ. Res. **42**(7), 26–32 (2021)
8. Luo, R.S., Yang, Y.S., Shen, J.L.: Analysis of principal nonintellectual factors. J. Math. Educ. **1**(1), 172–181 (2008)
9. Xu, H.Y., Zhang, H., Han, K., et al.: Learning alignment for multimodal emotion recognition from speech. In: Inter-Speech 2019, Graz, Austria, pp. 1–5 (2019)
10. Rohmanawati, E., Kusmayadi, T.A., Fitriana, L.: Analysis of students' mathematical communication ability based on Kolb's learning styles of converger and diverger type. J. Phys. Conf. Ser. **1808**(1), 12–50 (2021)
11. Felder, R.M., Silverman, L.K.: Learning styles and teaching styles in engineering education. J. Eng. Educ. **78**(7), 674–681 (1988)
12. Pan, Y.B., Cao, L.Z., Tan, M.L., et al.: The effect of VARK learning style survey on the teaching quality and satisfaction of dermatology students. China's Contin. Med. Educ. **14**(7), 101–105 (2022)
13. Sathishkumar, V., Radha, D.R., Saravanakumar, D.A., et al.: E-learning during lockdown of Covid-19 pandemic a global perspective. Int. J. Control Autom. **13**(4), 1088–1099 (2020)
14. Li, X., Shen, S.S.: The connotation and design of homework based on adaptive learning support system. Mod. Educ. Technol. **29**(1), 38–44 (2019)
15. Wang, Z.Y., Teng, J.M., Lei, M., et al.: Opportunities and strategies for the implementation of STEAM inclusive education enabling Double Reduction. Mod. Educ. Technol. **32**(8), 43–49 (2022)
16. Mosca, J.B., Curtis, K.P., Savoth, P.G.: New approaches to learning for generation Z. J. Bus. Divers. **19**(3), 66–74 (2019)
17. Strapparava, C., Mihalcea, R.: Learning to identify emotions in text. In: Proceedings of the 2008 ACM Symposium on Applied Computing, New York, United States, pp. 1556–1560 (2008)

18. Bahreini, K., Nadolski, R., Westera, W.: Towards multimodal emotion recognition in e-learning environments. Interact. Learn. Environ. **24**(3), 590–605 (2014)
19. Ammen, S.Y., Alfarras, M., Hadi, W. A.: OFDM system performance enhancement using discrete wavelet transform and DS-SS system over mobile channel. In: ACTA Press Advances in Computer and Engineering, Sharm EI Sheikh, Egypt, pp. 1–18 (2010)
20. Chen, Y.L., Cheng, Y.F., Chen, X.Q., et al.: Speech emotion recognition in 3D emotion space of PAD. J. Harbin Inst. Technol. **50**(11), 160–166 (2018)
21. Li, X.B., Pfister, T., Huang, X.H., et al.: A spontaneous microexpression database-inducement, collection and baseline. In: Automatic Face and Gesture Recognition (FG), 2013 10th IEEE International Conference and Workshops on IEEE, Shanghai, China, pp. 1–6 (2013)
22. Yan, W.J., Li, X., Wang, S.J., et al.: CASME II: an improved spontaneous microexpression database and the baseline evaluation. PLoS ONE **9**(1), 1–8 (2014)
23. Davison, A.K., Lansley, C., Costen, N., et al.: SAMM: a spontaneous microfacial movement dataset. IEEE Trans. Affect. Comput. **9**(1), 116–129 (2018)
24. Li, T.T., Tan, D.N., Tan, S.H.: Dimension, characteristics and function mechanism of online learning emotional experience. Adult Educ. **42**(10), 63–70 (2022)
25. Yerkes, R.M., Dodson, J.D.: The relation of strength of stimulus to rapidity of habit formation. J. Comp. Neurol. Psychol. **18**(5), 459–482 (1908)
26. Pekrun, R., Goetz, T., Titz, W., et al.: Academic emotions in students' self-regulated learning and achievement: a program of qualitative and quantitative research. Educ. Psychol. **37**(2), 91–105 (2002)
27. Li, X.Y., Yang, Y.S.: A study on the relationship between learning motivation, academic emotion and academic self-efficacy of Mongolian and Han students from high school. J. Inner Mongolia Normal Univ. (Nat. Sci. Edn.) **44**(6), 856–861 (2015)

Integrated Comprehensive Analysis Method for Education Quality with Federated Learning

Ruijin Wang[1] , Tin Chen[2]([✉]), Jinbo Wang[1] , Jinshan Lai[1] , Jingwei Li[1], Mengjie Zhang[1], and Xuxia Chen[1]

[1] School of information and software engineering, University of Electronic Science and Technology of China, Chengdu 611731, China
[2] School of Computer Science and Engineering, University and Technology of china, Chengdu 611731, China
brokendragon@uestc.edu.cn

Abstract. A thorough evaluation of education quality can help schools, governments, and related organizations evaluate education quality, detect persistent problems, act quickly, and raise teaching and educational standards. Traditional methods of assessing education quality, such as statistical analysis and teacher evaluations, suffer from limitations such as data fragmentation, privacy preservation and relying solely on one form of evaluation. We presented a method for comprehensively assessing education quality by incorporating federated learning (CEQFL) to fully utilize big data. First, under a unified evaluation model and indicators, universities act as terminal nodes to train the evaluation model using private data locally. Second, universities aggregate the model to the Ministry of Education for model aggregation and update the evaluation model parameters based on the aggregated data. Finally, using school data as experimental data, we demonstrate that CEQFL has strong education quality assessment capabilities.

Keywords: Federated Learning · Evaluation of Education Quality · Model Aggregation · Privacy Preservation

1 Introduction

Evaluation of education quality is a process that assesses and monitors the quality of education, and it is crucial for ensuring the development and improvement of the education system [8]. It guarantees the quality of educational institutions and teachers, identifies students' needs, improves teaching quality, monitors the progress of education, enhances education quality [1,3,5,7], and thus contributes to the growth of both society and the economy.

Many factors affect the evaluation of educational quality. Universities categorize these factors into two major types: student and teacher, which contain numerous specific indicators [4]. Moreover, different universities have distinct

J. Gan et al. (Eds.): CSEI 2023, CCIS 1900, pp. 439–449, 2024.
https://doi.org/10.1007/978-981-99-9492-2_37

perspectives regarding these factors [10]. Consequently, evaluating educational quality comprehensively presents a challenging task. Thus, we are required to undertake prolonged research and exploration while improving and innovating continuously to advance educational quality.

Statistics and survey results are heavily emphasized in current ways of evaluating teaching quality [2,12]. There are problems including laborious data gathering, insufficient evaluation, difficult data processing, and privacy invasion.

To comprehensively and accurately evaluate education quality and protect the privacy of students and teachers, we use federated learning to jointly train a generalized model for evaluation. Federated learning is a machine learning technique that enables collaborative training on decentralized data. With this approach, we can unify data formats and evaluation indicators, allowing for the application of standardized evaluation and comparison of education quality across different universities.

To build a generalizable and comprehensive model for evaluating education quality, CEQFL can specifically use data on teaching quality across universities. Sending model parameters rather than data can protect the privacy of the data. The data silo issue has been resolved.

However, there are certain differences in the evaluation indicators of education quality among different universities. This results in inconsistent inputs for education quality evaluation models, thus leading to heterogeneity in model structure and parameters. Therefore, training a comprehensive education quality evaluation model through federated learning presents significant challenges.

To overcome this substantial challenge, we first unified the inputs of the education quality evaluation model. We normalized the evaluation attributes' dimensions according to different universities to achieve consistency in dimensions. We used the processed data for model training and finally aggregated and updated the model until convergence.

The contributions of this paper are as follows:

(1) Proposing a novel cross-university education quality evaluation method based on deep learning.
(2) Designing a normalization method for education quality indicators.
(3) Using federated learning to safeguard the privacy of private data in the education quality evaluation process.

The structure of this paper is as follows. 1. Introduction 2. Related Work 3. Normalization of education quality indicators 4. Our Scheme 5. Experimental analysis 6. Conclusion and Future work.

2   Related Work

To measure the quality of education, we need to start with a series of indicators that reflect the quality of education, including government expenditure on education, student/teacher ratio, teacher qualifications, exam scores, and the length of time students are in school. It is necessary to ensure that every investment can serve these aspects to ensure the ultimate quality of education for all programs. Investing in education can enhance social wealth and growth, making it easy for individuals to improve their personal efficiency, productivity, and income.

To measure the quality of education, there have been many studies that measure indicators and methods from different perspectives and case studies. Nojavan et al. [13] proposed a hybrid fuzzy method for the performance evaluation of educational units based on service quality. The method includes four stages. First, based on the fuzzy SERVQUAL questionnaire, the students' expectations and perceptions of the service quality of the educational unit are evaluated, and gap analysis is conducted. In the second stage, the fuzzy analytic hierarchy process is used to determine the corresponding weights of the dimensions and subdimensions of SERVQUAL. In the third stage, the fuzzy TOPSIS method is used to rank the subdimensions of service quality in educational units. Finally, using the fuzzy DEA method, the efficiency of educational units is determined based on the evaluation results of their service quality. Yu H et al. [9] proposed the current research status of emotion recognition and data mining algorithms, improved the April oriTid algorithm, and constructed an online teaching quality evaluation model based on teaching needs. Ebtesam et al. [6] proposed using a combination of quantitative and qualitative methods to collect data through questionnaire surveys and semistructured interviews. The evaluation of English as a foreign language course at the University of Zavia indicates some shortcomings in the balance between program implementation, teaching resources, language skills taught, and student job evaluation. Yang J et al. [14] evaluated the quality of simulated teaching of the Basic Course of Nursing by using the fuzzy comprehensive evaluation method for undergraduate nursing students in a nursing college and analysed the quality of simulated teaching at Peking University. Li et al. [11] proposed establishing a fuzzy evaluation model for the quality of college English teaching based on the analytic hierarchy process. First, theoretical analysis is combined with model calculation to create an improved multiangle EIS to improve the quality of college English teaching. A quality evaluation model for college English teaching was constructed through quantitative and qualitative analysis, and fuzzy indicators were processed.

Although the above different methods can evaluate the quality of education on different indicators, their evaluation targets are all individual school entities and do not have universality. Therefore, this article proposes combining federated learning with education quality evaluation, using education data from multiple schools to jointly train the model, and finally forming a global education prediction model. This global model has better performance and generalization ability compared to local training in a single school.

3 Preliminary

3.1 Federated Learning

Decentralized machine learning technology called "federated learning" is intended to protect user privacy and reduce data transmission.

The objective of federated learning is to minimize the expected loss function of the collaborative model. The expression is as follows.

$$min_{\omega \in W} F(\omega) = \sum_{k=1}^{K} \frac{n_k}{n} F_k(\omega) \tag{1}$$

The model parameters ω belong to the parameter space W. n_k represents the sample size on device (or data source) k, and n represents the total sample size across all devices. $F_k(\omega)$ indicates the loss function on the k device, and K represents the number of devices. Because data distribution may differ across devices, federated learning needs to solve the issue of imbalanced distribution.

Training in federated learning is frequently carried out through an iterative process. The global model parameters are distributed to each device by the central server throughout each iteration. The devices then change the parameters locally using their own data and send them back to the centralized server. The updated parameters from all devices are combined by the central server using weighted averaging, and the result is used as the global model parameters for the following iteration. The model architecture is shown in Fig. 1.

3.2   Definition of Education Quality Evaluation Indicators

We have comprehensively considered the quality of education from the perspectives of students, teachers, and schools. We have developed 27 education quality evaluation indicators and have confirmed the validity of these indicators through questionnaires administered to both teachers and students. The above 27 education quality indicators are summarized and formed after investigating various factors such as schools, parents, students, and the Ministry of Education. Table 1 presents some of the 27 evaluation indicators.

Table 1. Description of relevant indicators

Number	Indicator names	Indicator descriptions
1	Students_num	The total number of enrolled students
2	Teachers_num	The total number of enrolled teachers
3	Avg_class_size	The average number of students per class
4g	Per_student_budget	The admission fee for each student
5	Graduation_rate	The graduation rate of the school
6	Library_size	The area occupied by library
7	Studen_satisfaction	The satisfaction rate of students obtained through a questionnaire survey
8	Teaching_equipment	The quantity of teaching materials and equipment in all colleges

3.3   Performance Index

$Top-k$: used to compute the proportion of correct labels in the top k results with the highest probability in the prediction results. Our experiment used $top-k$ as

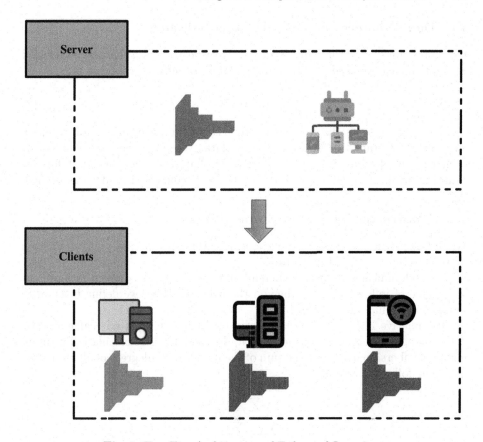

Fig. 1. Two-Tier Architecture of Federated Learning

the accuracy evaluation index. The common $top-1$ is the classification accuracy. The formula is as follows.

$$Accuracy = \frac{TP+TN}{TP+FP+FN+TN} * 100\% \qquad (2)$$

TP means that the actual class, that is, the real class of the sample, is positive, and the result of the model recognition is also a positive class; TN means that the true negative class of the sample is a negative class, and the model identifies it as a negative class; FN indicates that the false negative class, that is, the actual class of the sample is a positive class, but the model identifies it as a negative class; FP means that the correct category of the sample is negative, but the model recognizes it as positive.

4   Our Scheme

In this section, we introduce the data preprocessing of education indicators, the construction of evaluation indicators, and the federated learning model.

4.1   Data Preprocessing for Education Indicators

We represented the data samples of the 27 indicators as a feature vector and normalized each dimension. The normalization formula is as follows.

$$x_{norm} = \frac{x - \mu}{\sigma} \tag{3}$$

Here, x represents the raw data, μ represents the mean of the data, and σ represents the standard deviation of the data. We selected a batch of size B from the samples, creating a $B * 27$ matrix that served as the input for our neural network. For text vector data, only a fully connected model was needed.

4.2   Construction of Evaluation Indicators

We first constructed a set of evaluation indicators $A = \{a_1, a_2, ..., a_n\}$, where n represents the number of indicators.

For each indicator a_i, its membership function $\mu_i(x)$ was defined to represent the degree of influence that a_i has on the decision. Here, we define it as an S-shaped curve that varies with x.

The relative importance of each indicator in the decision was calculated by determining its weight ω_i. For indicator a_i, its weight can be calculated by dividing its membership degree by the sum of the membership degrees of all indicators using the following formula.

$$\omega_i = \frac{\sum_{j=1}^{n} \frac{\mu_i(x)}{\mu_j(x)}}{\sum_{j=1}^{n} \sum_{i=1}^{n} \frac{\mu_i(x)}{\mu_j(x)}} \tag{4}$$

Here, the numerator is the sum of the membership degrees of indicator a_i and other indicators, and the denominator is the sum of the ratios of the membership degrees of all indicators.

Finally, we normalized the weights of all indicators so that their sum became 1.

4.3   Federated Training of the Education Quality Evaluation Model

In this section, we mainly introduce the federated learning approach for the education quality evaluation model based on the education indicator dataset X and evaluation indicators Y.

First, device i used its local private dataset X_i to train the model M provided by the server. We denote the model trained on device i as M_i. The training process can be represented by an encoder as follows.

$$Y_i' = F(X_i) \tag{5}$$

Here, Y_i' represents the model prediction, and F represents the forward propagation of the model. Then, by comparing the predicted values with the true evaluation indicators, we obtain the model's loss value L_i. By taking the derivative of the parameters, we obtain the update value $\Delta_{(\omega_i)}$. The expression is as follows.

$$\Delta_{\omega_i} = \frac{\partial ||Y_i - Y_i^i||}{\partial \omega_i} \tag{6}$$

Device i updates the model parameters locally according to the following formula.

$$\omega_i(t+1) = \omega_i(t) - \eta \Delta_{\omega_i} \tag{7}$$

Here, t denotes the training iteration number, and η denotes the learning rate. Then, each device uploads the model parameters to the server, and the server updates the global model parameters using the following formula.

$$\omega_{t+1} = \sum_{i=1}^{K} \frac{n_i}{n} \omega_{i,t} \tag{8}$$

Here, ω_{t+1} represents the global model parameter after the $t+1$ th round of iteration; K represents the number of devices participating in training; n_i represents the sample quantity on the i-th device; n represents the sample quantity on all devices; and $\omega_{(i,t)}$ represents the local model parameter on the i-th device after the t-th round of iteration.

In each round of iteration, the central server distributes the global model parameter ω_t to all participating devices, and each device trains the model locally using its own data and sends the updated local model parameter $\omega_{(i,t)}$ back to the central server. The central server takes the weighted average of all devices' local model parameters to obtain the global model parameter ω_{t+1}, which is used as the global model parameter for the next round of iteration.

After the global model converges, we use test samples to validate the model performance.

5   Experimental Analysis

In this section, we will conduct an experimental analysis on the education quality evaluation method proposed in this article. First, we provide a detailed introduction to the experimental configurations we use, including experimental details, datasets, etc. Second, we analyse the experimental results, including accuracy analysis and comparative experimental analysis.

5.1   Experimental Configuration

Experimental details: In the federated learning setup, we simulated 10, 7 and 5 terminals for federated learning to conduct collaborative training and education quality evaluation models. We set the local training iterations of the terminals in federated learning to local epochs=3. Global iterations epochs=60. The number of samples for one training is batch size=32. The learning rate is set to lr=0.001. All the code is implemented using the Python language and PyTorch framework and runs entirely on the GPU.

Dataset and model: The education quality dataset we use contains 30 education-related attributes, including the number of students in schools, the number of courses offered, the number of awards won by schools, and the number of papers published. The dataset is collected and sorted by the teaching quality research team of our school. The corresponding labels have four levels, namely, A, B, C, and D. The designed neural network model also includes three fully connected layers, with the input of the model being thirty attributes of the training data and the output being probabilities at four levels.

5.2   Accuracy Analysis

Figure 2 shows a comparison of accuracy when 10 terminals participate in federated learning to evaluate educational quality. The accuracy of federated learning models can reach approximately 85%, which is 1–2 percentage points higher than that of traditional centralized learning. It can be seen that federated learning can combine different data on multiple terminals for training without reducing accuracy, and the achieved data can have invisible properties.

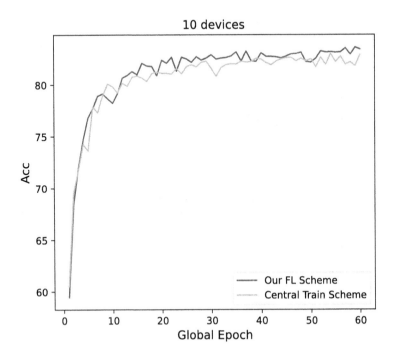

Fig. 2. Accuracy when 10 devices participate in federated learning

Figure 3 shows a comparison of accuracy when 7 terminals participate in federated learning to evaluate educational quality.

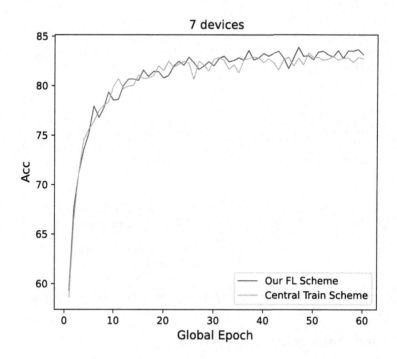

Fig. 3. Accuracy when 7 devices participate in federated learning

Figure 4 shows a comparison of accuracy when 5 terminals participate in federated learning to evaluate educational quality.

It can be seen that the fewer terminals involved in the evaluation of educational quality in federated learning, the closer the accuracy of the final model is to that of centralized learning, which also indirectly demonstrates the advantages of federated learning.

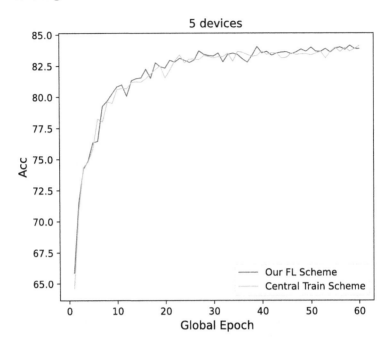

Fig. 4. Accuracy when 5 devices participate in federated learning

6   Conclusion and Future Work

This article proposes a method for evaluating educational quality using federated learning, which can effectively combine local data from different terminals to train a global model. The performance of the model will be better than that of the locally trained model. Considering that education quality datasets from different terminals may be independent and identically distributed, a method will be designed to meet this challenge in the future.

Acknowledgement. This work is supported by the National Natural Science Foundation of China under Grant (62271128), and the Sichuan Science and Technology Program Key R&D Project under Grant (2022ZDZX0004, 2023YFG0029, 2023YFG0150,2023ZHCG004,2022YFG0212,2021YFS0391,2021YFG0027).

References

1. Bakar, K.A.A., Supriyati, Y., Hanafi, I.: The evaluation of admission student policy based on zoning system for acceleration education quality in Indonesia: evaluation of admission student policy based on zoning system for acceleration education quality in Indonesia. J. Manag. Info **6**(2), 19–24 (2019)
2. Bichi, A.A., Musa, A.: Evaluating the effectiveness of teaching practice: experience of northwest university, Kanonigeria. Int. J. Soc. Stud. **3**(1), 104–112 (2017)

3. Bondarchuk, O., Balakhtar, V., Balakhtar, K.: Monitoring of the quality of the psychological component of teachers' activity of higher education institutions based on google forms. In: E3s web of conferences. vol. 166, p. 10024. EDP Sciences (2020)

4. Coffey, M., Gibbs, G.: The evaluation of the student evaluation of educational quality questionnaire (SEEQ) in UK higher education. Assess. Eval. High. Educ. **26**(1), 89–93 (2001)

5. Corbalan, M., Plaza, I., Hervas, E., Zaragoza, E.A.J., Arcega, F.: Reduction of the students' evaluation of education quality questionnaire. In: 2013 Federated Conference on Computer Science and Information Systems, pp. 695–701. IEEE (2013)

6. Ebtesam, E., Foster, S.: Implementation of CIPP model for quality evaluation at Zawia University. Int. J. Appl. Linguist. Engl. Lit. **8**(5), 106 (2019)

7. Harvey, L.: A history and critique of quality evaluation in the UK. Qual. Assur. Educ. **13**(4), 263–276 (2005)

8. Jeddi, F.R., Nabovati, E., Bigham, R., Khajouei, R.: Usability evaluation of a comprehensive national health information system: relationship of quality components to users' characteristics. Int. J. Med. Inf. **133**, 104026 (2020)

9. Jiang, L., Wang, X.: Optimization of online teaching quality evaluation model based on hierarchical PSO-BP neural network. Complexity **2020**, 1–12 (2020)

10. Kamalova, L.A., Raykova, E.: The quality and criteria of evaluation of educational work at the universities of Russia at the contemporary stage. Int. Electron. J. Math. Educ. **11**(1), 71–79 (2016)

11. Li, N.: A fuzzy evaluation model of college English teaching quality based on analytic hierarchy process. Int. J. Emerg. Technol. Learn. (iJET) **16**(2), 17–30 (2021)

12. Mammadi, A., Funtua, H.A., Muktar, U.A., Jibrin, B.: Impact of facilities and service quality on patient relatives satisfaction and patronage in University of Maiduguri teaching hospital, borno state, nigeria. Traektoriâ Nauki= Path of Sci. **7**(3), 3001–3011 (2021)

13. Nojavan, M., Heidari, A., Mohammaditabar, D.: A fuzzy service quality based approach for performance evaluation of educational units. Socioecon. Plann. Sci. **73**, 100816 (2021)

14. Yang, J., Shen, L., Jin, X., Hou, L., Shang, S., Zhang, Y.: Evaluating the quality of simulation teaching in fundamental nursing curriculum: AHP-fuzzy comprehensive evaluation. Nurse Educ. Today **77**, 77–82 (2019)

Author Index

Printed in the United States
by Baker & Taylor Publisher Services